HULDAH, EDDIE, AND ME

HULDAH, EDDIE,  ME

VOLUME I

BY
E. CALVIN GOLUMBIC

Huldah, Eddie, and Me - Volume 1

Copyright © 2009-2024 by E. Calvin Golumbic

First Edition
First Printing

Volume 1 Hardcover ISBN: 979-8-218-40984-5

Library of Congress Control Number: 2024908762
Printed in United States of America

No part of this publication may be reproduced, stored in a retrieval system, or transmitted in any form or by any means, electronic, mechanical, photocopying, recording, scanning, or otherwise, without the prior written permission of the author.

This publication is designed to provide accurate and authoritative information in regards to the subject matter covered. It is sold with the understanding that neither the author nor the publisher is engaged in rendering legal, investment, accounting, or other professional services. While the author has used their best efforts in preparing this book, they make no representations or warranties with respect to the accuracy or completeness of the contents of this book and specifically disclaim any implied warranties of merchantability or fitness for a particular purpose. No warranty may be created or extended by sales representatives or written sales materials. The advice and strategies contained herein may not be suitable for your situation. You should consult with a professional when appropriate. The author shall be liable for any loss of profit or any other commercial damages, including but not limited to special, incidental, consequential, personal, or other damages.

Publishing Assistance provided by:
Heimat Publishing, Crystal Heidel

Table of Contents

PREFACE i

INTRODUCTION iii

CHAPTER I 1
ARENT FOX: RETIREMENT FROM A LAW FIRM AND MY NIGHTMARES WHILE BEING THERE

CHAPTER II 7
GROWING UP IN THE TOWN OF LOCK HAVEN, WHICH WAS IN CLINTON COUNTY, PENNSYLVANIA, WITH MY FAMILY AND FRIENDS

CHAPTER III 16
GROWING UP IN THE TOWN OF LOCK HAVEN: ATTENDING A DEBATE PROGRAM IN THE SUMMER BETWEEN MY JUNIOR AND SENIOR YEARS OF HIGH SCHOOL AT NORTHWESTERN UNIVERSITY AND MEETING LOU BERES THERE FOR THE FIRST TIME

CHAPTER IV 20
GROWING UP IN THE TOWN OF LOCK HAVEN: DEBATING, MY ACADEMIC PERFORMANCE IN MY SENIOR YEAR OF HIGH SCHOOL AND MY COLLEGE CHOICES

CHAPTER V 24
GROWING UP IN THE TOWN OF LOCK HAVEN: MY BOYHOOD FRIENDS STEVE ROMEO AND ALLEN JOSLYN; THE TRIP TO NEW YORK IN A 1929 PONTIAC CONVERTIBLE AND A SUBSEQUENT SNOWBALL FIASCO IN THE SAME VEHICLE

CHAPTER VI 29
GROWING UP IN THE TOWN OF LOCK HAVEN: MY BEST FRIEND ALLEN JOSLYN; OUR IGNOMINIOUS TRIP UP BALD EAGLE CREEK TO THE TOWN OF BEECH CREEK IN A CANOE AS WELL AS FACING GRADUATION AND BEYOND

CHAPTER VII 35
NORTHWESTERN UNIVERSITY: TAKING A GREYHOUND BUS FROM STATE COLLEGE, PENNSYLVANIA TO CHICAGO, ILLINOIS AND, ULTIMATELY, TRAVELING BY AN ELEVATED TRAIN TO NORTHWESTERN UNIVERSITY, IN EVANSTON, WHERE, SUBSEQUENTLY, I DECIDED TO ROOM WITH MY OLD FRIEND, LOU BERES, IN SARGENT HALL DURING MY FRESHMAN YEAR

CHAPTER VIII 45
NORTHWESTERN UNIVERSITY, FRESHMAN YEAR: LIVING WITH LOU BERES DURING MY FRESHMAN YEAR IN SARGENT HALL

CHAPTER IX 49
NORTHWESTERN UNIVERSITY, FRESHMAN YEAR: THE BOARD JOB AT ALPHA CHI OMEGA; THE ANNUAL SNOWBALL FIGHT BETWEEN THE WAITERS AND THE SORORITY SISTERS; THE ANNUAL CHRISTMAS PERFORMANCE BY THE WAITERS; AND A SORORITY HOUSEMOTHER CALLED, "MRS. V"

CHAPTER X 58
NORTHWESTERN UNIVERSITY, FRESHMAN YEAR: GRADE POINT AVERAGE, FRATERNITIES, THANKSGIVING AND THE EVANSTON TOWNSHIP HOSPITAL

CHAPTER XI 63
NORTHWESTERN UNIVERSITY, FRESHMAN YEAR: SUMMER VACATION; FROMMS DRY CLEANERS, DRIVING A DRY CLEANING TRUCK, AND BROTHERLY MISBEHAVIOR

CHAPTER XII 66
NORTHWESTERN UNIVERSITY, SOPHOMORE YEAR: DAVE KNAPP, FRANKLIN GROVE, ILLINOIS AND THE ROCK ISLAND LINE

CHAPTER XIII 73
NORTHWESTERN UNIVERSITY, SOPHOMORE YEAR: THETA DELTA CHI; FRATERNITY BROTHERS, "RUSHING," "PLEDGING" AND THE ABOMINABLE LIVING SITUATION IN THAT FRATERNITY HOUSE

CHAPTER XIV 80
NORTHWESTERN UNIVERSITY, SOPHOMORE YEAR: SUMMER VACATION; FROMMS DISCOUNT BOOKLETS, CHARLIE HERLOCHER, STEVE ROMEO, ALLEN JOSLYN, JUDY MACAMOND AND THE GRAYSTONE

CHAPTER XV 86
NORTHWESTERN UNIVERSITY, JUNIOR YEAR, FALL QUARTER: LOU BERES AND JUDY HARRIS, DINNER AT WALKER BROTHERS, CLASSES WITH PROFESSOR MCGOVERN AND DATING NANCY PAUL

CHAPTER XVI 91
NORTHWESTERN UNIVERSITY, JUNIOR YEAR, WINTER & SPRING QUARTERS: LUCY JEFFRIES, THE PEMBRIDGE HOUSE AND "RAGGEDY ANN AND ANDY"

CHAPTER XVII 97
NORTHWESTERN UNIVERSITY, SUMMER VACATION, JUNIOR YEAR: FROMMS DRY CLEANERS, CHARLIE HERLOCHER AND SELLING DISCOUNT BOOKLETS AGAIN

CHAPTER XVIII 100
NORTHWESTERN UNIVERSITY, JUNIOR YEAR, SUMMER VACATION: CHARLIE HERLOCHER, MOLLY YEAGER, THE TANGLEWOOD AND THE CURTIN FAMILY

CHAPTER XIX 105
NORTHWESTERN UNIVERSITY, SENIOR YEAR, FALL QUARTER: LOU BERES WAS ELECTED PRESIDENT OF THE STUDENT GOVERNMENT, AFTER WHICH HE LOST HIS ACADEMIC SCHOLARSHIP AND, AS A RESULT, HE BECAME A PARKING ATTENDANT IN THE EVENINGS, WHICH CAUSED HIM TO BE SUBSEQUENTLY ADMITTED TO THE EVANSTON TOWNSHIP HOSPITAL, FOR A WEEK, BECAUSE OF EXHAUSTION

CHAPTER XX 110
NORTHWESTERN UNIVERSITY, SENIOR YEAR, WINTER QUARTER: WORKING WITH LOU BERES AT A FLORAL SHOP ON THE NORTH SHORE DURING MY CHRISTMAS VACATION; MY TRAIN TRIP HOME ON CHRISTMAS EVE; GIVING MY FRATERNITY PIN TO MOLLY YEAGER ON NEW YEARS EVE

CHAPTER XXI 117

NORTHWESTERN UNIVERSITY, SENIOR YEAR, SPRING QUARTER: SUCCEEDING IN MY SENIOR YEAR; BECOMING A WAITER IN THE SORORITY HOUSE; PROFESSOR MCGOVERN'S CLASSES; BORROWING WARREN BUTLER'S TUXEDO AND AUTOMOBILE FOR A SPRING FORMAL; THE END OF THE JUDY HARRIS AND LOU BERES RELATIONSHIP AND OUR GRADUATION

CHAPTER XXII 123

NORTHWESTERN UNIVERSITY, SUMMER VACATION FOLLOWING MY GRADUATION: SELLING FROMMS DISCOUNT BOOKLETS ONCE AGAIN; THE UNFORGETTABLE MEETING OF AN OLD LADY IN LEMONT; LUNCH WITH MOLLY YEAGER AND CHARLIE HERLOCHER AT THE "HUB"; AND FAILING A METROPOLITAN LIFE INSURANCE EXAMINATION

CHAPTER XXIII 132

PENN STATE UNIVERSITY, GRADUATE SCHOOL, THE PHILOSOPHY DEPARTMENT: EXISTENTIALISM AND ANCIENT POLITICAL PHILOSOPHY; STANLEY ROSEN AND RICHARD GOTSCHALK

CHAPTER XXIV 138

AMERICAN UNIVERSITY LAW SCHOOL, FIRST YEAR, FIRST SEMESTER: INITIALLY LIVING IN A SINGLE ROOM IN HARTNET HALL; SUBSEQUENTLY LIVING WITH MATT ZALE IN AN APARTMENT; AND THE BORING CLASSES AND INSTRUCTORS IN LAW SCHOOL

CHAPTER XXV 146

AMERICAN UNIVERSITY LAW SCHOOL, FIRST YEAR, SECOND SEMESTER: MEETING JUDY HARRIS ON A STREET IN WASHINGTON, D.C. AND SATURDAY NIGHTS WITH MATT ZALE AND THE CATHOLIC SECRETARIES

CHAPTER XXVI 150

GRADUATE SCHOOL, PENN STATE UNIVERSITY: RACHEL NEWMAN, ROBERT DOCKETY, BILL POICK, DAPHNE PARKER AND A LIFE-ENDING AUTOMOBILE ACCIDENT, SHORTLY BEFORE THEIR GRADUATION, WHICH HAD A LIFE-LONG IMPACT ON MY LIFE

CHAPTER XXVII 157

AMERICAN UNIVERSITY LAW SCHOOL, FIRST YEAR, SUMMER VACATION: THE POCONO MOUNTAINS; TYLER HILL CAMP; "A HAWK, A BEAR, AND A MOOSE," AND A SWEDISH GIRL NAMED GUNILLA HOLMIN

CHAPTER XXVIII 163

AMERICAN UNIVERSITY LAW SCHOOL, SECOND YEAR: A NEW BUILDING, BETTER COURSES AND INSTRUCTORS, AND A CORRESPONDING IMPROVEMENT IN MY GRADE POINT AVERAGE("GPA")

CHAPTER XXIX 166

AMERICAN UNIVERSITY LAW SCHOOL, SECOND YEAR: LIVING WITH BUD MENAKER ON THE THIRD FLOOR OF A TOWNHOUSE AT 1835 LAMONT STREET IN THE MOUNT PLEASANT AREA OF THE CITY, WITH A PROSTITUTE AND HER FIVE CHILDREN ON THE FIRST FLOOR AND AN ARMY MAJOR, WHO WOULD REGULARLY BEAT HIS GERMAN WIFE, ON THE SECOND FLOOR

CHAPTER XXX 173
AMERICAN UNIVERSITY LAW SCHOOL, SECOND YEAR, SUMMER VACATION: TYLER HILL CAMP, LIS JØRGENSEN, THE NARROWSBURG INN, MY MARRIAGE PROPOSAL AND HER SUBSEQUENT ACCEPTANCE

CHAPTER XXXI 193
AMERICAN UNIVERSITY LAW SCHOOL, SECOND YEAR; SUMMER VACATION: MARRIAGE IN THE TRINITY METHODIST CHURCH IN MY HOMETOWN, FOLLOWED BY A FOOTBALL GAME AT PENN STATE UNIVERSITY AND A SUBSEQUENT RETURN TO MY HOMETOWN TO SHOP AT "UNCLE JOE'S WOODSHED."

CHAPTER XXXII 198
AMERICAN UNIVERSITY LAW SCHOOL, SECOND YEAR: THE TWO BEDROOM APARTMENT ON THE THIRD FLOOR ATTIC OF AN INAUSPICIOUS ROW HOUSE IN THE ADAMS-MORGAN AREA OF THE CITY, WITH LIS, BUD AND CAL, IN A CONTEMPORARY DRAMA, ENTITLED, "THREE'S COMPANY"

CHAPTER XXXIII 208
AMERICAN UNIVERSITY LAW SCHOOL, SECOND YEAR: A CHRISTMAS STORY, ON OUR FIRST CHRISTMAS, WITH BUD, CAL AND LIS

CHAPTER XXXIV 214
AMERICAN UNIVERSITY LAW SCHOOL, SECOND YEAR: CAL AND LIS MOVE INTO A BLEAK ONE-ROOM EFFICIENCY IN THE CALIFORNIA HOUSE AND LEAVE BEHIND A COMICAL SITUATION IN THEIR OLD APARTMENT, INVOLVING, IN ONE INSTANCE, A CLOTHESLINE, A PAIR OF WET STOCKINGS AND A TERRIFIED BUD MENAKER

CHAPTER XXXV 225
AMERICAN UNIVERSITY LAW SCHOOL, THIRD YEAR: LIS HAS "MORNING SICKNESS" ON A BUS, SLEEPING PROBLEMS IN THE LATTER STAGES OF HER PREGNANCY AND TOO FEW MATERNITY CLOTHES

CHAPTER XXXVI 228
AMERICAN UNIVERSITY LAW SCHOOL, THIRD YEAR: THE ASSISTANT DEAN'S ANNOUNCEMENT, IN CLASS, THAT I WAS ABOUT TO BECOME A FATHER; THE AGONIZING TRIP TO THE HOSPITAL; THE DELIVERY ROOM SAGA; THE CORPORATIONS EXAMINATION THAT FOLLOWED, AND THE BIRTH OF MY OLDER SON, COURT EDWARD GOLUMBIC

CHAPTER XXXVII 242
AMERICAN UNIVERSITY LAW SCHOOL, THIRD YEAR: GRADUATION; AUNT NORMA AND UNCLE CALVIN AND RELIGIOUS DIFFERENCES WITHIN MY FAMILY

CHAPTER XXXVIII 245
AMERICAN UNIVERSITY LAW SCHOOL, THIRD YEAR: MY SUCCESSFUL STUDY FOR THE DISTRICT OF COLUMBIA BAR EXAMINATION IN THE LIBRARIES AT MARJORIE WEBSTER JUNIOR COLLEGE AND THE UNIVERSITY OF MARYLAND

CHAPTER XXXIX 250
FIRST JOB: CONGRESSIONAL OFFICE; I BEGAN MY FIRST JOB, AS A LAWYER, AS A LEGISLATIVE AIDE IN A CONGRESSIONAL OFFICE

CHAPTER XL 253
FIRST JOB: CONGRESSIONAL OFFICE; THE DIFFICULT SECRETARIES; ROBERT BAER COHEN AND HIS WIFE; PHILADELPHIA POLITICS AND STUDENT VOLUNTEERS

CHAPTER XLI 260
FIRST JOB: CONGRESSIONAL OFFICE; COHEN LOST THE ELECTION AND, YEARS LATER, I WAS INFORMED THAT HE MAY HAVE BEEN CONVICTED OF A FELONY AND, SUBSEQUENTLY, IMPRISONED, AND, EVEN LATER, I WAS INFORMED THAT HIS WIFE HAD DIED

CHAPTER XLII 263
SECOND JOB: DENNING & WOHLSTETTER; AMBIENCE, THE THIRD REICH AND THE FIFTH GRADE

CHAPTER XLIII 271
THIRD JOB: NEIGHBORHOOD LEGAL SERVICES PROGRAM; A PRACTICE IN FEDERAL COURTS AND ADMINISTRATIVE AGENCIES OF EVERY KIND, WITH DIVERSE CASES, INVOLVING POOR CLIENTS

CHAPTER XLIV 274
THIRD JOB: THE NEIGHBORHOOD LEGAL SERVICES PROGRAM; ITS NATURE, DIRECTOR AND DEPUTY DIRECTOR, MANAGING AND STAFF ATTORNEYS, OFFICE NUMBER EIGHT, DECOSTA V. MASON, RHODA LACKRITZ AND MY FIRST CASE

CHAPTER XLV 279
THIRD JOB: NEIGHBORHOOD LEGAL SERVICES PROGRAM; PRACTICING LAW IN OFFICE NUMBER EIGHT WITH LARGE CASELOADS, THE NATURE OF MOST OF THOSE CASES, AS WELL AS FOOD STAMPS AND A CREDIT UNION ROBBERY

CHAPTER XLVI 283
THIRD JOB: NEIGHBORHOOD LEGAL SERVICES PROGRAM; TRANSFER TO OFFICE NUMBER NINE AND THE ELIMINATION OF THE BACKLOG THERE BY USING VOLUNTEER ATTORNEYS; THE TRANSFER OF EDWARD SCHWAB AND THE ENGAGEMENT IN A NUMBER OF AFFIRMATIVE ACTIONS ON ISSUES OF LAW, WHICH, EVENTUALLY, RESULTED IN A SUPREME COURT CASE

CHAPTER XLVII 292
STONEGATE: LARS IS BORN AND COURT'S REACTION; SATURDAY MORNING TELEVISION CARTOONS AND A RECKLESS DEPARTURE FROM A CRIB

CHAPTER XLVIII 296
STONEGATE: WHILE LIVING IN A GARDEN STYLE APARTMENT AT 1835 PINEY BRANCH ROAD IN SILVER SPRING, MD., WE BEGAN TO LOOK FOR A HOUSE TO BUY AT "SIGNAL HILL" AND, SUBSEQUENTLY, AT "STONEGATE," IN MONTGOMERY COUNTY, MARYLAND

CHAPTER XLIX 305
STONEGATE: WE MOVED INTO THE SPLIT-LEVEL HOUSE IN STONEGATE WITH, INTER ALIA, A MAPLE BED THAT WAS USED NEARLY EVERY EVENING BY TWO OF MY CHILDREN, SUCCESSIVELY, TO SAIL OFF WITH OLD "BLACKBEARD," THE PIRATE, TO PLACES UNIMAGINABLE FOR MOST DISBELIEVING ADULTS

CHAPTER L 311
AMERICAN UNIVERSITY LAW SCHOOL, THIRD YEAR: I USED THE MONEY THAT WE HAD SAVED FOR MY LAW SCHOOL TUITION TO PURCHASE AN EIGHTEENTH CENTURY, CHERRY, CHIPPENDALE, "SLANT-FRONT" DESK, WHICH RESULTED IN MY WIFE UNFAIRLY TAKING OVER OUR FAMILY FINANCES

CHAPTER LI 318
FOURTH JOB: AMERICAN UNIVERSITY LAW SCHOOL; LAWCOR AND PROFESSOR NICHOLAS KITTRIE

CHAPTER LII 323
STONEGATE: MY YARD WORK, REPLICATING FORESTS FOUND IN CENTRAL PENNSYLVANIA WAS NOT UNLIKE THE YARD WORK DONE BY MY PARENTS, WHO WERE PROBABLY ENGAGED IN THAT KIND OF A PURSUIT, BECAUSE THEY WERE, GENERALLY, WITHOUT FRIENDS

CHAPTER LIII 330
STONEGATE: WELSH TERRIER; THE JOYS AND SORROWS ASSOCIATED WITH HAVING A WELSH TERRIER IN OUR FAMILY

CHAPTER LIV 334
STONEGATE: CAMP DEVITT; MY MOTHER WAS PLACED IN A TUBERCULOSIS SANITARIUM FOR SEVERAL YEARS AND, WHILE RECUPERATING THERE, SHE CONTRACTED SERUM HEPATITIS, FOR WHICH SHE WAS SUBSEQUENTLY HOSPITALIZED, FOR AN EXTENDED PERIOD OF TIME

CHAPTER LV 340
STONEGATE; KERRY BLUE TERRIER; MY KERRY BLUE TERRIER WAS PUT DOWN BY A VETERINARIAN BECAUSE, IN THE ABSENCE OF MY MOTHER AND FATHER AND, EVENTUALLY, MYSELF, THERE WAS NO ONE AT HOME TO TAKE CARE OF HIM

CHAPTER LVI 348
STONEGATE: LIS; OUR PRESCHOOL CHILDREN'S EATING HABITS DURING LIS' COLLEGE CLASSES; BEING A SUBSTITUTE TEACHER WITH EARLY MORNING TELEPHONE CALLS; THE FIRST DAY AS A PERMANENT TEACHER AND THE RESULTING "KEYS INCIDENT"

CHAPTER LVII 357
STONEGATE: LIS; ELEMENTARY SCHOOL READING GROUPS; FRIDAY NIGHT DINNERS; SATURDAY AFTERNOON MOVIES; SUMMER SWIMMING POOL AFTERNOONS; LUNCH AT DUKE ZIEBERT'S RESTAURANT AND THE BETTY FORD LETTER

CHAPTER LVIII 367
STONEGATE: COURT AND LARS; "LATCHKEY" CHILDREN WHO WERE NEARLY INVOLVED IN A FAMILY BATHROOM TRAGEDY IMMEDIATELY AFTER SCHOOL

CHAPTER LIX 373
MUSIC: FAMILY TRADITION; LARS PLAYED THE PIANO AND CLARINET AND COURT PLAYED THE TRUMPET THROUGHOUT MOST OF THEIR RESPECTIVE GROWING UP YEARS

CHAPTER LX 378

MUSIC: FAMILY TRADITION; AS IT RELATES TO MYSELF, MY MOTHER AND MY GRANDMOTHER, NOT TO MENTION MY SONS, SPANNING, AT LEAST, FOUR GENERATIONS

CHAPTER LXI 384

FIFTH JOB: CORPORATION COUNSELS OFFICE, APPELLATE DIVISION; APPLICATION AND ACCEPTANCE INTO A WORLD OF LITIGATION ON AN APPELLATE LEVEL

CHAPTER LXII 386

FIFTH JOB: CORPORATION COUNSELS OFFICE, APPELLATE DIVISION; FEATURING ECCENTRIC AND HIGHLY COMPETENT LAWYERS IN A DEMANDING APPELLATE PRACTICE

CHAPTER LXIII 394

FIFTH JOB: CORPORATION COUNSELS OFFICE, APPELLATE DIVISION; NATURE OF THE WORK, INCLUDING WRITING BRIEFS, DOING LEGAL RESEARCH, REVIEWING THE RECORD AND PRESENTING ORAL ARGUMENTS

CHAPTER LXIV 398

FIFTH JOB: CORPORATION COUNSELS OFFICE, APPELLATE DIVISION; A COURT-APPOINTED COUNSEL WHO HAD NEVER PRESENTED ARGUMENT IN AN APPELLATE COURT HAD A HEART ATTACK WHILE DOING SO IN ONE OF MY APPEALS

CHAPTER LXV 404

FIFTH JOB: CORPORATION COUNSELS OFFICE, APPELLATE DIVISION; I HAD TO ABANDON MY PLANS TO GO ON A VACATION WITH MY DANISH WIFE AND MOTHER-IN-LAW BECAUSE OF MY PROSPECTIVE PARTICIPATION IN AN EN BANC APPEAL

CHAPTER LXVI 412

STONEGATE: MY TWO YOUNG SONS; SWIMMING AND BASEBALL LESSONS, HUMOROUSLY DESCRIBED

CHAPTER LXVII 418

STONEGATE: MY TWO SONS; TENNIS LESSONS, TENNIS APPAREL AND PLAYING TENNIS, HUMOROUSLY DESCRIBED

CHAPTER LXVIII 424

STONEGATE: MY LITTLE LEAGUE REJECTION AND THE SUBSEQUENT DEVELOPMENT OF SELF-RELIANCE, REVISITED

CHAPTER LXIX 429

SIXTH JOB: THE PENSION BENEFIT GUARANTY CORPORATION, OFFICE OF THE GENERAL COUNSEL; HENRY ROSE, INSECURITY AND NON-DECISION MAKING

CHAPTER LXX 433

SIXTH JOB: PENSION BENEFIT GUARANTY CORPORATION, OFFICE OF THE GENERAL COUNSEL; MY PREDECESSOR WAS APPARENTLY REPLACED AS A LITIGATION HEAD BY HENRY ROSE BECAUSE OF MY WORK ON A SUPREME COURT BRIEF

CHAPTER LXXI 438

SIXTH JOB: PENSION BENEFIT GUARANTY CORPORATION, OFFICE OF GENERAL COUNSEL; I ORGANIZED A LITIGATION SECTION TO SUCCESSFULLY LITIGATE CASES IN FEDERAL COURTS, TRIAL AND APPELLATE, BY ELIMINATING MEDIOCRITY, DEMOCRACY AND DECENCY

CHAPTER LXXII 442

SIXTH JOB: PENSION BENEFIT GUARANTY CORPORATION, OFFICE OF GENERAL COUNSEL; AFTER ACHIEVING AN ENORMOUS AMOUNT OF SUCCESS IN PENSION LITIGATION, I DECIDED TO DEPART THE CORPORATION AND JOIN THE UNITED MINE WORKERS OF AMERICA HEALTH AND RETIREMENT FUNDS AS THEIR GENERAL COUNSEL

CHAPTER LXXIII 445

SIXTH JOB: PENSION BENEFIT GUARANTY CORPORATION, OFFICE OF GENERAL COUNSEL; DULCAN, FORD, HANRAHAN, AND ROSE REVISITED, YEARS LATER

We shall not cease from exploration And the end of all our exploring Will be to arrive where we started And know the place for the first time.

Excerpt from Four Quartets, Little Gidding V by T. S. Eliot (1943)

For the Dane.

Preface

I LIKE to tell stories; I have all of my life. My stories are usually about my life, or about those who have been part of my life. And for the most part, my stories are true, although my older son, Court, would probably disagree. He usually says that it is true that I like to tell stories, but it is hard, sometimes, to find the truth in them. Actually, I don't think that he really believes that there is nothing true about my stories. It is just that, in his opinion, I seem to have some difficulty in telling an uninteresting story, so I do whatever it takes to make the story more interesting, which, in his mind, means that I usually leave the truth behind or, at least, somewhat behind. I, on the other hand, would prefer to say that I like to tell stories that are true, but in an interesting manner, whatever that may mean, and who wants to hear an uninteresting story, anyway.

Because I have always believed that my family, or, at least, that part of it that I know, is quite interesting, I have decided to tell a story about what I know, or what have been told, about my interesting family. And in this instance, unlike in so many others, I have decided to write it down, so that those in my family who generationally follow me, in the years ahead, may have an opportunity to read it. Being able to read a story about some of their family that they do not know, because it has historically preceded them, literally by generations, may allow them to better understand what they have come from, where they are going and, likely, why, at least in part. Because those are very serious questions, not easily resolved during one's lifetime, that is probably the final and, maybe, the most important reason for telling the story . . . and writing it down.

In case there may be others, apart from my family, who find the story to be worthwhile, I think that is understandable. After all, my family may not be so different from yours, and I may not be so different from you, because, in the end, we are all members of the human family. Otherwise, a discipline like history, even with all of its nuances and interpretive aspects, would be meaningless. Since it is obviously not, my story may actually transcend my family, although not apparently, and it may actually be about your family, or even the human family, but I can't be sure of that. I can only be sure about the story that I am about to tell, and that it is about my family, including those who have gone before me and, in all likelihood, those who may come after me, if you understand anything about history and philosophy, that is.

Introduction

THE PHOTOGRAPHS of my mother, Huldah Winifred Davis, and my father, Edward Jacob Golumbic, were likely taken sometime shortly before their marriage. And in some respects, but only in those respects, this story really begins with that marriage. If you have some difficulty in understanding that fact, at least at this point, it is because you have not yet read the story, which is, in reality, their story. The significance of that fact is limited only by descendants and generations and time.

Edward J. Golumbic   *Huldah W. Davis*

CHAPTER I

ARENT FOX: RETIREMENT FROM A LAW FIRM AND MY NIGHTMARES WHILE BEING THERE

MY STORY, which is this story, begins, since it must have a beginning, on December 21, 1995, which, surprisingly, was my fifty-ninth birthday. More importantly, however, at least for this story, it was also the day that I essentially retired from the legal profession, after a little more than thirty years of practicing law. To be more specific, it was the day that I retired, as a partner, from the law firm of Arent, Fox, Kintner, Plotkin & Kahn (hereinafter, sometimes, "Arent Fox"), which was a large international law firm that was headquartered, at the time, at 1050 Connecticut Avenue in Washington, D.C. See the photograph of myself, as a partner at Arent Fox, in Exhibit 146 in the Appendix.

In the thirteen years that I was with the firm, I watched Arent Fox grow to become one of the five largest law firms in Washington D.C., and, likely, one of the fifty largest firms in the country. During that time, with the possible exception of my first and last years of working there, I was probably one of the ten most productive partners in the firm. In two or three of those years, with the possible exception of two or three individuals, I originated more business than all of the other partners in the law firm. I also maintained a caseload, nearly every year, that consisted of some of the most complex litigation in the firm, including a number of appeals, involving, in a number of those cases, issues of first impression.

Nearly all of that litigation took place in the United States District Courts and in the United States Circuit Courts of Appeals. Some of it even reached, in various stages and in various forms, the Supreme Court of the United States. The issues often involved significant constitutional questions and/or the construction of complex federal statutes. Damages, when they occurred, normally reached hundreds-of-millions of dollars and even, on occasion, billions of dollars. My clients in these cases, nearly all of whom were obtained by me, were ordinarily large institutions, including federal agencies, collectively-bargained multi-employer pension funds, and even, on occasion, the National Chamber of Commerce.

I suppose that you could possibly say, in light of those superlative descriptions, that my practice was a litigator's dream, but if you did, even in light of those descriptions, you would have been wrong. There was nothing, in any part of my thirteen years of practice in that law firm, that was "dreamlike." It was, metaphorically speaking, more of a nightmare, at least to me, anyway. That was because, among other things, the nightmare didn't end at 5:00 p.m. or even begin at 9:00 a.m. Rather, it captured nearly every waking moment of every day, and far too many sleepless ones at night, too. And it ordinarily required writing, speaking, meeting, arguing and thinking, not to mention the ubiquitous telephone conversations, for, typically, over sixty-hours each week, mostly in the office. I say, "typically," over sixty-hours, because I can't remember not working for any significant period of time during the week, even at home during the evenings, so I thought that it would be reasonably safe to say it that way.

I don't even want to talk about the travel, which I had to do all of the time, because the litigation was, generally, in federal district or circuit courts all over the country, and, therefore, so was I. Living in hotels for vast periods of time, while litigating cases away from home, was a rather lonely existence. It was made even more lonely, because I had more time, in those circumstances, to worry about seemingly irresolvable problems in my cases, which were pending in those courts, especially at night, when I couldn't sleep, because I was living in a hotel and worrying about irresolvable problems in my cases. And, of course, the food in the hotel was nothing like the food at home, so my stomach, which was already upset, because of the irresolvable problems, reminded me, depending upon the length of the trial, how miserable I was. On top of that, I did not particularly like to fly, which was ordinarily a transportation requirement, and my stomach, upon takeoff, reminded me of that, too.

Some of this may have been more tolerable, if there had been any collegiality, at all, in my firm, but large law firms were not built on collegiality; they were built on profit. And if you were not profitable, you were not in the law firm, not for very long, anyway. In case I have not already made myself abundantly clear, at this point, let me remind you of that fact now: It was important, no imperative, to be profitable! There was ordinarily a large overhead at a large law firm like mine, consisting of, among other things, a significant secretarial support staff, a large general services office, a two-floor law library, with numerous librarians to service it, a human resources office, with seemingly more personnel than the rest of the law firm, including all of the lawyers, and a substantial comptrollers office, which was necessary to calculate the cost of supporting all of those people. All of which was, seemingly, expanding, hourly, and, therefore, so should your work, calculated by billable-hours, if, that is, you wanted to remain profitable and in the law firm.

Assuming that you do remain profitable and in the law firm, at least up to that point, the question then becomes how profitable in relation to every other partner in the firm. That was an important question, because your partnership share of the economic pie, so to speak, was ordinarily determined by the answer. And if the answer would increase your share of that pie, assuming that the size of the pie remains essentially the same, that may mean that another partner's share would likely decrease. That, may I point out, was not a foundation for a good working relationship with the rest of your partners in the law firm. It was, rather, a foundation for jealousy and insecurity and instability, which was exaggerated by a daily report on the desk of each partner, every morning, when he arrived at work, showing the respective billings of every other partner in the firm for the previous day. In case any partner may have missed this daily opportunity to anguish in the morning about his comparative partnership status in the firm, based upon his billings for the previous day, a monthly report of a similar nature was kindly issued at the partnership meeting, which took place at the end of each month, and which made that meeting rather exciting or, possibly, depressing, depending upon where you were, based upon your billings, in the law firm.

It is no wonder, after reviewing some of those daily or monthly reports, that some of my partners seemed to have diminished in size, until they were eventually no more than two feet tall, and, at the same time, some of their counterparts seemed to have increased in size, until they were eventually ten feet tall. No matter what their respective size may possibly be, however, few of them ever appeared to be particularly human, not from my vantage point, anyway. They appeared to be my adversaries, maybe not in the same manner as the adversaries in my litigation, but adversaries, just as well. To say the least, none of them appeared to be my best friend!

Maybe, that explains why my compensation in the law firm never really seemed to reflect my productivity on an annual basis. Oh, I was handsomely paid, all right, but the amount never seemed to correspond, as it should have, to the amount of business that I originated each year. The amount of that business sometimes exceeded, in my belated estimation, six or even seven million dollars, in todays' inflated economy, but my income, which was based on my partnership allocation, or my "draw," never exceeded, by my recollection, a reasonable fraction of that amount, for the same period of time. Oh, I admit, once again, that my "draw," for most of those years, still amounted to a substantial amount of money, but it was not, in any conceivable way, related to my productivity, at least in originating new business, and that is without even considering the amount of my billable and non billable hours for each of those years.

Most of those billable hours were spent litigating significant cases in federal trial and appellate courts around the country, while most of the non billable hours were spent originating new business every year. With the remainder of my working time, I served on prominent boards, such as the Advisory Board to the National Chamber of Commerce Litigation Center, and I published articles in professional journals, with the view toward developing new business from their interested readership.

Those partners who ordinarily did less, in those respects, usually did more within the firm, by, among other things, serving on administrative committees. And they often used their participation on those committees to ensure that their compensation exceeded, or, at least, was inexplicably unrelated, to their productivity, at least in originating new business from outside of the law firm.

Outside of those pernicious facts, relating to the nature of the law firm and its administration, the work, itself, which was adversarial in nature, was often extraordinarily difficult, if for no other reason than the nature of the litigated cases. They often involved so much money, typically in the hundreds of millions of dollars, that our firm's malpractice insurance carrier may not have covered all of the amount at issue, and I was ordinarily retained as an insurance policy by an organization with a significant presence of in-house counsel. If I should lose the case, I would likely be sued for malpractice in, at least, the amount in dispute. And the general counsel of my institutional clients, with whom I normally worked in that litigation, carefully monitored everything that I was doing with that in mind.

Aside from the possibility of subsequently facing my client in a malpractice action, in the event that there was an unsuccessful outcome in the original litigation, I also had to confront the possibility that my client may, and often did, try to destroy incriminating evidence or even manufacture, after-the-fact, supporting evidence, in some of those cases. Obviously, in those kinds of cases, as well as in so many others, I had to be nearly as careful in dealing with my clients, as I was in dealing with my adversaries. Actually, now that I think about it, everybody was my adversary in those kinds of cases, except, possibly, the courts, and, on some occasions, they seemed to be, too.

It was, in short, a nightmare, albeit a financially rewarding one. Nevertheless, the fact is that my life practicing law in that law firm, and in those types of cases, with those kind of clients, involving such large amounts of money, seemed to be a continuous nightmare!

CHAPTER II

GROWING UP IN THE TOWN OF LOCK HAVEN, WHICH WAS IN CLINTON COUNTY, PENNSYLVANIA, WITH MY FAMILY AND FRIENDS

MY LIFE, however, has not always been like that. Actually, it began somewhat more comfortably, but still unceremoniously, in an inconsequential hospital, located in a comparatively small rural town, called Lock Haven, situated in Clinton County, Pennsylvania, where I was born on December 21, 1936. The location was rather beautiful, because of the presence of the Appalachian Mountains, which, literally, surrounded the town in a veritable chain. The valley formed by those Mountains, where the town was actually situated, was called the Bald Eagle Valley, after a reputed Native American Chief of a local tribe, known, at the time, as the Susquehannocks.

Interestingly, for unstated, but not unimaginable, reasons, the Susquehannocks subsequently removed themselves from the area, for a more hospitable environment, somewhere in the remote regions of Canada. Before doing so, however, they were kind enough to lend a version of their name to the West Branch of the Susquehanna River, which, together with the Bald Eagle Creek, reportedly named for the same Native American Chief, established most of the town's boundaries. Given those watery facts, I suppose that you might say, with a little bit of flair, that the town was once embraced by its Native American demographics, but it would probably be more accurate to say that the boundaries of the town were geographically named, in part, for its Native American ancestry.

Well, by now, you probably realize that the town was old enough to become historic; it was also commercial enough to survive well into the mid-twentieth century, which is when I grew up there, but not always at the same location. In fact, I moved several times during that growing up period, with my family in tow, naturally. And nearly as important, especially when you are trying to grow up in a small town, where community is a very serious sociological consideration, I tended to make friends rather easily, no matter where I lived, especially with those who were my age, or nearly so, and who lived nearby. So when I decided, while still in nursery school, to move all the way up to the third ward, and into a two-story, semi-brick house, located at 269 Susquehanna Avenue, which continued to be my residence during most of my formative years, Wally Smith, who was my age, and Charlie Lair, who wasn't, became my best friends, because, not surprisingly, they lived nearby. A photograph of Charlie, Wally and me, when we were no more than nine or ten years of age, kneeling beside Wally's dog, Sport, has been included as part of Exhibit 115 in the Appendix. See also the photograph of me, dressed in a sailor suit, when I was about five years of age, which is in Exhibit 144 in the Appendix.

Emilie Ann Hayes and her younger sister, Ruthie, actually lived next door, but that was different, because they were girls. And we didn't play with girls at the time, not noticeably anyway, so when we played "kick-the-can" or "capture-the-flag," we played with other boys our age, usually in the vicinity, but not with girls, even though they may have resided nearby, although to this day, I really can't explain why.

The mountains, of course, surrounded my home, so I played in them nearly all of the time. When I was younger, in elementary school, it was only hiking or building a treehouse with Wally Smith and Charlie Lair, or even sleeping, overnight, in Wally's cabin, at the foot of the mountain, right behind his house. Later, when I was a little bit older, around twelve years of age, I began to hunt some of the smaller game, which had been seen, repeatedly, on my younger forays into those mountains. Growing even older, as a student in junior high school, I started to hunt some of the larger animals, too, like deer, with a hand-me-down rifle, which I had received as a Christmas present. By the time that I had reached my early "teens," however, my universe began to expand beyond those mountains, and the street upon which I lived, to become as wide-reaching as my bicycle would take me.

Actually, I didn't have to travel very far, because a wide-reaching river was less than a mile away, the West Branch of the Susquehanna, and now, still in junior high school, I started to play there, too, or, at least, along its banks, at first, usually with my friends, Wally and Charlie. And following a discovery that we could actually stay afloat, by moving our arms in a swimming-like manner, shortly thereafter, measured more in months than by years, the river, as well as its banks, became just as important as the mountains in our still playful lives.

In fact, nearly every morning of every summer day, at least following the seventh grade, if not actually before, was spent swimming in it, every part of it, if you can actually say that something like a "dog-paddle" was swimming, because there were no lifeguards, or overly concerned parents, around to tell us that we couldn't. So we did everything that you could conceivably do, and then some, in and around that river, some of which was extremely dangerous and some of which was extremely exciting, probably for that very same reason.

It was far less exciting to go swimming in the afternoon at the facility established by the town at Price Park (now known as Hanna Park), because there were lifeguards there, and burdensome rules and regulations, too. And the girls our age, or nearly so, who routinely went swimming there in the afternoons, because of the lifeguards and the rules and regulations, not to mention their overly concerned parents, did not really become interesting, not until a few years later, so we generally avoided the community swimming facility, and the girls there, too, until we had grown older.

When we did grow older and learned how to drive, too, that made our universe, consisting of, among other things, the rest of the boys in town, if not in the county, readily available. With that automotive fact, my friendships and my interests correspondingly broadened, geographically at first, and, eventually, numismatically, too. The explanation for that recently acquired numismatic interest probably lay in psychology, if for no other reason than it was the beginning of an obsessive desire to collect almost anything and everything for the rest of my life.

The interest in this instance, however, had an address on Sixth Street, where my newly acquired friend, classmate and numismatic counterpart, Nevin B. Greninger, lived. Interestingly, at least from the perspective of a prospective coin collector, Nevin had a paper route, every afternoon, and of even more interest, for the very same reason, he was normally paid for his trouble in some form of coinage, ordinarily on the weekends, following which we carefully identified and retained those coins with some kind of an apparent numismatic value, at least to us. Over a few years of this kind of practice, not to mention a number of other forms of acquisition, we both began to accumulate a rather extensive collection of "Lincoln Head" Pennies, "Buffalo Nickels," "Mercury Head Dimes," and an assortment of even larger denominations, such as "Morgan Silver Dollars." We also began to collect "Indian Head Pennies" and other, much earlier, denominations, to the extent that we could afford too, anyway. Sadly, most of that collection has been sold, at this point in my life, as my "collecting" interests began to vary through the years, although I still retain two of my original "gold pieces," and a few other notable coins.

In any event, as the years progressed, and my age did, too, my interests returned, once again, to the "out-of-doors," and, eventually, I began to fish for trout in the headwaters of the great freestone streams in Clinton County, with my childhood friend, Wally Smith, and two of our classmates in high school, Louis S. Winner("Butch") and Donny Witmeyer. Even though it was difficult to reach those streams, deep in the mountains surrounding the town, Butch was able to drive us there in his family's Jeep, even though he had not yet reached sixteen years of age, which was the age that was ordinarily required to legally drive on public roads in the State of Pennsylvania.

At about the same time, I began to play a lot of tennis, too, nearly every afternoon in the summertime, with another high school classmate, Steve Romeo. In the mornings, however, while I went fishing with Wally, Donny, and Butch, Steve usually played baseball for one of the "little league" teams in our hometown. At the end of the season, he was selected to play on an "all-star" team, because he was an excellent baseball player. So was I, but I was never even selected to play on any one of those "little league" teams, even though I "tried out," in a manner of speaking, on two different occasions over a two-year period.

I didn't understand it at the time, and my friends didn't seem too, either. Indeed, I was, in the consensus of many of them, better than some of the kids who had already been selected. Well, a lot of years have passed, since that non-selection, and I suppose that I will never know why, but I do know that it was terribly important to me at the time, unreasonably important. Indeed, that I was not selected, and that there was no apparent reason why not, would trouble me for years!

It would not trouble me nearly as much as another event, however, which occurred much later in my formative life, and, unlike the former disappointment, the consequences of that troubling event are still part of my life, in one form or another. It occurred while I was still in high school, and while I was still working, in the evenings during the week and all day on Saturdays, at Derr's Stationery Store in Lock Haven. With some of the money that I had earned, while working there over several years, I intended to pay for a possible "junior" membership in the Clinton Country Club, so that I could play golf with my fishing friends, Wally Smith, Butch Winner and Donny Witmeyer, whose families belonged to the Club. Because my family could not afford to join, or may not have been interested in joining, or both, I decided to join, solely on my own behalf, by filing an application for a junior membership, which was sponsored, as required, by two members in good standing, Mrs. Winner and Mrs. Joslyn, mothers of my two friends, Butch and Allen. Notwithstanding their support, however, my application was subsequently denied, for reasons that I did not understand, not initially, anyway.

Apparently, Mrs. Winner did understand, because she was noticeably uncomfortable in informing me that my application had been denied, but she never explained the reason for her discomfort or the denial, so I was left to assume that they may have been interrelated. Mrs. Joslyn, on the other hand, was not uncomfortable, just angry, because, in her view, there was no justifiable reason why my application had been denied, at least none that had been explained, which I subsequently construed to mean that it was likely denied because my father was an undereducated Jew, who, even worse, in the eyes of the Board of Directors, came from a very poor family in town.

Somewhat distraught by my misfortune and, maybe, even a little despondent, as a result, because I had never been explicitly rejected by anyone or anything before, with the possible exception of that "little league" baseball "try-out," which was not the same in my eyes, I explained to Mrs. Joslyn that my father no longer belonged to a

Jewish synagogue, since his marriage to my mother, and, therefore, he may not really be Jewish, anymore, and although he had, admittedly, grown up in an impoverished circumstance, that was no longer the case, because we now lived in a very nice home and in one of the nicer neighborhoods in town. Mrs. Joslyn ambiguously replied that, "she understood and that maybe one day I would, too." Although I wasn't quite sure what she meant by that statement, I did understand two things: Mrs. Joslyn was an extremely nice person in a world made up of many others, who were not, and as much as I hated the thought, I had to learn to live with both kinds of people.

It was a lesson that would subsequently serve me well in high school, because I had decided, certainly by that time, not to let the ability, or lack thereof, of any one of my teachers affect my performance in their classroom. Naturally, I would have preferred to have competent teachers in every class, but not unlike the rest of life, what I wanted did not always materialize. And in that respect, it did not take me long to realize that some people do not belong in a classroom, teaching high school students, any more than they belong in any other profession, while engaging in that profession. Indeed, by the end of my three years in high school, which, essentially, marked the end of my life growing up in that town, I had concluded that you had to become extremely charitable to justify some people's existence on this earth, and, by the way, I am not limiting that unflattering conclusion to the educational profession. Nevertheless, such people do exist and, sometimes, their existence intersects with your own, in the classroom or outside of it, and it is important to learn how to function reasonably well in life despite that fact. So despite a number of my teachers, and a less than educationally conducive atmosphere in some of my classes, I did quite well in nearly all of them, all the way through high school.

In that I did, I also learned another lesson, which was not readily available on the baseball field or on the golf course. My genealogy, whatever that may possibly mean, did not, in the end, inhibit my performance, in any manner, in the classroom; or putting the matter somewhat differently, my parents, if not my grandparents, were not a limitation on an academic life based on merit, to whatever extent a meritocracy may have existed in those classrooms at the time. Whatever I did academically depended, for better or worse, upon me and me alone. For a young boy, who seemed to have to survive his questionable parentage, at least in part, and at least while growing up, that fact was quite reassuring, at least up to that point in my life, to the extent that anything was at the time.

It was also reassuring to have Allen Joslyn, another high school classmate, and long-time friend, as my debating partner during all three of my years in high school, because of his capability, if nothing else, at least according to some of the judges. And, moreover, it did not hurt that he, like me, was argumentative by nature, especially with each other, which was likely why we had been paired, together, as a team, by our debating instructor. That way she could avoid any problem that may result from placing either one of us with someone else, who was more placid by nature, which seemed to work out quite well for both of us, because none of us had an opportunity to beat the other in a debating contest, although I believe that, sometimes, we both regretted that fact. An old photograph of the two of us playing chess, another competitive part of our high school lives, has been so identified and included as Exhibit 1 in the Appendix.

After several years of defeating debaters in intra-state competition, found mostly in high schools throughout Berks and Bucks County, Pennsylvania, we were both interested in seeing how well we would fare against some of the debaters found, elsewhere, throughout the country. So we each applied to so-called, "high school institutes for debate," taking place over the summer between our junior and senior years in high school, at the University of Colorado, in his case, and, in mine, at Northwestern University. Having been subsequently accepted in both cases, Allen headed off that summer to the University of Colorado, and I, in turn, headed off to Northwestern University . . . in what would become, for me at least, a life-changing event!

CHAPTER III

GROWING UP IN THE TOWN OF LOCK HAVEN: ATTENDING A DEBATE PROGRAM IN THE SUMMER BETWEEN MY JUNIOR AND SENIOR YEARS OF HIGH SCHOOL AT NORTHWESTERN UNIVERSITY AND MEETING LOU BERES THERE FOR THE FIRST TIME

I DON'T remember much about the trip to Chicago and, ultimately, to Evanston, Illinois, where Northwestern University was located, in order to participate in the summer debate program there. I do remember a fair amount about the program, itself, however, although the years have dimmed my memory somewhat. Among a number of other things, I remember that it was the first time that I had actually lived away from home. It was also the first time that I had lived in a dormitory, while eating three meals a day in a cafeteria, on a college campus, too. It was also the first time that I, an only child, ever had a roommate . . . from Knoxville, Tennessee, no less. And it was the first time that I had ever interacted with others, my age, who were from all over the country, which was somewhat unnerving, because most of them were capable of doing everything and anything really well, including debate during that summer program.

I suppose that all of those firsts may explain, but only to some extent, why my performance in all four of my speech classes that summer was no more than mediocre, a description that, unfortunately, continued in the debate competition, itself, held at the end of the summer and that summer program. Actually, in hindsight, I probably should not have even characterized my performance in that competition as mediocre, because my teammate and I were eliminated in the very first round. That was really quite disappointing, especially because of all of our preparation, but it was not too surprising, because I had begun to realize, long before that competition began, that there were some remarkably talented individuals in that summer program, from all over the nation, too, including two who had won the national high school debate contest, in the prior year, and one who had won the national high school extemporaneous speech contest that year, too. They had far more experience than I did, especially on a national level, and, probably, far more talent, too. For all of those uncomfortable reasons, if not more, I began to realize, shortly after my arrival, that my ability to compete with them was a tremendous opportunity, because I would probably grow from the experience, even in defeat.

Well, even though I was defeated in that debate contest, in the first round, too, I really did grow over the course of that summer program. Among other significant things, I grew into someone who realized, probably for the first time, that the world was much larger than the one in which I had grown up, and, of even more consequence, that the world was inhabited by a lot of people, even at my age, who were unlike those with whom I had grown up, for more reasons than I care to explain at this point. And, finally, of possibly even greater consequence, if that were even remotely possible, I realized that I may actually belong in that world . . . the larger one, I mean . . . although maybe somewhat tenuously at that point. That realization, even after a loss in the first round, was almost exhilarating!

Some of my newly acquired friends, over the course of that summer, did much better in that debate competition. One of them, Lou Beres, actually reached the finals, where, after an excellent performance, he and his teammate emerged victorious. And Lou was given an award, following that performance, for being the outstanding debater in the entire competition, something that I remember quite well, because we were in the same public speaking class, which took place every morning that summer. It was there, during that class, that we first became acquainted, and that classroom acquaintance subsequently ripened into a friendship, as a result of the animated conversation that briefly took place at the doorway to his room, nearly every evening, following my dinner in the cafeteria at Sargent Hall.

Indeed, upon reaching the entrance to our residence hall, which I believe is still known as the Hinman House, I would normally walk, resolutely, down the hall on the first floor of the dormitory, toward the back stairs, leading up to the second floor, where my room was located. But I would routinely stop at the open door to the third room on the right, because standing there, just inside the doorway, obviously waiting for me, was one of the residents, who generally had a smile as large as his affable personality. And I would briefly engage in a light-hearted conversion with the young man, right there in his doorway, who I had earlier discovered, from our public speaking class, was Lou Beres from Pekin, Illinois.

Those light-hearted conversations, brief as they were, took place nearly every evening, at about the same time and at the same place, which, of course, was the doorway to his room on the first floor of the Hinman House. And they were about everything and anything that two "rising" high school seniors could possibly discuss, in, roughly, a ten-to-fifteen minute interval, including his girlfriend back home in Pekin, Illinois, and, unfortunately, my lack of a counterpart back home in Lock Haven, Pennsylvania.

I remember that he told me, during one of those conversations, that his high school girlfriend was driving up to see him on the following day, and that he was really looking forward to seeing her again. I also remember that he told me that his girlfriend put a star on the outside of her correspondence with him, which, apparently, occurred weekly, and which probably had some significance at the time, but which I must have forgotten at this point in my aged life. Nevertheless, whatever it may have been, it must have diminished over time, because the relationship did not survive his senior year, or, if you will, the last star on the last piece of correspondence, but my new-found friendship with Lou did . . . for a lifetime! That, however, is quite another story and, for purposes of this story, a story yet to come.

CHAPTER IV

GROWING UP IN THE TOWN OF LOCK HAVEN: DEBATING, MY ACADEMIC PERFORMANCE IN MY SENIOR YEAR OF HIGH SCHOOL AND MY COLLEGE CHOICES

THE MORE immediate story, however, began to take place on my return to my hometown for the beginning of my senior year of high school and, among other academically related things, rejoining the debate program for that year. Now, however, I was a different kind of a debater, likely due to my summer experience, and so, too, was Allen Joslyn, probably for the same summer reason. For those experiential reasons, over the summer, of course, if not simply because of our irascible personalities, our debate coach decided to pair us together, once again, on the first team. I liked the idea, because it meant that there would be no real solution to the ever pending question of whether Allen was a better debater than me; Allen disliked the idea for the same uninformative reason.

Nevertheless, I was not unmindful that some questions may be better left unanswered, and by avoiding the answer and, instead, "barnstorming," once again, across the eastern part of the State of Pennsylvania, we won debate-after-debate in school-after-school. In the end, we were quite a team, maybe somewhat different as debaters, if not as individuals, but that just meant that we, as individuals, were a different kind of winning team in debate competitions, which, to be quite frank about it, was really our only concern.

Even aside from debate and debate competitions, I was also a different kind of student in my senior year of high school, because, among other improbable things, I began to work with far more efficiency in my courses and with far more interest in the subject matter. I also manifested a driving ambition to raise my grade point average even higher, for reasons apart from Allen Joslyn, probably for the first time in my academic life. And I began to consider, by late fall of that year, where I would like to go to college in the following year. In that respect, there had never been any doubt in my mind, as I was growing up, that one day I would go to college, even when I was a lowly student in elementary school. My parents expected no less, even then, and although they were no longer a significant presence in my life, because of my mother's unfortunate institutionalization during my junior and senior years of high school, some parental expectations linger on from childhood, sometimes over the course of one's life, even when we are no longer aware of that fact, and even when they are no longer around to remind us.

Well, mindful of expectations, at least of the parental variety, I decided, at some point during the fall of my senior year, that, notwithstanding all of the financial problems associated with my mother's unfortunate institutionalization, I should still try to go to college and, toward that end, begin an application process, related to that purpose, reasonably soon. I just didn't know where I should apply, or how I could conceivably afford to go there, wherever that may possibly be. Because most of those questions seemed to be beyond my ability to answer, and my parents were no longer available to assist me in doing so, for reasons that have already been discussed, but which will be more fully addressed in subsequent chapters, I sought the assistance of Mrs. Joslyn, the mother of my best friend and debating partner, Allen Joslyn, and she did try to help with everyone of those perplexing questions. Notwithstanding her counseling and kindness, however, I was fast learning that the answer to very difficult questions in one's life was not really subject to answer by someone else, even someone as kind and as helpful as Mrs. Joslyn. So, eventually, I began to rely on myself, for the most part, which really meant that I was relying on someone who was inexperienced, at best, and inept, at worst, in the college application process.

My inexperience, not surprisingly, limited my choices to my experience, such as Penn State University, located in virtually the next town of State College; Dickinson College, because it was not much further away, in Carlisle, and I had known some people who had gone there; Bucknell University, because it was even closer, in Lewisburg, and I had known some people who had gone there, too; and, finally, Northwestern University, because of my experience there last summer, while attending the high school debate program, even though it was in another state, quite far away, and I probably couldn't even afford the transportation costs of getting there.

In the end, however, after an agonizing period of indecision, defined more readily by months, that "on-campus" experience proved to be the deciding factor in making my first choice Northwestern University, even though, rationally speaking, I probably couldn't even afford to get there, let alone go there. But, then, when making a major decision in life, one in which you were really unprepared to make in the first place, why rely on reason, so I didn't. I sent in my room deposit, constituting part of the savings from my work that year at Derr's Stationary Shop, shortly after receiving an acceptance letter from Northwestern University, which, if you can believe it, has been included in Exhibit 20 to the Appendix.

It certainly is worth noting, at least at this point, that my inexperienced decision to attend Northwestern University, if you can call it that, was truly a transformative one, especially in hindsight, which, of course, I did not realize at the time. Nevertheless, I can honestly say now, that it would change my life forever, for reasons that will become clear, or, possibly, somewhat clear, as this story progresses and I do, too, in the story.

In any event, having said that, some things in life are so significant that you can remember them, quite vividly, even though they may have occurred almost a lifetime ago. And, indeed, it was over seventy years ago that I received that acceptance letter, which, in reality, was simply a one-page, two sentence, statement, formally admitting me into the freshman class, for the following academic year, at Northwestern University. That letter, with that scant, but transformative, information, was handed to me by my father, unopened, just after he entered the house, following the end of his work, for the day, late one afternoon. Within the hour, he would undoubtedly leave, once again, to visit my mother, thirty miles away, in a tuberculosis sanitarium in Lycoming County, a trip that he made nearly every evening, while she was institutionalized there.

I was bedridden at the time with the flu and, interestingly enough, Dr. Long, our family physician, was in attendance as a result. Before he began examining me, however, I opened the letter and, after quickly reading it, informed him and my father, who was still standing nearby, that my application had been accepted by my first college choice, Northwestern University. They both immediately smiled, and Dr. Long congratulated me on my acceptance to, in his subsequent words, "such a fine university." Actually, to be quite honest about the matter, my malaise, because of the flu, my mother's institutionalization, because of tuberculosis, my father's general absence, because of that fact, and Dr. Long's presence, because of all of those things, seemed far more significant at the time!

CHAPTER V

GROWING UP IN THE TOWN OF LOCK HAVEN: MY BOYHOOD FRIENDS STEVE ROMEO AND ALLEN JOSLYN; THE TRIP TO NEW YORK IN A 1929 PONTIAC CONVERTIBLE AND A SUBSEQUENT SNOWBALL FIASCO IN THE SAME VEHICLE

STEVE ROMEO had long since replaced Butch Winner, Donny Witmeyer and Wally Smith, as my trout fishing buddy, because the others had gone off to a boarding school at the Mercersburg Academy in Mercersburg, Pennsylvania. So that left Steve, as the only friend my age, who was still at home and who was still willing to join me on the great freestone streams in Clinton County, nearly every weekend in the springtime of that year, our senior year in high school. In the summertime, though, Steve and I replaced trout fishing trips with tennis matches, nearly every evening, after work, and on most weekends, too. I was probably a better trout fisherman, but Steve was probably a better tennis player than me. He would probably agree with the latter and disagree with the former, but, unfortunately, for far more people than just myself, he is no longer on this earth to do so.

Actually, Steve was really not a disagreeable person. To the contrary, he was generally well liked by most members of our class, which is probably why he was elected to be the class president that year. Nevertheless, although generally affable, and recognized as so by his classmates, he was still a little bit different from most of them, possibly not unlike myself, I suppose. Although I was not able to explain how we were different, I just knew that we were. Actually, that difference did not really become ostensible, not until many years later, when the two of us, in our different ways, engaged in lifestyles, as adults, that differentiated us, for better or worse, from those with whom we rejoined at our class reunions, nearly every five years, for the rest of our respective lives, and I am speaking about more than geography here.

On the other hand, Allen Joslyn was so different, even in high school, that it was sort of uncomfortable to be one of his best friends. After all, no boy in high school wants to stand out, not as being different, anyway, and Allen Joslyn stood out, and as being different, too, really different! And I was afraid that his difference may have been perceived to be contagious, and that I may have been perceived as being already infected. Oh, it was not just his manner of dress; actually, he dressed rather well. In fact, he was named the best dressed guy in our class in the school yearbook. But when you think about it, that just illustrates my point. It probably would have been a whole lot better if he would have dressed a little bit more like the rest of the guys our age in high school.

Allen, however, was never interested in being like everyone else in high school, and, I should add, he was not interested in doing what everyone else did in high school, either. I mean, he actually decided to join the Clinton County Historical Society, even though every other member, except one, was at least eighty years of age. And half of them actually needed "walkers" to get to the meetings, while the other half fell asleep half-way through them. That is precisely why the one exception to this aged spectacle, which happened to be me, decided to quit. Fortunately, I did long before my classmates discovered that Allen had not!

Oh, sure, I liked history and I liked historical things, too, especially if they originated in, or were related to, Clinton or Centre Counties, but not that much. I was in the end, and I continued to be, mindful of what was possible, as a teenage boy, growing up in the backwater of Clinton County. I am referring here to the boys who had grown up in a rural county, in the mountains of central Pennsylvania, where some people hunted deer all year long, even without a license, and those that did not, did not care about those that did!

Usually, those kinds of fellows were interested in more contemporary automobiles, the faster the better, which they could easily identify, but not easily afford. Nevertheless, cost aside, it was the more recent models, especially with a sleek design, featuring, so-called, elongated "fins," which ordinarily caught their attention. Not Allen Joslyn, though, oh, no, he drove a different kind of automobile, because he was a different kind of person, which, in the former case, could be more accurately described as a 1929 Pontiac convertible, whose canvas top stopped working, years ago, which is probably why it had been discarded in the earlier part of the twentieth century, when the heater and the mechanical brakes still efficiently worked.

Actually, even when Allen owned the car, which was in the middle of the century, the mechanical brakes still worked, but only in a manner of speaking, because the automobile would not fully come to a stop, not until it had traveled for about another forty or fifty feet, from the point at which they had first been continually applied. That, however, did not stop us from driving the car to New York City, over our Christmas vacation that year, our senior year in high school, on a supposedly educational trip to visit the United Nations. Unfortunately, the car still had an inadequate heater, which, to the extent that it still worked, was offset by the lack of a top, on our eighteen-hour winter trip to New York. So when it began to snow, several hours after being on the road, we simply put an old army blanket over our heads, which we had, thoughtfully, brought along for such a possibility. Now reasonably secure from the winter's worst, we cheered, wildly, every time that we passed a dog, a human being, or a stalled automobile, which was about the most that we could conceivably accomplish in that department and in that automobile. We also cheered, although less wildly, when the speedometer, which was no longer really working, either, actually hit twenty-seven miles per hour on the downhill side of the infamous "seven mountains," over in Centre County.

Well, difficult as it may be to believe, especially now, when youngsters entertain less hazardous adventures, usually because of their overly-concerned parents, we never encountered one problem, at least that was irresolvable, during our whole interstate trip on that holiday vacation. But we did one afternoon, several months later, shortly after school ended for the day, when most of our high school classmates had begun their long, wintry walk home in the snow. Allen, who had become more academically bored than usual that day, decided, shortly before classes had come to an end, that his life would dramatically improve if we, including, unfortunately, me, filled up his convertible with snowballs, immediately after school. That way, we could become a moving fort, in which we could pelt everyone, meaning every other classmate in sight, with snowballs, while quickly, alright slowly, moving away, hopefully long before they could effectively retaliate.

The idea seemed like a pretty good one at the time, certainly if you happened to be a seventeen- or eighteen-year-old boy, although, as it turned out, it was not a particularly smart one, irrespective of your age. Oh, sure, we did hit a number of our classmates with an assortment of hastily made snowballs, and we did move out of their way, before they were able to effectively retaliate. But Allen, who could not hit a large building, if it was right in front of him, with any kind of a missile, snow-like or otherwise, decided, for some insane reason, probably known only to God, and, unfortunately, to him, to throw a snowball at an elderly woman, shoveling snow off of her sidewalk, right in front of her house, on West Church Street. And, miraculously, even if you are a nonbeliever, he hit her on top of the forehead, which, unfortunately, at least for me, knocked off her glasses.

The chances of that ever happening again, may I remind you, had less statistical probability than Christ returning back to earth, which, by the way, was our subsequent defense at the police station, shortly after we were arrested, obviously because of that statistical improbability. Our defense, however, did not prevail with either the police or our parents, who were subsequently summoned, because of that statistical improbability, once again, and who, upon discovering what had miraculously happened, imposed an incomprehensible sentence, or so it seemed, at the time, requiring us, as I recall, to make some kind of an effort to grow up.

For two teenage boys, creative on occasion and injudicious on far too many others, who intended one day, with an appropriate amount of education, to become lawyers when they grew up, this whole, sordid, snowy, scenario did not prove to be an auspicious beginning; or, on the other hand, when you consider that rather carefully crafted theological defense, " on-the-fly," no less, maybe it really did!

CHAPTER VI

GROWING UP IN THE TOWN OF LOCK HAVEN: MY BEST FRIEND ALLEN JOSLYN; OUR IGNOMINIOUS TRIP UP BALD EAGLE CREEK TO THE TOWN OF BEECH CREEK IN A CANOE AS WELL AS FACING GRADUATION AND BEYOND

HAVING ARRIVED relatively unscathed by the end of our senior year of high school, with the possible exception of that unfortunate snowball incident, I was beginning to realize that Allen Joslyn's difference, which could probably be measured by an intelligence quotient factor, could also become a problem for me, even apart from his higher-grade point average. No better evidence of that fact comes to mind than the notorious canoe trip from our hometown up the Bald Eagle Creek toward Beech Creek, a small, quaint village, located about twelve or thirteen miles away, in the southwestern part of Clinton County.

I say, "notorious," because, by the time that ridiculous trip was over, the whole town had become involved, and not in any kind of a constructive way, either, which meant, of course, that our names, along with the only two murderers in the history of Clinton County, would likely go down in infamy! Unlike those two, however, we gained our notoriety, because of my overly-creative and injudicious friend, Allen Joslyn, who decided that we could easily take, in a manner of speaking, a canoe all the way up the Bald Eagle Creek, from Lock Haven to Beech Creek, not to mention a return on the very same day, which was a round trip of about twenty-five miles, over which we would have to carry the damn thing about half the time and paddle against a very strong current on the way up for the rest of the time.

To overcome the problem with the current, and my pessimism, I might add, Allen decided to build a small motor, an extraordinarily small motor, that, in his questionable opinion, he "could easily hook up to the side of the canoe, because of its size." That way, as explained to a dubious me, we would not have to face that strong current, with no more than a paddle, on the way up that miserable creek. To overcome the acknowledged portage problem, and my continuing pessimism, he decided to include me, in a moment of enormous benevolence, so that, in his words, I may share in "the glory of making such a trip," not to mention, in my words, "the unbelievable burden of carrying that damn canoe over miles of a rocky terrain!"

That I agreed to go on that "hair-brained" journey is beyond understanding; that I did go is beyond justification. I certainly had difficulty justifying it to the general inquiry, subsequently conducted by the local police, my family, his family, the local newspaper, the local radio station, and every other member of our class, their parents, and the concerned citizenry of the town, if not in the county, nearly all of whom had begun a county-wide search for us, in one form or another, meaning by land, water and air, when we did not reappear before nightfall!

I did try to explain, however, that the whole trip turned out to be a ridiculous fiasco, at least to anyone who cared to listen at that point. For one, the motor kept breaking down, about every half-mile, and while Allen was trying to fix it, which was continually, I might add, I had to paddle against an unbelievably strong current, for miles, literally for miles! In fact, his hands were in the water, trying to fix that damn motor, more than they were on a paddle, and that was during the whole miserable trip up that stupid creek. For that injudicious reason, I don't think that we ever made more than one mile in an hour, at anytime during the whole futile effort, which explains why the sun was starting to go down, late in the afternoon, and we were not even half-way up that stupid creek!

I pointed that out to Allen . . . that we were not even half-way up there and that the sun was starting to go down, which meant, of course, that it was probably getting to be quite late in the day, and I suggested that we turn around and go back, before it actually became too dark to see, anymore. Allen, who, by this time, had lost what little sanity he had left, somewhere out there on that miserable creek, refused, and he justified his refusal by the early afternoon time on his wristwatch, which, of course, had stopped, hours ago, because it was not waterproof and, along with the rest of his left arm, had been in the water for most of that ill-fated trip, while he was trying to fix that stupid, half-assed, motor!

Finally, however, his sanity, or what little remained of it, returned, miraculously, about an hour later, probably because of the darkness, and he agreed, at that point, to turn around, halfway up that "godforsaken" creek. Hours later, while paddling back down, about as fast as we could, now in almost complete darkness, we were met, at various intervals, by a number of motorized crafts, not to mention their alarmed passengers, who enquired whether we had seen two teen-age boys in a green canvas canoe, reportedly last seen somewhere further up the creek. The last one, which actually had a searchlight, noted the green color of our canvas canoe in the darkness, not to mention the two teen-age idiots who happened to be in it, and, disgustingly, informed us that nearly everyone, and I really do not mean to qualify that noun in any manner, was looking for us! Apparently, however, he was not quite accurate, because some of the more realistic ones had already given up the search, because they believed, by that time, that we had probably drowned somewhere up that ridiculous creek on that impossibly stupid journey.

Actually, looking back now, it may well have been easier for both of us if we had, in fact, drowned, because our fate, which was waiting for us, on our return back down there at the boat dock, where we had started, turned out to be even worse than death, because it would linger on, for days and weeks, and even months, and, ultimately and tragically, especially when you are trying to grow up in a small town, years!

Unfortunately, however, as you may have suspected, at least at this juncture in my story, we didn't drown. Instead, we paddled, in a panic now, the rest of the way down that "god-forsaken" creek, in the dark, to meet a large part of the town, most of whom were impatiently waiting for us, having already been informed that we were actually alive, and on our way back, and the remainder of whom clearly believed, without saying so, that we really should have drowned for being that stupid! Our parents, on the other hand, were clearly pleased that we had not. They were not especially pleased, however, to pay for the cost of the search, especially by the airplanes!

I do not remember anything more about that canoe trip that is worth remembering, which may almost be a tautology, other than, possibly, one thing. Both of my parents were standing on the dock, with all of the others, and with enormously concerned faces as we appeared. And that was the first time, which I could recall, that my mother had ever been out of the house, since she had returned home, following her lengthy convalescence in the tuberculosis sanitarium and hospitalization thereafter. And my father, who ordinarily would have been working at that time of the evening, selling life insurance, was standing right beside her.

Because of his work and her institutionalization, at the risk of being somewhat repetitious, my parents were not a very significant part of my life during my high school years. And following her return during the latter part of my senior year, my mother was still too weak, because of a prolonged recovery period, to even go to my high school graduation, and, frankly, I don't know whether my father attended the event either. If he did, it was all by himself, and he apparently didn't stay after the ceremony, because I didn't see him, following the procession out of the auditorium and into the lobby, where most of the parents were waiting to greet their graduating sons and daughters. It is possible that the absence of my mother, because of her convalescing situation, dampened the whole experience for him, or, possibly, there was something else, which I would not fully understand until much later in my life. So in his absence, I spent the rest of the evening, following the ceremony, with Steve and Allen, as well as with several other of our classmates, some of whom I would not see, following our summer vacation, for the rest of my life. A photograph of me at my high school graduation is part of Exhibit 115 in the Appendix.

Because we were going our separate ways in the fall of that year, to different universities, if nothing else, and because they remained my best friends at the time, even out of the classroom, I spent as much time as possible with Steve and Allen that summer, doing all of the things that we had been doing together over the last four years. I could not help thinking, however, that there seemed to be a very strong current that summer, inevitably sweeping everything before it, including the three of us, and like a raging river, at flood stage, it was literally and metaphorically carrying everything along with it, including us, whether we liked it or not. And it was not lost on me at the time that there seemed to be something rather foreboding about what lay ahead, probably for all of us, even though it may have been somewhat different for each one of us, although I didn't really understand what that may have been.

I did understand, however, that things would likely change in the days ahead, for all three of us, and that there seemed to be a lot of anxiety about that kind of a change, even if it meant no more than simply growing up, especially when you don't fully understand the ramifications of doing so. I just understood that things would never be quite the same, not, at least, as they were that summer, and that there was something very special about growing up where we did, and when we did, and even, for the most part, how we did.

CHAPTER VII

NORTHWESTERN UNIVERSITY: TAKING A GREYHOUND BUS FROM STATE COLLEGE, PENNSYLVANIA TO CHICAGO, ILLINOIS AND, ULTIMATELY, TRAVELING BY AN ELEVATED TRAIN TO NORTHWESTERN UNIVERSITY, IN EVANSTON, WHERE, SUBSEQUENTLY, I DECIDED TO ROOM WITH MY OLD FRIEND, LOU BERES, IN SARGENT HALL DURING MY FRESHMAN YEAR

I DON'T remember very much about the day that I left at the end of that summer on a Greyhound Bus for Northwestern University. I do remember that my mother, who was still convalescing in bed, came downstairs to the kitchen, in order to watch me carry my things out to the car, where my father was waiting to drive me to State College, the location of the Greyhound Bus Station, about an hour away. But I don't remember whether my mother hugged me, or shook my hand, or simply said goodbye, before I walked out of the kitchen door for the last time, although it was probably the latter, because that is what we ordinarily did in my family in uncomfortable circumstances like that.

My father had come home from work at lunchtime, in order to drive me there, which he subsequently did, once I had finished loading everything into the trunk of his car. Notably, we did not say very much to each other during the trip there, probably because we had so many things to say to each other, over a lifetime of no real conversation, that we really couldn't fit it all into one hour, the time that it took to reach the Greyhound Bus Station in State College, so we decided not to try!

Upon our arrival, about three hours before the bus departed the Station for Chicago, my father parked the car and helped me unload my things from the trunk and carry them into the Station, where they were placed behind the ticket counter for safekeeping. After purchasing my ticket and placing identification tags on all of my bags, I came back outside, to find my father standing over by the car, waiting for me. As I approached him, he handed me my portable radio, which I had apparently forgotten in the backseat, and, then, we stood there for a moment, looking away from each other, somewhat uncomfortably, while searching for something to say. When it had become uncomfortably apparent that neither one of us could really think of anything, I simply shook his hand, because, you know, that was what we ordinarily did in my family in uncomfortable circumstances like that.

Then, somewhat sadly, I watched him turn around, slowly walk back toward the car and, once seated, start the engine and pull away towards home, at least what was once my home, anyway. At that moment, at that elucidating moment, I realized, probably for the first time, that we, my parents and myself, were destined now, if not before, to take different paths in life, and that this moment was probably the very beginning, right there in the Greyhound Bus Station in State College, Pennsylvania!

With that in mind, I wonder now, as I have for years, which one of us was more fortunate at the time, my father, who could go back home again, and did, or me, who could not, and did not! That's right, whatever may be the case, one thing was for sure, especially looking back now, unlike my father, I could never really go home again, not in the same way, not even if I wanted to, and, trust me, at that moment, I wanted to. I wonder, now, while still looking back, if my sadness . . . and words cannot adequately express my sadness, as I watched my father pull away, and begin his trip back home . . . was because I sort of understood that inability at the time.

Because the bus did not leave until later in the afternoon, I decided to spend the intervening time, by walking across the street to the Penn State campus, in order to visit two former high school friends in their dorm room, who were going to the University at the time. I was mindful that those two would probably be the last high school friends that I would likely see for some time, maybe even for years, if not, actually, for a lifetime.

I doubted, on the other hand, that I would actually know any of the students at Northwestern University. In fact, to be even more realistic, I didn't even know exactly how to get to the University, in suburban Evanston, once I reached the Greyhound Bus Station in Chicago. That I went anyway, that I boarded a bus for, roughly, a fourteen-hour trip to a huge city, in another state, in those kinds of circumstances, is a serious statement about a young man from a small rural town, in one of the poorest counties, in the State of Pennsylvania, which may explain much about the rest of his life, not just at Northwestern University, but in the years that have followed, even as the author of this story.

In any event, I don't remember much about the actual trip, other than it involved a lot of states, a lot of miles, a lot of flat land, a lot of boredom and not much actual sleep, all of which, I suppose, should not be unexpected on a bus trip of that duration. Taking the rest of the afternoon and virtually all of the night, we arrived fairly early in the morning, on the following day, at the Greyhound Bus Station in Chicago. The only interruption to all of those miserable miles, occurred when we stopped at a bus stop, somewhere outside of a small town in the middle of Ohio, at about eight o'clock in the evening, so that the passengers, who chose to do so, could use the bathroom facilities there, and, if they were so inclined, find something to eat at a cafeteria located there, too. While waiting for them to rejoin me on the bus, following use of those facilities or that cafeteria, I quickly finished a sandwich that my mother had thoughtfully packed for, obviously, that kind of a situation. If something else occurred on that trip, which was at all consequential, and, frankly, there must have been something, given all of those miles, I simply cannot remember it.

I will never forget, however, something that occurred shortly after we reached our destination at the Greyhound Bus Terminal in Chicago. Within minutes, following the departure of the passengers from the bus, I picked up my things, which had been stored, along with a number of other items for a number of other passengers, in the baggage compartment underneath the bus. Now, with everything uncomfortably secure, in both of my hands and under both of my arms, not to mention over my shoulder, I immediately departed the Terminal, walking straight out of the side door and onto the streets of Chicago. There, somewhere within the infamous "Loop," in downtown Chicago, I immediately began looking for an elevated train station, so that I could board a northbound to Evanston, where the Northwestern University's undergraduate campus was located.

Wandering about, somewhat bewildered, not to mention somewhat bedraggled, from way too little sleep, I labored under the weight of my two suitcases, my "forty-five" record player, my portable radio, and a large laundry bag, containing, among a number of other things, my electric alarm clock, my leather toilet case and a pair of tennis shoes in it.

Frustrated, now, by my inability to find any evidence of an elevated train station, after what was beginning to seem like an endless search, but which, realistically, was probably no more than a five- or ten-minute effort, I finally asked several passersby, in an ad seriatim fashion, how to find a nearby station. Although each one was kind enough to provide some kind of an explanation, if not an implicit direction, which did not essentially differ, I still could not find the damn station. In fact, I couldn't even find the street, where it was supposedly located, so after wondering, aimlessly, around the "Loop," probably in "proverbial circles," looking for what had been repeatedly described as "nearby," I finally asked a nicely dressed, middle-aged, black lady, standing next to me on a street corner, obviously waiting for the light to turn, if I was anywhere near an elevated train station. Smiling, slightly, the woman studied me, for just a moment, realizing, likely from all my paraphernalia, if not my inane question, that I was probably a newcomer in her city, and, thereupon, she advised me that I was going in the wrong direction. Following which, after exchanging a few inconsequential, but pleasant, words, she offered to take one of my suitcases and walk there with me.

Somewhat uncomfortable now, because my intrusion on a street corner may actually have been unwelcome, I thoughtfully protested that, with a little bit of guidance, I probably could find it on my own. Nevertheless, following a brief, but polite, discussion, I finally relented, because, as the lady accurately pointed out, I obviously had not been able to find the station on my own. And, thereafter, while talking with each other in somewhat of an animated fashion, as though we had known each other for some time, we walked, together, each one of us carrying some of my luggage, on the way to a nearby elevated train station, and, for that matter, the rest of this chapter, if not the rest of my academic life.

Interestingly, prior to that time, I had never met a black person, not in my circumscribed life. Indeed, I had never even seen one before, outside of the "movies," that is. In fact, outside of my previously brief encounters, in a futile effort to discover the whereabouts of an elevated train station, I had never even talked to someone on the street who I did not already know, or, at least, know of, in a manner of speaking. Indeed, prior to that time, I had never been in a city larger than Williamsport, Pennsylvania, a relatively small city, located in a nearby county, with a population that must not have exceeded forty thousand people at the time. And except for the prior summer, in which I had attended the debate program at Northwestern University, I had never even been outside of the State of Pennsylvania. In fact, although it may be hard to believe, especially now, I had never even been outside of Clinton County, where I had grown up, except on some cursory visits, for various parental purposes, to Centre and Lycoming Counties, which border it.

Maybe, in some inadequate way, all of that explains why I remember that black lady so well, even now, after nearly sixty-five years. She was only a part of my life for the five- or ten-minute interval that it took us to walk to an elevated train station, somewhere in the inner city of Chicago. But given my immediate circumstances, being effectively lost on the streets of Chicago, she was a very important part at the time, which, obviously, transcended the five- or ten-minute instance of our acquaintance!

I often thought about that fact, as well as the five or ten-minute act of kindness, during the year in which Ann Powell (Stuart), who has a similar complexion, came to live with us, and, legal niceties aside, became, in reality, our daughter, or as she was prone say, "our granddaughter." Well, whatever the filial case, I was always mindful that, by engaging in our relationship with Ann, who has become an important part of our family, over a lifetime, I may have discharged a debt, a sixty-five-year-old debt, to a kindly, well dressed, middle-aged, black lady, who helped a lost country boy negotiate the streets of Chicago, a long time ago, for a five or ten-minute disruption in both of their lives.

Well, in case you may be wondering, at least at this point in my digression, with the kind assistance of that black lady, I finally reached and, subsequently, boarded an elevated train, which, eventually, traveled northward toward Evanston, where I had every reason to believe that I would find the undergraduate campus of Northwestern

University. Arriving no more than twenty minutes later at the Noyes Street Station, which I remembered, from the summer before, to be the closest stop to Sargent Hall, the dormitory to which I had been assigned, I departed from the train, descended, clumsily, with all of my paraphernalia, from the elevated platform to the street. And I, immediately, began lugging all of it, for about four blocks, eastward, toward Sheridan Road, which, I recalled, bordered the undergraduate campus of Northwestern University.

Crossing with the light, I slowly made my way onto the campus, walking directly across the parking lot in front of Sargent Hall, on my way over to the Hinman House, just a few minutes away, where I had stayed the summer before, and where I had been informed, by correspondence over the summer, that I could pick up my room assignment. Thereafter, with my room assignment in hand, following a brief, but pleasant, discussion with a University Housing Official, I walked back across the parking lot to Sargent Hall, no more than twenty yards away, entered the building, following a short trip up the steps to the entrance, stopped, briefly, to catch my breath in the lobby, and, finally, climbed three flights of stairs to the third floor, still clumsily lugging all of my paraphernalia. At that point, I walked, somewhat tentatively, a short distance down the hallway, checking the numbers on each door, rather carefully, until I finally reached my assigned room, number 302, which was on the right side, facing the parking lot.

After opening the door with a key, which had been given to me along with my room assignment, I decided to put all of my things on the floor, right next to the bed, located on the right side of the room, which, in due time, I did, noting, at the same time, that my assigned roommate had not yet appeared. Immediately thereafter, I began the monotonous, but necessary, job of unpacking my clothes and putting them away, mostly in the built-in drawers and closet on my side of the room, located next to the doorway. In the midst of that mechanical effort, necessary as it was, I was left with the distinct impression, as I continued to sit there on that cold tile floor, still unpacking my things, that everything around me in that barren room was institutional, and that, one day, I would likely be, too, as a student on that university campus, but I couldn't imagine it, not yet.

Notwithstanding my institutional circumstance, or, at least, the perception thereof . . . over what seemed like only minutes in that still sterile room, but which must have been more like twenty, or even thirty, given the amount of my unpacked things at that point . . . an event occurred, which I can only describe as fortuitous, even now, and which would eventually change my life at that university and, likely, well beyond, possibly for the rest of my life. The event, if we can appropriately call it that, was initiated by a pronouncement, made by a sonorous, bass-baritone voice, with which I had become well acquainted, but which I had not heard since the end of the debating program, during the previous summer, at that university.

The melliferous voice did no more than simply pronounce my name, "Cal Golumbic," in the most articulate fashion, as was its custom. And since that was my name, which was being used in an unfamiliar environment, but in a more than familiar manner, it caused me to immediately look up and to discover, to my outright astonishment, the personage of Lou Beres, who was now standing right there in front of me, in a half-opened doorway, with a smile that seemed as big as the future that lay before us!

Lou then said, while still standing there, that he had "noticed the 'wingtip' cordovan, dress shoes" that I was wearing and that I had previously worn on occasion, during our summer debating program, the year before, as he was walking by the half-opened doorway, on the way down the hallway, toward his own assigned room. "Struck by the sight of those shoes," once again, and "having never seen them before on anyone," other than myself, he said that it caused him "to immediately stop, look up, and there," in a manner of speaking, I was, and, as it turned out, we were, for the next four years, and, as I have already stated, in somewhat of a different manner, for the rest of our natural lives!

Lou's next words, upon entering the room, were, in that characteristically, sonorous, base-baritone voice, "Cal, it's great to see you!" Funny, how you can remember something like that, after all of those years, over seventy of them to be nearly exact. Although I don't remember much about the conversation that followed, there must have been quite an amount, because the discovery of each other, within an hour of our arrival, at a university that was essentially unknown to each one of us, was unquestionably consequential to both of us.

In fact, I clearly remember, even now, being overjoyed at finding someone at that university, who I already knew and who I had always liked, even before I had finished unpacking my clothes, on the very first day of my arrival. I also remember, quite clearly, since it would impact the rest of my life, that somewhere during the conversation that followed, most of which has been lost to history, Lou suggested that we go back to the Hinman House, where we had received our room assignments, to see if we could have our assignments changed so that we could room together.

Well, following his suggestion, something that I did, continually, over the next four years, we did go back; we did get our room assignments changed; and we did room together, not just during our freshman year, in that dormitory, but during our sophomore and senior years, as well, in a fraternity that we subsequently joined together. But I am already getting a little ahead of my story, at this point, probably because I began to remember, all over again, how fortuitous it was that the remarkable young man from Pekin, Illinois, who would subsequently become my best friend at that university, and, for that matter, the rest of my life, just happened to walk past my room, only minutes following my arrival, and noticed my "wingtip" cordovan shoes on that fateful day, which, when you think about it, became the very first day of the rest of our lives, together, at a great midwestern university!

CHAPTER VIII

NORTHWESTERN UNIVERSITY, FRESHMAN YEAR: LIVING WITH LOU BERES DURING MY FRESHMAN YEAR IN SARGENT HALL

IN FACT, to be quite honest, if not quite repetitive and, certainly, quite reflective, a significant part of my life over the next four years at that university was defined by my association with Lou Beres. But my course selection for the very first quarter was not; unfortunately, the choices were solely mine; so I really had no one else to blame for my poor academic performance that quarter. I don't know what I had in mind, in making that selection, other than, possibly, a secret desire to fail out of school, which, by the way, I nearly did. That way, of course, I would have no alternative, other than to go back home, where I couldn't fail, because I didn't have to try.

Lou, on the other hand, did quite well that quarter, academically and socially, which, of course, was our very first quarter at that university, and which made his success all the more surprising, because of that fact. I was never quite sure how he did it, because he was usually gone for most of the day, returning to the room shortly after dinner at his board job. Following a brief, but cordial, greeting, we would ordinarily open our books, previously residing on our desks, and begin studying together for the rest of the evening, without talking very much about the rest of the day, which, of course, had taken place earlier in the day. At some point, however, much later in the evening, when he had obviously concluded his studies, Lou would typically rise from his desk and, without saying a word, walk over to his bed, which was only a few steps away, where he would typically kneel down at the very end, underneath a large wooden cross, previously hung by him from an overhead cabinet door handle. Then he would fold his hands in supplication, rest on his knees and bow his head in prayer.

At about the same time, nearly finished with my own studies, too, I would quickly rise from my desk and quietly slip past Lou, on my way over to the door to our room, which I would quietly close, so that he would not be disturbed. Following the conclusion of his evening prayer, no more than a few minutes later, Lou would typically rise, walk straight over to his closet and, without any delay, put on his pajamas and slippers. After doing the same, but not nearly as efficiently, I normally joined him at the doorway, where he had been impatiently waiting, after which we would begin to briskly walk down to the bathroom, at the other end of the hallway, so that we could brush our teeth, among other unmentionable things, and, in my case, quickly shower, something that I had always accomplished in the evenings, even now.

Following my brief accomplishment of that evening habit, I would hastily rejoin Lou, standing just outside the bathroom door, in the hallway, impatiently waiting for me once again, and, thereafter, the two of us would normally return back down the hallway to our room, walking together once again, but far more slowly this time, bidding a good evening to a number of newly acquired dormitory friends, from all over the country, still studying in their rooms, with half-opened doorways. Upon reaching our own room, nearly at the other end of the hallway, we characteristically engaged in a brief period of conversation and, sometimes, laughter, too, generally about the days' events and nonevents, while, at almost the same time, straightening up our desks, but only somewhat, and laying out our clothes for the following day. And at inexplicably diverse points, but seemingly related, we would noticeably pause for a few moments, in an unstated acknowledgement of the end of another difficult day, in the lives of two slightly anxious college freshmen, who were roommates then and friends now.

Without any hesitation at that point, or, at least, not much, we ended our evening together, in that now comfortable dormitory room and at that still uncomfortable university, by crawling, once again, into our respective pull-out beds, located on the opposite sides of the room, and pulling the covers up and over the end to another full and challenging day, while, at almost the same time, saying goodnight to each other and, in our own silent ways, to our respective families, who have not yet become distant afterthoughts, even though they have remained in Pekin, Illinois and in Lock Haven, Pennsylvania.

After which, I typically reached over and turned out my desk lamp, the only light still remaining on in the room, and, at almost the same time and in the same motion, I turned on my small portable radio, which was also within reach on my desk. And, finally, we, who had become roommates from disparate worlds, and who had come together in this one, managed to fall asleep, listening to the comforting sounds of classical music, compliments of Pierre Andre, who would play that genre until, in his own nightly words, "dawn." That, of course, is when we would ordinarily rise to face another trying day, in the academic life of two young college freshmen, who were trying, on a daily basis, to become a viable part of a great midwestern university, one of which, I might add, was doing so, far more successfully than the other, at least at that point.

All of those nightly occurrences in a midwestern university dormitory, depicted rather precisely hereinbefore, almost approached the status of a ritual, or, maybe, on a more religious note, a rite, taking place nearly every evening that quarter, as well as in the second and third quarters, too. And for reasons that I cannot explain, at least not at this point in my life, or at this point in my story, which, of course, bear a marked similarity, that nightly ritual or rite, involving those two young men, one of whom is no longer living now, but still a living part of this story, has resurrected itself in my memory, continually now, fully in the late winter of my years.

Actually, in somewhat of a haunting fashion, those evenings in that university dormitory, and in that room, with that young man, who was my roommate then and my best friend now, speak to me often, about what we were at the time and what we became, in the end, not just at that four year university, but in life, itself, his and mine, which, in his case, is so much more than a simple grave marker can say and, in mine, a story can tell!

CHAPTER IX

NORTHWESTERN UNIVERSITY, FRESHMAN YEAR: THE BOARD JOB AT ALPHA CHI OMEGA; THE ANNUAL SNOWBALL FIGHT BETWEEN THE WAITERS AND THE SORORITY SISTERS; THE ANNUAL CHRISTMAS PERFORMANCE BY THE WAITERS; AND A SORORITY HOUSEMOTHER CALLED, "MRS. V"

I CAN'T tell you what Lou did during the day that quarter, our first quarter, or even during that year, our freshmen year, at that university, other than to say that, like me, he probably attended classes most of the time. Classes, however, usually ended earlier in the afternoon on most days, at least for most people, including me, so I would typically return to my room and take a nap or, alternately, relax in my room with some of my newly acquired dormitory friends, who, generally, occupied rooms nearby on my floor, the third floor.

Lou did neither of those things, however, which would leave most of his activities for much of the afternoon, unaccounted, at least for purposes of this story. I did not think much about that unaccounted fact at the time, probably because, as my grades reflected, I did not think much about anything at the time, in class or out. As the quarter progressed, however, one thing became quite clear, even to someone like me, who found clarity at the time to be quite challenging, whatever Lou did during those hours, he must have done it with a lot of people, because a lot of people voted for him to become the freshman class president, which is obviously why he won that election.

Some of the people who voted for Lou were girls, who lived, among other locations, in sorority houses, located in quadrangles, with entrances on either end, on the southern part of the campus. One of those sororities was called Alpha Chi Omega, where Lou worked at a "board job" in the kitchen, washing dishes at breakfast, lunch, and dinner, seven days a week, with the exception of Sunday evening. Actually, there was no meal plan on that evening, not anywhere on campus, including the sorority houses, so everyone, who was living in a university residence, typically frequented an off-campus dining site, like "Walker Brothers," which was located nearby, and which was reasonably inexpensive, too.

Although I knew that Lou was working at a "board job" for his meals, I did not realize that it was at a sorority house, not until much later in the quarter, the first quarter of our freshmen year, when he informed me and asked, at the same time, if I would be interested in working there, too. Because I could not really afford to continue paying for my meals in the cafeteria at Sargent Hall, where I had been eating them with other freshmen on my floor, I told him that I would be grateful for such an opportunity, and, toward that end, I asked him to let me know when there was an opening.

Shortly thereafter, he did, and, following an interview, I was subsequently hired by the "house mother," Olga Volkman, who the waiters in the kitchen and the girls in the sorority house affectionately called, Mrs. "V." The "board job" was an economic lifesaver at the time, for which I received a meal every time that I worked, which was at breakfast, lunch and dinner, and, as it turned out, so much more, which I will subsequently discuss, at some length, at a later point in this chapter. At this point, however, I think that it is important to point out that it would not be the last time that Lou Beres would economically intervene on my behalf, by providing me with a great employment opportunity, over the course of our four-year association, as students, at Northwestern University.

With that acknowledgment, let me also note that his success in this instance, which enabled me to begin work in the kitchen at that sorority house, was the beginning of some sort of a social life, in a broadly construed sense of the concept, for a country boy out of a small, rural town, who was now a college freshman and clearly out of his element, in every dimension, at a great midwestern university, located in a large, sprawling, suburban area of Chicago, Illinois. Given that rural consideration, if not limitation, it is not too difficult to understand that the country boy had, in fact, never even heard of sororities, before stepping onto that college campus, let alone associated with sorority girls in any one of them.

Admittedly, my association was quite limited at the time. Most of them did not even know my name that quarter. I was merely an employee in the kitchen, nothing more, who just happened to be a college freshman on that campus. Nevertheless, I was around them on a daily basis, while working there, and being around sorority girls that often was more than a sufficient social life for an awkward college freshman, especially when you consider that I received breakfast, lunch, and dinner at the same time.

With that in mind, together with so many other things that occurred over the four years of my association with the girls in that sorority house, some of which are subsequently discussed in more detail, I actually think, upon reflection, that one of the more important parts of my education at that university took place at that "board job," even though it was never part of the subject matter in any one of my courses over my four academic years there. Nevertheless, an education may well be more broadly defined, and learning that individuals, like most of those sorority girls, who came from circumstances distinctly unlike mine, economically, if nothing else, were still just individuals, who, in some cases, merited a much closer look, in a manner of speaking, was distinctly educational. And I learned that and so much more while working at my board job, over a four-year period, at that sorority house.

That, of course, is not to diminish the other facets of my educational life at that university, including my classes, my professors, and even my fellow students. But I do believe that I learned more about life, washing dishes in the kitchen and, subsequently, waiting tables in the dining room of that sorority house, than I did anywhere else on that campus, even including the classroom. And in those rare moments when you may have forgotten where you were, what you were doing there, and how well you were expected to be doing it, Mrs. "V" was always there to remind you! She was a very wise woman, whose history was unknown to me, but it must have been notable, because she was a very accomplished individual, who demonstrated the kind of confidence that you only see on those who were, and who were aware of it.

I also learned, more mundanely, how to appropriately set a table, wait on a table and clear a table in a sorority house. And over the four years of my employment there, I learned how to come in the back door, after pushing a buzzer to do so, put on one of the white coats hanging down in the laundry room and clip on one of those horrendous bow ties down there, too, before starting to work as a waiter, by walking up the back stairs to the kitchen and out through the swinging doors into a dining room full of noisy sorority girls, eating breakfast, lunch or dinner, and talking and laughing, as usual, all at the same time, seemingly oblivious to the presence of waiters like me.

Actually, those girls were not so oblivious, not to our presence, while waiting on their tables, as I would subsequently discover over the years of working there, because they included us in a number of their functions, formally and informally, during the course of the school year. Referring to the latter, we were always included in, if not made the involuntary subjects of, the annual "snowball fight," between the girls and the waiters, which traditionally occurred right after the very first snowfall for the year, and right after we had finished cleaning up the kitchen and the dining room for the evening, so that we could automatically leave through the back door to our respective residences.

The imbroglio, for want of a better descriptive word, actually began, just as soon as we opened the back door, in order to depart for our residences, on and off that campus. At that moment, that very moment, we were unfortunately, but not unsurprisingly, met with a hail of snowballs, even before we were able to get completely out of the door, by nearly all of the girls in the sorority house, who were standing right behind a rather impressive snowy structure, referred to by them as a fort, no more than seven or eight feet away.

A three-year-old, which, in those circumstances, was not an unfair characterization of what confronted us, could not miss their target at that distance, and they, those screaming and laughing three-year-olds, did not. Covered with snow, from head to foot, which, quite frankly, does not begin to adequately or accurately characterize our poor state of affairs at that point, we simply struggled to do no more than just get out of the back door and, gamely, if not pathetically, fight back!

Obviously, the sorority sisters of Alpha Chi Omega, nearly all forty of that laughing and hysterical throng, gave fairness in a snowball fight a new dimension. It would become my first real lesson on relationships, between men, which, before becoming covered with all of that snow, we had once been, and women, which, before engaging in all of that screaming and laughing at our snowy plight, they had once been. Yes, I can safely say that, because of that traditional snowball fight, every wintry year for four years, I became quite dubious about finding some sense of fairness in the "fairer" sex, in the years that followed.

I must acknowledge, however, that the "waiters" . . . a generally descriptive term for all of those who were employed at that "board job," irrespective of their actual service in the dining room . . . gained some smattering of retribution during their vocal performance at the traditional dinner for the sorority sisters of Alpha Chi Omega, occurring shortly before our vacation over the Christmas holidays. At the end of that performance, which was musically conceived and performed by the waiters, we gave out awards to the delight of most of the girls. I say, "most of the girls," because some of the others, who received the awards, were often less than delighted, because of the nature of some of those awards!

One award, for example, which was traditionally given to the girl, who we would most like to flush down the kitchen drain, and subsequently described as such, because of her demanding nature in the dining room, was called, "Miss Drano." So following a lengthy speech, explaining in agonizing detail why we believed that girl had earned that award, it was ordinarily given to her by the head waiter, followed by the boisterous laughter of the rest or her sorority sisters. Another award, which was given to the girl whom we would most like to give a bath to in the pots and pans sink, followed by a quasi-anatomical speech why, was called, "Miss Pots and Pans." Actually, I always believed that the recipient of that award was secretly thrilled to receive it, and that the girls, who did not, were secretly jealous of her good fortune, or good figure, whichever feature you may decide to choose, the waiters, of course, having chosen the latter!

Another award was called "Miss Vestibule," because, as explained in another lengthy speech by the head waiter, it was given to the girl who "made-out" the most in the vestibule, whatever that may have meant, just before "Mrs. V" ushered out the co-perpetrator from fraternity row and, then, locked the front door on another, nearly compromising, situation on a Saturday night. This, of course, was a far more dubious distinction, especially as a publicly noted one, in the nearly Victorian era of the nineteen-fifties, which, nevertheless, found a significant amount of competition among the overachieving, romantically inclined, sorority sisters of Alpha Chi Omega. Indeed, as it was pointed out by the headwaiter, who traditionally gave this particular speech, some of his Kappa Sigma fraternity brothers were enormously grateful to have been "saved" by "Mrs. V's" late-night interventions on their behalf, from "a morally precarious situation," created by some of "the love-starved sisters" of Alpha Chi Omega.

Another waiter, Rich McCormick, immediately jumped to his feet and said that his fraternity brothers at Alpha Tau Omega, "were equally grateful for those late-night interventions," for the very same inappropriate reasons. Obviously, he continued, "Some of those sorority sisters were repeat offenders, no matter what fraternity was involved." Following that, he announced our choice of the "one deserving the scarlet letter," among the great many in contention, after which he gave her the award, which, by the way, was decorated in scarlet paper.

There were about one hundred coeds in that sorority, including the pledges, during any one of the four years in which I worked there, about forty of whom actually lived in the sorority house, itself. The rest lived in the freshmen dormitories, the Northwestern University Apartments, as sophomores, and some off-campus housing as juniors. Nevertheless, they all had dinner in the sorority house every Monday evening, because of their "chapter" meeting on that day, which active members were required to attend. Because there were so many of them at dinner on that evening, normally close to one hundred girls, the pledges and some of the upper class women, on sorority scholarships, routinely helped us in the kitchen. As a result, those of us who worked in the kitchen grew to know most of those girls quite well, and, eventually, most of the other girls in the sorority, too, over our four years there, because of subsequently serving them, as waiters, in the dining room, upon, eventually, becoming juniors and seniors at that board job and at that university.

After all, we spent three meals a day, seven days a week, together, with a previously noted Sunday evening exception, of course. And even though it was in different capacities, as servers and served, we were, in the end, just young men and women, who were college students on a university campus, and that was a far more prevailing characteristic, which seemed to transcend almost everything else, including that employment distinction, noted hereinbefore.

As waiters, of course, we may have been required to come to work through the back door, but that sorority house in the southern part of that elongated campus, beside Lake Michigan, where nearly all of the classrooms were located, was home to nearly every one of us, almost as much as it was to the girls, who resided there. In fact, we probably spent more time in that sorority house, than we did in our respective fraternities, located some distance away, in the northern part of campus. Like our male counterparts on fraternity row, we also entered the front door when we were not working there, which was before, between, and after classes. At that time, we were nothing more than college guys, who were hanging out in a sorority house, where we, unlike most of our male counterparts on that campus, knew nearly every one of the girls in that house, because we worked there, seven days a week.

Not surprisingly, or, at least, it should not be, some of the waiters eventually married some of those girls, and all of us eventually dated one or two of them, sometime during our four years on that college campus. We were, in the end, more than just coeds and college guys on a university campus; we were good friends, some of whom happened to be residents and some of whom happened to be waiters in that sorority house.

That is certainly one of the reasons why I concluded, earlier in this chapter, that some of my greatest lessons at that university did not necessarily occur in a classroom; some of them actually occurred while I was working, or otherwise present, at that sorority house. I learned, little by little, over the four years of being there, that I was not, in many respects, so different from most of those who were living there, even though I worked for them as a waiter, and even though our economic and cultural situations, if not origins, may have been distinctly different.

Oh, sure, I wasn't exactly like most of them, either; I don't think that I ever had any doubt about that fact. But, amazingly, I eventually began to feel somewhat comfortable around most of them over time, and I was around many of them, every day, for much of the day. That familiarity, of course, did not obliterate our differing circumstances, or origins, but it clearly began to mollify the impact, until, eventually, the differences began to seem almost trivial, if not irrelevant, on that college campus.

In some respects, the consequences of being a waiter at that sorority house, even for that comparatively short period of time in my life, numbering no more than four years at that university, never really ended, not sociologically, anyway. I began to become a different person, with a different perspective, not only about myself, but about others, who were seemingly unlike myself, because of my work at that sorority house, which seemed, at the time, to be nothing more than a day on the job, so seemingly inconsequential, but so meaningful, in so many ways, the limit of which was defined by a lifetime.

CHAPTER X

NORTHWESTERN UNIVERSITY, FRESHMAN YEAR: GRADE POINT AVERAGE, FRATERNITIES, THANKSGIVING AND THE EVANSTON TOWNSHIP HOSPITAL

ACTUALLY, JOINING a fraternity seemed far more consequential at the time. Not at first, however, because I did not even know what they were, not before I arrived on that campus, anyway. Consequently, I did not go through "formal rush," during orientation week of my freshman year, which most freshmen did, because it was permitted, if not encouraged, by the University.

As the first quarter progressed, however, I began to learn a little more about the fraternity system, such as which ones were considered to be better than some of the others, mostly because of the freshmen in my dormitory, who happened to have joined some of them. So knowing little more than that about fraternities, from little more than those sources, I enrolled in "open rush" during the first quarter of my freshman year and, by doing so, visited a number of fraternity houses, pursuant to their invitations.

The visits were generally interesting and informative, and, maybe, even a little bit stressful, too, and they seemed to be divided into two kinds of functions, if I may be permitted to categorize them in such a manner. The so-called, "smokers," involved, you guessed it, a lot of smoking and a lot of smoke, mostly as a result of a lot of burning cigarettes in the mouths of a lot of the fraternity members. This kind of a smoke-filled gathering ordinarily occurred in the living room of the fraternity house, shortly after dinner, apparently because smokers generally like to "light up" at that point. To give the smoke-filled room some sense of dignity, not to mention the smokers, fraternity and non-fraternity members, alike, were required to dress for the occasion, ordinarily in "coats and ties." Notably, conversation was at a minimum, even by the fraternity members, probably because it was somewhat difficult to talk with a cigarette in your mouth. So everyone engaged in a lot of hand-shaking and smiling, with everyone else, which was done, repeatedly, throughout the evening.

To my amazement, the smiling, which seemed to be ubiquitous among the fraternity members, seemed to be readily accomplished even with a cigarette in their mouth. Although to be quite honest about the matter, I was never completely sure about that accomplishment, because I could not see very well, due to all of that smoke in the room. In fact, with that amount of smoke, especially in that short amount of time, it would lead one to believe, which I did, that the smoke alarms would likely be set off at any moment. But, then, upon reconsideration, I changed my mind, because it seemed far more likely that those smoke alarms probably had already died, years ago, likely from lung cancer.

There were also the so-called "dinners," staged, if you permit the expression, in overly-filled dining rooms, in which most of the fraternity members, more commonly known within the fraternity system as "brothers," spruced up their table manners, in order to impress those of us who were their guests, more commonly known within the fraternity system as "rushees." Not unlike the "smokers," however, everyone, "brothers" and "rushees," alike, considered the gathering to be important enough to dress for the occasion, once again in "coats-and-ties." And with their most gregarious personalities, demonstrated in between mouthfuls of food, all of the "brothers" took great pains to create a convivial atmosphere, not only at the dinner table, but elsewhere, as well, if elsewhere subsequently figured into the social occasion.

In the midst of all of that conviviality, not to mention all of that food, it was useful for the "rushees" to mention, quite incidentally, of course, some of their more impressive credentials, such as being on the high school football team, or having already dated someone in one of the better sororities on campus. Because I had done neither, not at that point, anyway, I simply had to rely on my good looks, all one hundred and thirty-six pounds of them, which were uniquely fitted into a five-foot ten inch frame, complimented by a charcoal black suit, offset by a pink buttoned-down shirt and a coordinated pink and black regimental tie, with a matching belt and a pair of argyle socks, no less, all of which was supported by a pair of "wing-tip" cordovan dress shoes. Apparently, that was more than sufficient, because, after a number of visits, I received bids from a number of fraternities to join their membership.

When I realized that they wanted me, and that I actually had a choice between them, I became far more cautious, deciding that I had better find out something more about them, before joining any one of them. Even more importantly, I decided, once I had an opportunity to think more about it, which did not occur very often during my freshman year, that it was probably incumbent upon me to discover why they wanted me, so that I could be reasonably sure that they would not change their mind, once they realized that they may have made a mistake. So I decided, in the end, not to make a decision, prematurely, and, in the meantime, turned my attention toward righting my academic ship, which, as the result of my first quarter grades, had been listing badly.

With that in mind, I chose my courses far more carefully for the following quarter, which would become my second quarter on that campus, with a view toward a selection that I would like, and in which I would likely do much better, probably for just that reason, if nothing else. I also chose a course of conduct that quarter that would likely assist me in doing much better, essentially for that diligent reason. In other words, I decided to work; I decided to work very hard, in and out of class, and, in fact, I did. I studied every conceivable minute that I did not have to work at my board job, or on the weekends, helping people with their lawn work. To some extent, I substituted study for sleep, eating, and, where possible, breathing, with reasonably satisfactory results, I might add, because I had a "3.5" grade point average out of a possible "4.0," at the conclusion of my midterm examinations, which was an "A-" at that university, and I never looked back!

I was on my way, or, at least, I thought that I was, but I had such a long way to go, metaphorically speaking, and I knew that. I suppose, however, that if I had any idea of just how long, I probably would not have returned, following my summer vacation that year. I really had no idea of just how difficult my academic life would become, over the next three years, but I clearly understood how difficult it was at the time. I did not have to be a clairvoyant to realize that those who were sitting beside me in class were academically better prepared, for whatever reason, to be in that class and at that university.

It also did not take me very long to realize that I could not realistically afford to be there, either, notwithstanding my board job and my weekend yard work. Actually, I couldn't even afford to go home for Thanksgiving, so I didn't. Instead, I, unfortunately, spent my first Thanksgiving, away from home, in the Evanston Township Hospital, where the University Infirmary sent me, because of a fear of appendicitis, growing out of an acutely painful abdomen, probably the result of being away from home at that holiday time.

Because it was so painful, and because the Hospital could not readily diagnose why, I couldn't even eat anything on Thanksgiving Day, let alone eat some kind of a traditional Thanksgiving dinner. So, instead, I spent my time in that hospital, and on that traditional holiday occasion, by feeling sorry for myself, and, in between, trying to preserve what little dignity I had left, by refusing to allow a female resident to conduct a rectal examination, normally utilized, I was angrily informed, to discover an inflamed and/or an enlarged appendix.

Looking back now, especially from an eighty-six-year-old perspective, that stubborn refusal, which may have seemed slightly ridiculous at the time, especially to that female resident, would carry me a long way in life, especially with what often seemed to become almost insurmountable difficulties, transcending even those lying ahead at that four-year university. With that in mind, I guess that one could possibly say, while continuing to look back, that my "holiday-in-the-hospital," so to speak, was quite fortuitous. Otherwise, I may not have begun to develop the kind of resolve that would become necessary to carry me through the difficult academic and professional days that lay ahead!

Actually, while still looking back, I believe, after some further consideration, that such resolve was probably formed long before my subsequent academic days out west. Its origins can probably be traced back to the economically and culturally challenged circumstances, which were part of the rural life of my childhood, in the mountains of central Pennsylvania. Indeed, that kind of resolve probably explains my decision to leave home, on a bus, for a university that was roughly six hundred miles away, in a large, sprawling, metropolitan area, in another state, for which I was quite unfamiliar, if not unsuited, at the time. And that kind of a resolve probably explains why I never gave up during my freshman year, notwithstanding all of my struggles, even though I may not have really understood why. In fact, it really took me a lifetime to understand why, and, at virtually the end thereof, to be able to explain it, over the course of this story.

CHAPTER XI

*NORTHWESTERN UNIVERSITY,
FRESHMAN YEAR: SUMMER VACATION;
FROMMS DRY CLEANERS, DRIVING
A DRY CLEANING TRUCK, AND
BROTHERLY MISBEHAVIOR*

STILL, ON so many occasions that I can barely recall them all, I would have liked to have given up and to have gone back home during my freshman year. I really did not belong at that university, academically or culturally, and I could not afford to be there financially, either. All of which explains, at least partially, my overwhelming desire to leave over the course of that year. So no one should actually be surprised when I tell you that I was more than happy to see that miserable year, my freshman year at that university, come to an end. I was so happy that I packed my trunk, in which my family had previously forwarded most of my clothes, about a month before the spring quarter had come to an end, and my final examinations had begun. Lou, who you will recall was my roommate during that time, assisted me in that regard with a newly found sense of humor, by covertly packing some stones in the trunk, which I did not discover until unpacking the thing, shortly after I had arrived home for the summer in Lock Haven, Pennsylvania.

Following an informal interview, or what went down as one in my hometown at the time, I was hired by Fromms Dry Cleaners to service the route of each one of their drivers, for one week, while they were on a vacation. To be able to do that, I helped each one of them for a two-week period, prior to their departure, in order to learn their route. Naturally, by the end of the second week, I grew to know the driver, as well as his route, and reasonably well, too, and that, in itself, became reasonably educational, sociologically speaking. That, however, was just the beginning of my education that summer, especially that kind of an education, while working for Fromms Dry Cleaners.

Among other things, I learned a lot about the communities where we picked up and, subsequently, delivered the dry-cleaning, which were generally rural and quite poor in Centre County. I also learned a lot about the lives of the individuals, who drove the dry-cleaning trucks, and who operated the machinery in the dry-cleaning plant, for what proved to be a rather meagre living in both cases. And almost inadvertently, because I was not deaf, I learned something about their families, too. I learned, among a number of other things, that they were all rather marginal, with insufficient incomes, who led rather challenging lives, likely for just that economic reason, if nothing more. If there was anything about them that was not marginal, it was their resentment; there was nothing marginal about that!

I also learned something about the owners of the dry-cleaning establishment. Among other things, I learned that they were not marginal, not economically, anyway, but their manner of being and of doing business often seemed marginal, if not untoward, sometimes. Although I no longer remember all of the reasons for reaching such a critical conclusion, I do remember how much they disliked one another, probably because they were always trying to take advantage of each other in their business operations. That, in itself, seemed at the time to be a questionable way of being, especially to another family member, and, on top of that, a very poor way of conducting a business, too.

By the end of my summer work, however, I put aside my sociological views on the dry-cleaning industry, if not my critical commentary on misbehavior therein, because the fall was rapidly approaching and, with it, my sophomore year at a midwestern university, a far more immediate concern, for which I still did not feel fully prepared. Nevertheless, because of the nature of that summer work, and the circumstances of those who were employed there, not to mention their marginal families, the return for my sophomore year was far less traumatic.

I began to realize, if I had not before, that the university, for all of its inherent difficulties, presented a real opportunity for change. I was not exactly sure what that change might be, not at the time, but, at least, I had some ill-defined sense of what it might be. It might be a change from the nature of that summer employment and from the circumstances of the people who were employed there. I had begun to realize, certainly by the end of that summer, that the individuals who worked there were rather limited in their horizons and in their opportunities, too, and that I might, eventually, leave those limitations behind, by boarding a train to Chicago and, eventually, Northwestern University.

CHAPTER XII

NORTHWESTERN UNIVERSITY, SOPHOMORE YEAR: DAVE KNAPP, FRANKLIN GROVE, ILLINOIS AND THE ROCK ISLAND LINE

MAYBE THE biggest change was geographic, and that didn't change, either, not during my sophomore year, or, for that matter, my remaining years at that midwestern university. I had never been to the Midwest, not before going to that summer debating program, and I had spent most of that summer in the library. As a result, I never knew, outside of a book or two, anything about the great midwestern plains, where a road can go on in a straight line, indefinitely, right off into the sunset, and you may have to travel for ten miles, or even more, before you can actually leave behind the fence on just one farm.

I really did not discover those geographic facts on the shores of Lake Michigan, where Chicago and, just a few miles north thereof, Northwestern University was located in Evanston, Illinois. I actually discovered the great midwestern plains, or, at least, the northern part of them, on road trips west during my freshman year, with my newly acquired university friend, Dave Knapp, to his hometown of Franklin Grove, Illinois. Although Dave had obviously grown up in a different part of the country, geographically speaking, it had become rather evident, rather quickly, that we had actually come from the same sort of circumstances, economically and culturally, with, of course, some variations, which, generally, did not seem to be all that important at the time.

One of those variations, which subsequently became important during his freshman year, was his economic inability to continue as a student at that university during the following year, which, of course, would have been his sophomore year at Northwestern University. Even with his scholarship, which was substantial, Dave simply could not afford the costs of being at that university, even though he worked, every afternoon, for a landscape contractor in the area. In fact, Dave could not even afford a meal plan in the cafeteria at Sargent Hall, which, of course, was our residence that year, so, with that in mind, one of his dormitory friends would go back in line for an extra plate of everything for Dave, but meat, which, with that protein exception, did not cost him any more under his meal plan. And that gratuitous gesture by one of his dormitory friends was Dave's meal plan during his freshman year at Northwestern University. Even as a college freshman, on a campus that was beyond my ability to adapt at the time, especially economically, that seemed to be a material difference in our economic situations.

After all, although I could not easily afford to be at the University, I certainly could afford to eat there during my freshman year, because of my board job at the sorority house. And I could also afford the cost of my books, because of the money that had been earned by me during the previous summer, while working back home for Fromms Dry Cleaners. I could not afford much else, however, and I guess that Dave realized that fact, because he would often take me along on his trips back home for the weekend to Franklin Grove, Illinois. That way, as he would often say, it would save me the cost of an evening meal on Sunday, which, as you may recall, was not included in my board job at the sorority house.

Looking back now, from more than my eighth decade on this earth, I would have to say that my weekends with the Knapp family, which consisted of his mother and brother, in Franklin Grove, Illinois, were some of the more memorable moments of my freshman year at Northwestern University. In fact, the trip, itself, was nearly as memorable as being there. The endless farms that we encountered were larger than any that I had ever seen, or even imagined, when I was growing up in Clinton County, where a fifty acre "truck farm" was considered to be huge.

The land on those gigantic midwestern farms was typically covered, depending upon the season, with corn, rye, wheat or barley, or some combination thereof, which had a certain appeal, in and of itself, that is hard to describe, other than by scale. Even the roads, which were never more than two lanes, after we left the metropolitan area, and which were not often paved, but, rather, covered by some form of crushed stone, had a certain definable interest. I say, "definable," because you could define them by a straight line, and even a straight line takes on a certain amount of interest, which was certainly noticeable and, maybe, even esthetically pleasing, after a few hundred miles. And when the sun began to set, as it often did, on that line, which, as you may recall, was really a two-lane road, going on, endlessly, into the sunset, it . . . the line or the road, whichever you may choose . . . took on a certain amount of character, which was almost surreal in nature.

The town of Franklin Grove, itself, which, of course, was ultimately our destination, was also quite interesting, for non-linear and more personable reasons. Not surprisingly, but still of some interest, I could see characteristics of Dave in his mother, Margaret, and even in his lackluster brother, Russell. I found that brotherly characteristic to be especially interesting because Dave Knapp was anything but lackluster, as he would capably demonstrate throughout the rest of his very successful life, academically and professionally.

His old girlfriend from high school days was equally interesting, but for differing reasons. Without being more specific, in order to avoid censorship problems, it is, at least, worth noting, in other respects, that she still continued to live there, in that small community, in which there was really not much to do, personally or professionally. And consistent therewith, when we met her, although it was rather briefly, she was not doing very much at all. Nor, for that matter, did she say very much, probably because she did not have very much to say, not to her old boyfriend, not anymore, having replaced him with another one, who was far more available, at least geographically.

Apparently, she had decided, not unreasonably in her mind, that her future lie in proximity, not promise. That kind of an unimaginative decision made by that kind of a hometown girl was not lost on me. It was a decision made by so many of the risk-adverse young ladies with whom I had grown up, who also saw their future in proximity, by staying home in order to marry someone who had also stayed there, with no more promise than their own.

I also met some of Dave's high school friends of the male variety, too, who, not surprisingly, did not appear to be noticeably different from their homegrown female counterparts, with the possible exception that they played basketball and baseball with him on his high school teams. When you include the owners and the patrons of the pool hall, the grocery store and the drugstore, which consisted of nearly every store in town, I believe that I must have met nearly everyone in town, which was not so surprising, because there could not have been more than a few hundred of them.

The town, itself, was not structurally like anything that I had ever seen before in my limited life, at least not at that point. It consisted of wooden structures of various designs, although no more than fifty of them, with a few brick exceptions, mostly churches, and a raised wooden sidewalk in front of them, ending, abruptly, on both sides, in farmland.

Maybe, the most unusual thing of all, at least to this eastern observer, was a small, unobtrusive building, off by itself, but still on the main street, which housed a central telephone operator, who managed the telephone calls for every home in town, which was possible, because they were all on the same line. So if you wanted to call someone in town, which really wasn't necessary, because you could just as easily walk over to their house, you just picked up your telephone receiver and asked the operator, by her first name, of course, to connect you, which was possible, because, as you will recall, they were all on the same telephone line. Given that fact, you could conceivably listen to everyone else's telephone conversations, if you were so inclined, which, I am sure, limited, by necessity, the variety and intimacy of the conversations that took place on that telephone line.

All of this, quite obviously, left an indelible impression on a young country boy from the mountains of central Pennsylvania, who was a long way from home at the time, and who was not terribly comfortable in being so. Indeed, that probably explains why, after all these years, I still remember so much about that town and the people who lived there. But I remember one of them far more than the others, probably because he left that town, although smaller and midwestern, in order to try to become something more and, maybe, something else, elsewhere.

Dave Knapp, as you may have surmised by now, did not come back for his sophomore year at Northwestern University. Instead, he transferred to a smaller school in the northwestern part of the state, appropriately called Northern Illinois University, located in DeKalb, Illinois, which was much smaller, less expensive and, in his subsequently disapproving words, "less demanding." I was privileged to hear those words, in person, because I actually went down there to visit him, for a long weekend, early in the fall quarter of my sophomore year, by taking a train out of the Union Station in Chicago, on the musically renown "Rock Island Line," which was, in my retrospective opinion, far more attractive in song, than in reality. Nevertheless, I, like the train in the song, traveled westward on that line, except, in my case, with far too many people, which was the reason why I had to stand all the way, on a round trip, to and from Dekalb, Illinois. I bet the person who wrote that country song never had to stand both ways on that old, rickety line. Otherwise, he might have thought better about eulogizing a "common carrier" in an unrealistic melody about a commonly overbooked railroad line.

The visit, itself, was not much better than the trip, probably because of how unimpressive the school seemed to be, which, truth be told, reminded me somewhat of the similarly unimpressive teachers college at the time in my hometown. I guess that unimpressive comparison was not lost on Dave, because the first thing that he did, following my arrival at his new university, was to criticize the quality of the education that he was receiving there. Nevertheless, it was not lost on both of us, at that point in his life, that he really could not afford to go back to Northwestern University.

Apparently, however, somewhat later in that year, his sophomore year, Dave decided that he could not afford to continue at Northern Illinois, either, not if he wanted to eventually enroll in a first-rate graduate program in business, like the one at Northwestern University. So he apparently left Dekalb, sometime during that academic year, in order to join the Army, which, at least in his mind, offered him far more academic opportunities through the "G.I. Bill."

Well, history did not prove that academic decision to be a miscalculation, because, following his four-year tour of duty, Dave came back, as an undergraduate, to Northwestern University, compliments of the "G.I. Bill," with a fistful of U.S. Army money, a newly acquired wife and some well-earned direction. As a result of that direction, not to mention the "G.I. Bill," he not only finished his undergraduate education at Northwestern University, with an even higher "GPA," which was, in itself, quite commendable, but he also went on to the graduate school in business, located at the downtown campus, finally graduating with an "MBA," from Northwestern University, thanks, among other things, to an excellent fellowship.

I did not learn about Dave's four-year sojourn in the Army, or about his subsequent return to Northwestern University, for his pre and post graduate degrees, until many years later, having departed for other academic environs, on the east coast, several years prior thereto. In fact, Dave Knapp faded from my memory over the remainder of my years at Northwestern University, and that situation did not effectively change thereafter, not until I came across his name in an alumnae magazine article, approximately thirty years later. According to that article, he, too, had married and become a father, and, of no less consequence, become a reasonably successful corporate executive, residing at the time in Pittsburgh, Pennsylvania.

CHAPTER XIII

NORTHWESTERN UNIVERSITY, SOPHOMORE YEAR: THETA DELTA CHI; FRATERNITY BROTHERS, "RUSHING," "PLEDGING" AND THE ABOMINABLE LIVING SITUATION IN THAT FRATERNITY HOUSE

AT ONE point during the first quarter of my sophomore year, I decided to join one of the fraternities that had already given me a "bid," a year earlier, probably as part of my campus coping skills, if nothing else. Belonging to a fraternity, it seemed to me, could lift the seemingly insurmountable burden of feeling so alone and unsupported in my continuing effort to adapt to this unfamiliar and demanding way of life, which, of course, was as a student at a midwestern university in a large metropolitan area. I was hoping, in geometric terms, that Euclid was right, and that the whole, of which I would become a part, as a member of that fraternity, would become greater than the sum of its parts, including poor little me. So toward that "greater" end, I joined Theta Delta Chi, which, at the time, was not a particularly distinguished fraternity on that campus, but, then, neither was I, personally speaking.

The irony, of course, is that I joined that undistinguished fraternity, because it seemed far more comfortable than joining Sigma Alpha Epsilon, which was also interested in me and which was one of the more distinguished fraternities on that campus. I used the word "irony," because I joined a fraternity to become something else, something more, and, maybe, even something better, through that membership, and I ended up choosing one, whose membership was, likely, more like me. That irony would, sadly speaking, follow me for years, in whatever I chose to do, academically and professionally. It seemed that I, like most people in life, would often choose, to my detriment, comfort over promise, security over risk, and the past over the future. It would become an inherent struggle, and, maybe, even a failure, that would, unfortunately, describe most of my choices throughout the rest of my life. Indeed, with the exception of my marriage, I would not, metaphorically speaking, choose to join something like a Sigma Alpha Epsilon, for roughly another thirty years, when I decided to join my law firm of Arent Fox. Instead, I spent the intervening time, trying to develop into something that would become someone, who actually believed that he belonged at that fraternity and at that firm.

Nevertheless, I never gave up the struggle during that academic year, my sophomore year, because the alternative was unacceptable; remaining the same was simply unacceptable at the time. I am not sure that I could have reached that conclusion simply by self-perception, but I certainly could by looking back at where I had come from, and those who had remained there. In that respect, I understood that I had grown up with them, and that I was probably like them, but I did not want to remain that way, not anymore. One year at Northwestern University, if nothing else, had made that abundantly clear!

It was still hard, however, to address the consequences of that recently formed opinion, because my life at that university did not get any easier during my sophomore year. It was hard, for example, to call a sorority girl for a date, when you knew that she actually belonged there, whatever that may have meant, and you could not even afford to be there. And in the event that she was actually willing to go on a date with someone like you, there was no way that you could afford to take her anywhere, other than to the library, in order to study, with, possibly, coffee afterwards. It was also hard to go to classes, every day, hoping that your performance would receive higher marks, comparatively speaking, when you knew that the others, seated around you, had a better academic background, because of the quality of their boarding school education. And it was especially hard to do well enough in those classes to be able to go on to graduate school, or even to law school, which was something that I had always wanted to do, because my challenging past seemed to be insurmountable, academically, culturally and, especially, economically. Nevertheless, as I have said before, hard as it may have been, or seemed to be, it was still not as hard as not trying, if you do not mind a "double negative," even when I was sure, sometimes, that I would fail to succeed. As I had learned in just one year at that university, I could live with failure, sometimes, but not with a failure to try! That's right, I could live with loss on occasion, but not with lost hope!

I wasn't sure, however, whether I could actually live another year in that fraternity. The sleeping situation, when you possibly could, which was infrequent, was abominable! We, all forty of us, slept in the same room, up in the attic, which was on the third floor of that fraternity house, if you can picture that. The nightly cacophony of sounds rivaled the practice session of a symphony orchestra, not only in volume but in dissonance. Moreover, for those, like myself, who were not interested in sleeping, nightly, in the Arctic Circle, it was a wintry nightmare. Anything approximating warmth did not exist up there; we were in the attic, and the attic, like most attics, was unheated!

Then there was the Wisconsin factor, for want of a more appropriate description, which was, unfortunately, coupled with French doors, which was a more accurate, architectural description. That's right, there were, for reasons that defied architectural explanation, French doors up there, in that unheated attic. Even worse, there were a number of my fraternity brothers from Wisconsin, the northern part of Wisconsin, who also slept up there, and who insisted upon sleeping next to those French doors, which they also insisted upon opening, every night, even in the dead of winter. I can't tell you how often I woke up with snow on top of my bunk, because of a snowstorm the night before, even though my bunk was over against the opposite wall, as far away from those doors and those idiots as geographically possible!

The room downstairs, on the second floor, where I and eight others studied, or, at least, tried to study, was small, overpopulated, noisy and, generally, disgusting, with remnants of half-eaten snacks strewn about the desks, not to mention yesterday's partially full Styrofoam coffee cups littering the floor. For all of those reasons and, probably, some that I have likely forgotten, I never studied there after a while. Instead, I began to study in the Charles Deering Library, located on the southern part of the campus, along with the rest of the class buildings, which rivaled, in architecture, a number of medieval gothic counterparts in Western Europe.

The midwestern version, however, was introduced by mammoth, arched doors, made of oak, which opened into cavernous rooms with stone floors, upon which sat Windsor-style chairs and matching oak tables, nearly room size in length, accompanied, all the while, by the calming background noise of slow-moving, oversized, floor fans, nearly reaching the ceiling in height. All of which gave the distinct impression of quiet solitude, which would have made a cloistered monk feel right at home, and which almost shouted, to any academic entrant, that this was a place for serious study!

Because I was interested in serious study, as well as the attractive coeds, who ordinarily studied there, too, I would, religiously, a term seemingly appropriate in this context, go over to the Deering Library, in the early evening, right after my board job at the sorority house. To whatever extent that it may be said that I succeeded, academically, at Northwestern University, in the years that followed, credit must be given to the Library, and to those studious coeds, but none to my fraternity. Academics were an afterthought within the four walls of that physically challenged fraternal structure, especially in every one of those "study rooms" on the second floor.

You would never believe that to be the case, however, during the conversations that normally took place during "formal rush," when freshmen were permitted to "rush" fraternities, a questionable part of orientation week for college freshmen, occurring just before registration for the fall quarter. At that time, my fraternity brothers would typically extoll the academic virtues of belonging to our fraternity, supporting that questionable proposition by advising the "wide-eyed" freshmen . . . who had never seen those congested study rooms, upstairs, on the second floor, let alone the freezing communal sleeping arrangements in the unheated third-floor attic . . . that our overall grade point average("GPA") for the fraternity house was over a 3.0. Actually, the GPA was probably over a 3.25, for each of the years that I belonged to that fraternity. Credit for that over-achieving fact, however, should more appropriately be given to the innate intellect of my fraternity brothers, not to mention their nightly habit of joining me, and the studious coeds, for an evening of study at the Charles Deering Library.

"Formal rush," by the way, can be fairly described as time-consuming and a waste of time, which certainly could have been better used for more important pursuits, such as preparing for registration and buying books for classes, thereafter. Instead, there were endless meetings of the "brotherhood," to discuss, endlessly, how we could convince some of the college freshmen, who were "rushing" our fraternity, to actually join it. And, of course, during my sophomore year, when I was a lowly pledge, I, and my pledging counterparts, had to do the brunt of the work required to clean up the place, which had been allowed to deteriorate over the summer months, when it had been essentially unoccupied, so that its appearance would be dramatically improved before the commencement of "formal rush." To some extent, a rare extent, it could conceivably be said that some of the "brothers" also helped with those kinds of house cleaning duties at the time.

Nevertheless, I, at least, escaped the lunch and the dinners during "formal rush," and some of the digestive aftereffects, because of my board job at the sorority house. I did not, however, escape the evening "smokers," where most of the "brothers" "lit-up" like a chimney and some of the freshmen "rushees" did, too, whether they had ever smoked or not. The smoke, on occasion, became so dense in the living room, where those unfortunate evenings occurred, that you could barely see the person standing next to you.

If honesty be required, I was allergic to that smoke, and if it be further required, most of the smokers, too. But I had decided, long before joining that fraternity, that as much as I may have disliked the whole "brotherly" scene, smoke-filled and otherwise, that fraternity was going to make a difference in my life, somehow, at least for the next two years of it, anyway. And if I am really going to be honest, it did, for so many reasons that I am unable to even begin to recount them all.

I can certainly say, however, that whatever difference that fraternity may have made in my life, especially as a college sophomore, may be attributed to the membership at the time. They were all rather bright, at least bright enough to get into that academically challenging university and, eventually, to distinguish themselves, academically, if nothing else, while being there. On the other hand, I considered it, at the time, to be an unbelievable achievement to just come back for another two years and to eventually graduate. Eventually, however, being in that fraternity, where my fraternity brothers had unending and unnerving aspirations, began to change my lack thereof, comparatively speaking, into some kind of an indefinable desire to become something that I was not, and that I could not even imagine ever becoming at one time, which was one of them!

Nevertheless, even though I was nearing the completion of another academic year at that university, with a far more distinguished academic performance, not to mention an ambivalent membership in a fraternity, I was still torn between wanting to go back home and live the rest of my life with others like me, or to try to become something different, something that, so far, I was not, at least not yet, anyway. Thankfully, however, I was given a reprieve, from this seemingly irresolvable dilemma, by a summer vacation, and the comfortable prospect of going back home to what I was and what I was used to being, and being around.

CHAPTER XIV

NORTHWESTERN UNIVERSITY, SOPHOMORE YEAR: SUMMER VACATION; FROMMS DISCOUNT BOOKLETS, CHARLIE HERLOCHER, STEVE ROMEO, ALLEN JOSLYN, JUDY MACAMOND AND THE GRAYSTONE

I HAD even become accustomed to the train ride back home for a summer vacation, all eight hours of it, most of which took place overnight. Thankfully, my father was always waiting in the railroad station, quite early in the morning, in Altoona, Pennsylvania, which was the closest terminal to my hometown, about two hours away at the time, but not "as the crow flies."

It was always exciting to get off of that train, at just about daybreak, and to look around at those mountains, the Alleghenies, which had been so much a part of my life growing up in central Pennsylvania. I was nearly back home now, where I had grown up and where I still belonged. And in the short amount of time required to drive back across those high-crowned, "Pinchot" roads, vernacularly named for their originator, Governor Gilbert Pinchot, I would be back in my hometown and, more importantly, at least it seemed so at the time, those with whom I had grown up, many of whom had been my boyhood friends, and a few of which, notwithstanding distance and time, always would be

My parents, however, were quite another matter. I never really considered them to be my friends, not when I was growing up, but they were certainly an important part of my life then, just differently so. I'm not sure that I thought very much about it when I was growing up, but I certainly thought a lot about it during that summer vacation, following my sophomore year, and when I did, it sort of made me uneasy, sometimes, because they seemed to have changed from the parents that I had remembered from that time, and I sort of missed the earlier version, for reasons that I could not explain at the time. But, then, maybe it was just me; maybe my parents were not any different at all; maybe they just seemed to be different, from my vantage point as a sophomore, about to become a junior, by the end of that summer, at Northwestern University.

My tennis game didn't seem to be any different, though, not while playing with my old high school friend, Steve Romeo, nearly every evening after work, down at the tennis courts at the local college. Steve was home for the summer, too, having completed two years at Franklin and Marshall, where he was doing quite well in their premed program. Aside from that academic fact, which did not seem so important that summer, he was still the same old Steve, more than willing to join me in doing some of the same old things, one of which was to play tennis, nearly every evening, after dinner, until it had become too dark to play anymore.

That, of course, is when we would pack up our tennis gear, throw it all in the trunk, jump into the car and head down to the Graystone, or, maybe, over to the Old Corner, both of which were in town, or even out, along the Renovo Road, to the Casalomma, several miles out of town, all of which were long-standing "watering holes" for our underaged generation.

Arriving there in short order, we would typically join Allen Joslyn and Charlie Herlocher, old high school friends, who, like us, had nothing better to do, especially at that customary drinking hour. See, in that respect, the photograph of Allen Joslyn, Charlie Herlocher and myself, years later, likely in our late fifties, or, even, in our early sixties, celebrating the newly restored offices of "Herlocher Foods," in State College, Pennsylvania, which can be found in Exhibit 139 in the Appendix.

Situated now in one of the over crowded booths, which seemed to typify the seating arrangement in that kind of place, we drank too many beers throughout the evening, played too many games of darts, at about the same time, and, in between, talked and laughed, far too loudly, about everything, until, literally, closing time. At that point, which was shortly before midnight, we rose, more slowly now, departed from the booth, awkwardly, of course, said our goodbyes to everyone and, thereupon, headed home, over now barely visible roads, defined more readily by the consumption of alcohol than by headlights.

That way, following a night of interrupted sleep, because of a "beer-laden" evening, prior thereto, we would still be able to get up, early the next morning, shrug off a debilitating "hangover," go to work, once again, in a meaningless summer job, followed by a customary tennis match, right after dinner . . . and, then, do the same drunken things, all over again, that evening, too, at a local bar, just as though growing up in that town and in that manner would never have to end.

Work that summer, at least during the first half, consisted of driving a dry cleaning truck, once again, for Fromms Dry Cleaners, when, of course, the regular driver on that route was on vacation. Early in the second half, however, Phil Fromm asked me to sell discount booklets, which he had already ordered, to help him obtain new dry-cleaning customers in some of the villages and towns in nearby Centre County. Because I needed a car to do that, I asked Charlie Herlocher to join me, which he did, and the two of us used his car to sell those booklets, for a dollar-and-a-half-a-piece, which we could keep, all over the towns and the countryside in Centre County.

Each one of us usually made about thirty dollars for no more than six hours of work each day, six days a week, which, to say the least, was not taxing. Sometimes, however, we would discover a really good Fromms' customer, like an automobile repair shop, with a lot of uniforms to clean, and we would sell them up to twenty booklets, within just a few minutes, and, then, quit for the day. Naturally, that did not exactly excite Phil Fromm, because we were not supposed to sell the booklets to his customers, not the old ones, anyway. The booklets, as you already know by now, were supposed to be sold to potentially new customers, who would get a discount on their dry cleaning, by using the coupons contained therein. Nevertheless, we sold the booklets to anyone who was willing to buy them, irrespective of whom they had previously used as a dry cleaner, even if that dry cleaner happened to be Fromms Dry Cleaners, because we knew that Phil Fromm would probably not discover that fraudulent fact, not until we were back in college, early in the fall.

A much greater worry was the license requirement in the Borough of State College, which prohibited anyone from soliciting or selling anything within the Borough, without paying an exorbitant fee for a weekly license. Because the fee was that exorbitant and the license lasted no more than a week, we never paid the fee nor, in turn, obtained a license that summer. That, however, did not stop us from selling an enormous amount of discount booklets within the Borough of State College.

That driving ambition, questionable as it may have been, may explain a lot about the similarities between the two of us at the time. And I am more than proud to say that, aside from our lifetime friendship, ending only with his recent death, there were many!

Well, at the very least, we worked in the same job that summer for a similar amount of money, and we refused to pay for a license to do so. I also believe that we may have gained something from having done those things, or not done them, as the case may be, which may explain, somewhat, our not dissimilar futures. The more immediate future, however, took us back to our respective universities in the fall, Penn State University and Northwestern University.

Once I departed that fall for Chicago and, eventually, Northwestern University, I didn't think much about Charlie, not anymore, not until the following summer, anyway. But I did think a lot about Judy Macamond, a girl that I had dated during the latter part of that summer, although not too seriously, but, apparently, serious enough to think about her, sometimes, after I had returned to the Midwest and to that University.

Following graduation from high school in Emporium, Pennsylvania, a small town about two hours north of my own, situated in the heart of "Penn's Woods," so to speak, she enrolled, as a summer student, in the small teacher's college in my hometown. I don't remember whether we met on that campus, where I often could be found playing tennis, or elsewhere in town, where I often could be found at one of the more celebrated local drinking establishments. But I do remember that I rather liked her, not too long after I began to date her, which was somewhat unusual at the time, because I don't remember liking myself, very often, in those days, let alone someone else. Nevertheless, I seemed to have been able to overcome that challenging problem, at least somewhat, during the latter part of that summer, for whatever reason, most of which was probably related to the girl.

We really did not do much of anything that was particularly noteworthy that summer, at least not that would make you think that it was noteworthy. Usually, we would just join Allen Joslyn, Charlie Herlocher and Steve Romeo, or any combination thereof, for a few beers and some popular music at, among other frequented "joints," the Graystone, a local bar in town, which featured, as part of its cosmopolitan atmosphere, a sign over the urinal in the men's room, which read, "men with short props should taxi close to the runway." I guess that sign was appropriate, not necessarily because of the short props found on many who taxied there, especially after an evening of heavy drinking, but because the bar was located right behind the town's municipal airport. In any event, aside from the location, when I think about the bar, itself, not to mention those who "taxied" there, I find it to be amazing that there were not any misspellings on the sign!

In fact, the atmosphere in the place could best be described as sociologically intriguing, although, by now, I guess that you may have already figured that out. Nevertheless, the girl and I spent a lot of our evenings there, just talking among ourselves, or with others, while ignoring the Cretans at the bar, and listening, at the same time, to some of the latest "hits" on the jukebox. As a result, not just of being there and doing that, I can safely say that, for reasons that I can no longer remember, she became the very first real friend that I ever had, who did not have to worry about that aeronautical sign in the men's room.

Looking back now, I think that there was something really significant about that fact, which probably had more to do with the person who liked her than with the girl that he liked, although to be quite fair about the equation, the girl was more than likable. Nevertheless, I also think, for whatever it may be worth, that the person who liked her was probably somewhat different from the one who left on a bus for Chicago, all by himself, a long time ago, historically, if not philosophically, speaking.

CHAPTER XV

NORTHWESTERN UNIVERSITY, JUNIOR YEAR, FALL QUARTER: LOU BERES AND JUDY HARRIS, DINNER AT WALKER BROTHERS, CLASSES WITH PROFESSOR McGOVERN AND DATING NANCY PAUL

I ACTUALLY began to develop something like a history, in the fall quarter of my junior year, on the campus of Northwestern University, or, at least, something worth recording at the time as a history. To begin with, I had successfully completed two years at a university where I, initially, did not believe that I belonged, for academic, economic, and cultural reasons, if nothing else, and that, in my mind, was worth historically noting. That I had not done anything particularly noteworthy at that university, at least not up to that point, should, in the interest of accuracy, also be historically noted. But that was about to change, in my third year of trying to belong, and, maybe, even becoming noteworthy, at a notable midwestern university, called Northwestern University!

The meaning of noteworthy, of course, can depend upon the person being noted, or even upon the situation in which he has been noted. Lou Beres, for example . . . who remained my good friend, although no longer my roommate, because I had decided to rent a room, just off campus, for my junior year . . . remained especially noteworthy on that campus during that year. Having become the freshman class president and the sophomore representative to the student governing board, Lou had now decided to run for the junior class presidency, which he won, handily, not a surprise to anyone who knew Lou, which, likely, included nearly everyone on that campus. Within months, he also became, almost by popular demand, the president of our fraternity, Theta Delta Chi. And notwithstanding a fairly demanding schedule, following the assumption of both positions, he found time to date and, eventually, enter into a serious relationship with Judy Harris, a member of Kappa Kappa Gamma, one of the very best sororities on campus, not just in my opinion, but in the opinion of others as well.

In between such noteworthy events, social as well as political, Lou and I joined each other for coffee, sometimes, in Scott Hall, a poor excuse for a student union, which, by the way, has been replaced, in the intervening years, by a real one, if not a worthy one, so I have been told. I also saw Lou on Monday evenings, when our fraternity, together with nearly every other one on campus, held their chapter meetings. And, of course, we continued to work together at our board job, for breakfast, lunch, and dinner at Alpha Chi Omega.

Oh, yes, I nearly forgot to note that Lou and I had dinner, together with Warren Butler, a very good friend of ours, nearly every Sunday evening at Walker Brothers, an undistinguished restaurant located, rather conveniently, near the southern part of campus, whose only real appeal was proximity and cost. My meal, for example, always consisted of the sirloin butt steak, which was an unappealing special, consisting of a minuscule piece of sirloin steak, well-aged, if not historically so, and mashed potatoes, also suffering from the same historical problem. Together with tax, the cost never varied from the standard fare of $1.03, without a drink, of course, which likely explains my consistent choice of that underperforming dining establishment, because I nearly always finished the week, before that dinner, with exactly one dollar and ten cents in my pocket.

Obviously, I was on a very structured, self-imposed budget, which made my life during the week equally structured, so that my expenditures during the week became as predictable, and as well-planned, as my life on that campus. And my predictable and well-planned life on that campus invariably ended, each week, with a dinner, together with Warren and Lou, on Sunday evenings at Walker Brothers, consisting of the sirloin butt steak special, costing me exactly one dollar and three cents. That invariable fact gave rise to the widely used expression on that campus during that year, especially on fraternity row, that, "good grades are as hard to come by at this university as money in Golumbic's pocket," in obvious reference to my Sunday evening financial situation at Walker Brothers. The expression, if you care to know, became widely used because Warren and Lou were widely known on that campus, having been elected to various offices through the years, and it became widely known that I was a friend of theirs, who happened to join them every Sunday evening for dinner at Walker Brothers, because, as you are already aware by now, I could afford too!

I'm not sure, however, that I initially appreciated such questionable notoriety, being of a pecuniary nature, but, subsequently, it dawned on me that such recognition, although possibly somewhat dubious, was still recognition. And recognition, in any form on that campus, was, in reality, quite noteworthy, especially for a boy recently removed from the limitations inherent in his origins, found in a small town in the mountains of central Pennsylvania.

Moreover, to my amazement, that recognition apparently extended, for whatever reason, even further than I realized that year, geographically speaking, all the way down to the southern part of campus, where the sororities were located, because Nancy Paul, one of the best-looking girls in Alpha Chi Omega, whose father, I was told, owned a "mitten factory," somewhere in Appleton, Wisconsin, became sort of interested in me, or so she said. Not surprisingly, I couldn't believe it at first. After all, how can you believe that you are twenty feet tall when you know that you are not, notwithstanding an opinion to the contrary by one of the most beautiful girls in that sorority? Well, after what must have been a frustrating period of convincing by Nancy, I eventually believed her, and I became twenty feet tall, at least for several months, after which she discovered the arithmetic truth and dumped me! A photograph of the lovely young lady, as I remember her, who, at the time, was a coed on the campus of Northwestern University, has been included as Exhibit 101 in the Appendix.

Like all painful lessons, however, there is always something to be learned, even by an idiot like me, and I learned a lot about myself from that brief relationship, if, in fact, I may be so bold as to call it one. Above all, I learned that there was something about me that made someone, quite special, believe, although all too fleetingly, that I may be different from the person that I had always assumed that I was, which may well have been measured in more than feet and inches!

I also became a different person, academically, in my junior year, likely because of a different work ethic, if nothing else, and my grades began to show the consequences thereof, in every one of my classes that year. Most of those classes, of course, were in my major, political science, and in my minor, history, or some related subjects in the liberal arts department. By that time, I had already finished all of my "distribution requirements," some of which had been rather uninteresting courses, taught by rather uninteresting instructors. Now, however, I no longer had to take those kinds of courses, and I assiduously avoided those kinds of instructors. Instead, I chose my political science and history courses very carefully, with the choice usually predicated upon the professor teaching the course.

My favorite, by far, was an erudite, charismatic, eccentric, internationally renowned professor in the political science department, named William Montgomery McGovern, whose teaching style I would emulate, to a certain extent, many years later, with some success, I might add, when I, too, would stand in front of a classroom on a college campus. In any event, I took every course that professor McGovern offered, over my remaining two years at that university, which usually meant two a quarter, and they varied from political philosophy to those involving near and far eastern studies. No matter the nature of the course, however, he was enormously entertaining and widely knowledgeable, about nearly everything imaginable, and his courses reflected that fact, which made them absolutely amazing. Besides, he had a fascinating habit of characterizing some of the students in his classes with nicknames, usually in order to illustrate some point in his lectures. And, interestingly enough, I became the "chicken chaser," a name, or a characterization, which he used to describe the womanizing lifestyle of some of the more historically flamboyant figures in government and politics through the ages.

Now some may find it to be somewhat uncomfortable to be characterized by such a moniker, especially by a professor in a class full of your peers. But I can assure you that there was nothing like recognition from a recognized academic figure, which, in this case, was a popular political science professor, to help you believe that you may possibly belong at a university of those academic dimensions. Indeed, by that characterization, questionable as it may have been, I became, if you will, a student, who was obviously worth recognizing, publicly in that instance, in a classroom full of students of corresponding academic dimensions. That, may I add, was, in my book at the time, more than worthwhile!

CHAPTER XVI

NORTHWESTERN UNIVERSITY, JUNIOR YEAR, WINTER & SPRING QUARTERS: LUCY JEFFRIES, THE PEMBRIDGE HOUSE AND "RAGGEDY ANN AND ANDY"

LUCY JEFFREYS, a pledge at Gamma Phi Beta, which was also an excellent sorority on that campus, probably would have agreed with professor McGovern . . . that I was a "chicken chaser," that is . . . because she was the "chicken" that I was "chasing," for the remainder of that year, the winter and spring quarters of my junior year at that university. A photograph of the young lady, as she appeared at that time, is in Exhibit 142 in the Appendix.

She was introduced to me by, who else, Lou Beres, who apparently had become acquainted with her earlier in the year and, being Lou, realized, with her in mind, that I needed some social assistance in the dating department on that campus. With that in mind, my mind, that is, I don't remember the first time that we went out on a date, but like the beginning of all relationships, there must have been a first time, and because that time was the beginning of a relationship, there must have been more times that followed. But I can't remember much about them, either, other than to say that they must not have involved any real expenditures, not on my part, because my pockets were just as empty on Saturday evenings with Lucy Jeffries as they were on Sunday evenings with Lou Beres and Warren Butler.

Apparently, that is why we took a lot of walks, everywhere on and off campus, and, absent the money for taxi fare, I had to walk several miles south of campus to the Pembridge House, her freshmen dormitory, to pick her up for a date on a Saturday night, probably to go walking. I made that trip enough times to remember, even now, roughly sixty-five years later, and I distinctly remember that it was remarkable that I did not freeze to death before I arrived at her dormitory, during the winter quarter, when the wind, blowing off of the lake, drove the thermometer down below zero. Because I didn't, and because I continued to brave the elements, or, more specifically, the cold wind off of Lake Michigan, the relationship survived the snow, the wind, the walk and the winter, but, unfortunately, it did not survive the year, probably because of a number of things, mostly related to me, of course. For one, she was a Christian Scientist, or, at least, she claimed to be, and I did not understand her distaste for medicine and those who dispensed it. And, sadly, after some time, most of which had been relatively good times, I began to dislike the distaste, in frequently issued opinions, which, not surprisingly, resulted in an end to what had once been my very first serious relationship, especially of any duration.

It was not that I intended to become a medical doctor, or a lobbyist for the American Medical Society, or anything like that. It was just that I couldn't fathom disliking anything, not for religious reasons, anyway, especially if the religious reasons did not make a lot of sense to me, and that religion, if it qualified as being so, did not make a lot of sense to me. On the other hand, I could certainly understand disliking a religion for non-religious reasons, or, maybe, even for religious reasons. After all, religion, it seemed to me, had a lot less to do with God, and a lot more to do with ungodly institutions, often mired in bigotry or, simply, the dislike of their institutional counterparts.

In any event, to be that religious for unscientific reasons, postulated by Mary Baker Eddy, years ago, seemed to me to be a bit medically ridiculous, if not religiously so, and, unfortunately, I told her so one day. I say, "unfortunately," because her reaction could not be characterized as charitable, or within any possible parameters of Christian forgiveness.

Moreover, to compound the injury, she did not forgive my simultaneous efforts to improve her campus attire, either, which, unfortunately, suffered from a distinctly Western influence. In that regard, she had grown up in Denver, Colorado, which I distinctly remember, because Westerners, like her, never did understand the so-called, "Ivy-Look," associated at the time with those fortunate enough to go to "Ivy League" schools.

No, she was a westerner, who dressed like one. When I tried to point that out, the objectionable nature of her wearing apparel, I mean, only as a helpful courtesy, mind you, she not only rejected my suggestions of how she could successfully overcome that western fact, she rejected me, too. She even rejected my gift of a pair of brown and white "saddle shoes," in her size, too, which were currently in vogue among the gentler sex on eastern college campuses, and which I thought were probably a good place to start, sort of working from the ground up, so to speak. A photograph of the young lady, on a happier day, wearing those brown and white saddle shoes on campus, has been included as Exhibit 102 in the Appendix.

Eventually, however, I decided, after some weeks of agonizing indecision, that the rejection, although initially painful, was probably a good thing, because I was not doing very well in the language class that we had decided to take together, and now I was free to drop the class. Moreover, I had always found it to be rather uncomfortable to be interested in someone who was doing that much better than me in a class that we had decided to take together.

Nevertheless, despite those noted benefits, I could not avoid thinking about the girl during the days and the weeks and, eventually, the months that followed, probably because, if honesty be required, she was a very attractive young woman, exceedingly so, a very nice young woman, exceedingly so, and a very talented young woman, too, for which an appropriate adverb does not readily come to mind. Indeed, with respect to the latter, I remember that she actually created outfits for us to wear to a costume party, which was being "thrown," so to speak, by her sorority at a hotel, downtown, in Chicago. Drawing on her experience as a theater major, she created those costumes out of the simplest things, and the result of such simplicity, not to mention her creativity, was a very appealing representation, in costumes, of the fictional characters, "Raggedy Ann and Andy." Photographs of the two of us in those creative costumes, confirming the girl's extensive artistic talent, have been included for your review as Exhibit 2 in the Appendix.

Actually, her creative ability may have been exceeded, to the extent that one can exceed that kind of ability, by her academic achievements in every scholastic area. The girl was bright; there was no question about that. And her stratospheric grade point average was rather uncomfortable for one whose average was certainly "well-grounded," a term that I am not about to define at this point in my underachieving story. Indeed, it was hard, sometimes, to be around someone, every day, because we were around each other nearly every day, who was that attractive, that talented and that bright. It certainly resulted in an enormous amount of conflicting feelings on my part. Even worse, I couldn't be sure whether those feelings were about her, or about me, or about both.

I suppose that it would not be fair to conclude this chapter without acknowledging that I received a telephone call from the young lady about a year later, not quite a week before my graduation from Northwestern University. At the time, I was studying for my last final examination, in my room, on the second floor of the fraternity house, when I was informed that a telephone call was waiting for me, downstairs, in the vestibule, where the only public telephone in the fraternity house was located. When I discovered who it was, after descending the steps to the first floor and entering the vestibule, it was quite a surprise, to say the least, because I had not seen, nor heard, from the young lady for nearly a year, encompassing nearly my entire senior year.

Nevertheless, following a few minutes of polite, but somewhat awkward conversation, at least on my part, she informed me, in a rather straightforward manner, that, her final examinations having been concluded earlier in the day, she was now about to fly home, for the summer, to Denver, Colorado, and that, she wanted to wish me well before departing and to congratulate me on my prospective graduation from Northwestern University.

Then she added something, almost as an afterthought, because it followed a brief pause in the conversation, or, at least, in her conversation. And in a voice that was all too familiar, but which I had nearly forgotten, in the one-year interlude, she said, "I know how hard it has been for you here, Cal, but just think how far you have come in four years. You are an amazing person, Cal, we all knew that; someday, you will, too!"

Frankly, after thinking about that telephone conversation, for nearly the entire week, before my graduation, that is, I was left, in the end, with no more than a failure to understand why she would bother to call me, especially after all of that time. I guess, however, in looking back now, which, of course, is exactly what I am doing, following a considerable amount of time, amounting to nearly a lifetime, that it had something to do with a concept found all too infrequently in life, especially in my life, called "kindness." And although it is somewhat uncomfortable to acknowledge, even now, the girl was always a very kind person. In fact, that attribute may actually have been a defining one, which, possibly, may have overshadowed all of the others, and which, probably, explains why I have never forgotten about the girl, even now, a little over sixty-five years later. Maybe, it also explains, but only in part, why it was rather sad to learn of her demise, a number of years ago.

I am also aware of some of the other reasons for that sadness, which, I believe, are abundantly clear from the story that has already been told. Other reasons, which may not be quite so clear, have something to do with the wisdom that comes from being alive, whatever that may mean, for as long as I have been alive. And somewhere during that life, especially as I have lived it, I began to understand the significance of that kind of a friendship between a college boy and a coed on a college campus, long after it may have seemed to be of any consequence to either one of them. If you can understand that, then you can certainly understand why the boy, who has now reached four score and six on this earth, has one great regret about his relationship with that former coed, who became one of his very best friends on a college campus, a long time ago, which is that he never thanked her for what she has done for him . . . for virtually a lifetime!

A number of photographs of the young lady, while attending formal dances that year, with yours truly, have been included as Exhibit 103 in the Appendix.

CHAPTER XVII

NORTHWESTERN UNIVERSITY, SUMMER VACATION, JUNIOR YEAR: FROMMS DRY CLEANERS, CHARLIE HERLOCHER AND SELLING DISCOUNT BOOKLETS AGAIN

WHEN I came back to my hometown for a summer vacation, following my junior year in college, I was a different person. Oh, I probably still looked the same, or nearly the same, which a photograph will certainly confirm in Exhibit 3 in the Appendix, but I wasn't the same, not even remotely the same. Among other things, I was someone who had survived and, possibly, even thrived, from a year-long relationship, or nearly so, and on top of that unbelievable fact, I had survived, if not thrived, over three taxing years, as a student, at a great midwestern university.

I was also someone who had grown to like the majority of my classes, many of which were taught by a professor that I especially liked. And I had succeeded in liking a coed, somewhat and sometimes, who was probably brighter than me, and who was certainly more talented, and, believe it or not, who once liked me, too. That was a lot of "liking," for someone who did not particularly like getting on that bus for Chicago, three years ago, but in those three years, I had apparently become a rather "likable" fellow, and, even more importantly, I began to like that fellow, too. Oh, all right, somewhat and sometimes.

With this new perspective, somewhat and sometimes, I began to work, once again, for Fromms Dry Cleaners. Not much had changed in my absence, other than the owners, Ruby and Phil Fromm, seemed to dislike each other even more, and their employees seemed to dislike both of them even more, with the possible exception of one of their drivers, a rather unusual fellow, known as Harvey Walker. The man had such a resolute affinity for everything and everybody, including the two Fromm brothers, that it often seemed to be infectious. For that reason and, probably, a number of others, he was extraordinarily well-liked by nearly everyone with whom he came in contact, and that certainly included most of those to whom he delivered dry-cleaning. And with my newfound perspective, somewhat and sometimes, I liked him, too, although I did not really have much of an opportunity to work with him that summer.

Instead, I spent most of my time working with Charlie Herlocher, once again, selling discount booklets anywhere and everywhere that we possibly could, and to anyone and everyone that could afford to buy them. I hasten to add, for posterity's sake, if not the judicial system, that we did not particularly care whether they lived within the dry cleaner's service area or whether they were already one of its customers. Since the objective of those discount booklet sales, enunciated by Phil Fromm, on a number of occasions, was to gain new customers within the service area, he was not too happy with us, midway through that summer, when he discovered that he had to send dry cleaning trucks to counties outside his service areas, because people in those locations had purchased discount booklets from us. That discovery nearly resulted in our mid-summer dismissal, but he relented after I explained that, in all likelihood, he would double his profits, because we had doubled his territory.

I'm not sure that Phil was thoroughly convinced that he would "double his profits," but he seemed to become more amenable to the possibility when his brother subsequently entered into the discussion with his usual pessimism. Phil would have been willing to extend his territory to the moon, even before NASA had reached it, by space exploration, if Ruby did not believe that it was possible. And, of course, we had only extended his dry cleaning territory to several counties outside his normal service area, and Phil didn't need any assistance from NASA to service those counties; he just needed to add a few more trucks, a far more feasible enterprise. Actually, now that I think about it, he should have been grateful, considering the cost of space travel, not to mention the logistical nightmare, that Charlie and I did not sell a lot of those discount booklets to the "man-in-the-moon"!

In any event, I remember Phil walking away from the two of us, during one of our heated exchanges, relating to the sales of those discount booklets outside of his service area, while, at the same time, expressing some concern about our overly ambitious entrepreneurial skills. And with that obviously in mind, muttering, "I must have been half-crazy to turn a Jew and a Dutchman loose out there among my customers." I assumed, at the time, that his reference to a Jew must have been a reference to me, although to be completely accurate about the subject, I only satisfied one-half of the definition. Charlie, on the other hand, had no difficulty satisfying the definition of a Pennsylvania "Dutchman," or, more accurately, a Pennsylvania German. Not only was he part of that community, but so was his way of being. He was, habitually, a very hard worker, with an overriding desire to succeed in life. And in the years that have followed, over sixty-five of them to be exact, he has done a lot of things, most of which were entrepreneurial in nature and in all of which he was enormously successful, which, if truth be told, is probably a gross understatement!

CHAPTER XVIII

NORTHWESTERN UNIVERSITY, JUNIOR YEAR, SUMMER VACATION: CHARLIE HERLOCHER, MOLLY YEAGER, THE TANGLEWOOD AND THE CURTIN FAMILY

BY THE end of that summer, following my junior year in college, which had otherwise been fairly uneventful, outside of a few work-related problems, which have already been noted, Charlie decided to improve my social life, by suggesting that he would like to "fix-me-up" with a college girl from Penn State University. His suggestion came after we had finished selling discount booklets for the day, and while we were eating dinner later that evening at the Tavern Restaurant in State College. It was the same restaurant, by the way, where, not too far in the future, I would become a waiter during another pivotal point in my life. That, however, is another story for another chapter in this story.

So returning to that evening in the Tavern, following the end of our dinner together, Charlie informed me, almost as an afterthought, that he was going to call a Penn State coed for a date, immediately after we paid the check, and that, if I agreed, he would ask her to suggest another coed, who might be willing to go out with me at the same time, so that we could go on a "double date," somewhere in the area. Well, I agreed, he called, she suggested Molly Yeager, a rising sophomore at Penn State University, who was living that summer with her family, in nearby Bellefonte, and the rest, as they say, became the beginning of a history, or a relationship, or even both!

Well, whatever it was destined to become, it began that evening at a local bar, where you could also dance, called, "The Tanglewood," located along the Jacksonville Road, which was really Howard Street extended, just outside of the town of Bellefonte, Pennsylvania. There, in a little more than a rustic bar, located, virtually, in the backwoods of Centre County, we danced and talked and laughed for hours, over the course of that evening, with and without Charlie and his date, in what would become the beginning of something that was so special that it would last for nearly four years, but the effects of which would last far longer, probably for a lifetime!

Molly had grown up in a small town that was, virtually, next to mine, no more than twenty miles apart, and in a county that was next to mine, which probably explains, in part, why her cultural background was not unlike mine. Like me, she reeked of rural central Pennsylvania, but with some notable exceptions, possibly the most notable of which was her mother's maiden surname of "Curtin," and the genealogical history associated therewith. In fact, her mother, Eliza Curtin Yeager, was the great-granddaughter of Roland Curtin, an historic figure in our area, who, inter alia, founded a town, just outside of Milesburg, Pennsylvania, called, you guessed it, "Curtin," where he became a prosperous and prominent businessman, making iron ore throughout most of the nineteenth century.

Thereafter, the Curtin family became so prominent in the surrounding area that streets in nearby Bellefonte and State College were named, in each instance, "Curtin Street," likely named after Roland's son, Andrew Greg Curtin, Molly's great-great uncle, who became the Governor of the State of Pennsylvania during the Civil War. To commemorate that gubernatorial fact, the town erected a statue of the gentleman, which was placed in front of the courthouse, shortly after the Civil War. A photograph of that statue, with the two of us, among others, paying our respects, as college students, has been included as Exhibit 4 in the Appendix.

My family, on the other hand, could never be historically characterized as prominent. I guess that you could possibly say that we were prominently undistinguished, but that would probably be a non-sequitur. In any event, none of us, to my knowledge, were ever a governor . . . of anything! Actually, to be quite honest about the matter, I'm not sure whether some of my forebears could even spell the word, not in the English language, anyway.

Nor did anyone ever name a town after us, or even a street, for that matter. And If I am going to be totally honest, I don't even know of an alley that carries our name. Nor are you going to find a statue of any one of us anywhere in this universe, or any other, for that matter. That is because we, as a family, did not do anything, historically speaking, that is worth remembering, let alone, significant enough, to be commemorated with a statue. Gosh, genetically speaking, we're not even statuesque!

History, I am sure, will reveal, if you can even identify us historically, that we, as a family, did little more than get ourselves born, make some ambivalent effort to get through life, without achieving any distinction in doing so, and, then, die, in all likelihood, in a rather ignominious manner, recorded, somewhere, by a simple gravestone and, possibly, a record or two.

Still, families aside, including their historical differences, Molly and I had an overriding factor in common: We were both college students at the time and at two great universities, no less, who were, because of those academic dimensions, if none other, upward bound, whatever that may have meant. That was the great equalizer, which served as the basis for a certain amount of commonality, despite the apparent historical and familial differences. In short, we were, notwithstanding those differences, just college students, which has often served as a fundamentally sound basis for dating and, as it turned out in this instance, even a significant relationship.

Every relationship, of course, has some kind of a beginning and ours could best be described as beginning rather slowly. I say, "slowly," because the relationship consisted mostly of walks, around her hometown, which were about all that I could afford, and which were accomplished by moving rather slowly while doing so. Actually, the only real alternative was probably running, and it seemed sort of inappropriate to begin a relationship by running. That actually seemed more appropriate in trying to get out of a relationship, and, I must say, far more typical. Since this was just the beginning, we chose to move rather "slowly."

In doing so, I discovered, as the weeks progressed, that I had chosen to like someone who, despite the historical and familial differences, came from the same area with a similar culture and, essentially, familiar values. The girl, in short, turned out, over time, to be a lot like me that summer, which, eventually, presented a real problem, because I was not at all satisfied with what I was at the time. In fact, I still wanted to become something more, or, at least, something that I was not, which, at that point, I could not define, but which, nevertheless, might be more to my liking, or, at least, what everyone else might like.

Because I believed that I had not yet succeeded, despite an academic effort at that point, I was still apparently stuck, somewhat, with what I was, which, unfortunately, I saw, during the last few weeks of that summer, in the countenance of that coed. And even though I really liked the girl, which is a classic understatement, that presented a real quandary, because how do you continue to like someone that is so much like a person that you do not like . . . at least not very much or very often. That, I can tell you, is not easily accomplished, and I had some lingering difficulty in accomplishing it over the remainder of that summer.

Nevertheless, I worked very hard during the remaining weeks of that summer to resolve that dilemma, because, by then, I had begun to realize that the girl was really special. And by the end of that summer, I had grown to really like the girl, despite the perplexing similarities. Nevertheless, for the first time in nearly three years, I actually looked forward to returning to school, because, if you can believe this, I sort of realized that it was probably the only real chance that I had to become unlike the person that I really liked. So filled with ambivalence over a relationship, because of what it represented, I boarded a train, shortly after Labor Day, for Chicago, and change, and my last year at a midwestern university, known, then and now, as Northwestern University!

CHAPTER XIX

NORTHWESTERN UNIVERSITY, SENIOR YEAR, FALL QUARTER: LOU BERES WAS ELECTED PRESIDENT OF THE STUDENT GOVERNMENT, AFTER WHICH HE LOST HIS ACADEMIC SCHOLARSHIP AND, AS A RESULT, HE BECAME A PARKING ATTENDANT IN THE EVENINGS, WHICH CAUSED HIM TO BE SUBSEQUENTLY ADMITTED TO THE EVANSTON TOWNSHIP HOSPITAL, FOR A WEEK, BECAUSE OF EXHAUSTION

IN SOME ways, but only in some, my senior year seemed, in a four-year comparison, to be a rather uneventful academic year. On the other hand, it probably seemed that way because, unlike the previous three, I seemed at the time to be able to handle most things on that campus reasonably well, both inside and outside of the classroom, even though some of them were quite significant. Maybe the most significant, if not the most harrowing, was Lou Beres' decision to run for president of the student governing board. Although it is certainly true that the decision, itself, was quite dramatic, if not complicated, it seemed to pale in comparison to what eventually followed. Lou, for one, did not receive the nomination of his party; consequently, after a brief period of reflection, in order to consider his next move, he ultimately decided to run for the position as an independent. That had never been done before at that university, not in its history, so it would probably be an understatement to say that his decision was not met with any form of approval by major members of the administration at Northwestern University.

Nevertheless, after a lengthy and hard-fought campaign, in which every building, every classroom and every tree on campus, contained the sign, "no matter how big the parties, the people are bigger," Lou Beres' magical bass-baritone voice prevailed in meeting-after-meeting, dorm-after-dorm, sorority-after sorority and fraternity-after-fraternity. Indeed, that captivating voice, employed in those university circumstances, gave birth to the eventual campus-wide expression, "Lou Beres, the golden-throated Greek," which was eventually captured, in word and in personage, in a full page of the class yearbook. It . . . the person . . . also captured the election, in which Lou received over twice as many votes as the other two candidates, combined, a remarkable outcome, to say the political least.

Lou's political success that year made him an even more popular and recognizable personality on that campus, assuming, of course, that such a thing was at all possible, and that, quite frankly, would have been a rather risky assumption. Well, apart from any such risk or any such assumption, you should not be surprised to learn that my friendship with Lou resulted in a more wide-ranging recognition on campus for this personality, too, for the rest of that year, my senior year at that university. Likely, for that reason, I became involved in a lot more campus activities, while acquiring a lot more friends at the same time. I actually became, in spite of myself, somewhat of a campus personality.

Just as the trajectory of our lives on that campus seemed to be soaring, now in the fall quarter of that year, something happened one day, which was certainly unanticipated and which nearly destroyed Lou's chances of finishing his senior year at Northwestern University. It occurred on an otherwise uneventful Friday afternoon, when, as usual, Lou and I returned to the fraternity house, our classes having ended for the day, in order to pick up the mail, put our books away, and prepare to walk down Sheridan road to Scott Hall, that poor excuse for a student union, in order to have coffee with a number of our friends, before, eventually, leaving for our board job at the sorority house, about an hour later.

Lou always received a lot more mail than I did, given his extensive campus activities, so I sat down on a chair to await the completion of his mail opening. As we would both subsequently discover, however, somewhere in the middle of that stack was a letter from the Dean of the School of Speech, in which Lou was enrolled as a public speaking major, informing him that his scholarship had been revoked for the remainder of his senior year, ostensibly because his grade point average had fallen below some form of an "A" . . . to a "B+".

Can you imagine that, a "B+"? Hell, most of the students on that campus, including this one, would have metaphorically killed for a grade point average like that, over a nearly four-year period. And as hard as it was to believe, probably for both of us at the time, and in my case even now, they were going to take away his scholarship for the last two quarters of his senior year, because of that kind of a "GPA."

Initially, Lou didn't say anything about the contents of the letter, or about the letter, itself. Instead, he just put it down on his desk and quietly sat down on a chair, nearby. Then, after a few minutes, at least it seemed like a few minutes, he put his head down in his arms, on the desk, and he began to softly cry. Surprised by what was now happening, I got up from my chair and walked over to his desk, as quietly as I could, picked up the letter and read it, myself. Stunned, for a moment, by its contents, as well as Lou's uncharacteristic response, which was continuing, and which I had never seen before, and which I would never see again, I walked over to the door to our room and quietly shut it. Then, still shaken, I sat back down on my chair, as quickly and as quietly as possible, and I waited, because I didn't know what else to do.

For about another five or, maybe, it was even ten minutes, I can't really be sure, anymore, neither one of us said a word . . . about anything! By that time, Lou seemed to have regained most of his composure and, eventually, he rose from his desk and, without saying a word, began to open the rest of his correspondence. When he finally put the last envelope down on his desk, apparently finished, we rose, together, descended the stairs to the first floor of the fraternity house and, mechanically, opened the mammoth front door to a university that was still a major part of our four-year lives. After which, we proceeded to walk down Sheridan Road to Scott Hall, without saying a word about the letter, or about his scholarship, or about how he could possibly finish the year without it, or about anything else for that matter. And, as usual, upon reaching Scott Hall, we descended the stairs to the snack bar, down in the basement, where we sat down with a number of friends so that we could have coffee and some meaningless conversation with them.

It is not too much to say, at least at this juncture, that it must have occurred to both of us, as we sat there with our friends, that our lives, as a result of what had just transpired, would never be quite the same. In Lou's case, the immediate consequence of that scholarship loss was the acquisition of a job, downtown, somewhere in Chicago, working as a parking attendant, nearly all night, every night, seven days a week, for the remainder of his senior year. Moreover, midway through that year, Lou collapsed at a meeting, and he was immediately taken to the Evanston Township Hospital, for diagnosis and treatment. The diagnosis, not surprisingly, was exhaustion and the treatment was complete bed rest, for over a week, in that hospital.

In my not unreasonable opinion, that hospitalization was, unfortunately, the short-term consequence of the inexplicable loss of that academic scholarship. The long-term consequence, which was just as unfortunate, if not more so, was the likely long-term affects on his health, resulting from that kind of sleep deprivation, especially over that extended period of time. And although the status of one's health, or lack thereof, and the causes therefor, are ordinarily a complex medical phenomena, especially over a lifetime, it is my not unreasonable opinion, once again, that the demands of those sleepless quarters were likely related to a subsequent malaise, lingering over a lifetime, which, ultimately, resulted in a premature death, or, at least, one occurring far sooner than most life insurance mortality tables might have predicted!

In my case, assuming that it is at all relevant at this point, the consequences of that scholarship loss differ in nature, but they are of no less importance, not to me, anyway, because they have resulted in the premature loss of my very best friend, years later. And that mortal fact, with its unjustifiable origins, years earlier, has also given rise to an indelible confirmation of a long-held belief that God has not created a perfect universe. In the ungodly world in which I have lived, over the course of a lifetime, events seem to periodically occur, within its historical parameters, that have resulted in an enormous amount of unfairness, not to mention irremediable loss, to some individuals, if not to many, who clearly deserved more, much more! Indeed, within any applicable ethical system, theological or Aristotelian, Lou Beres deserved more, much more, then and now!

CHAPTER XX

NORTHWESTERN UNIVERSITY, SENIOR YEAR, WINTER QUARTER: WORKING WITH LOU BERES AT A FLORAL SHOP ON THE NORTH SHORE DURING MY CHRISTMAS VACATION; MY TRAIN TRIP HOME ON CHRISTMAS EVE; GIVING MY FRATERNITY PIN TO MOLLY YEAGER ON NEW YEARS EVE

MY RELATIONSHIP with Molly Yeager continued over my entire senior year at Northwestern University, while she remained a sophomore at Penn State University, and it was defined by daily correspondence and a weekly telephone call, the cost of which was shared, equally, by the two of us. It was the only fair thing to do, because the weekly cost of those five-minute telephone calls and the postage on those one-page letters, written in between, was considerable, especially when you consider that we were just college students, from unenviable economic circumstances at the time.

Aside from the costs, however, I don't believe that the five-minute telephone calls or the one-page letters turned out to be much of a problem. We really did not have a whole lot of time to do anything other than to say, within the allotted five-minute time or the one-page space, that we thought enough about each other to write or to call, which, when you think about it, really says a lot . . . about each other, about the relationship and about responsibility.

With the same object in mind, being responsible, that is, I worked at a floral shop over the first part of my Christmas vacation that year. It was located about twenty minutes north of campus, in a suburban town on the "North Shore," called Winnetka. Naturally, I got the job because of Lou, who started working there on the weekends, several weeks prior thereto, and who recommended me, when he learned that they were looking for a few more college students to work over that holiday period.

Lou and I worked every day, seven days a week, during that holiday period, from eight o'clock in the morning until, at least, ten o'clock in the evening, and even later, on some days. It was really hard, dirty work, no matter what we were doing, but especially when we were "flocking" Christmas trees. To do that, we used some kind of a chemical, which was guaranteed to become banned by the Environmental Protection Agency, upon the Agency's inception, years later. Since the chemical had not yet been banned, and we were still using it, almost every day, to "flock" some of those Christmas trees, by turning their exterior into a frothy white, it caused a lot of concern on both of our parts, especially when we couldn't scrub its derivative white coloring off of our hands and arms during a nightly shower.

Nevertheless, irrespective of its seemingly irremovable quality, we were still quite willing to risk death or disability for ten dollars an hour, our hourly wage, because of unpaid tuition bills, among other associated university obligations, such as fraternity dues. Indeed, so that we could save every dollar of that meager amount, toward those unpaid ends, Lou and I stayed in our "closed-for-vacation" fraternity house, and we traveled back and forth every day in his recently acquired Studebaker coup, which had a significant history and which had been sold to him at a deep discount, because of that historical fact, by his uncle, who apparently owned a dealership back there in his hometown of Pekin, Illinois.

Interestingly, that nondescript, second-hand automobile, which is an overly fair characterization, seemed to be more important to Lou than almost anything else on this planet, other than, possibly, his girlfriend at the time, who, of course, was Judy Harris. I guess that you could say, with some degree of accuracy, that it was the beginning of Lou's love affair with the automobile industry, which continued on, with more conspicuous acquisitions, throughout the rest of his life, often with an international flair, especially as he grew older.

In any event, forgetting for the moment about those four-wheel expenditures, which occurred in the years ahead, our work at that floral shop came to an end, during that holiday season, at about six o'clock in the evening on Christmas Eve. Thereafter, we returned to the fraternity house, now full of Christmas spirit, probably for the first time during that industrious holiday period, with the postponed realization that the holiday, itself, was nearly upon us. Now thinking about home, and the most efficacious way of getting there, we quickly showered, changed our clothes, and finished what little remained of our packing, after which Lou drove me downtown to the Union Station in Chicago.

After dropping me off and, belatedly, wishing me a "Merry Christmas," he immediately turned the car part way around and headed due west, toward his home in Pekin, Illinois, which was, at least, a several-hour drive, to spend Christmas with his family. I, in turn, boarded a train, about an hour-and-a-half later, to Altoona Pennsylvania, which was the railroad station nearest to my home and which was about an eight-hour trip on the rails, but which actually seemed much longer this time, probably because I couldn't sleep very well during most of the trip, anticipating, especially as the train drew nearer, spending Christmas, at last, with my family and, eventually, with a coed from Penn State.

When I arrived at the station in Altoona, quite early on Christmas morning, my father, as usual, was standing there, along with a few others, in the parking lot, waiting to pick me up. After briefly shaking my hand and helping me to carry my luggage to the car, while exchanging a word or two, not to mention an obligatory smile, we finally pulled out of the parking lot, shot straight through a blinking red light, turned quickly onto the main road out of town, and, at that point, began the long drive over Gilbert Pinchot's high-crowned roads, endemic in the area, to my hometown of Lock Haven, Pennsylvania.

As usual, my father and I hardly exchanged a word with each other during the whole trip, aside, possibly, from a few words that could, in all likelihood, pass as appropriate pleasantries. I guess, in looking back now, that there was not a whole lot more that we were comfortable in saying to each other, and that there was so much more to be said, which was evidently so uncomfortable for both of us to say, that we had decided, a long time ago, not to say anything more at all.

Naturally, following our, roughly, two-hour trip, my mother was waiting for us at the front door, having seen the car pull up in the driveway from the bay window in the living room, where she was standing, even though it must have been no later than seven o'clock in the morning. After coffee and a nice breakfast, during which we engaged in some meaningless discourse, mostly about my western work over that holiday period, interspersed with moments of uncomfortable silence, we, eventually, arose from the kitchen table, almost in unison, as though it was according to some unwritten script, and began to walk, in a single file order, into the living room. There, just inside the doorway, we stopped for a moment, as we were accustomed, in order to admire the brightly lit Christmas tree, which, together with seasonally wrapped presents on the floor, occupied a large part of the living room.

Traditionally decorated by my mother with, among other cheerful things, a number of antiquated balls, placed here and there, old fashioned, multicolored, tree lights, interspersed among the branches, tinsel everywhere, and a well-worn angel on top of it, which had belonged to earlier generations of her Pennsylvania German family. With all of that in mind, the tree, as usual, captured part of our family history at that seasonal time, and illuminated our family's presence that year, and every year, in a most festive manner.

Following an appropriate amount of comments about the beautifully decorated tree, we quietly sat down in our favorite chair and, without saying another word, slowly and carefully began to open our gifts, which, of course, were almost entirely from each other. I don't remember much about those gifts, probably because there wasn't much about them that was really worth remembering, likely being some form of wearing apparel, distinctive only by age, gender and necessity. But I do remember, quite distinctly, that the most significant gift that any one of us could have received on that holiday occasion remained unopened. I'm speaking here of a conversation that did not take place, among those three individuals, who were members of the same family, and who loved each other, but who no longer understood each other, and who could not speak about that fact, or about anything else that mattered, not of any consequence, anyway . . . then, and, for that matter, the rest of their respective lives!

We had, little by little, become strangers over the course of my university years, who were unnerved by that fact, but who were still uncomfortably civil to one another in each other's presence. We had simply replaced the intimacy of my childhood with the civility of estrangement over the course of those four years. Indeed, we were killing each other, in a manner of speaking, with civility, every day of that estranged existence, over that holiday period. But, then, civility, even in the face of estrangement, seemed like the responsible thing to do, and, as you may have discovered, certainly by this point in my story, we were a responsible people, speaking here of my family and of their culture and of generations.

To escape estrangement, but not necessarily civility, I responsibly removed myself during that holiday period, whenever I could, to the equally unnerving hospitality of the Yeager family. I say equally unnerving, because that family was not unlike my own, aside from the historical differences of course. Unlike my own, however, that family had a coed that I had been writing to and speaking with over the fall quarter of my senior year. And during that time, through that correspondence and those conversations, I had discovered that the young lady continued to possess a lot of qualities that I really liked, if not admired, with a certain amount of ambivalence of course. Indeed, those qualities and that coed seemed to be reason enough to visit the residence, over the latter part of that holiday season, at 231 North High Street, in nearby Bellefonte, where she continued to live with her parents, while a sophomore at Penn State University.

Actually, I visited her home almost daily over the remainder of that holiday season. Doing so allowed me to have a much greater association . . . in person, thank you very much . . . with the coed, and the qualities, which happened to be residing at that address. That daily association, however, resulted in certain consequences, by the end of that holiday season, which seemed almost inexplicable, if not slightly ironic at the time. Among other things, I grew to like, as she often said, her parents even more than I did the coed, notwithstanding my inability to see the difference between the two of them, or even between her parents and my own, for that matter. And that similarity between our respective parents was really confusing because I had a lot of difficulty being around my own parents at the time. And if that was not enough confusion in my life, not to mention the irony, I began to realize, more and more, or should I literally say, day-by-day, just how much that coed and I were alike. And as I have repeatedly said, it was certainly confusing at the time, if not slightly ironic, to like someone more than myself, who was, for all practical purposes, somewhat like myself. Well, notwithstanding the lingering confusion and, possible irony, I decided to keep the coed in my life, even though, in a few weeks, I would have to return to the Midwest, where my university was located. And with that midwestern return in mind, not to mention my growing affection for the girl, I decided to give the girl my fraternity pin . . . on New Year's Eve!

Days later, leaving confusion and irony behind, with the girl and my fraternity pin, I returned, for the last two quarters of my senior year, to Northwestern University. And for reasons that I do not understand, even now, she accepted everything . . . the pin and the absence and me . . . even though the pin, with its inherent promise, came from a totally perplexed individual, who, shortly, would be nearly eight hundred miles away, trying to complete a major academic milestone at a midwestern university.

I have decided to end this chapter, almost as an afterthought, by noting that, for reasons that I still do not understand, my favorite Christmas, to this day, is the one that I have just depicted in this chapter, which began with my work over that holiday season in the metropolitan area of a midwestern world, so different from my rural origins in the culture and terrain of more mountainous regions in central Pennsylvania. And it ended with my decision to return home, over that holiday period, to that terrain and to that culture, which formed, if not framed, my origins, and, consistent therewith, to become "pinned," although ambivalently so, to a young lady, who was, in fact, part of those origins.

The conflict, if we may call it that, resulting from being part of both worlds, manifested so dramatically over that holiday season, has been part of my life forever, and, for similar reasons, so, too, has the memory of the young lady.

CHAPTER XXI

NORTHWESTERN UNIVERSITY, SENIOR YEAR, SPRING QUARTER: SUCCEEDING IN MY SENIOR YEAR; BECOMING A WAITER IN THE SORORITY HOUSE; PROFESSOR McGOVERN'S CLASSES; BORROWING WARREN BUTLER'S TUXEDO AND AUTOMOBILE FOR A SPRING FORMAL; THE END OF THE JUDY HARRIS AND LOU BERES RELATIONSHIP AND OUR GRADUATION

NOW PINNED with, admittedly, a certain amount of concern about what that may eventually mean, apart from having a very bright, beautiful, and delightful Penn State coed in my life, at some distance, of course, I went back to Northwestern University, at the end of that holiday season, to continue changing my life, or myself, or both, in the last quarter of my senior year. I had an innate sense, which had commenced long before that time, that it was important to keep on moving, even if it was only geographically. That way, I would not be stuck with where I was and what I was, because of what was there, whatever that may have meant.

Actually, none of that seemed quite so important, anymore, not at that point in my life, because I was not the same person that had begun college, nearly four years ago. See my photograph, as a member of the graduating class of 1958, which has been included in Exhibit 147 in the Appendix. I was now a spring quarter senior, who had already finished over three years of academic adjustment at that university, difficult as that may have been, and who, by now, knew how to do this "university-thing," and how to do it reasonably well. I had not merely learned how to study, or how to take notes, or how to take examinations, or, more generally, how to do well academically, I had also learned how to be confident about that fact, too. And although I may not have been a "quick study," after all of that time, I did study now, every waking moment, sometimes, and some other kinds, too, with the result that I was actually beginning to thrive, academically, if nothing else, by the end of my education at Northwestern University.

Maybe that is why I actually began to like that year, my senior year, especially the spring quarter of that year, which, of course, was my last quarter at that university. That quarter occurred, of course, like all spring quarters, during the springtime, and the springtime has always been a wonderful time on a college campus, and that was no less true, that year, on the campus of Northwestern University.

Interestingly, however, the previous springtimes on that campus did not seem to be quite so wonderful to me. Maybe that was because, among other things, I was not able to fill my course schedule with political science courses taught by Professor William Montgomery McGovern, who was a monumental intellect, and who could make a cumbersome course, like those in political philosophy, come alive, with unceasingly interesting lectures, which was a rarity on any college campus.

On the other hand, maybe that change in my springtime perspective was because I was able to leave the kitchen sink behind at my board job and become a waiter during my senior year at Alpha Chi Omega. Becoming a waiter was far more fun, serving forty good-looking sorority girls three meals a day in the dining room, rather than gaining dish-pan hands by washing dishes in the kitchen beside grumpy old Al Pearsal. By the end of that spring quarter, I had actually gained forty new female friends, renewed hands and even more social self-confidence.

On top of all of that, assuming that it was possible to top all of that, I had never gone to the formal dinner-dance held by my fraternity in the springtime, not in any one of the three previous years at that university. To do that, in any one of those years, I would have been required to rent a tuxedo, not to mention an automobile, because the event was formal, and it was always held in one of the more grandiose hotels, miles away, in downtown Chicago. And the cost of both seemed impractical, if not insurmountable, in those, seemingly, more challenging years. This year, however, which, of course, was my senior year, everything seemed to have changed, and I don't mean the cost, either. In fact, the cost was still the same, but I wasn't! Whatever I was, whatever I had become, wanted to go to that "spring formal," irrespective of cost or anything else!

Still, in more rational moments, usually occurring late at night, the cost seemed to be somewhat daunting, even to the newer me, so I borrowed a "tux" from my good friend, Warren Butler. After that, all I needed was a ride, so I asked Lou if I could ride with him in his new dilapidated automobile. Unfortunately, however, that car was in the shop, once again, but he had been able to borrow Warren's car, and, fortunately, he had room for me in the back seat. With that transportation problem resolved, I was now on my way to my first fraternity "spring formal," and without any appreciable cost, too, because I had been able to borrow Warren's "tux," and ride with Lou in the car that he had borrowed from Warren.

Several days later, however, while we were both working at our board job in the sorority house, Lou said to me that we really should invite our "old buddy, Warren," to our "spring formal." I agreed and Lou subsequently invited Warren, who immediately accepted, even though he did not have a "tux" to wear or an automobile to drive, because they had already been borrowed by Lou and me. So believe it or not, Warren had to subsequently rent a "tux" and an automobile, in order to go to our "formal," which he did, and which made a delightful story that the three of us recounted, over-and-over-and-over, among ourselves and our friends, laughing, endlessly, each time that we did, often over coffee on Friday afternoons at Scott Hall, or at dinner on Sunday evenings at Walker Brothers. See the photograph of Lou Beres and myself, taken years later, when we were ushers in Warren Butler's wedding, which has been made part of Exhibit 101 in the Appendix.

Not every story ended so joyously that quarter, however, especially the one involving the relationship between Lou Beres and Judy Harris. Lou, as you may recall, had dated Judy rather seriously for most of our junior and senior years. Unfortunately, however, not all things seemed to continue indefinitely, not in this universe, anyway, and their relationship definitely ended, but only over a painfully protracted period of time that spring quarter, the last quarter of our senior year. In fact, the relationship was never really the same following the end of our junior year, but it survived, fitfully, over the summer, in which they were away from each other, and, then, it tried to resurrect itself, once again, when they came back to school for the fall quarter of our senior year. That resurrecting effort, and it was an effort, on both sides, too, was only partially successful, however, for reasons that, in part, seemed to have transcended them both.

Two of those transcendent reasons may have resided back home, where Judy's parents resided, in the suburbs of Cleveland, Ohio. As parents of more than some means, they did not seem to be able to bring themselves to believe that their daughter should tie her future to the amorphous prospects of the son of a poor, immigrant, Greek family. The third reason resided back on campus, in the form of an excessive amount of pride on the part of an overly accomplished, highly capable, son of that poor, immigrant, Greek family. Those reasons, pride and parents, alike, seemed to have kindled a combustible situation that caused the relationship to burn out, slowly, over the course of the rest of that year, our senior year at that university.

The end, when it finally came, occurred, somewhat dramatically, at the end of our classes in the spring quarter of that year, just before graduation. Apparently, Lou had realized that it was inevitably coming, sometime before it actually happened. Nevertheless, in order to forestall the inevitable, he asked me to pick up his cap and gown, several days later, on graduation day, and, then, wait for him, before the procession was actually scheduled to commence, by the south gate to what was then known as Dyke Stadium. That way, in his words, "he would be able to meet me there, just before the ceremony actually began," and quickly put on his cap and gown, with just enough time for both of us to join the rest of our graduating class, as they began to proceed, to the traditional sound of "Pomp & Circumstance," into the Stadium.

In the meantime, he drove to Cleveland, Ohio, or, rather, the suburb of Bay Village, where Judy had gone home for the summer, following the end of her final examinations, in order to try to salvage whatever was left that was salvageable about their relationship. Because nothing really was, he returned to campus, two days later, which was on the day of our graduation, arriving about twenty minutes before the ceremony was actually scheduled to begin and, eventually, reaching the south gate, where I was waiting with his cap and gown, approximately fifteen minutes later. That left no more than five minutes before the band began to play, "Pomp & Circumstance," and the graduating members of the class of "1958," including Lou Beres and Cal Golumbic, began to march into the Stadium!

Our graduation ended a four-year long journey, together, through the halls of Northwestern University. During that time, we had grown into young men, who had, through it all, become very good friends. We had also become accustomed to seeing each other almost every day, rooming together during our freshman, sophomore and senior years, or relaxing together, in between classes, at the fraternity house or the sorority house, or even studying together, sometimes, at the Charles Deering Library, or, possibly, having coffee together, with friends, on a Friday afternoon at Scott Hall, or even having dinner together with Warren Butler on a Sunday evening at Walker Brothers, and, of course, working together, as waiters, for three meals a day at our board job at Alpha Chi Omega. That, of course, would all come to an end with our graduation from Northwestern University.

Following the graduation ceremony, photographs of which are part of Exhibit 115 in the Appendix, we briefly visited with each other's family, which, of course, were present to witness, in my case, the first graduation of a family member from a four-year college, and in Lou's case, the second graduation of a family member from a four-year college. Thereafter, following a brief visit to the fraternity house to pick up our luggage, both of us, with our overly proud families in tow, departed from a university that had been our challenging, but growing, home, for four academic years, and we returned, at least for the time being, to the now unfamiliar environs of our family homes in Pekin, Illinois and Lock Haven, Pennsylvania.

We would not see each other again, for nearly ten years. Lou would not see Judy Harris ever again. I, however, would run into her, quite by accident, four years later, on the streets of Washington, D.C., where I was attending law school at the time, but that, as they say, is a story for another day, or, maybe, even another chapter.

CHAPTER XXII

NORTHWESTERN UNIVERSITY, SUMMER VACATION FOLLOWING MY GRADUATION: SELLING FROMMS DISCOUNT BOOKLETS ONCE AGAIN; THE UNFORGETTABLE MEETING OF AN OLD LADY IN LEMONT; LUNCH WITH MOLLY YEAGER AND CHARLIE HERLOCHER AT THE "HUB"; AND FAILING A METROPOLITAN LIFE INSURANCE EXAMINATION

I JOINED Molly Yeager, by design, nearly every day during that summer, following my graduation from Northwestern University. Often, it was twice-a-day. The first time ordinarily occurred when Charlie Herlocher and I decided to take a break, for lunch, on the Penn State campus, following our early morning sales of discount booklets once again, in and around the State College area . . . without a license of course! Fortunately, Molly was working that summer on the campus of Penn State University, doing secretarial work for some faculty members in the Agricultural Department, which meant that she was ordinarily free for lunch, somewhere on campus, but for no more than half-an-hour.

With that in mind, Charlie would typically park his automobile in one of the university parking garages, impermissibly, of course, at which point we normally walked over to the student union, known at the time as the "HUB," for lunch. Upon entering the cafeteria, encompassing nearly the whole first floor, Charlie typically secured a table, over by the windows, while I turned around, departed the building by a side door, before commencing a long walk up "Ag Hill," to the agricultural building where Molly was working, and where she would typically be waiting for me, just outside of the front door, usually in something "summery," which she described as a "shirtwaist dress," which was of assorted colors, the choice depending upon the day, if you really care to know. After a hug and some small talk, usually about our day so far, which, to be quite honest about the matter, was not nearly as memorable as the hug, we typically walked back down the hill together, hand-in-hand, to join Charlie, for what would become a half-an-hour lunch in the cafeteria at the "HUB."

God's universe, during that descent down "Ag Hill," on our way toward the "HUB," never seemed more perfect, not to those two young students, not during those memorable moments, anyway. Just two college students, a coed and her college guy, on their way down to have lunch on a college campus, once again, for no other reason than they liked each other, a lot! We can assume, of course, that those fleeting, lyrical moments, full of unending expectations, have not yet been confronted by the realities that lie beyond that academic setting and those idyllic moments.

Well, let's leave such maudlin moments, not to mention the consequent observation, and return, once again, to our three notable college students, now at the conclusion of Molly's half-hour lunch break, when she would ordinarily note the time, rise from the lunch table, always over by the windows, and give one of the two remaining college fellows, now standing, a hug, all over again, which, trust me, was no less memorable. Then, following a more civilized goodbye to both of them, the coeducational part of this summer story normally turned and walked, briskly, out of the building, back up "Ag hill," on the way back to a more mundane part of her day, commonly called secretarial work, in a university agricultural office.

No less conscientious, but, possibly, a little bit more mercenary, Charlie and I would usually follow suit, in a less coeducational manner, of course, especially in our choice of a bathroom. Thereafter, following a no-nonsense departure from the men's room, the building and, subsequently, the campus, in an impermissibly parked car, naturally, Charlie and I would normally spend the rest of the afternoon, or, at least, a part thereof, depending upon our earlier success, selling discount booklets in every farming village and town in Centre County.

By doing so, we normally made a lot of money for very little work, in a short amount of time, every day, six days-a-week, that summer. Unlike us, however, Molly did not work on Saturdays, so Charlie and I would usually drive down to her hometown on those days, where she was still living with her parents, in nearby Bellefonte, so that we could join her for lunch there, usually at a restaurant located at the time on the corner of Spring and High Streets, called "Blaskos."

After parking his car on High Street, right beside the restaurant, without putting any money in the parking meter, a fairly common practice that you may have already noticed by now, Charlie normally entered the restaurant, found a seat, over by the window once again, where he could easily watch for us, and impatiently waited, while I quickly walked around the corner and up the hill on North Spring Street, to the residence at 231 North Spring Street, where Molly was dutifully waiting for me, outside the front door of her home, usually around noontime. Then, in what had become a lunchtime ritual, but this time off-campus, Molly and I would walk back down the hill from her house, hand-in-hand, once again, to join Charlie, who was still impatiently waiting at a table, over by the window, at that restaurant.

I should probably point out at this point in my story, that, all things being considered, especially at this point in my life, which unfortunately follows the fairly recent departure of both of those individuals from this earth, not to mention from my life, those fleeting moments have become part of an all too intrusive memory, if not some kind of a worthwhile history.

Outside of those all too brief lunch interludes with Molly and Charlie, during the week and on Saturdays, I can't say that any one working day that summer, selling discount booklets, was any more noteworthy than any other, with possibly one notable exception. On that noteworthy day, Charlie and I were spending the morning, as usual, selling dry cleaning discount booklets in Centre County. On that morning, however, we were selling the booklets in the farming village of Lemont, a small, quaint, Pennsylvania German community, at the foot of Mount Nittany, where the Nittany Lion was reputed to have once roamed, many years ago, or, at least, before it decided to relocate and to retire on the campus of Penn State University, where it has become the name, if not the inorganic mascot, of their, once, very proud football team!

Significantly, because it is of great significance at this point in my story, if not in my life, my mother had grown up in that farming village, in a large, brick, turn-of-the-century farmhouse, located at the corner of Mountain and Pike Streets, the latter of which is now more often known as Branch Road. The house was owned at that time, and built before that time, by her aunt and uncle, Hannah and John Grove, who had long since retired from farming land that they owned, for nearly half a century, located in or around the farming village of Shiloh, not too far away, in Centre County.

On that atypical day, in which I was selling dry cleaning discount booklets in the same farming village where my mother had grown up, I typically introduced myself at the doorway of every residence, by saying, with only minor variations, that "my name is Calvin Golumbic, and my mother was Huldah Davis, who grew up in the village, while living with her aunt and uncle, Hannah and John Grove." That introductory sentence usually garnered some kind of a familiar response, generally indicating that the people in that particular residence did, indeed, remember my mother, and her aunt and uncle, with the only difference being how well.

Toward the end of that morning, however, as I approached the outer limits of the village, just before Branch Road leaves Lemont, crosses Route 45, the main road to State College and, then, eventually enters the tiny farming village of Puddintown, on its way over to Houserville, I encountered a, seemingly, enfeebled, elderly woman, in a wheelchair, dozing somewhat, in the partial sunlight of a flagstone patio, right in front of her house, or, possibly, her family's house.

She had a distinctly withered face, likely from way too much farm life, thinning gray hair that was pulled back into a bun, commonly found on elderly women in rural areas, and the kind of sallow complexion that aged people typically acquire, who are no longer able to care for themselves and who are now relegated to a more stationary life, indoors. And I could not help saying to myself, as I approached the steps to the patio, "that she was as thin as a scarecrow," which, given her initial appearance, was not an inapt description. Based on those telling characteristics, I initially estimated that she must have been somewhere between ninety and ninety-five years of age . . . at the very least.

For probably that aged reason, or for reasons that I no longer remember, I initially thought about just walking around her, without saying a word, on my way across the patio and up the steps to the front door of the house. But mindful of not being rude, especially because my mother had grown up in that village, I quickly changed my mind, especially when the elderly woman partially turned her head, for just a moment, apparently to look at me. So, instead, I stopped for a moment on the flagstone patio, right beside her, and with a well-worn smile on my face, turned, slightly, toward the woman and announced, once again, in a rather conversational voice, who

I was and my consequent family connection to that village, just as I had with every other resident, in every other residence, that I had visited that morning in that town.

Not really expecting much more than a smile, in return, if that, I was noticeably surprised, because she immediately made a very distinct, although an unintelligible, response. In fact, I found the words to be not only strange, but nonsensical. At the very least, they seemed to be completely out of context or, more accurately, without any context at all. Indeed, absent a subject of that seemingly meaningless statement, by name or otherwise, it was impossible to understand to whom she was referring, when she said that, and I quote, "it was tragic that she took her life like that." And there was absolutely no reason for me to believe, especially in those circumstances, that the pronoun, "she," in that meaningless statement, had anything to do with me, or any other member of my family, living or dead, who happened to be of the feminine gender.

So I discounted the whole linguistic episode, almost immediately, as the unintelligible ramblings of an enfeebled old woman. I say "almost," because, try as I might, over the next few minutes and, subsequently, hours, which tantalizingly followed, I could not, "for the life of me" get her, or her puzzling words, out of my mind. And I could not stop wondering why she would say anything like that to me . . . seemingly in response to my announcement of whom I was and my relationship to those in my family who had once lived in that farming village.

In the end, I was left, as I walked away, with some kind of a ridiculous statement about an unnamed suicide, which appeared, on its face, to be unrelated to anything or anybody that I knew, and which was likely the delusional statement of an enfeebled old woman, who was probably mentally unstable at her age. Yet, I must admit, if I may repeat myself, that I was still somewhat unnerved by the fact that the elderly woman, unstable or not, found some reason to make that statement to me, after I had just announced who I was and my consequent family history in Lemont.

Well, in any event, I sold a lot of dry-cleaning discount booklets to a lot of people who lived in that town and who knew my mother and my great Aunt Hannah Grove. They seemed to be more than happy to purchase a discount booklet from the nice young man, who was related to both of them, even though, given their Mennonite or Dunker lifestyles, they probably never had, nor ever will have, anything to dry clean in their entire lives. Aside from their kindness, however, I don't remember anything else about any of those people, probably because there wasn't anything else worth remembering about any one of them. But I do remember, even to this day, that elderly woman in the wheelchair, who seemingly spoke in riddles, which, not surprisingly, made no sense at all to me at the time.

I also remembered her later that day, when I had lunch with Molly Yeager at Blaskos restaurant on High Street in Bellefonte, which, as you may recall, was normally what I did on Saturdays, although, generally, with Charlie Herlocher, too. But when I told Molly about the puzzling, and slightly unnerving, encounter with that elderly woman in Lemont, earlier that day, it did not seem to really interest her, let alone concern her, if, indeed, the encounter should have been at all concerning or, for that matter, interesting, to anybody. So we moved on to more interesting things to discuss, which, at the time, seemed far more interesting, such as our plans for the evening, in which I agreed to drive back up to her home, after dinner with my parents, in order to spend the evening, mostly at the renown Hofbrau House, located on Bishop Street, in historic Bellefonte, in order to consume a sizable amount of pizza and beer, with the possibility of acquiring a few more hugs from my favorite coed at the time, before departing for home, at way too late of an hour.

For reasons that I cannot explain, even now, I decided not to discuss that uncomfortable encounter with my parents at dinner that evening, even though I had been selling discount booklets, earlier in that day, in Lemont, where my mother had grown up and, in all likelihood, may well have known many of the people who still lived there, including that strange elderly woman.

The rest of that summer seemed comparatively uneventful, probably because it was, at least until the day came, almost at the end of that summer, when my father asked me, after I had returned home from selling dry cleaning discount booklets, earlier in the day, what I planned to do about finding work. I assumed at the time that he meant, "real work," the forty-hours-a-week, with benefits, kind, since I would not be going back to college in the fall. Because I did not have any of those kinds of vocational plans, not at the moment, anyway, and I told him so, my father suggested, apparently out of some concern that his only son may become a vagrant, that I take a "management intern examination," given by his employer, the Metropolitan Life Insurance Company.

Because his only son had recently graduated from a great midwestern university, I guess that my father, along with his manager, who administered the examination, thought that I would be more than qualified, upon successfully passing that examination, to enter an intern program and, eventually, become a manager for their Company. Apparently, however, the "management intern examination" must have thought otherwise, because the examination failed me, which must have embarrassed my father, enormously, not to mention my hopeful mother, although they were both kind enough not to say so.

Since I had never wanted to become like my father, or even remotely like him, and I went eight hundred miles away to a midwestern university, in an effort to avoid doing so, you should not be surprised to learn, at least at this point, that I was greatly relieved that I had failed that examination, or, rather, that I had not succeeded in qualifying for an opportunity to become like my father, whichever way that you prefer to look at that ironic situation. To this day, however, I cannot explain how I happened to fail, since I did not, knowingly, try, and, quite frankly, it was not at all a very difficult examination. Apparently, there must have been some sort of divine intervention, for which I have always been eternally grateful, although not necessarily religiously so.

Nevertheless, there was something else about that examination that was even more important than my failure, which, in the interests of historical accuracy, should be noted here. My father, in short, had arranged it, and with the only company that he had ever known, undoubtedly because his only son had graduated from college, and did not have a job, or even any vocational plans, and he worried about him, which he had for lifetime . . . without, of course, ever saying so!

CHAPTER XXIII

PENN STATE UNIVERSITY, GRADUATE SCHOOL, THE PHILOSOPHY DEPARTMENT: EXISTENTIALISM AND ANCIENT POLITICAL PHILOSOPHY; STANLEY ROSEN AND RICHARD GOTSCHALK

MY FAILURE on the insurance examination reminded me that I could not live the rest of my life without some kind of employment . . . the unimaginably real kind, that is. Because I could not imagine it, however, I decided to avoid it, at least for the time being, by going on to graduate school. So with that in mind, I decided to apply for admission, as a graduate student, to the Philosophy Department at Penn State University. That seemed like a reasonably smart thing to do at the time, because my only real interests were avoiding work and not avoiding Molly Yeager, both of which I could accomplish by going back to college, as a graduate student, where Molly was a coed, at Penn State University.

Within several weeks, I discovered that I was successful on both counts, by a letter of acceptance from the Philosophy Department, even though I had only taken one course in philosophy, although a number of courses in political philosophy, as an undergraduate student at Northwestern University. That only one course in philosophy, as an undergraduate student, could, conceivably, be sufficient for admission to a graduate program in philosophy was beyond my understanding, other than, possibly, divine intervention, once again, for which I will be . . . well, you know.

Now armed with divine intervention once again, and an acceptance letter from the Philosophy Department, enabling me to enroll as a graduate student at Penn State University, I began, by the end of that summer, to look for a place to live in State College, where the main campus was located, and where I would be attending classes in the graduate school of the Philosophy Department. I also began to wonder, at the same time, how I could possibly afford to live, as well as to go to college, there, at least in a manner that was consistent with my non-working lifestyle, up to that point, anyway. The only real, if not unreasonable, answer seemed to be some form of work, but more like the imaginable discount booklet sales kind, not the unimaginable forty-hours-a-week, with benefits, kind. And with that kind of imaginable work in mind, if not in a substantial part of my past, especially in the State College area, I decided to rent a single room on the second floor of a boarding house, located at 409 South Allen Street, which was reasonably inexpensive, because it was unreasonably small. And, thereafter, I began to sell dry cleaning discount booklets, nearly every evening, mostly to students who lived in rooming houses, not unlike mine, and who probably would never have any use for them. And if you are still wondering, I did it without a permit, once again!

Shortly thereafter, I also applied for, and subsequently received, a teaching assistantship, which covered the cost of my tuition and also paid me, to my unending surprise, not to mention my eternal gratitude, approximately $1800 a year, in living expenses, for, once again, work that was not the unimaginable kind, which, in case you may have forgotten, was one of the reasons why I was going to graduate school in the first place. That amount, coupled with free tuition and my discount booklet sales in the evenings, generated more money than I had ever made up to that point in my entire, unproductive, irresponsible life. For that reason alone, I was enormously proud of myself. I had succeeded in becoming a wealthy vagrant, which exceeded even my irresponsible expectations at that point in my life. And as a result of my unproductive, irresponsible lifestyle, I was about to become well-educated, thank you very much, in philosophy, no less. Moreover, I was not unmindful that completing several more years of this kind of irresponsibility, in academic pursuits, too, with pay, no less, could result in a Ph.D. and, eventually, the same kind of unproductive work obtained by my faculty . . . with benefits, no less. That's right, I could avoid work by working as a college instructor!

With that noble ideal in mind, I went to my very first philosophy class in graduate school, which was in the fall semester of that year, 1958, and which, obviously, was attended by others like me, who had the same kind of thing in mind, namely irresponsible and unproductive faculty work. The amazing thing is that, irrespective of irresponsibility, or my intended lifestyle, whichever seems to be more appropriate at this point, I really grew to like all of my philosophy classes over the course of that semester. Maybe not at first, of course, because the subject matter was a bit foreign to me since I did not have much of a background in it. So I probably had to work a little harder than the other graduate students, academically, that is, who had majored in philosophy as an undergraduate student. But by reading secondary sources, on my own, I eventually caught up, and I subsequently discovered, in the process, that I really liked the study of philosophy, and that, even more importantly, I was rather good at it.

Maybe that was because the study was, among other academic things, a process of self-discovery, analogously speaking. Possibly, that is why I, who was so conflicted about almost everything in my life, such as my girlfriend, my parents, and, especially, myself, to name just a few, became so interested in existentialism, which was a philosophic prescription for self-examination, or, if you will, self-understanding. But I continued to be interested in political philosophy, the origin of which was in my undergraduate days, especially the ancient kind, because that field provided a basis for understanding others, historically and politically, if not sociologically and religiously, and I was no less interested in understanding others, especially with those academic subjects in mind.

I also grew to like two of my philosophy professors, Stanley Rosen, an ancient political philosopher, and Richard Gotschalk, a European existentialist, both of whom were fairly young men, who had recently obtained their doctorate degrees, and who had begun their college teaching careers, as instructors, in the Philosophy Department at Penn State University. I liked them because, like Professor McGovern, during my undergraduate days, they were extremely good at what they did, which was teaching college students, although somewhat differently from Professor McGovern, likely because, in this instance, they were graduate students, which was yet another profitable lesson, especially for a one-day college instructor, even aside from the subject matter.

It seemed that I had developed a real affinity for competent academicians, especially the philosophic kind, and a real anathema for the incompetent ones, for which there were far too many in the world of academics, not to mention in other worlds, too. This was quite a revelation, if not a confirmation, and, personally, a very important one at that. Maybe the fault, if there happened to be such a thing, in learning, or the deficiency thereof, may lie, on occasion, with the learned and not necessarily with those learning. Maybe, I may have been more than my undergraduate grades, especially for the first two years, which were quite good, but not really great, possibly for all of those deficient faculty reasons. And, maybe, I may eventually become more, in an academic manner of speaking, if not in a subsequently professional one, than those who gave those grades to me, at least in some cases. The answers, of course, to all of those questions, or to any one of them, may not be easily found, especially during one's college days, but if they are to be found, they can probably be found, somewhere and sometime, in subsequent years, with the greatest of all instructors . . . experience!

So far my experience, upon the departure from Clinton County, years ago, has been, with the exception of some unremarkable summer employment, essentially academic, with some coeducational refreshment mixed in there, too. That experience, limited as it may have been, certainly resulted in my perception, at least by that time, that I was no longer just like those that I had left behind in Clinton County. On the other hand, I was not completely sure whether Clinton County had completely departed from me, either.

It could well be, of course, that such a departure did occur, at least somewhat, following a successful performance in some instance or instances, or in some course or courses, or in some semester or semesters, or even in some academic year or years, but there was no guarantee that I would continue to be that successful in another instance, or in another course, or in another semester, or even in another academic year. Such success, in short, to the extent of its existence, was no guarantee that the limitations of my origins would not rear their ugly head, somewhere or sometime, in the near future, while I was still trying, academically at this juncture, to become something else, by becoming something more. That concern, that ambivalence, if you will, was still sufficient, in and of itself, to drive me onward, toward other tests, other trials, other risks, to see if, indeed, I would not fail, as I had once feared, on the day that I left home for a midwestern university, seemingly, a lifetime ago.

By "onward," I meant, if nothing else, a geographic move. I was interested in such a move, because I had geographically returned to central Pennsylvania, in order to go to graduate school at Penn State University, so that I could be near to a coed that I liked, who was a student there. Although my return could well be construed, by most reasonable minds, to be a progressive move, because it also involved going on to graduate school, the move was still unsettling, geographically, if nothing else, because it was to a locale, with all of its inherent limitations, where I had grown up. And, of course, my interest in a coed, who lived there and who went to college there, too, was equally unsettling, for the same geographic reasons, if nothing else.

So after several years of being settled and unsettled, a little over three to be exact, as a graduate student in the Philosophy Department at Penn State University, I decided, upon graduation, photographs of which are part of Exhibit 116 in the Appendix, that both the University and the coed may be holding me back from becoming something, which I could not describe at the time, but which I was reasonably sure that I could not find in either locale . . . the school or the girl. Consequently, I decided to change locations, academically and coeducationally, so that I may be able to become what I did not understand, but that I was sure that I would, when I became it, sometime in the future, somewhere else.

Unfortunately, I knew that leaving the school and the girl would be, in each instance, a heart-wrenching experience, because I really liked them both, in quite different ways of course. Among so many other indescribable things, I liked what they were, institutionally in one instance, and personally in the other. And I was more than aware of what they had meant in my life, certainly up to that point, which, even now, is quite hard to describe, especially in a historical perspective, and my perspective is, by its nature and years, historical. If, however, I must try, I can safely say that whatever I am today can be traced back, in so many different ways, to my association with both of them. Their definition of what I was, academically, in one instance, and personally in the other, provided me with an opportunity to believe that, possibly, someday that may become true.

CHAPTER XXIV

AMERICAN UNIVERSITY LAW SCHOOL, FIRST YEAR, FIRST SEMESTER: INITIALLY LIVING IN A SINGLE ROOM IN HARTNET HALL; SUBSEQUENTLY LIVING WITH MATT ZALE IN AN APARTMENT; AND THE BORING CLASSES AND INSTRUCTORS IN LAW SCHOOL

UNFORTUNATELY, OR, maybe, even fortunately, whichever you prefer to believe at this point, I now believed that any opportunity for self-advancement lay elsewhere, in another academic setting and, maybe, with another coed, although the latter being unidentifiable at that point in time. After all, the university and the coed, who had believed in me, could possibly have been wrong; I couldn't be sure. Therefore, I decided to try something else, educationally at first, and in a different and more difficult environment, where success was hardly guaranteed, but where success may eventually guarantee a greater economic and social return, and with it, a greater sense of self-appraisal.

With that in mind, among so may other inexplicable things, I decided to apply to law school, which I did, but only upon the successful completion of my oral examinations and the approval of my thesis, followed shortly thereafter by my graduation with a Master of Arts Degree from the Philosophy Department at Penn State University.

My application was subsequently accepted by, among a number

of other nondescript law schools, the Washington College of Law at the American University, where I began to attend class in January of 1961. At the time, I hoped, as I began my legal studies, that I would not see the same kind of political hostility among the faculty that was so prevalent among their counterparts in graduate school. By "political hostility," I mean the kind of animus that existed among the various members of the faculty in the Philosophy Department, because of their varying views on the subject. And as a graduate student, if you were liked by some members of the faculty, because of your interest in, or subscription to, their particular views on the subject, or simply because you were likable, some other members may, and often did, dislike you for the very same reasons or, even worse, for no reason at all. Of course, those on the faculty who happened to like you, because of your similar philosophic views, would often try to protect you from those who did not, if they could, but often, because of the situation, they could not, and when they could not, the situation often became quite unpleasant.

I can think of no better example than my oral examinations, as a graduate student, in the Philosophy Department at Penn State University. Because I was perceived to be a disciple of Dr. Stanley Rosen, and his views on political philosophy, as well as Dr. Richard Gotschalk, and his views on existentialism, those members of the faculty who disliked one or the other, or both of those views, and/or their proponents, made my life quite trying during the examination. Indeed, it would have been difficult enough if Stanley Rosen had been present during the examination, but, in fact, he was in another country, on a sabbatical leave at the time. Consequently, I was completely on my own in discussing political philosophy, much to the delight of those who detested Dr. Rosen's views, which was nearly as much as they detested Dr. Rosen, himself. Thankfully, Dr. Richard Gotschalk happened to be there, during the examination, and he continually intervened on my behalf during my discussion on existentialism, but it was still a long, tortuous afternoon, probably for both of us.

Following that examination, I decided that I would never go through anything like that again, which would have been required, "in steroids," if I had decided to go on for a Ph.D. So I can certainly say that intra-departmental politics, which were all too prevalent in the graduate school faculty at the time, were another factor in my decision not to spend the rest of my life making very little money as a college instructor. Instead, as you are aware by now, I decided to enroll in law school, which I did, where I hoped that merit would replace mendacity.

Because the law school was located in Washington D.C., I had to find a place to live in the Nation's Capitol. So I borrowed my parents' car, not having one of my own, and I drove to that city to find a room to rent, because I really could not afford anything much larger. And after spending a rather unproductive day, searching, I finally found something that seemed quite suitable, but not much more. It was called Hartnett Hall, which, in reality, was nothing more than a so-called, "rooming house," consisting, in that instance, of a number of buildings that were located just off of Dupont Circle. There, I could rent a single room, which I did, not far from the law school, for a nominal weekly fee, which also included three modest meals a day, in a cafeteria owned by the rooming house. The meal plan was financially attractive but gastronomically atrocious. I knew, however, that I could live with atrocious, if I could just afford it, which was far more important in my life at that time.

The breakfasts turned out to be generally acceptable; you really can't kill eggs and bacon, even if you tried and, trust me, they tried. They were far more successful with the lunches, however, because each and every one of them seemed, metaphorically speaking, like "death-warmed-over," which I know is a cliché, even a very poor cliché, but quite an applicable one in this instance. The dinners, esthetically speaking, were better eaten without opening your eyes; your taste buds, of course, had already been destroyed by the lunches.

Nevertheless, I survived the food, and I gradually grew to enjoy some of the dining room company, which changed, continually, depending upon the person that you happened to be sitting with, which could include any one of the hundreds of individuals, who happened to be renting a room in one of those buildings. Some, I might add, were more attractive than others, probably because the organization seemed to be a preference for young secretaries, just starting to work for the government, after having recently graduated from a high school in a small town, somewhere in the middle of America.

Not all of my dining companions, however, turned out to be secretarial. One of them, who joined me for dinner one evening, happened to be a young lawyer from Wisconsin, who had recently graduated from the University of Wisconsin Law School and, almost immediately thereafter, moved to Washington, D.C., to become a lawyer for a federal agency. Since he, like me, did not have a place to live, or eat, when he came to town, he, like me, accepted the low rent and poor food hospitality of Hartnett Hall. And several days later, after several more dinners together, I accepted his hospitable offer to join him in renting an apartment that he had recently found on Cathedral Avenue, just a few blocks from the National Zoo, right off of Connecticut Avenue, Northwest.

His name was Matthew Zale, although his surname was originally, "Zelibobka," but somewhere, sometime, someone in his family, who happened to precede him, generationally speaking, decided to change it to simply, Zale, which, therefore, became the surname of the person with whom I shared an apartment for the remainder of that semester, my very first semester in law school. That historical fact became far more consequential than I ever imagined, which, unfortunately, for this story, at least, I can fully remember. But I do remember that our association, in that apartment, became an interesting story, which has been subsequently noted in this story, over the latter part of my first semester in law school.

The earlier part of that semester, however, was not much to speak about, not academically, anyway. If, however, I had to do so, I really could not speak about very much that I liked; I certainly did not like most of my courses. They were, in fact, quite boring, with the possible exception of criminal law, which I probably liked because I had already embarked on a life of crime, for a number of summers, with my good friend, Charles Herlocher, by failing to purchase a license to sell dry cleaning discount booklets in State College, in case you may have already forgotten. And it occurred to me that, following my graduation from law school, the two of us may be able to continue such a questionable enterprise, without any concern, anymore, because, in the event of our apprehension, we would not have to retain a lawyer to defend us.

Apart from that questionable prospect, the courses during the first semester seemed to be somewhat meaningless, if not personally irrelevant. For example, I simply could not find anything about the course on "property" that seemed to be at all applicable in my life. At the time, I had never, in fact, owned any real or personal property, not of any consequence, anyway, not even an automobile. And I lacked the imagination, or even the inclination, or, more realistically, the opportunity, to try to acquire any of it, personal or real, not in the immediate future, anyway. I did, however, pay a little more attention during the week in which the instructor discussed "lost or abandoned property." I could, in fact, imagine acquiring property, somewhere, someplace, or sometime, that someone had lost or abandoned, especially along a stream, while I was trout fishing. I have always liked to fly fish and, maybe, someone might be absent-minded enough to lose or abandon a key to a rather expensive summer cottage along a stream, somewhere, which I might be fortunate enough to find. Oh, I know, that really doesn't seem to be very plausible. Well, neither did the rest of the course!

The course on the federal rules of civil procedure was even "worse," if you can imagine that, and I will leave the meaning of that subjective adjective to your creative imagination. If, however, you are somewhat challenged in that creative department, let me point out that it was a course in which you had to memorize the federal rules about an arcane subject, called "civil procedure," in civil litigation, no less, which, by its very nature, was probably a non-sequitur. I mean, come on now, are you really serious, "civil" litigation? The only thing "civil" about "civil litigation" is likely its non-criminal nature.

Moreover, even aside from suffering from a lack of civility, the rules did not seem to have any rhyme or reason, other than that they were just there and that you had to learn them, so that you could follow them, in order to engage in litigation . . . "civilly," of course. Otherwise, you could possibly lose your case for procedural reasons, if not "uncivil" ones, and be sued by your clients, in an "uncivil" manner, for having done so.

That about summarizes what I got out of that course, and I told the professor as much on the four-hour final examination, which did not exactly excite him, and which could possibly explain his uncivil behavior, in giving me less than a generous grade on that examination and in that course. Oh, sure, my inability to remember all of those stupid rules . . . the "civil" ones, I mean . . . may have been a contributing factor to his "uncivil" behavior.

Then, of course, you have to ask yourself, as I did at the time, what kind of a professor spends a lifetime mastering arcane legal rules that are as illogical as they are boring. The answer that readily came to mind is really not too difficult: A very boring person who, unfortunately, also happens to be a law professor! And, trust me, except for Fred Danforth, Tony Morella and Dean John Sherman Myers, who were comparatively young men, who had left a successful practice of law, in order to challenge young minds in the classroom, they were that boring, each and every one of them, each and every day, in each and every one of my classes.

Also, the fact that each and every one of them, except Fred, Tony, and "the Dean," were in their late nineties, without any guarantee that they would live long enough to reappear for another boring performance on the following day, let alone the following week, did not help. A feeble voice, barely heard, even from the front row, even from the middle of the front row, where we all tried to congregate, was not what you would call a rousing voice, giving rise to a vibrant course on, for example, irrelevant subject matter or, if you prefer, illogical and arcane civil rules.

Indeed, it occurred to me, somewhere during that first semester, that whatever professional opportunities were once available for enterprising young lawyers, must not have been available for those pathetic "has-beens," who were now my instructors in law school. And for financial reasons, which were distinctly less rewarding, those legal misfits retreated, as a result, into the ivy-covered universe of semi-retirement, health benefits, summers off, a modest income, and a life of very, very low expectations.

My low expectations, as a result, remained essentially the same for the remainder of that semester, and I wasn't wrong, either. Nothing, absolutely nothing, changed! The days full of boring courses, taught by ancient, pathetic professors, droned on, mercilessly. The only real interest on my part, day-after-day, was discovering whether they would still be alive at the end of the semester, using that term, of course, rather loosely. Short of that possible drama, the days, the endlessly boring days, simply followed one another, without interruption by any real interaction on the part of the law professors, or whatever you want to call them, with the law students, who had long since decided that there was no benefit in trying to interact with the living dead. And worse yet, if that concept were, by any means, still applicable, if you wanted to become a lawyer, by graduating from that law school, there did not seem to be any real means of escape.

CHAPTER XXV

AMERICAN UNIVERSITY LAW SCHOOL, FIRST YEAR, SECOND SEMESTER: MEETING JUDY HARRIS ON A STREET IN WASHINGTON, D.C. AND SATURDAY NIGHTS WITH MATT ZALE AND THE CATHOLIC SECRETARIES

ONE DAY, however, I did escape from that unfortunate classroom situation, even though it was only through a momentary encounter, on a relatively warm day, during my second semester in law school. The encounter occurred while I was on my way back to class, early in the afternoon, following lunch with several other first-year law students, at a restaurant located, several blocks away, on Pennsylvania Avenue.

At a crosswalk, just a few blocks away from the law school, and several blocks away from an area known as "foggy bottom," I happened to look up, quite fortuitously, while heavily engaged in a conversation with my law school associates. At that moment, I noticed, quite serendipitously, three young women, roughly my age, descending from a curb and proceeding straight across the street, directly in front of us. From my rather poor vantage point, walking directly behind them, one of girls looked amazingly like the back of Judy Harris, Lou Beres' former girlfriend, four years ago, at Northwestern University.

Momentarily dumbstruck at the possibility, right there in front of me on a street in the Nation's Capitol, hundreds of miles away from where and when we were last together, not to mention the intervening years, I decided to walk slightly ahead of my conversational associates, without seeming to and without explaining why, so that I could get a better look. And when I reached a point that was nearly abreast of the three, allowing me to partially see their faces, from the side, of course, I exclaimed, quite excitedly, "Judy Harris"! because I could now see that it really was Lou's old girlfriend. With that rather animated announcement, the young lady immediately stopped, together with her two associates, turned slightly toward me, so that I was now clearly within her view, and with an obviously surprised look on her face, she said, in an equally animated manner, "Cal Golumbic," followed by a rather large, developing smile.

With that rather instantaneous recognition, by both of us, my dull world of ancient, non-distinctive professors and boring classes on irrelevant subject matter, with meaningless arcane legal rules, changed abruptly. There, standing on that street corner with law students that I no longer remember and three young ladies that I did not know, except one, of course, I was transported, while trying to catch up with her life and mine, back to an undergraduate time at a midwestern university. And I began to remember how far that I had come in my challenging undergraduate life there. Indeed, following four uncommon academic years, I belonged at Northwestern University. By my junior year, I had academically, culturally, and socially earned the privilege. And because of most of those categorial accomplishments, graduate school had become somewhat of a "walk-in-the-park," at least in comparison, even though some of the professors did not particularly like the philosophic paths that I had decided to take. The point, however, is that it didn't make any difference; I had become a different student, or, at least, a different person, as a graduate student at Penn State University. At that point, I could do almost anything in any academic institution and do it quite well. And looking forward, which is equally, if not more important, that is going to be no less true in law school, notwithstanding the ancient professors and the arcane subject matter.

My accomplishments, if you will, were speaking to me, in the form of a beautiful, bright and remarkable young woman, standing there, right in front of me, on a street corner in Washington, D.C. Actually, when I think about it now, we probably didn't talk very long, while standing there, because of the situation. After all, there were also other people standing there, two of whom were her friends, and they eventually said, somewhat impatiently, that they needed to return to the State Department, where all three of them were apparently working at the time. So I ended our conversation by inviting Judy to a party, hosted by my roommate, Matt Zale, in our apartment on Cathedral Avenue, on the following Saturday evening, which she immediately accepted.

Actually, it was not at all difficult to extend that invitation on "the-spur-of-the-moment," as they say, because Matt Zale was always hosting a party in our apartment on a Saturday evening. Having finished law school and securing a good job in a federal agency, Matt only needed to find a wife to round out the expectations of those whom he left behind in Wisconsin. And he was "hell-bent" on fulfilling those expectations, nearly every Saturday evening, at our apartment on Cathedral Avenue!

On the following Saturday evening, which, of course, is the date on which I had extended an invitation to Judy Harris, it was not much different. There was a party at our apartment, once again, hosted by my roommate, Matt Zale, in which there was an ample amount of beer, laughter, good food and girls, naturally, who were clearly, in the eyes of Matt Zale, not to mention those remaining back home in Wisconsin, available prospects. Each and every one of them seemed to be Catholic, single and secretarial, all Wisconsin requisites for an acceptable marriage. Unfortunately, however, the night ended, as they usually did, at least while I was living there, with the departure of each one of those Catholic secretaries and, with that, the disappointment of all those Matt had left behind in Wisconsin.

I was not disappointed, however, not on that evening, because Judy Harris did appear, even though it was quite late, and even though she did not intend to stay very long, a fact that she made quite clear upon her arrival So for that time limiting reason, we immediately walked out into the kitchen, away from the others, who were still socializing in the living room, where we could talk by ourselves without any interruption.

Now, off by ourselves, we continued our street corner conversation, which was mostly about our lives that followed the years in which we were together, as students, at Northwestern University. Eventually, however, after we had exhausted our "reunion-like" subjects, Judy informed me that she was in the foreign service, and that she had been assigned to an office somewhere abroad. She also informed me that she would be leaving within a week for her post, which she apparently did, because I would never see her again, but I would never forget her, not for the remainder of my life, for a myriad of reasons, many of which have already been set forth, previously, but not excluding our days, together with Lou Beres at Northwestern University.

Interestingly, I did learn, years later, almost fifty-five of them to be exact, that she had married an Italian, sometime in the intervening years, and that she was living at the time in Italy. In a telephone conversation, shortly after learning of her whereabouts, I informed Lou of those geographical and matrimonial facts. Thereafter, he obtained her address from the alumnae office at Northwestern University, and, apparently, corresponded with her, briefly, sometime before his death, a year or two later. I guess that Lou never forgot about her either!

CHAPTER XXVI

GRADUATE SCHOOL, PENN STATE UNIVERSITY: RACHEL NEWMAN, ROBERT DOCKETY, BILL POICK, DAPHNE PARKER AND A LIFE-ENDING AUTOMOBILE ACCIDENT, SHORTLY BEFORE THEIR GRADUATION, WHICH HAD A LIFE-LONG IMPACT ON MY LIFE

THE LOU Beres and Judy Harris story was not the only time that I became aware that everything did not seem to end so nicely in this universe, although I don't remember thinking about it in those terms, not at the time. Instead, I simply thought that what happened was terribly unfair, if for no other reason than it happened during the week before graduation and it involved the death of two graduating students, one of whom had been a very good friend of mine. Their death and the tragic circumstances in which it occurred gave rise to the story that I am about to tell in this chapter.

The story, like all stories, even those with happier endings, had a beginning, which, in this case, occurred sometime during the week before their graduation from Penn State University in 1960. At that time, Molly and a number of her graduating sorority sisters in Chi Omega, who were, generally, "pinned," decided to throw a party with their "pin-mates," including me, in celebration of their upcoming graduation. The date was chosen, which happened to fall on the afternoon of the following Saturday, just days before their graduation, and the menu was planned, consisting of, essentially, several kegs of beer, and a lot of hot dogs and hamburgs, with probably little else, although I have no knowledge of that fact.

Unfortunately, I had to tell a disbelieving Molly Yeager that I could not attend, because I needed to work on a paper for one of my graduate courses in philosophy that weekend. Notwithstanding that fortunate fact, as you will subsequently discover, the day arrived and Rachel Newman and her fiancé, Robert Dockety, who we simply called "Doc," and Daphne Parker and her fiancé, Bill Poick, joined a number of other graduating sorority sisters, and their respective "pin-mates," at a barn, located somewhere near a little farming community, called Tusseyville, several miles away from the University, for a day and, possibly, an evening of drinking, eating, dancing, laughing, talking and reminiscing.

Several of those in attendance on that day had been rather good friends of mine, such as Rachael Newman and her fiancé, Robert Dockety, probably because Rachael was in the same sorority as Molly. Others, like Bill Poick, who was also a graduate student at the time, I knew independently, and in differing circumstances. In Bill's case, we were regular dinner companions, and, at one point during that year, I had "fixed-him-up" with Daphne Parker, another member of that sorority, with whom he subsequently became engaged in the months that followed. Those individuals, and a number of others, not unlike them, apparently spent much of the afternoon, on that day, socializing with each other in a manner in which I have already suggested.

I, on the other hand, spent an uneventful afternoon, or, rather, part of the afternoon, at my desk, writing a paper and, at the same time, feeling somewhat sorry for myself, at varying intervals, because I was unable join the others in their revelry. In my absence, Molly apparently decided to remain at her home, which, as you may recall, was located several miles away in Bellefonte. It promised to be an uneventful, if not a dreary, day, for both of us, or, at least, one of us, anyway.

That promise, if you can call it that, was interrupted, however, by what turned out to be a very disturbing telephone call from Molly, who immediately said, as soon as I picked up the receiver, "Cal, something terrible has happened"! Before I could make any kind of an enquiry, she immediately went on to say, "there was a terrible automobile accident and 'Doc' and Bill were killed." Since she really did not know anything more about the accident, and said so at the time, we must have ended the conversation, shortly thereafter.

Disturbed now by what had apparently just happened, not to mention the subsequent conversation thereon, I quickly arose from my desk and, in doing so, knocked some of the pages from my paper down onto the floor. Amazing, isn't it; I can still remember doing something like that. I can also remember that, right after picking them up, I began to prepare to leave my room, with a clear destination in mind.

Finishing the paper now seemed to be an almost irrelevant exercise. Reaching some of those who were most closely affected by what had just transpired, in my absence, of course, seemed, quite reasonably, to be far more important. So after stopping at the front door of my room, for just a moment, in order to inform my roommate where I was going and why, I began to walk, as quickly as possible, down Allen Street, where my rooming house was located, across College Avenue and up onto the campus, where I eventually headed over to the Chi Omega Suite in Haller Hall, which was part of the South Halls.

Arriving there, without any kind of a delay, I discovered that a number of Molly's sorority sisters had gathered downstairs in their suite, as I had suspected, which was located on the first floor of their dormitory and accessible by a door from the lobby, which I quickly used to enter. Inside, I discovered that her sorority sisters had effectively formed a semi-circle around Daphne Parker, who must have already learned that her fiancé, Bill Poick, had been killed in the accident, because she was now slumped over on the floor, sobbing, inconsolably. After quietly seating myself, almost directly across the room from her, beside several of her sorority sisters, she happened to look up, momentarily, noticed my arrival and, while still partially sobbing, said, in a quivering voice, which was barely audible, "Oh, Cal, I'm so grateful that you fixed me up with Bill. I'm so grateful for the year that I had with him."

Funny, or maybe not, I still remember those words, those exact words, as they had been spoken, even now, nearly sixty-five years later. I also remember that Bill and Daphne had planned on getting married, shortly after graduation, and that those plans, like so many others involving those fateful couples, would quite obviously die with one of the planners.

I also remember that Rachel and Doc, not only had made wedding plans, including a date, but that they had already sent out invitations. Moreover, to reach that stage in their relationship, it had not been an easy road, or one that was most frequently traveled, because it had required a lot of compromise, on both of their parts, and a certain amount of diplomacy with regard to the rest of the interested world, because Rachel was Jewish and Doc was not, a religious scenario that was rather unusual in a relationship at that time.

It was a scenario that usually presented a number of insurmountable problems, long before anybody ever talked about wedding plans, let alone engaged in them. In fact, young college students like that, who were Jewish and who were not, usually did not survive a second date, unless, of course, they had not disclosed that difference by that time. But Rachel and Doc did, not only to each other, but eventually, to everyone else, including their respective families. And we . . . their friends and families . . . knew that they, and what they had in that relationship, were pretty special, especially given their religious circumstances.

I never did see Rachel at any point during that tragic afternoon; she wasn't in the sorority suite at the time, or even thereafter, I was subsequently informed. Days later, I learned that she had been incorrectly informed that Doc had survived the accident, and that he was in critical condition in the emergency room of the Centre Community Hospital, where she had immediately gone, leaving her disbelieving sorority sisters behind, at what had once been a boisterous celebration, only to discover, upon reaching the Hospital, that it was one of the other four passengers who had survived. Unfortunately, Doc had died at the scene of the accident!

Following their discovery of what had tragically taken place, earlier in the day, involving Rachel and Doc, her parents apparently came up to the University, the very next day, out of a justifiable concern for their daughter's wellbeing, and, while there, persuaded her to go back home with them to Alexandria, Virginia. Not surprisingly, she never came back for her graduation, which occurred several days later. The rest of her graduating sorority sisters, including Molly, did attend, but they graduated under a very distinct cloud that day, which darkened what ordinarily would have been a joyous day, not to mention, in some respects, the rest of their formerly optimistic lives.

I am left, as I write this story of Robert and Rachel and Bill and Daphne, and of loss, once again, with the same weighty considerations that have burdened my life for some time, which are less philosophic and more theological in nature, and which, as you may have noticed, have already been alluded too, in a disappointing manner, in several other contexts.

In any event, I would not see Rachel again for more than twenty years, but I did have an occasion to visit her parents in Alexandria, Virginia, shortly after I enrolled in law school in Washington, D.C. Rachel told me, years later, when I visited her in New York, where she had been living and working for some years, that her parents never mentioned that visit. I guess, upon reflection, that they were concerned that my visit, given my former association with everyone involved in that earlier tragedy, including and especially their daughter, would, possibly, bring back uncomfortable memories for the young lady, who was, understandably, still struggling, even at that point, to recover from such a devastating loss. Actually, the whole deathly episode became a very bad memory for all of those who happened to be her friends at the time and, quite obviously, it continues to be a bad memory for, at least, one of them now.

Given that fact, I can't explain why I decided to visit her parents, during the beginning of my classes in law school, other than, possibly, because they happened to live in the area. Maybe, however, I wanted to tell them something: Maybe I wanted to tell them that God had not created a perfect universe! Actually, on second thought, I probably didn't have to tell them that; as the parents of a young woman who had suffered such an irredeemable loss, they probably already knew!

Before concluding this unfortunate chapter of my life, and, more importantly, theirs, I should historically note that many years ago, I wrote a publishable article, entitled, "Robert and Rachel." The subject, if not the subjects, have obviously haunted me for much of my life, which probably explains why it, and they, have been captured at this point in my story; or, to put the explanation somewhat differently, their story has quite obviously become part of my story, which is the reason why it is in this story. If there was ever any doubt about that storied fact, and there has never been any doubt in my mind, it has been resolved, believe it or not, by the "later-in-life" move by Lis and I to spend our retirement years in Rehoboth Beach, Delaware, where waiting for me, in a manner of speaking, were Doc's two younger sisters, Joan and Lynn, and his two younger brothers, David and Grant, all of whom were, and are, residents of that beach community. Even more bizarre, if that is really an appropriate term here, the latter of those two young men, who was merely six years of age at the time of his brother's death, and who has grown older with the rest of us in the interval, has become one of my best friends in that seaside life.

Nevertheless, I want to set aside that friendship for the moment, but not the death of that family member and the circumstances in which it occurred, not to mention, of course, the lingering loss suffered by a young woman, now grown older with us all. It is because of that death and in those circumstances, as well as the miraculous recovery by that woman over a lifetime, which I have been privileged to witness, that I have written their story, here, in this story, and, yes, there, in that unpublished article. Because it, referring now to the latter, may become lost in the dust bin of history, upon my fairly eminent departure from this earth, I have also decided to include the unpublished article as Exhibit 104 in the Appendix. I also note, for historical purposes, that the article has remained unpublished, notwithstanding the obviously compelling nature of the subject matter, solely because of an understandable privacy objection by one of the protagonists, who still remains on this earth, and who still continues to give new meaning to her life, over the intervening years, notwithstanding that loss, and who still continues to remain one of my oldest and dearest friends!

CHAPTER XXVII

AMERICAN UNIVERSITY LAW SCHOOL, FIRST YEAR, SUMMER VACATION: THE POCONO MOUNTAINS; TYLER HILL CAMP; "A HAWK, A BEAR, AND A MOOSE," AND A SWEDISH GIRL NAMED GUNILLA HOLMIN

WITH AN imperfect universe now in mind, theologically speaking, I knew that I had to work much harder in law school. Meeting Judy Harris on that street corner certainly confirmed that fact. And when I began to waiver, because of the arcane subject matter or the lack of faculty proficiency, just thinking about how hard Lou had worked to save that relationship, including that last-minute drive to Cleveland, Ohio, which almost caused him to be late for his own graduation, served as a reminder. So, too, did that terrible automobile accident, in which Bill and "Doc" were killed, just days before their graduation. And every time that I would think about how unfair it was that Lou had lost his scholarship and, with it, any financial opportunity to go on to law school, something that he had always dreamed about doing, ever since he was a high school student, it served as yet another reminder of why I should work that hard in law school, notwithstanding those diminishing factors. It had something to do with an imperfect universe and my need to survive in it!

Indeed, that was why I would always go back home to work for the summer during my undergraduate and graduate years. It always seemed to be reasonably safe there. Oh, sure, there was always something rather limiting about it, too, ordinarily giving rise to a rather serious case of intellectual claustrophobia by the end of the summer. Still, after spending nearly eight years at one university after another, in which I had to face dragons that lurked externally as well as internally, there was always something reassuring about going back home to work for the summer, where I had grown up, amidst unending mountain ranges and a great river, all of which I loved, as well as a family that loved me, even though they no longer understood me.

Moreover, I don't remember any of my friends dying in automobile accidents when I was growing up, or, for that matter, unfairly losing their scholarships, or even seeing their relationships come to a catastrophic end, despite all of their efforts to the contrary. None of those things seemed to have been part of my life growing up, not where I lived, anyway, but they seemed to have become part of my life, as an undergraduate and graduate student, at two different universities, and, what's more, the lives of some individuals, who were part of my life at those universities.

Now, however, it seemed like my reasonably secure life growing up in my hometown was just some kind of a historical illusion, which, with the advent of more reality than I may have liked over the last eight years, was gone forever. Now it seemed like I really couldn't go home again, not in a manner of speaking, not even for summer work. Maybe Thomas Wolfe was right, when he wrote, in his iconic novel, *Look Homeward Angel*, that, realistically speaking, "you can't go home again!"

So with summer work in mind and admonitions from Thomas Wolfe, not to mention more reality than I might have wished over the recent years, I decided, this time, to find work for the summer in New York City, which I realized at the time was really an imperfect universe, but which, fortunately, had all sorts of employment opportunities, even for summer work, in that kind of a universe.

Unfortunately, however, after only a few weeks of residing in that imperfect urban universe, I couldn't stand the heat anymore, afford the costs of my rental room anymore, or, for that matter, deal with the claustrophobia on the city streets anymore, even though some of the job offers were rather attractive, if not tantalizing. So, after a few weeks of suffocating urbanization, I decided to avoid the heat, the costs, and the claustrophobia, by finding work in a summer camp, located somewhere in the Pocono Mountains, by reviewing advertisements for camp counselors in the classified section of the New York Times. And following my telephone response, on that very day, no less, I was subsequently interviewed by one of the owners of such a camp, Bill Heft, who was also a physical education instructor at the Boys High School in the Bedford Stuyvesant Section of Brooklyn, New York.

Immediately following the interview, Bill Heft hired me, and, in doing so, advised me that, although the salary for the six-week period, in which the camp would operate that summer, was only $200, I would probably make more than $1000 in tips, not to mention receive "board and room," or should I more accurately say, an opportunity to eat excellent kosher food and sleep in a rundown bunkhouse.

The amount of those prospective tips, together with lodging, even of that kind, as well as three excellent meals a day, kosher or not, was a lot of compensation at the time for summer work, especially when you consider that it was for umpiring baseball games, every day, in the sunlight, too, teaching tennis, twice a week, in the sunlight, once again, and, finally, chaperoning dances with senior boys and girls, three times a week, in the evenings, which included, believe it or not, free ice cream at the canteen, where the dances were held. And aside from a few other, more mundane, considerations, such as ensuring that civilization would continue in my bunkhouse, that is exactly what I did for the entire six weeks!

Oh, yes, I also did a few other things to make that summer

worthwhile, which were of a distinctly more questionable nature, such as playing tennis with the campers for their canteen coupons, allowing me to purchase anything that I wanted from the canteen, including ice cream, with the coupons that I had won. And to make life even more enjoyable than simply eating free ice cream at the canteen, compliments of the overprivileged and underperforming tennis-playing campers, I gave a number of the other counselors nicknames, which, in my unquestioned judgment, corresponded to their appearance, or their personalities, or, sometimes, both. So, Howard ("Howee") Puro, who looked like a bear, talked like a bear, walked like one, and ate, literally, like a bear, became . . . "the Bear." And Howard ("Howee") Pike, who looked like a hawk and unsuccessfully tried to fly like one, by jumping off of the junior boys' bunkhouse roof, with a pair of wings made by the arts and crafts counselors, became, you guessed it . . . "the Hawk." And "Lefty" Cohen, who was as big as a moose, and moved as slowly as one, became, you guessed it, once again . . . "the Moose."

I'm not sure whether they enjoyed becoming a "Bear," a "Hawk," or even a "Moose" that summer, but I sure as hell did! And beating the little overprivileged campers out of their canteen coupons, at tennis twice a week, was probably not kosher, which probably borders on being a cliche in that summer situation, but after dying one whole year long in the stultifying atmosphere of a law school classroom, I decided to reclaim my life, or, at least, the more jovial part of it, even though it was being reclaimed at the expense, literally, of the campers and, metaphorically, some of their counselors.

At the same time, and of no less consequence, I also began to date one of the best-looking counselors in the whole camp and, maybe, in the whole world, whose name was Gunilla Holmin, and who happened to be from Stockholm, Sweden. Shortly after we began dating, she informed me, at one of the local bars, where we spent most of our evenings laughing, drinking and dancing, that she was part of an international program, that provided college-educated counselors from Europe, for rather nominal fees, to summer camps in America. And that it was her good fortune, in obvious reference to the commencement of our summertime relationship, that she was assigned that summer to the Tyler Hill Camp in the Pocono Mountains.

I had never dated a Swede before that summer; actually, I had never even met a Swede before that summer; in fact, I did not even have the remotest idea of where Sweden was located, although I had always assumed that it must be somewhere in the northern part of Europe. So dating one for the duration of that summer, six weeks in all, turned out to be a rather novel experience, and even an educational one, too. Yes, even though education was not on my mind, not on the very first day that I saw her, I actually learned an enormous amount about another culture, in another country, on another continent, from one of its more attractive citizens, by the end of that summer.

In that respect, my world had grown larger, but so too had my problems. They no longer simply resided with the individuals and the circumstances of my childhood in central Pennsylvania. They had succeeded in gaining admission to a number of great universities across this great nation, numbering three at the moment, and now they had even managed to bridge the Atlantic Ocean, and to become international in nature. That's right, now I had an international problem, which, in reality, was a Swedish problem, a very, very attractive one.

The problem was that I rather liked the Swedish camp counselor or, at the very least, the things about her that made her Swedish. Nevertheless, at the end of that summer, which was at the end of that camp season, she was going to reclaim that Swedish distinction, by going home to Sweden. Since I was neither Swedish, nor financially capable of going there, where I probably didn't belong, anyway, I decided, somewhat sadly, to return to my law school, where I probably did belong, even though I did not particularly like the process of belonging. A photograph of the young Swedish counselor and her date, who happens to be your raconteur, together with another couple, on a day-off trip to the "Big Apple," has been included as Exhibit 18 in the Appendix.

CHAPTER XXVIII

AMERICAN UNIVERSITY LAW SCHOOL, SECOND YEAR: A NEW BUILDING, BETTER COURSES AND INSTRUCTORS, AND A CORRESPONDING IMPROVEMENT IN MY GRADE POINT AVERAGE("GPA")

LAW SCHOOL seemed to become different in my second year . . . in all kinds of ways. Among other things, the building was different, because the law school had moved over the summer, from a townhouse at 2000 G St. Northwest into a new building on the campus of American University. It was built, essentially, through the financial benevolence of the Dean, John Sherman Myers, who made a fortune, as a counsel to a number of mutual funds on Wall Street, years ago, and who, in retirement, decided to buy himself, or, rather, build himself, a law school and become its Dean.

The Dean, who was obviously quite successful in a lifetime of practicing law was equally successful as an educator, too, being a sterling lecturer, and after a semester of attending classes in his new building, I can safely say as an architect, too. Indeed, it was uplifting, if there ever was such a concept in the study of law, to go to class in the new building. Moreover, the architectural flair seemed to have improved the lecturing style of some of the older professors, who now inhabited new classrooms, and who only last year gave new meaning to the ancient words, "the living dead." Now, at least, they were "dead-men-talking," to paraphrase a less ancient phrase, and, for the first time, I could actually hear them and, mercifully, for my grade point average, understand them, too.

Moreover, the law school also hired several new instructors, none of whom were eligible for Medicare, and some of whom were actually dynamic. Because of the nature of the new building, especially the architectural design, and the new instructors, if not a partial resurrection of the older ones, too, my grade point average became equally dynamic. In fact, I actually became a reasonably good student by the end of my second year, as measured by my class standing, in a subject matter that still seemed, on the whole, to be somewhat arcane and less than interesting.

I had great difficulty, for example, calling the subject of personal income taxation interesting, even though I received the book award in the class, which was the award given to the student with the highest grade in the class. On the other hand, I found my class on criminal procedure to be quite interesting, and I received the book award in that class, too, probably for just that reason. The rest of the courses, during both semesters of that year, were somewhere in between, in terms of interest, that is, but where they fell on that scale did not seem to affect my performance, anymore, because I did quite well in all of them.

Nevertheless, no matter how well I was doing, and I really was doing quite well now, the law, as a subject matter, continued to seem rather dull to me. Moreover, not only was the subject matter rather dull, consisting of endless rules and exceptions, and even exceptions to the exceptions, but spending each and every moment of every day memorizing them seemed mindless. In fact, every time that I heard a professor conceptually speak about "thinking like a lawyer," which happened nearly every week, it struck me that the concept was really a non-sequitur, because lawyers, or, at least, law students, did not, in my opinion, really have to think; they simply had to memorize. And I missed thinking, really thinking, about thoughtful subjects, which was a large part of my study of philosophy in graduate school. But then I would quickly remind myself that lawyers were well compensated, even though it was for seemingly mindless activity. So, in the end, I decided not to think about it . . . the mindless activity, I mean . . . which was not too difficult to do in that kind of study, if you really think about it, anyway.

CHAPTER XXIX

AMERICAN UNIVERSITY LAW SCHOOL, SECOND YEAR: LIVING WITH BUD MENAKER ON THE THIRD FLOOR OF A TOWNHOUSE AT 1835 LAMONT STREET IN THE MOUNT PLEASANT AREA OF THE CITY, WITH A PROSTITUTE AND HER FIVE CHILDREN ON THE FIRST FLOOR AND AN ARMY MAJOR, WHO WOULD REGULARLY BEAT HIS GERMAN WIFE, ON THE SECOND FLOOR

ONE DAY of no particular consequence, three of us, who were second-year law students, decided, early in the first semester of that year, to live together in a two-bedroom apartment, because it would be cheaper, among other practical things. So after some searching, in which we looked for something that was reasonably close to the law school, not to mention affordable, we decided, upon discovering that the cost of rentals in the area was beyond our means, to rent an apartment some distance away, in a far more dubious area of the city. And we found just what we were looking for on the third floor of a townhouse at 1835 Lamont Street, N.W., in the Mount Pleasant area of Washington, D.C., which was a "transitional" neighborhood, if you don't mind the use of a euphemism.

Because of the nature of the area, where you were fortunate to survive a walk from the bus stop to the townhouse, just three blocks away, the rent was incredibly low, especially for our "furnished" two-bedroom apartment, and, therefore, quite suitable for three impoverished law students, who, by the way, were without any furniture of their own. And, fortunately, we even received a further discount, because we agreed to live on the third floor, which, in reality, was nothing more than an attic, without a door to the entrance. You just had to walk up three flights of stairs and, without having to knock on a non-existent door, step right into our living room, which, together with a run-down kitchen, two miniature bedrooms, and a historic bathroom, with an elongated hallway in between, masqueraded as some sort of an apartment, with rather primitive furnishings.

None of this would have posed a problem, however, if the first floor had not been inhabited by a prostitute, who, by the way, never heard of birth control, and who, consequently, had five young, illegitimate children, as well as one on the way, noticeably so, at the time. The children, however, were not the real problem, at least not initially, anyway; it was her patrons! They came calling, day and night, and, sometimes, quite late at night, requiring us, quite often, to wake up and walk down the hallway to our living room, in our pajamas, where they were standing, while, quite loudly, calling out her name. Because we wanted to go back to bed, as soon as possible, without having to worry anymore about uninvited guests, standing out there in our living room, we ordinarily told them that they had to walk back down the three flights of stairs to the first floor, in order to find what they were looking for, if, by the way, you don't mind the use of another euphemism.

Because some of them were barely able to climb up the three flights of stairs in the first place, as the result of a significant amount of alcohol consumption, they were not in any kind of condition to walk back down. So, we often had to sublet, without fee, of course, the living room floor, for the night, to some of the more inebriated patrons, who, by the way, rarely, if ever, expressed any form of gratitude for their nightly accommodations.

Others, who had reached the third floor, not to mention our

doorless apartment, but just barely, and who suffered from the same kind of alcoholic problems, would often become rather surly, especially when they realized that they had expended all of that energy to climb up three flights of stairs, for no reward, so to speak, the reward being lodged back downstairs on the first floor, with all of her children. Those patrons . . . who had become rather surly . . . acted as though it was our fault that we had chosen to live on the third floor and that she had chosen to live on the first, and that they had chosen to walk up all of those stairs in between, after, I may add, drinking far too much to do much about anything, including the achievement of the original purpose for which they had entered the townhouse in the first place, which, as you may recall, was lodged back down there on the first floor, still with all of her children.

We also had a problem on the second floor, too, but that was not because a prostitute lived there. No, we had an army major living there, who liked to beat the hell out of his German wife, Helga. If he did not like it, you could have fooled us, because he did it, quite often, and usually people do not repeat what they do not like. The German wife did not particularly like it, though, and she usually indicated that fact by screaming, quite loudly, at least loudly enough for all of us on the third floor to hear.

We, the three law students on the third floor, found all of this . . . the beating and the screaming . . . to be quite disturbing. At the very least, it was difficult to study with all of that commotion going on, several times a week, too, and usually in the evening, unfortunately, when we were trying to study. Because we couldn't and, more importantly, because we found the whole sordid mess to be quite disturbing, we did whatever we could to stop it. That usually took the form of Bud Menaker, our larger law school roommate, getting his shotgun down from the upper shelf in his bedroom . . . which he ordinarily used for small game hunting, not in the city, of course, but in the countryside, outside of Harrisburg, Pennsylvania, where he had grown up . . . and racing down the stairs to the second floor with a gun in hand. Meanwhile, my other law school roommate and I, of distinctly smaller proportions, would usually take a seat on the stairs, in-between the second and third floors, to watch the evening's festivities, well away from the action, of course, periodically shouting encouragement to our well-armed third-floor roommate, who, by the way, was now standing, menacingly, in front of the door to the apartment on the second floor, where all the mayhem had been taking place.

At about that time, Bud would normally begin pounding on the second-floor door to that apartment, shouting, at the same time, "John, stop it, John!" followed by, after a brief pause, "I know what you're doing, and I want you to stop hitting her!" Almost immediately, the screaming would stop, which, if nothing else, was a tribute to Bud's size, if not his armament. Whereupon, Bud would usually say, "John, I want you to open the door," and, after several minutes, he usually did, which, quite obviously, was another tribute to the same sizable proportions of our roommate, who continued to remain well armed. Then, following a brief discussion with John, who was now standing, rather uncomfortably, in the doorway, probably because of his comparatively diminutive size, if not his lack of armament, Bud would typically insist upon Helga's belated appearance at the doorway, too, and, in response, she would subsequently comply, although slightly more disheveled. Then, after a few minutes, in which Bud would survey the damage, or the victim, whichever seems more applicable in this situation, he would ordinarily ask her, if she was all right, to which she ordinarily responded, "Yes," even though she did not appear to be.

Now, they . . . the beater and the beaten . . . would ordinarily reenter their second-floor apartment and lock their door, on yet another dramatic evening at 1835 Lemont Street, N.W. And we . . . the "night's saviors" . . . would ordinarily climb nobly back up the stairs to our questionable abode on the third floor, where we would begin to study all over again.

One day, however, of possibly greater consequence, at least in an elucidating manner, Bud met the Major, on the steps to the second floor, shortly after returning from class, and, after exchanging some unaccustomed pleasantries, asked him, rather pointedly, why he was always mistreating his wife, and so often, too. Apparently, the Major responded, by informing Bud that it was because she was in competition with the tradeswoman on the first floor, except that she did not charge any fees for her services, and, apparently, she was rather successful in her benevolent endeavors.

To be quite honest, as well as reflective, we ultimately found both floors, as well as their dramatics, to be rather annoying, but no more than that, just annoying. The fatherless children on the first floor, however, became more than annoying, given their mother's frequent absences during a large part of the day. In fact, because of their unsupervised circumstances, on almost a daily basis, those children became a matter of major concern to all three of the angelic protagonists, who were still living on the third floor, because they were generally of preschool age.

Bud Menaker, however, became absolutely obsessed by their predictably precarious situation, and he developed a rather annoying habit of sharing his obsession with the rest of us on the third floor, on a daily, no, hourly, basis, and often while we were trying to study. In order to address that inability to study or, at least, avoid the obsession, I suggested to Bud, one evening, that he do something about his obsession, or our problem, whichever you prefer in this context. And, unfortunately, or possibly, fortunately, depending upon your particular perspective at this point, he did, early one afternoon, because the five-year-old, who was the older of the five children, was carrying the baby around in the backyard, in the wintertime, while it was snowing, and neither one of them had on a coat.

Enraged, the overly sanctimonious Menaker called the District of Columbia Child Welfare and Protective Services Agency (hereinafter the "Child Welfare Agency"), within minutes, and after reporting what he had just witnessed, which was five, unsupervised, pathetic, little waifs in the backyard snow, without any coats, he asked the Agency to send someone over, immediately, to observe the questionable situation themselves, and, finally, to address the problem, by removing the children, so to speak, into the protective custody of the Child Welfare Agency.

Obviously concerned now, by what they had just heard from our overly intrusive roommate, two highly motivated social workers appeared on the scene, rather quickly, so that they could observe the flagrant coatless situation, too. And shortly after having done so, they apparently became as disgusted as our overly intrusive roommate, or nearly so, because they impounded all of the children, except the one not yet born, because of the difficulty inherent in that situation, and made them . . . the five now crying and terrified children . . . wards of the Juvenile Court, subject to the custody of the Child Welfare Agency.

Their mother, who was plying her trade, elsewhere, at the time, was less than happy when she returned home to discover that her crying and terrified children were now in the custody of the Child Welfare Agency, courtesy of two highly motivated social workers from that Agency and a "do-gooder" law student from the apartment on the third floor. Indeed, her language, when she subsequently discovered that her children had been impounded, and why, which, by the way, traveled all the way up to the third floor, and probably beyond, could have melted the snow outside, brought on a precipitous springtime and made the lack of winter coats on those poor, little, unsupervised waifs irrelevant. It certainly made the three of us retreat back up three flights of stairs to the safety of our doorless, third-floor, attic apartment, and hide behind our law school case books, so that it would appear as though we had nothing to do with any of this, and that, in fact, we really had been studying during the whole time. Nevertheless, upon being subsequently informed, by the social workers, of Bud's complicity, her language, among other things, clearly cast doubt on the legitimacy of Bud's ancestry.

I dare say that, following the departure of those five little terrified children into the care and custody of the Child Welfare Agency, if the three of us on the third floor had ever considered availing ourselves of the services ordinarily provided by the now childless individual on the first, which, I can assure you, would never have happened, such an unlikely endeavor would have been futile, anyway, because the cost of such an enterprise, however one might like to define "cost," not to mention "enterprise," would have been prohibitive, if you can understand what I mean!

CHAPTER XXX

AMERICAN UNIVERSITY LAW SCHOOL, SECOND YEAR, SUMMER VACATION: TYLER HILL CAMP, LIS JØRGENSEN, THE NARROWSBURG INN, MY MARRIAGE PROPOSAL AND HER SUBSEQUENT ACCEPTANCE

HAVING COMPLETED my second year of law school by now, I was doing rather well inside and outside of the classroom. Oh, admittedly, I had not become completely comfortable with what I saw in the mirror every morning, but I had, in hindsight, become somewhat comfortable with others . . . well, at least, one other, anyway. And I was even getting somewhat comfortable with the study of law, even though the thought of spending the rest of my life engaging in that profession was not especially comforting.

Nevertheless, putting aside that discomforting thought, I had, in fact, now successfully completed two years of law school. And as I began to think about finding some kind of summer work, away from the rules and the exceptions that made my academic days deadly dull in the classroom, I began to think once again about sunlight and fresh air, as well as canteen coupons, tips and kids, all of which you could find in a summer camp, and all of which I liked, except, possibly, the kids. So, following the conclusion of a telephone conversation with Bill Heft, once again, the owner of such a camp, where, of course, I had worked the previous summer, I decided to accept his kind offer to spend another summer wearing shorts and

"T-shirts," playing tennis, cheating kids out of their canteen coupons and doing it all with "bears, hawks, and a moose."

The decision, at the time, seemed to be a comparatively insignificant one, but that summer, not to mention the events that transpired over the course of that summer, while employed as a counselor at that camp, would prove to be otherwise. Indeed, what seemed like another simple decision, to avoid or delay a dull life of legal rules and exceptions, at least for another summer, turned out to be a decision that would eventually change my life, dramatically, and in ways that I could not even have begun to imagine, and for the rest of my life, too! Yes, in what seemed to be no more than a summer interlude, in a summer camp in the Pocono Mountains, once again, I would come face-to-face with my future, or a substantial part of it, by subsequently engaging in a momentous decision to take a risk, which would, eventually, change my life forever, and which would add dimensions that were incalculable and, yes, unforeseeable!

The unforeseeable that summer, and in that summer camp, came in the form of a twenty-three-year-old girl from a small city, called Frederikshavn, in the northern part of Denmark. The city was located on a seacoast of that country, and her home, which, in reality, was an apartment, nearly overlooked that sea, the North Sea. This particular summer, however, the girl left that apartment and that sea coast, as well as that city and that country, to participate in an international program, in which university graduates from Western Europe, who would begin working as teachers in the fall, of which she would become one, were recruited by the program to spend the summer, or, at least, six weeks of the summer, in a children's camp, located somewhere in the United States. Thereafter, they would ordinarily tour part of the country, for the rest of the summer, by bus, arranged, again, by the program, according to their geographic choice.

This particular teacher, or, more accurately, about to become a teacher, in or about her hometown in the fall, whose name was Lis Jørgensen, was scheduled to spend nearly six weeks of that summer, as a swimming counselor, or a lifeguard, if you prefer that kind of a description, at the Tyler Hill Camp in the Pocono Mountains, just outside of Honesdale, Pennsylvania. Coincidently, if not magically, and, maybe, even divinely, that was the same summer camp where I had been working the summer before, and where I was about to begin working, once again, as a tennis counselor. Because of that coincidence, or, possibly, because God's universe had significantly improved, I happened to see one of the most beautiful creatures that I had ever seen . . . in a swimming suit, no less . . . just before I entered the dining hall, for lunch, on my very first day in that camp, that summer. From inquiries made while eating my lunch, I subsequently learned that the creature . . . because anything that looked like that could not be fully human . . . was the new Danish swimming counselor.

Well, in light of that fantastic fact, I quickly finished my lunch, for fear that the whimsical creature may actually disappear, and I made a rather hasty departure from the dining hall so that I would be able to walk over to the lakefront, as quickly as possible, where I had been informed that such creatures normally reside. There, I discovered that the creature had not, in fact, vanished, but had, instead, joined Artie Sunshine, the head counselor on the girls' waterfront, as a lifeguard, for the entire afternoon. I also discovered that the creature was not only indescribably beautiful, but, unfortunately, quite tall, or, at least, seemingly so, from my vantage point, which was, seemingly, not quite so tall.

Later, when the creature became more fully human, following a number of evening associations, more commonly referred to as "dates," at least in this country, I would discover that we were about the same height, when I was wearing shoes and she was not, which was often the case that summer, because she was a lifeguard and, therefore, spent most of her time down on the lakefront, where you did not ordinarily need to wear shoes. Whereas, I spent most of my time on land, that summer, mostly on the tennis courts, cheating kids out of their canteen coupons, where you did need shoes, but not necessarily ethics!

I also wore heavily worn Bermuda shorts and a nondescript T-shirt nearly every day that summer, because that was sort of a "scruffy" camp counselor uniform, and that uniform, "scruffy" or not, was tolerated by Bill Heft, one of the camp owners, as you may recall. On the other hand, he would go absolutely apoplectic if he saw a counselor wearing tennis shoes, but without any tennis socks. For some reason, which defied logic that summer, or any other summer, for that matter, he seemed to think that you were not fully dressed if you did not have on a pair of socks. If that assumption had been correct, which it was not, I would never have been fully dressed that whole summer!

In any event, the creature, now having turned into an incredibly beautiful lifeguard, did not wear socks, either, not during the day, anyway. After all, she did not need to wear shoes as a lifeguard, so why would she need to wear socks? Not surprisingly, it was far easier to save someone from drowning, without wearing shoes and socks, but it was far more appropriate to save them while wearing a bathing suit. And for that cultural reason, among possibly a number of others, she always wore a dark blue, one-piece, bathing suit, while working down there on the girls' waterfront, every day, and almost everywhere else in the camp, even, sometimes, in the dining hall, too.

Out of some sense of decorum, however, she usually wore a dark blue pullover sweatshirt over top of her bathing suit, when she was somewhere else in camp, like in the dining hall, but that sweatshirt did not begin to cover one inch of those long and, remarkably, lithesome legs, so I noticed them on every occasion in which I could. They were, I can assure you, the most gorgeous legs that I had ever seen, which was probably why I took every opportunity to look at them, when I was, inconspicuously, down at the girls waterfront, or, unobtrusively, in the dining hall, or, later at night, on a casual date, or even after I had fallen asleep, while I was obviously dreaming.

Her eyes, by the way, were just as captivating, but not just because of the color. Oh, they were blue all right, but sort of a steely blue, which kind of captured her character. Yeah, there was a lot of character in those steely blue eyes. You could just see the extent, because those eyes were huge, big enough to see her Viking forebears, and, likely, what they did to the poor Angles, Celts, and Saxons, who happened to get in their way. That's right, with those penetratingly big, blue eyes and that severe northern European countenance, she looked like an incredibly beautiful and, maybe, even a little bit dangerous, Viking! Someone who could walk through fire unharmed, "because ice doesn't burn"!

This Viking, however, did not have blonde or even reddish-blonde hair, not that I could see, anyway; nor did she have a fair or ruddy complexion, like most of her northern ancestors. No, this Viking had distinctly brown hair and a rather dark complexion, ostensibly, anyway, with a noticeably dark beauty mark on her cheek, if that's what you want to call it, which made her seem even more dangerously exciting . . . almost mythological, I would say!

See the photographs of the young lady, sometimes with yours truly, taken at or near the camp grounds, which have been included as Exhibit 140 in the Appendix. See also the photograph of the young lady, following the successful completion of her studies at a university in Denmark, taken at or around that time, which has been reproduced below, and which has been included in Exhibit 106 of the Appendix.

Well, I happened not to be intimidated by mythological creatures, not even if they happened to look like the one illustrated above, not even if they happened to be walking the earth, even in summer camps, notwithstanding the reported fact that their ancestors may have slain medieval dragons, at least according to the Icelandic Fables. So with only a slight hesitation, measured in mere days, I asked this Norse goddess to join me for an evening of dancing and drinking, as well as talking and laughing, assuming that a goddess, like that, was capable of doing some of those things, at the Narrowsburg Inn. After a brief moment, in which she did not respond, consisting of at least one thousand years, she nodded, which I construed, gratefully, if not gleefully, to be an affirmative response.

Actually, that her response was affirmative should not, in hindsight, have come as such a surprise, even though it did. After all, I was the same person who had finished four years as an undergraduate student at Northwestern University, where I had become a fairly large personality on campus, at least by my senior year, and a reasonably good student as well. In addition, I had finished more than three years as a graduate student at Penn State University, where I had become an even larger personality on that campus, and an even better student there, too. And with my two large personalities in hand, not to mention an undergraduate and a graduate degree to go along with them, I was now about to become a third-year law student at the American University, with the potential of becoming an even larger personality, economically speaking, if nothing else, practicing law.

Well, I'm not sure that the mythological creature understood how fortunate she was to be on a first date with someone like me, because she was rather reserved during the whole evening, hardly even talking, let alone laughing, notwithstanding my impressive personalities and academic accomplishments. And for that matter, we never even got around to any form of serious drinking and dancing. That made me think that I had better spend another evening with her, so that she could get to know me, not to mention my personalities, much better, and, of course, all of my academic accomplishments, too. So I asked her to join me, and my personalities and accomplishments, the following evening for another round of drinking and dancing, as well as talking and laughing, once again, at the Narrowsburg Inn, even though there did not seem to be a lot of talking and laughing during the previous evening, other than by me.

Quite frankly, the following evening turned out to be even more equivocal than the previous one, which made me wonder if she did not particularly like dancing and drinking, or, possibly, it was talking and laughing, or, maybe, it was even the Narrowsburg Inn, or, possibly, it was all five of them, because the problem, if there really was one, was certainly not with my overly educated, overly accomplished and overly impressive personalities. So if there really was a problem, other than her seeming inability to talk very much or laugh at all, I was sure that it could be easily resolved by a further discussion about myself, and my overly educated and accomplished personalities, on another evening of talking and laughing, by both of us this time, at the Narrowsburg Inn, which, of course, would be the third evening, because I had obviously not succeeded in that kind of a discussion on the first two.

Well, when I had finished that kind of a discussion on the third evening, after several hours, by the way, her reaction could be fairly described as inexplicably nonexistent. As a result, after a few moments of uncomfortable silence, on both of our parts, I came to the conclusion that, because of a language barrier, if not a cultural one, she obviously did not understand what I was talking about, which, in its simplest terms, was why I was so impressive!

Actually, looking back now, I suppose that it was understandable that someone from another country, unfamiliar with our language and our culture, would have some difficulty in understanding the significance of my previous discourse, spread out over three evenings, concerning my academic achievements, if nothing else. If, on the other hand, she was at all familiar with our language and our culture, I was sure that she would have been duly impressed by what I had to say, which was, in its simplest form, once again, what I had educationally done, because I certainly was!

Since she was not, or, at least, did not seem to be, obviously because of that language and culture barrier, I asked her to join me once more, for another evening of drinking and dancing, as well as some talking, too, and, who knows, maybe even a little bit of laughter, on both of our parts, at the Narrowsburg Inn, which she did. By now, however, you can probably surmise what actually transpired over the course of that evening, too, and, by the way, not much changed over the rest of that week as well.

By then, which was, in fact, by the end of that week, the person who was duly impressed did not speak Danish at all. Actually, by then, it had become somewhat difficult to speak at all, because the person, who had been silent during most of that time, and who had been seated directly across from me nearly all of that time, began to look so fantastic that I actually thought that she was beginning to approach perfection. So, by the end of that week, I just sat back and quietly admired them . . . the perfection and the girl!

Now that I think about it, and I have had a lot of years to do just that, the whole week was sort of ironic: I spent nearly every evening explaining what I had done and how well I had done it, so that the girl would understand how fantastic I was, while she did not do anything other than look fantastic the whole time, and her fantastic appearance was far more impressive than my fantastic explanation in the end. Because of that distinction, between her appearance and my explanation, which had become readily apparent by the end of that week, I was obviously far more impressed with her, by that time, than she was with me!

Actually, to be quite honest about it, which, admittedly, is a little uncomfortable at this juncture, I don't believe that I learned very much about the young lady, or what she was like, not by the end of that week, aside from what she appeared to be like, but I do know that I had become absolutely captivated by what I didn't know, if you can esthetically understand that. And if you can't, that is simply because you were not sitting directly across from her, like I was, every evening, for a whole evening, for the whole captivating week!

Oh, sure, there were some other impressive things, too, like the way that she spoke, when she did speak, which was not very often, only when it seemed to be necessary, which required a lot of judgment, something which, quite obviously, I had not yet accomplished. But when she did speak, she spoke in English, of course, the British kind, which should not have been so surprising, because she was about to become an English teacher . . . of the British kind . . . in

Denmark.

Well, I loved that British accent, almost as much as I liked looking at the person who had it. And when she did speak, with that accent, it gave me a perfectly good excuse to look at her, which I did, because I had an excuse, since she was speaking with that accent, which was British.

I also loved the way that she dressed, especially during the day, even though it was no more than a one-piece blue bathing suit, with a pullover blue sweatshirt, or even in the evening, when she wore tight-fitting blue jeans, with that pullover blue sweatshirt, once again. Not everyone was capable of looking that great in a one-piece blue bathing suit or a pair of tight-fitting blue jeans, and I am not even going to address that blue pullover sweatshirt.

Trust me, if you happened to see her in that bathing suit during the day, down at the girls' waterfront, or you happened to be sitting directly across from her in that casual outfit, every evening at the Narrowsburg Inn, you would have agreed with me: The girl had taste! Well, to be quite honest about it, which, admittedly, is not too difficult at this point, anything that looked like that could dress like that!

What's more, she was really smart, which was something that I did not learn until much later, because I did not care about it until much later, which was when she began to speak, which was much later. Then I learned, as the result of a seemingly casual comment, during the course of a conversation, one evening, that she had done well enough in high school, and on her subsequent "student examinations," given by the educational department in her country, to become one of the fortunate three or four students, from her high school, to be selected to go on to a "gymnasium," in the language line, at an institution somewhere in or near her hometown. And upon graduation, two years later, from that "gymnasium," she completed another three years at a "teachers training college," nearby, where, together with her two years at the gymnasium, she acquired a real proficiency in five contemporary foreign languages, English, Norwegian, Swedish, German and French, and she studied Latin, as well, for four years, no less. Given her proficiency in so many languages, gained at so many institutions of higher learning, it was quite obvious that this young lady was not only highly educated, but quite capable as well. You could just see that, all of that, when you sat directly across from her, like I did, every evening, for a whole week, at the Narrowsburg Inn!

She was also extraordinarily kind. I realized that fact when she refused to allow me to pay for her drinks on the very first evening that we spent together at the Narrowsburg Inn. I am sure that her refusal was out of some consideration for my dire financial situation, as a penurious law student, which was just as challenging that summer, as it was in every other summer, not to mention in every other winter, fall, and spring, too, of my university years. What's more, she had just graduated from college, too, and she had not yet begun to teach at a full-time job, so she really did not have any more money than I did. And of even more consequence, if that were at all possible, she always wore sandals in the evening, and she walked barefooted down on the lakefront during the day, obviously because we had a height problem on our hands. She had quite a lot of it, and I didn't, not much of it.

On top of that, when you stop and think about it, as I often have throughout the years, she was kind enough not to be married, engaged, going steady, or even seriously dating someone else, not at the time, or, at least, she was kind enough not to mention it. Now that was really being kind, when you stop to think about it, as I did, during every one of those evenings, in which I was seated directly across from her at the Narrowsburg Inn, thinking about what a beautifully-kind face she had!

She also had an enormous amount of character and determination. You could see that right away, and need I remind you that I was seated directly across from her every evening, all evening, for a whole week, looking at just those characteristics . . . the determination and the character, I mean. Gosh, she even supported herself, all the way through "gymnasium," and the "teachers training college," too. That is certainly an indication of a lot of character, as well as a lot of determination, too. I could see that, all of that, all evening, every evening, while I was seated directly across from her at the Narrowsburg Inn!

Her values were just as apparent. For one, she loved children; that's why she wanted to be a teacher, so that she could help little children grow up to become fine young men and women. What a noble thought, and she didn't even care about the poor pay scale, either, which was certainly another noble thought. And she loved her family, every one of them, her brother and sister, as well as her mother and father, the latter two being an even more noble thought . . . from my uncomfortable perspective, that is!

Also, I just couldn't get over the remarkable things that she had already done with her life, like deciding to come to this country for the summer, as a camp counselor, and at the very same camp where I happened to be a counselor, no less. Of far less significance, but still worth noting, she also had been a lead vocalist with a dance band during her last year in college, which played, on the weekends, all over the northern part of Denmark. And then there were her numerous fashion modeling jobs, on a number of different occasions over the years, for which there are numerous photographs, documenting that fact, some of which have been included as Exhibits 5 through 10 in the Appendix.

She had also spent part of a year working in London, England, as an "au pair," whatever that is, for an English family, so that she could gain a greater proficiency in the use of the English language. It was obviously with a view towards subsequently coming to America, and working in a summer camp, where I also happened to be working, so that we could spend our evenings together, among other things, speaking English at the Narrowsburg Inn. I should also add, with a due amount of appreciation, that she was always discreet enough not to employ her mastery of the language, at least not in a manner that might disclose my own diminished use, comparatively speaking, during our rare nightly conversations at the Narrowsburg Inn. Indeed, it might explain, if an explanation need be required, her general reluctance, during those evenings, to express some form of response, in an appreciating manner, to my discussions about what an amazing person I had become.

On top of all that, if one could realistically top any of that . . . referring, of course, to her sojourn in England, mastery of the English language, while working there, and its subsequent discrete use in our evening conversations at the Narrowsburg Inn . . . she and a girlfriend spent a semester in Italy, studying the Italian language at a university in Perugia, or, at least, the girlfriend apparently did. I subsequently learned, many years later, that she apparently spent most of her time pursuing a different form of study, which, admittedly, was Italian-related. Well, whatever, not everything in this universe is perfect, not even, according to the Icelandic Fables, Norsemen, or, as in this case, Norse women. And far more importantly, here she was, if you will, a Norse goddess, who was preparing to work with me for six weeks at a summer camp in the Pocono Mountains in the United States, which, when you think about it, probably means over forty-two nights of being together at the Narrowsburg Inn. That delightful proposition, if you continue to think about it, as I did, is, metaphorically speaking, light years away from the Italian peninsula!

There were other aspects about her person, more genealogical, if not regal, in nature, which were not quite as easily seen at the time, but which became far more impressive, as the weeks moved by at the Narrowsburg Inn. I am speaking about her father, who had been knighted by the Queen of Denmark, for his clandestine activities, as a leader of the "underground movement," in the northern part of Jutland, occurring amidst the German occupation of Denmark during the Second World War. When you consider that "knighted" fact, as I did, for weeks, the possibility arose in my mind that it may have elevated the Norse goddess, as his daughter, into some form of European royalty. And if I just stuck around, long enough, I might become ennobled, or, at least, crowned, by association, or admiration, or osmosis, or something like that. And, truth be told, I have always considered myself to be a "princely" sort of fellow. See a photograph of her parents at about that time period, if not sometime before, in Exhibit 143 in the Appendix.

Well, by the end of that week, I was forced to leave any consideration of some form of royalty behind, as a subject for further imagination, and on a much better day, too, because, by that time, I had discovered that she planned on traveling with her international organization to another part of the country, by bus, for about two weeks, following the end of her employment at the summer camp. And, thereafter, she planned to return to her hometown, although by an airborne path, and teach English and German to the students in the school system there, beginning, sometime, in the fall of that year. That information, imparted in somewhat of a casual manner, during one of our evenings, together, toward the end of that week at the Narrowsburg Inn, was not received particularly well by an incredulous recipient, who, of course, is the teller of this romanticized tale, at least at this point.

When he . . . the teller of this now "dramatic tale" . . . realized that the young lady was about to embark on a career of teaching in the fall, which, admittedly, was a noble endeavor, he also realized, at the very same time, that the school system was unfortunately located across a vast ocean, somewhere in another country, called

Denmark. And, moreover, even if he liked to travel, which he did not, he also realized that he could not afford to travel, not all of the way across an ocean, not to another country, even assuming that the daily demands of law school would not pose a significant problem, which was an uncomfortable assumption at the very best! Having said that, or should I more appropriately say, having realized that, it did not require an extended amount of logic to also realize that the Norse goddess was about to depart from his life, probably forever, in a relatively short amount of time.

As a result of discovering such disturbing travel information, internationally, too, relating to an incredible creature, because, by now, the girl had reassumed the proportions of a mythological creature, I experienced something that had never occurred before, not in my entire self-absorbed life, which was an overwhelming interest in somebody other than myself. That, actually, should not have come as such a surprise, not to someone like me, who, at the time, had an opportunity to consider all of her remarkable qualities. I mean, how could anyone not be that interested in someone with that kind of experience, that kind of character, that kind of determination, that kind of a value system, that kind of genealogy, that amount of education, and who was that kind, that talented, that smart and who dressed like that. And, of course, that is without even considering that she actually looked like that!

Frankly, after being with the creature every night that week, I became so overwhelmed by the eventual departure of all of those sterling qualities . . . which, of course, I could observe from my seat, sitting directly across from her, every night, for the whole night, at the Narrowsburg Inn . . . I actually forgot about my week-long effort of self-promotion. And, instead, I decided, in an epiphany, that the best way to promote myself, now and, probably, for the rest of my challenging life, would be to marry this pinnacle of perfection and, metaphorically, shine in her reflected glory! So for reasons that were actually apart from her impending departure at the end of that summer, which were obviously not hard for me to articulate at the time, and even now, over sixty-five years later, I asked the girl to marry me!

I guess, in looking back now, that my proposal was probably not a very good idea, not at the time, anyway, because it had obviously come after no more than one week! Oh, don't misunderstand me, I didn't make a mistake about the "reflected glory," just the proposal to obtain it, not after only one week, at least she didn't seem to think so at the time. I could tell that because my premature proposal was met, so to speak, with that characteristic silence, where she simply stares intently across the table at you, with those overly wide, piercing, steel-blue eyes, just as though you had never asked the question, and, therefore, she never had to respond to it!

Since I did not feel that this was an acceptable response, being somewhat equivocal in nature, I asked her again, every evening during the following week, which we also spent together, doing and not doing the very same things at the Narrowsburg Inn, and which was followed by the same silent and, I guess, salient response, with the exception of the last evening of that week! On that evening, following my proposal, offered, once again, at the conclusion of another monumental evening at the Narrowsburg Inn, she said, after a few moments of penetrating silence, in which her normally steel-blue eyes seemed to come on fire, that if I ever brought up that matrimonial subject again, she would not go out with me, not anymore, because I was beginning to make her very uncomfortable!

To avoid the discomfort, but not the creature, I never brought up the subject again, not over the rest of that summer. But I continued to see her, at a distance every day, while walking past the girls' waterfront, where she continued to work as a lifeguard, and every evening, in a much closer proximity, while drinking and dancing, as well as talking and laughing, but, in the latter case, only by me, somewhere at a bar in the Pocono Mountains.

By the end of that summer or, more specifically, the end of that camp season, it seemed that we had grown to know each other rather well, certainly on a nightly basis, not to mention on some of the undocumented sojourns on our days off, each week, while hitchhiking, together, across the Delaware River, in order to spend the day somewhere in the Catskill Mountains in New York State. At least, given that amount of time and all of those instances, it certainly seemed that way to a young law student, who was already twenty-six years of age, seemingly old enough to know what he was doing, and what he wanted to do, which was to marry the girl at the time. Apparently, the girl didn't disagree, not by that time, anyway, because, one evening, during the last week of that summer camp, she informed me that she had sent home for her birth certificate, and a few other documents, that may be required to marry in this country. At the same time, she also informed me that she had notified her prospective employer that she would not be returning in the fall to work as a teacher in that school system in Frederikshavn, Denmark.

Elated by these belated announcements, I presumptuously assumed, at the time, that it was safe to ask the girl if she loved me, which I did, but, unfortunately, she did not and told me so. Thankfully, however, she immediately added the following encouraging caveat, which was that she may over time, and that we would just have to wait and see, but that the prospect, in her mind, did not at all seem to be an unreasonable possibility.

Now, both thrilled and terrified, at various intervals in the same moment, because I may be able to marry someone who may not love me, I departed for home, several days later, at the end of that camp season, to inform my parents of my ironic situation, maritally speaking. Because my parents did not believe that I would ever marry anyone, or, more probably, that anyone would ever want to marry me, which, of course, may be redundant, or maybe not, they seemed to think that the possibility of my marriage to anyone, at any time, including this time and this person, was a fortunate possibility, no matter in what kind of conditional circumstances or how perilous they may seem to be.

Consequently, with possibly some latent reservations, which, naturally, remained unexpressed at the time, my parents seemed to be somewhat pleased by the possibility, so much so that they assisted me in making several of the hasty arrangements for a wedding in my hometown, such as retaining a photographer and an officiating minister in the church where I had grown up. They also purchased an attractive, white, wedding dress for Lis, with a white "pillbox" hat to match, and a nice contrasting corsage. All of which, or nearly so, has been captured in one of the three black and white wedding photographs, which were taken at the time, one of which I have so identified in Exhibit 1 and included in the Appendix.

Meanwhile, Lis, who had been traveling around the country, as a tourist, for several weeks, following the end of the camp season, was rather pleased to learn of the arrangements, especially relating to the wearing apparel, because, as she later said, she really did not have anything to appropriately wear as a bride for her wedding. In fact, she was so pleased that she decided to cut her tour short and to subsequently join me in my hometown, by bus, no less, to discuss the wedding arrangements with me, not to mention my parents, who, by the way, still could not believe their good fortune.

While waiting for Lis to arrive, standing alone at the bus station, I had an opportunity, for the first time, to review the prospective wedding vows, provided earlier in the day, by the newly acquired minister, including the passage requiring a promise, on the part of each matrimonial participant, to remain married, "until-death-do-us-part," which, I must admit, was a good bit longer than I had ever imagined. Now, more than slightly unnerved, by such an interminable promise, because, as a college student or, at least, one not too far removed, I had always thought in terms of days, or weeks, or, possibly, even months, or, maybe, if everything was really going quite well, a year or two, at most, in a relationship!

Frankly, I couldn't even begin to imagine living by myself for a lifetime, let alone living with someone else for that long. And, unfortunately, I told her so at the bus station, where we met, upon her arrival, which, I am constrained to add, did not elicit a very understanding response. In fact, to be quite honest about the matter, if honesty be required at this rather unnerving point, she became rather upset, and said something about being "humiliated," because she had already notified her prospective employer, not to mention her parents, that she would not be coming back to live and/or teach in her hometown, which, of course, was in Frederikshavn, Denmark. And, now, nearly in tears, she continued, after a few minutes, by adding that her parents now believed, because of a similar notification, that their daughter would be married within days.

Well, admittedly, it had now become rather uncomfortable to be nonchalantly standing there, in the presence of someone who had become that upset, because of something that I had done, or, as in this case, possibly undone, in nothing more than a moment of honesty, if not reality. Nevertheless, I knew that I could live with discomfort or, if you will, the consequences of my indecision, in these consequential circumstances; after all, I was not the one who was going to be "humiliated." And although I was slightly embarrassed, but only "slightly," because my parents were certainly aware of what I had promised, in a matrimonial way, but they were already aware that their son was more than capable of leaving behind those that he had loved or, if you prefer, once loved. In fact, I had done just that, without even blinking an eye, years earlier, when I left my parents, upon my graduation from high school, to go to Northwestern University, miles away, in Chicago, Illinois. And I am not even going to mention a subsequent departure from the lives of a number of young ladies, who had once graced my life, and in a rather significant manner, too, in the interval. So the damages in my case seemed to be rather slight, if not historic, and given that, they were certainly something that I could live with, if, eventually, I had to, and, more importantly, I probably did not have to live with them over an extended period of time, like "a lifetime."

What I could not live with, however, was her subsequent angry threat, because the girl had now become quite angry, to immediately go home, which, as you may recall, was internationally inaccessible to a poor law student like me. And I may not have been able, at the time, to conceive of a lifetime together, let alone promising one, but I could certainly conceive of a tomorrow, and I could not imagine a tomorrow without her, at least not without an enormous amount of pain. As a result, I had an epiphany, another one, and I decided, right there at the bus station, that "tomorrow" outweighed a "lifetime" and, therefore, I agreed to marry the "tomorrow," and forget about the "lifetime!"

CHAPTER XXXI

AMERICAN UNIVERSITY LAW SCHOOL, SECOND YEAR; SUMMER VACATION: MARRIAGE IN THE TRINITY METHODIST CHURCH IN MY HOMETOWN, FOLLOWED BY A FOOTBALL GAME AT PENN STATE UNIVERSITY AND A SUBSEQUENT RETURN TO MY HOMETOWN TO SHOP AT "UNCLE JOE'S WOODSHED."

WELL, IF you are still wondering, I did marry the girl, and it was in a simple wedding ceremony, which is probably an overstatement, carried out on a Saturday morning on September 28, 1963. The wedding ceremony was conducted by a minister, who I did not know and who I no longer remember, in the Trinity Methodist Church, which I do remember, because it was the same one in which I had grown up in my hometown of Lock Haven, Pennsylvania. The only people in attendance were my disbelieving parents, who were there to witness a historic event, rivaling, in their minds, the possibility of Christ's return on earth, and two people, who, unfortunately, went to the wrong wedding, probably for the same theological reason, and who, subsequently, apologized for having done so, immediately following the ceremony. Possibly not an auspicious beginning for the greatest decision that I had made, over the course of my indecisive life, at least up to that point!

Following the ceremony, the two of us joined my parents for lunch at the Tavern Restaurant, located in nearby State College, and, thereafter, we spent the first part of the afternoon at a football game, taking place, nearby, at Beaver Stadium, which was on the campus of Penn State University, where the undefeated Nittany Lion football team was playing the undefeated UCLA Bruins, for the number one ranking in the country. My new Danish wife, however, was not particularly happy about spending her wedding day, or at least half of it, at a football game, which she had never witnessed before that occasion, and, therefore, which she knew absolutely nothing about, and, finally, which she found to be absolutely ridiculous! "I mean, really," she repeated, endlessly, "grown men, dressed up in those stupid outfits with matching helmets, running all over a large manicured field, for absolutely no apparent reason, other than some obsessive desire to destroy each other in periodic episodes of violence, all of which seems to be supervised by a number of older men, dressed up in prison uniforms, who periodically stop the mayhem by blowing a whistle, emphatically, and they call that ridiculous scenario a game?"

Departing from the stadium at the end of the first half, at the insistence of my newly acquired Danish wife, with the score tied and the fans, including your noble author, going absolutely berserk, in a "once-in-a lifetime" football game, I began to imagine, for the first time, by the way, marriage over a "lifetime," rather than a "tomorrow," and I began to wonder, in a worrisome manner, what else in my life, which was important to me, was going to be reduced by marriage, or, more specifically, my marital partner, to the "ridiculous," beside a football game between two undefeated teams, who were playing for a possible national championship.

Looking at my life in that manner, because I was now beginning to look at my life in "lifetimes," caused me to have some real concerns, which increased dramatically, when, following our premature departure from the football stadium, we drove back to my hometown, in order to join my parents on a visit to "Uncle Joe's Woodshed," in order to buy sheets and pillowcases, if you can believe that. By now, referring to the moment in which we departed from the "Woodshed," I had stopped thinking about "universities" and "football games" and "national championships," and other so-called "ridiculous things," and I began to imagine my life in terms of "sheets" and "pillowcases" and "Woodsheds," especially of the "Uncle Joe" variety, for which I had absolutely no interest whatsoever. And as a result, I began to become somewhat despondent about the prospect of a lifetime of avoiding such "ridiculous things," in order to acquire such "non-ridiculous things," as sheets and pillowcases, at places not unlike "Uncle Joe's Woodshed." What's more, or, maybe, even worse, if you can find it in yourself to believe that, I had just spent part of the first day of the rest of my life, following a marriage, with my parents and in my hometown. And because I could not afford to go anywhere else, we . . . consisting now of my newly acquired Danish wife, which, of course, was of the "non-ridiculous variety," and my deeply despondent self, which, of course, was of the "ridiculous variety" . . . were going to spend the first night of our marriage with them, too, in my home, in my old bedroom, sleeping, or whatever, in my old single bed!

By the following day, having already done so, I was no longer "despondent;" I was beginning to become seriously depressed. That was because I had spent the last ten years of my life trying very hard to get away from my hometown, and those who lived there, including my parents, by educating myself in various universities around the country, only to end up married, just like my parents, and, even worse, on the first day of my marriage, or, should I more accurately say, first night of my marriage, ending up in my parents' home. On top of that, assuming, of course, that you could really top all of that, I spent part of that day, which was on my wedding day, looking for sheets and pillow cases, in a provincial store, in my hometown, which was something that my parents would likely have done in similar circumstances. That kind of symmetry was not why I had spent virtually the last ten years of my life in universities across the country, the last two of which were spent as a student in a law school.

Even worse, if that were at all possible, on the following day, two days after my marriage, I had to return to law school, which was never my favorite endeavor, with the newfound realization that the purpose in doing so, becoming a lawyer, that is, may actually accomplish nothing. For even if I succeed, it may well be, given everything that has just transpired over the last several days, including a marriage, I may still not be able to escape from what I came from, and where, or what I was, and why. Whatever that was, in short, may well be, at least in some significant way, what I am, for as long as I will be!

With that depressing thought, because despondency had now reached the epic proportions of a major depression, I decided not to think about it, not any more than I had to, anyway, which, quite honestly, was still far too much and far too often. Instead, I decided to return to law school, with my newly acquired Danish wife, who, hopefully, had not yet realized what a hopeless idiot she had just married.

The return, of course, was actually to the third-floor attic of a townhouse, located at 1835 Lamont Street, N.W., which I had shared, the year before, with Bob May and Bud Menaker. Now, however, I was returning with another person, a girl sort of person, who, quite possibly, may have some misgivings about sharing a bedroom with Bob May. Realizing that problem, before it had actually become a problem, Bud, who, by now, was quite used to resolving problems on the first and second floors, now addressed the prospectively new one on the third floor, by telling Bob May that three people could not fit into that bedroom, and that he, Bud Menaker, was not interested in sharing his bedroom with anything other than an attractive Jewish law student, among others similarly qualified, and, then, only on a Saturday night.

Because he no longer appeared to fit into any one of the two bedrooms, located in that third-floor apartment, Bob May graciously decided to move on to another living arrangement, somewhere else. And, thereafter, "I," or, rather, "We" . . . because I was now married and, by becoming so, had moved on from an "I" to a "We" . . . moved into the bedroom that Bud did not occupy, by himself, on six nights and, if all went well, with an attractive Jewish law student, among others, similarly qualified, on the seventh. I say, "Jewish," because Bud was Jewish and, not surprisingly, interested in Jewish things, especially if they were at all attractive and in law school.

My overriding interest, however, was someone else at the time, who was sharing my bedroom, for all seven nights of the week, and who was not Jewish, or even a law student. She was a Dane, who had recently married me, and although I didn't know it at the time, because I was still not very good at thinking in "lifetimes," she would become a continuing and consuming interest, for the rest of my natural life, as, among other explicable and inexplicable things, my wife. But that interest, as well as its continuation, will have to wait for the rest of this consuming story, of which it and she are a substantial part.

CHAPTER XXXII

AMERICAN UNIVERSITY LAW SCHOOL, SECOND YEAR: THE TWO BEDROOM APARTMENT ON THE THIRD FLOOR ATTIC OF AN INAUSPICIOUS ROW HOUSE IN THE ADAMS-MORGAN AREA OF THE CITY, WITH LIS, BUD AND CAL, IN A CONTEMPORARY DRAMA, ENTITLED, "THREE'S COMPANY"

ACTUALLY, THREE people living together, only two of whom were married, in a "walk up," two-bedroom apartment, in a third-floor attic, without a front door, which was part of an inauspicious row house in a transitional part of the city, was hardly the beginning of a fairytale marriage. In fact, given all of those challenging circumstances, involving all three of those individuals, it may have been way too much reality. The kind that leads to some interesting situations, if not some unanticipated problems.

One of them was the constant and continual criticism of the situation by other interested parties, including and especially parents. The criticism arose, of course, because the situation was, at the time, "unusual," to use our words, or "unheard of," to use theirs. But it was not lost on us, any one of us, that most people simply do not like what is unusual, even if it works, and this situation did work, eventually, but only after a lot of effort by all three of those individuals living there.

To begin with, we had to decide upon a division of labor, which we did, but only after some prolonged discussions, measured by days. Nevertheless, it eventually worked out rather well, following a decision that, among other things, Bud and I would cook dinner, alternating the effort weekly, because we arrived home from classes early in the afternoon, and, therefore, we would be able to have dinner prepared by the time that Lis arrived home from work, making contact lenses for Sterling Optical Company. Moreover, following dinner, all of us would help each other to clean up the table and carry the dishes out into the kitchen, placing them somewhere near the sink, allowing Lis to wash and dry them and, thereafter, put them away in the cupboard. A little later in the evening, having finished up her work in the kitchen, Lis would straighten up the apartment, by way of light housework, while Bud and I studied in our respective bedrooms. And Bud and I would more thoroughly clean the place, from top to bottom, on Saturdays, while Lis was working at that time for the Sterling Optical Company. Bud also agreed to pay the monthly rent, on behalf of all of us, and we agreed to reimburse him for our half, which was probably why Bud decided to teach Lis how to draft a check, probably to him, for our part of the rent. Finally, Bud and I agreed to go food shopping together, every Wednesday afternoon, after class. It was also decided, almost as an afterthought, that if any other things would possibly arise, requiring some kind of attention, by one or more of the three of us, they would ordinarily be resolved on an ad hoc basis. Surprised, by all of that organization . . . well, what did you expect from two budding lawyers and a "would-be" schoolteacher!

Although that schedule certainly allowed us to live together in a reasonably efficient fashion, it did not ensure that we would live together in a continuously harmonious fashion. But then, how could you expect continuous harmony in a situation where three people were trying to live together, two of whom were recently married and those two were also trying to learn how to live with each other, let alone live with a third person, too. Part of the problem, if, arguably, there ever was a problem, arose when the third person, in this tripartite situation, notably Bud Menaker, would become involved in the marriage of the other two, by, among other things, taking sides, on occasion, in minor domestic disputes. That, of course, is assuming that the two recently married individuals, living in that tripartite situation, could have possibly reached the proportions of becoming "domestic," which, by no means, was a sure thing.

Well, domestic or not, Bud did take sides, on occasion, when his marital counterparts had something that may have approached the concept of a "disagreement," which occurred in his presence, of course. In one of those situations, Bud and I had returned to our apartment, right after class, sometime earlier in the afternoon. Shortly thereafter, Lis, who had apparently left work somewhat earlier than normal that day, likely because of a "beauty shop" appointment, came walking up the stairs, while supporting, at the same time, something on top of her head, which she subsequently described as "a stylish new hairstyle." Well, in my esthetic judgment, which, admittedly, was unqualified, it was certainly "new," but there wasn't much about it that was "stylish," unless, of course, grotesque was in style, and I simply hadn't realized that fact!

Now, admittedly, I had not taken a great amount of interest in my new wife's hairstyle, or lack thereof, before we were married. I was far more interested, as you may recall, in other, far more pleasing, aspects of her domain at the time. Now that we were married, however, my interest, if that is an appropriate use of the term in these circumstances, broadened to include that which was on top of her head, too, and I did not particularly like what I saw there, not at the moment, anyway, which was what she and/or they, at the "beauty shop," had done to it. Out of some sense of discretion, however, which, admittedly, has never been my strong suit, I did not immediately say anything about it; I just did not say anything at all . . . about anything . . . and for some period of time, too. Apparently, however, that prolonged silence on my part, being somewhat unusual, was construed by everyone else living in that apartment, notably Bud and my wife, to indicate some sort of a stylistic disapproval on my part, although they didn't immediately say so.

Instead, in an atmosphere now overladen with ambivalence, if not outright hostility, we all sat down for dinner, without saying a word to each other, and, following that, we ate our dinner, without saying a word to each other, and, finally, having finished our dinner, we all stood up to leave the table, without saying a word to each other . . . with one notable and subsequent exception: Bud Menaker turned around, briefly, on the way to his room to study, so that he was now facing the two of us, Lis and myself, and he said, and I now quote, "well, I like it!"

Briefly shaken by this unfortunate and unwanted intrusion into my marital domain, on behalf of the grotesque, no less, I was initially taken back, but quickly regained my composure and, believe it or not, disingenuously responded that "I like it, too." Whereupon, Lis decided to avoid the whole esthetic problem, assuming that there really was one, by not responding to either comment, probably because there was little more that could have been realistically added to what had already been said. So the evening, involving hair and our three young protagonists, in their third-floor attic "walk up," who were trying to live together harmoniously, but now melodramatically, ended in silence, which often, as it did in that instance, says a lot.

Some situations, however, involving those three individuals, who were trying to live together harmoniously, did not always end in silence. In one of them, for example, the three of us happened to be walking together to the grocery store, in the springtime, when a very attractive, scantily clad, young lady came walking toward us, probably on her way home from a shopping trip. I certainly noticed her, but I did so discreetly. Bud, who has never been discreet in situations like that, was not in this instance, either. His head actually turned around, like a turret on a tank, as the "barely-there," twenty-something, passed by the three of us. Lis, who had noticed both things . . . that the passerby was "scantily clad" and that Menaker had noticed that fact, too, and for a noticeably prolonged period of time . . . was not happy, and she said so, too!

When her initial disapproving response seemed to have no impact, she stopped, dead in her tracks, turned toward the offending Menaker, whose head was still slightly turned in the direction of the rapidly disappearing "barely-there," and said, rather pointedly, "that's rude!" Bud, who was probably thinking rather rude thoughts at the time, or worse, turned around, rather quickly, to face his accuser. Unfortunately, however, he could muster nothing more, by way of a defense, than a statement of the obvious, which was, "I'm not married to you," which, of course, was technically correct, but not particularly helpful, not in those questionable circumstances.

Standing there now, no more than a block away from the grocery store, and having just been confronted by an unexpected assault on one of his favorite pastimes, if not his actual favorite, outside of Saturday nights, of course, Bud looked visibly shaken. Although his demeanor changed, somewhat, in the days and the weeks that followed . . . in which we happened to encounter similarly dressed young women in the same kind of circumstances . . . I don't believe that Bud did. Rather, I believe that Bud began to think, over time, that we, who were married, would probably be happier if we lived elsewhere, and, more importantly, maybe he would, too, especially on a Saturday night.

Any doubt about that fact was probably resolved, several weeks later, when Bud invited a girl down for the weekend, which he had dated the prior year, while working as a counselor at a summer camp, called Pine Mere, in the Poconos. The girl was quite nice, quite attractive and, what's more, clearly met the Menaker standards for pulchritude, ethnicity, and education, enough to qualify for a date on a Saturday night. The trouble, however, was that this girl did not go home on a Saturday evening, probably because her home was several hundred miles away, somewhere in Ontario, Canada. Because of that distance and a number of other things, which shall go unreported here, because of a certain amount of delicacy, if not decency, the girl "slept over," as the kids like to say, in the other bedroom, with Bud.

This, in itself, did not seem to pose any real problems on the following day, not for the girl or Bud or me. After all, she was certainly of "the age of consent"; she did not snore, at least not loudly enough to keep me awake; and she did not talk in her sleep, at least not that I could hear, anyway. In fact, she was not intrusive at all, except, possibly, somewhat in Menaker's bed, which, for your prurient interest, was a single bed, not really constructed for two inhabitants, even in circumstances like those. But that fact, for unreported reasons, did not seem to bother either Bud or the attractive Jewish law student that night!

Oh, sure, the single bed may have interfered with their sleeping ability, somewhat, but, on reflection, I don't think that sleep was a matter of major concern to either one of them. So on the face of it, the "arrangement," which I have always found to be a nice way of describing that kind of a situation, seemed to work out rather well for everyone, except one, and I happened to be married to that one at the time.

Unfortunately for the "arrangement" and any form of continuation thereof, she was not at all happy about the situation. We . . . which now included everyone, but the attractive Jewish law student, who, by now, was well on her way back to law school, somewhere in Canada . . . discovered that unhappy fact, early in the afternoon, on the following day. At that point, she . . . the unhappy, narrow-minded one, to whom I happened to have been married . . . indicated, quite clearly, to the rest of us, still remaining on the premises, that she had some misgivings about the situation, which happened to occur, in the other bedroom, on the previous night.

Moreover, later that day, when we were having dinner together, the Danish morality police asked Bud if he was going to marry the girl, the implication being that the "arrangement," if I may still use that judicious term, morally required a subsequent act, or, as the case may be, a contract, both of which would ordinarily be construed in matrimonial terms. I don't think that Bud would have disagreed that the "situation," or the "arrangement," if I may still use those loosely fitting terms, may have required a number of things, but, in his opinion, those things were ordinarily required during the "situation" or the "arrangement," the nature of which, I may add, will continue to remain undefined, out of a continuing sense of delicacy, if not decency.

Moreover, Bud . . . now relying upon at least one thousand years of historical precedence . . . strongly disagreed with any implication that the "situation," or the "arrangement," euphemistic language still being employed by the author, required a marriage between the participants, sometime thereafter. And in support of his strongly held opinion, he pointed out that, otherwise he would, by now, be married to more people, presumably of a more feminine nature, than he could possibly count, and that marriage to more than one person, at the same time, would be against the law, and, of course, as a law student, he had every intention, if not an overriding obligation, to follow the law.

As a fellow law student and a guy at that, I was as impressed with Bud's legal argument, as I was with his conjugal history. On the other hand, the Danish morality police were no more impressed with that history than with that argument, probably because she was not a guy, or a law student, or both. Apparently, Bud realized that fact . . .

that she was not impressed . . . because he never brought another girl home, thereafter, even on a Saturday night, to "sleepover," as the kids still like to say.

Consequently, we never had to confront that problematic situation again, which, of course, consisted of a continuation of that conjugal history, any misgivings about the continuation, and a rejection of any subsequent marital obligation growing out of the continuation of that history. That, in the end, seemed to make every one of the individuals, who happened to be living together in that third-floor attic "walk up," happy, except, possibly, Bud, who considered his "relationships" . . . a term that I have deigned to use in this context, even though they never seemed to have lasted longer than a Saturday night . . . more important, in some respects, than life with his marital counterparts, even though we, unlike they, stayed over with him for the rest of the week, too.

Not all of our marital problems, however, were related to our living situation with Bud Menaker. Some of them were simply monetary, in any kind of a situation, and simply required a working solution. So I went to work, before, after, and in between classes in law school, teaching college students in the afternoon at Marjorie Webster Junior College, and at night at the Strayer Business College. At the same time, Lis continued working, full-time, making contact lenses for several optometrists at the Sterling Optical Company. Even then, however, with my two part-time jobs and her one full-time job, we struggled, economically, with tuition payments, among so many other indefinable financial obligations, which probably explains why we walked so often in the evenings, and on the weekends, too. At the time, we really couldn't really afford to do much else.

As a parenthetical note, if such things may be permitted to exist in this context, I believe that it is worth noting, at least at this juncture, that we have continued to walk, routinely, even now, nearly 65 years later, notwithstanding that time and effort have placed us in a far better financial situation. Maybe the continuation of our peripatetic practice, over all of those years, should not, in retrospect, be so surprising, notwithstanding that financial distinction in the interval After all, historians have continually reminded us that, "history repeats itself."

Well, forgetting about historians and gratuitous historical notations, at least for the moment, and returning, once again, to our more financially insecure days, while living with Bud Menaker, in a third-floor, attic "walk up," I have previously noted that we walked a lot because "we really couldn't afford to do much else at the time." Actually, on second thought, that's not quite accurate, because Lis became pregnant about three months after we were married. And although there really were not any significant expenditures into our lives before that pregnancy, with the exception, of course, of my law school tuition payments, the projected medical costs of continuous pre-natal care and a hospital delivery were terrifying, mostly because we did not have any health insurance!

Because we did not and because we said that we did not to our empathetic primary care physician, Dr. George Boinnis, who was kind enough to (1) ignore Lis' nostalgic recollections of socialized medicine in Denmark, on nearly every occasion in which she happened to visit his office; and (2) advise us that he would talk to an obstetrician, who was a friend of his and who normally delivered babies for a substantial fee, and ask him to deliver this one for virtually free. The obstetrician, who turned out to be Dr. Enos Ray, obliged, by charging us just two hundred dollars ($200), for all of the prenatal visits to his office and for the actual delivery, which, in monetary terms of the day, let alone today, was probably tantamount to being free!

The medical fee of just two hundred dollars ($200), for all of those medically related services, not to mention my continued sanity, as a result, caused me to reappraise my view of the American Medical

Society, not to mention its entrepreneurial medical participants. Moreover, based on my original, and more realistic, appraisal of that organization, and its overly entrepreneurial participants, that fee clearly qualified Dr. Ray for heavenly rewards, because of his virtual renunciation of earthly ones, at least in this instance. At least, I thought so, until Dr. Ray advised me, at the time of the delivery, that the cost of the next pregnancy . . . which, in his opinion, would likely occur sometime after I had graduated from law school and had begun working as a lawyer, redefining my economic situation . . . was going to be significantly more, so that it would offset his losses on this one. Since there was, indeed, another pregnancy, roughly three years later, following my graduation from law school and the commencement of my employment as a lawyer, Dr. Ray did, indeed, charge me a larger amount, which seemed at the time to be an unconscionable amount, for his services related to the subsequent pregnancy, if not for the original one, too, which, incidentally, restored my original view of the American Medical Society, as well as it's greedy participants!

Even after we, the marital two, put pregnancies, obstetrics, and the American Medical Society behind us, economic problems continued to haunt me and worry Lis, and we tried to address those problems, by not spending any more money than necessary, which included the possible purchase of an automobile, even a used automobile, although we really needed one, any kind of one. So we had to prevail upon whatever was remaining of Bud's charitable disposition, which was not much, not after the recent Saturday night morality episode, to drive us to the grocery store. When Bud was not available, or his charitable disposition, we would simply take a bus or, possibly, walk, and bring our grocery bags back home, in either case, on a bus, to the obvious consternation of the bus driver, as well as a majority of the standing patrons, on a typically over-filled bus, during, believe it or not, "rush-hour," on many occasions!

CHAPTER XXXIII

AMERICAN UNIVERSITY LAW SCHOOL, SECOND YEAR: A CHRISTMAS STORY, ON OUR FIRST CHRISTMAS, WITH BUD, CAL AND LIS

IN ALL fairness, I should point out that Bud's frustration, literally and metaphorically, over his Saturday night deprivations, seemed to diminish, significantly, as we approached the oncoming Christmas season. And the Dane, fortunately, now became far more concerned with Christmas, than morality or, more specifically, Danish Christmas traditions, as opposed to Menaker morality traditions. Moreover, since the Dane was now approaching Christmas, while living in America, approximately two thousand miles away from those traditions . . . the Danish ones, I mean . . . she became, for the very first time, quite homesick. And as a result, she began a rather irritating habit of advising us . . . Bud and myself . . . what her family would be doing on that particular day, back home, in Denmark, to mark the advent of the Christmas season.

Because our irritation over this holiday habit eventually changed to concern, Bud said to me, after class one day, while we were on our way back home, that we should buy a Christmas tree, and some decorations, too, because the presence of the tree and the decorations might improve her spirits . . . referring, of course, to his second roommate and my first wife. At the same time, he also thoughtfully said that he would pay for the tree, on condition that none of this would ever be disclosed to his rabbi, and that I should pay for the decorations, all six of them, because that was about all that I could afford. That way, according to the thoughtful advice of Mr. Menaker, Lis and I could probably reuse them, in subsequent years, with, hopefully, some decorative additions on Christmas trees of our own one day.

It was a great idea and I told him so . . . referring, of course, to the tree, the decorations and their subsequent use by the marital component of this unusual living arrangement . . . after which we, one married and one not, set out, shortly after dropping off our books, to buy a Christmas tree and, lest we forget, six decorations. Since Bud never had a Christmas tree, while growing up in his Jewish home, he wanted the largest one that we could possibly find, and after several visits to several tree stands in several nearby neighborhoods, we found a really large one, large enough to satisfy the Menaker standard for a large Christmas tree!

Apparently, it was the size that every Jewish kid imagines a Christmas tree should be, if, in fact, he were permitted to have one in his home, while growing up. Well, that tree . . . the Menaker one, that is, or, if you prefer, the one that he picked out . . . was, at least, fifteen feet tall, if it was a foot! And with that oversized selection and subsequent purchase, my Jewish roommate was in Christmas tree heaven!

The tree was so large that we could barely lift it, let alone carry it all the way back home, which, without having to carry the tree, was really not so far away. With the tree, however, it was quite another story, or walk, if you prefer to look at it that way, but we did lift and carry it, all the way back home, by me carrying the trunk and Bud lost, somewhere, up there on the other end, near the bushy top. That was where he wanted to be, however, so that, in his words, his "rabbi would not recognize him," in the midst of all of those branches, in the unlikely event that he happened upon this holiday spectacle, involving a Jew, a half-Jew and an outlandish non-Jewish Christmas tree! When we . . . the Jew and the half-Jew and the non-Jewish

Christmas tree . . . finally reached home, without detection by his rabbi, I might add, we struggled, mightily, to get that damned monstrosity up three long flights of seemingly interminable stairs!

After that, we . . . the Jew and the half-Jew and the non-Jewish Christmas tree . . . set about trying, with some limited success, initially, anyway, to erect the damned thing in the living room. Finally, however, with a sense of accomplishment now, we . . . like the "three-wise-men," who biblically preceded the two of us, by also traveling a great distance under extraordinarily difficult circumstances, for a seasonal purpose . . . ended our journey, like our biblical counterparts, by simply standing there, viewing with awe, if not adoration, the reason for our seasonal journey, which, in this case, was an upright Christmas tree, extending all the way to the ceiling, not to mention Bud Menaker's Christmas tree expectations, as well.

Well, with our seasonal epic now ended, or, rather, erected, we . . . Jewish and half-Jewish alike . . .began to place all six semi-secular decorations, spaced judicially, of course, over the entire fifteen feet of our magnificently erect Christmas tree, which, according to Bud, now reflected what every Jewish boy imagines, as a child growing up, with no more than his imagination to serve him at Christmas time. Thankfully, it was quite clear in this instance, without resorting to any form of imagination, that our enormous ceiling on the third-floor attic, which must have extended right up to the roofline, quite nicely accommodated our spectacularly oversized and under-decorated Christmas tree.

Pleased by what we had now accomplished, and, possibly, because Bud's rabbi had not yet discovered that fact, we sat down, in what remained of our now undersized living room, to further admire our holiday handiwork and, just as importantly, to await the Dane's discovery of Christmas . . . Jewish style or, if you prefer, Menaker style.

Upon discovering the fruits of our afternoon labor, in all of its magnificence, after working all day and, following that, climbing three flights of stairs to our "walk-in" abode, the Dane just stood there in the entrance way, in obvious amazement, just looking at the tree, the first one ever purchased by her Jewish roommate, Bud Menaker, and decorated, in part, by her half-Jewish husband, Cal Golumbic. Although the tree was way too big for its surroundings, at least in circumference, and not very well shaped in any surroundings, which was obviously why it cost so little, and, moreover, the decorations were virtually nonexistent in that coniferous spaciousness, there was a transcendent symbolism, in that moment, involving all three of those people and that tree on that holiday occasion. A symbolism that transcended the Atlantic Ocean and the holiday traditions of two great countries on two separate continents, and that joined together, literally, two of the world's great religions, Christianity and Judaism, and, finally, three people, only two of whom were married, who lived together and who cared enough about each other to do something like that to celebrate the holiday season.

After a few minutes, in which she still seemed to be somewhat transfixed by the tree and the holiday moment, the Dane walked over and sat down beside her two Jewish roommates, one of whom she had married and the other not, and they all just sat there, quietly together, admiring the gigantic, misshapen, sparsely decorated, unlit Christmas tree. Then, after a few minutes, without saying another word, they all stood up, nearly at the same time, and walked out into the dining room together, where, quite happily now, they had dinner together, once again, during which the Dane, now quite animated, began, once more, to inform her two roommates about the holiday season in Denmark. Funny, the stories no longer seemed to be quite so irritating, not anymore, anyway.

After dinner and after the stories and after the dishes were "done," so to speak, which is when Bud and I would normally have retired to our respective rooms to study, something quite different and quite special happened, at that point, in this storied holiday occasion.

We decided, without saying a word to each other, to stay in the living room with our Danish roommate, while she continued to talk about the holiday season in Denmark. Then, all of a sudden, in the midst of it all, she decided, inexplicably, to teach her two Jewish roommates to sing a number of Christmas carols . . . in Danish, would you believe! With that, I was initially afraid that she may have gone a little bit too far, and that Bud may have felt somewhat uncomfortable, in trying to learn how to sing Christian Christmas carols . . . in Danish, no less.

To my amazement, however, if not his, he quickly and enthusiastically mastered the Danish words to the classic, if not iconic, German Christmas Carol, "Silent Night," which he proudly sang on that Christmas Eve, and on every other Christmas Eve, for years, in which he would traditionally join us to celebrate a Danish Christmas, "American style," or should I more appropriately say, "Jewish style," or, maybe, I should even consider saying, "Menaker style."

Well, however you would prefer to say it, the Christmas Eves that Bud would celebrate with his two former married roommates, in the years that followed, were generally not unlike the one that the three of them celebrated, together, on that very first Christmas Eve, although maybe more in spirit than in decoration, because, by that time, we . . . the marital two . . . had succeeded in leaving destitution behind, permitting a far more decorative display during those subsequent holiday seasons, including on the Christmas trees.

Unfortunately, however, I never did learn how to sing that traditional, if not iconic, carol in Danish, over the course of those subsequent Christmas holidays that we traditionally celebrated together. Nevertheless, the carol, the tree, that evening, and whatever it may have meant, given the celebrants, stayed with us and we with each other, not just on that Christmas Eve, or on those that traditionally followed, but on every day and in every way for the rest of our lives on this earth!

On another, more parenthetical, note, this time of a far more maudlin nature, the Dane and I lost our old roommate, and lifelong friend, to an unfortunate malaise last year. Until that time, he continued to be part of our lives, in various ways and at various events, including holiday events, on occasion, over the years. Those events aside, but not the years, the Dane has always adored the man, for obvious reasons, and in my own peculiar way, I guess that I did, too, probably for the same reasons. Although such words were never spoken between the two of us, not during his lifetime, I assume that he left this world with that understanding.

CHAPTER XXXIV

AMERICAN UNIVERSITY LAW SCHOOL, SECOND YEAR: CAL AND LIS MOVE INTO A BLEAK ONE-ROOM EFFICIENCY IN THE CALIFORNIA HOUSE AND LEAVE BEHIND A COMICAL SITUATION IN THEIR OLD APARTMENT, INVOLVING, IN ONE INSTANCE, A CLOTHESLINE, A PAIR OF WET STOCKINGS AND A TERRIFIED BUD MENAKER

ONE DAY, just before class began, Skippy Weinstein, another second-year law student, asked Bud how he was going to celebrate the oncoming Jewish holiday, which, apparently, was on the following day. Initially, Bud was speechless, but after a couple of uncomfortable moments, he replied that he had, quite honestly, forgotten about the holiday, and, therefore, that he didn't know how or where he would celebrate it.

Later that afternoon, on our way home from class, Bud said, laughingly, that he had been living with us for so long that he had almost forgotten that he was Jewish, which, I realized, of course, was a statement made more out of jest, than fact, but, maybe, just enough fact to become subsequently consequential. And in that respect, I wasn't too far wrong, because a few weeks later, Bud said, on the way home from class once again, that it may be better for us . . . referring to the marital component of his living situation . . .

if he moved out and we . . . the same marital component . . . had an opportunity to live by ourselves. After all, Bud said, somewhat thoughtfully, Lis is now pregnant, and the two of you should probably think about planning a life together, with the baby, somewhere else, without me.

All of this, of course, may have been true, but it was also true that we . . . the marital component . . . had never addressed such an imposing issue, if not a problem, not among ourselves, not at any time, probably because we had no way of financially resolving it. Bud, of course, could change his living situation far more easily, and, if necessary, live by himself, or, at least, no longer with us, because, among other things, he could easily afford to do that. That distinction, which was a financial one, between Bud and ourselves, probably gave rise to Bud's considered statement to me, just a few days later, that we . . . all three of us, or, maybe, even four, if you count the unborn member of our household . . . "needed to move on." And after a number of agonizing discussions, followed by some rather hastily arranged searches, all of which were prompted by Bud's statement, we . . . the marital component . . . finally did "move on," into a one-room efficiency, because we could not afford to pay for anything larger.

The one-room efficiency was located in the California House, located on, you guessed it, California Street, just off of Connecticut Avenue, Northwest, in Washington D.C. The one room was not a very large room, but it did have a kitchen, consisting of a rather small, partially working, stove, an even smaller refrigerator, which really did not refrigerate very well, and something that appeared to be a well-worn sink, all on one wall, if you can actually picture that! If you really can't, maybe it might help you to look at the rest of the walls, in that comparatively small room, because they were essentially unadorned, covered by what must have once been a dull gray paint, probably put on by Methuselah, several thousand years ago, on a break from helping his grandson, Noah, load the Ark. The floor was made of some kind of a strange, inanimate composite, probably unknown to most contemporary geologists, or even chemists, for that matter. And I am sure that it was last cleaned by Methuselah, too, at least it looked that way.

There was also a closet, which was a comparatively small "walk-in," in which we planned to house the newly arrived addition to our growing family, along with some clothes and furniture that were seemingly appropriate for a human being of that dimension, and that we had been fortunate enough to secure, on its behalf, over the last few months. Given the amount of that furniture and those clothes, however, it was more than obvious that the "newly arrived addition" would still have a lot of closet space.

Oh, yes, I almost forgot, there was just one window in that dreary place, which, unfortunately, did not have much of a view. Actually, the view was of a dark gray cement wall, on the apartment house next door, which was no more than ten feet away. Looking at that wall, however, which, unfortunately, I did far too often, even before we moved in, was far better than looking at the furnishings, in what purported to be a furnished efficiency, which I tried not to do, not too often, anyway The furnishings, if you want to call them that, were so old and so shabby that they would have been rejected by an antique dealer in the early middle ages, or even a junk dealer in an earlier time period.

Most of them consisted of "over-stuffed" chairs, which had a distinctly "dusty-like" appearance, and a "moldy-like" smell to go with them, probably because most of them were filled with dust and covered with mold, at least underneath. You could tell that when you worked up enough courage to sit down on one of them, or troubled yourself to look underneath it, and, believe me, it took that much courage, not to mention that much willpower. The over-stuffed sofa, which suffered from the same dusty and moldy problems, pulled out into an incredibly, uncomfortable, "bed-like" phenomenon, for which there is no appropriate adjective in the entire language. It was the only one, by the way, in the whole place, which, eventually, posed a real problem, because Lis could not comfortably sleep on it, not during the latter stages of her pregnancy, anyway. So we borrowed a fold-out cot from my parents and purchased a large piece of plywood to place under the rather flimsy mattress, if you can honestly call that flimsy thing a mattress, in order to provide more support for her back. That way, she would be able to sleep on the cot, although not necessarily in a comfortable manner, without developing some form of a back problem, by the time that the baby was born, several months later. Nevertheless, even with the inherent discomfort of sleeping on a cot, without any real mattress, but, instead, a plywood substitute, that was a far better alternative, with backs and supports in mind, than sleeping with me, and the dust and the mold, on the over-stuffed, non-supportive, sofa, turned-into-something-like-a-bed.

Still, I should point out that when you are young and seriously in love, as well as full of optimism, which, generally, seems to follow, it is not hard to believe that anything, in a living situation, is acceptable. Well, I was quite young and seriously in love, at the time, and just as optimistic, as a result. For that optimistic reason, almost anything, in a living situation, would have ordinarily been acceptable, except for that miserably furnished hovel! The thought of living there was more than depressing; it was downright disgusting! Everything in that one-room efficiency, by way of furnishings, if nothing else, looked as bleak as that dumb gray wall, just outside of the only window in the whole disgusting place, and we had not even moved into it yet!

The thought of doing so provided the subject matter for a series of nightmares, over the next several weeks, all of which were surreal and none of which made any sense, probably for that surreal reason. Returning, nevertheless, to the more immediate nightmare, or should I more appropriately say, one-room efficiency, we began, notwithstanding its condition, to slowly move our things, along with ourselves, from the third floor "walk-up," apartment, which we shared with Bud Menaker, and which was, of course, in the attic of the townhouse at 1835 Lamont Street, N.W. in Washington, D.C. Aside from ourselves, those things consisted, substantially, of our clothes, numbering no more than four maternity dresses belonging to Lis, made by her mother, which she wore nearly every day to work, one at a time, naturally, as well as the few outfits that I had accumulated over my years as a college student, which I wore nearly every day to law school, one outfit at a time, of course.

To a much lesser extent, numerically speaking, they also consisted of some eclectic furnishings that we had managed to accumulate, during the short time that we had been married, which hardly seem worth mentioning, but in the interest of historical accuracy, if nothing else, included two unmatched table lamps, once belonging to the previous inhabitants of our third floor, "walk-up" apartment, an old metallic kitchen table, with unpainted wooded legs, without any accompanying chairs, I might add, once belonging to my parents, and a barely performing electric toaster, once belonging to my great Aunt Hannah Grove, probably as a wedding present, in the earlier part of the twentieth century. Together with some mismatched kitchen utensils and dishes, once belonging to Goodwill, which even they were unable to sell, not until we came along, anyway, those meager chattels formed the essentials of our tangible possessions at the time.

More importantly, for our story, at least at this point, those pedestrian possessions, as well as their penurious owners, eventually began to shift westward, as we have already said, like the American history before them, toward California Street. And with that, our sense of humor, so prevalent over the last year of our living arrangement with our third-floor roommate, Bud Menaker, nearly vanished, along with our persons. I say "nearly," because, just before we made our final move, ending our unconventional living arrangement with Bud, in the third-floor "walk up," attic apartment, which we shared with him, something happened, late one evening, which reminded all three of us, if not an unborn fourth, that our "arrangement," if you still do not mind calling it that, had often been fun, and even, on occasion, hilarious.

On that particular evening, exhausted from the "move," taking place over the previous four days, Lis and I went to bed, rather early, and within minutes, we found ourselves sound asleep. At about one o'clock in the morning, however, we were rudely awakened, by an ungodly shriek, followed by a profusion of profanity. Awakened by the tumult, Lis immediately jumped out of bed and onto her feet, confused and slightly frightened, after which she turned around, looked back at me, still in bed and barely awake, and asked, pointedly, "where did that noise come from?" Answering, sleepily, I conjectured "down the hall, probably somewhere near the bathroom." With that, admittedly, unreliable information, Lis turned back toward the bedroom door and began to walk, cautiously at first, out into the hall, while still in her pajamas, with me, now fully awake, out of bed and following closely behind, on our way down the hall, toward the bathroom.

Arriving at the bathroom door, probably within minutes, she hesitated, momentarily, in the dark hallway, and, then, seemingly assured about what she was about to do, carefully reached around the corner and turned on an overhead bathroom light, in what had previously been a forebodingly dark and questionable room, given the unidentifiable and unexpected, previously noted, noise at that hour.

Hesitantly, now, we both peered around the corner, and there, standing in the light's full glare, disclosing the evening's stark drama, was our roommate, Bud Menaker, with several of Lis' wet stockings draped partially around his neck and face and head, with the other ends still attached to a clothesline, inexplicably strung across, what appeared to be, the upper reaches of the bathroom.

Unbeknown to both of us at the time . . . Bud and myself, that is . . . apparently, Lis would habitually wash out her stockings, late at night, after which she would hang them up to dry on a rope that she had strung across the bathroom, earlier in the evening, from one end to the other, a little above eye level. All of this, as she subsequently explained, normally took place after we . . . consisting of the same two males . . . had finished studying for the evening and fallen asleep. The reason for this seemingly aberrational conduct, which occurred shortly before retiring, herself, for the evening, as she continued to explain, was because of some discomfort in hanging up her wet stockings in a bathroom ordinarily used during the day by two men, only one of whom she had married.

Apparently, Bud had discovered that unfortunate fact before I did, quite accidentally, by the way, and quite late at night, too, on the way to the bathroom, in the dark, naturally, and, not surprisingly, he did not look too happy about it at the time. Actually, now that I think about it, he looked absolutely ridiculous . . . with those wet stockings partially draped around his neck and face and head. He also looked sort of terrified, if not somewhat angry, and, of course, a little bit sleepy, all at the very same time, if you can honestly picture that!

Well, we . . . meaning the marital two . . . did picture that, at that surprising moment, after which we just stood there, looking at him, for several minutes, trying, in my case, at least, not to laugh, before, eventually, helping him to unravel that mess. Finally, as the last wet stocking fell harmlessly to the floor, I could no longer contain myself, and the partially hidden smile, on my formally disbelieving face, turned into outright laughter, followed by a rather indiscrete statement, that "this is probably not the first time that Menaker had a pair of women's stockings wrapped around his head!"

The verbal indiscretion on my part was eventually followed, after a few moments of general disbelief, by laughter, on the part of all of us, even Bud, even, if you can believe this, "the Danish morality police!" When the laughter began to subside, but only somewhat, I quickly added to my indiscretion, by noting that, "this is probably the first time, however, that it occurred accidentally," which caused the formerly diminishing laughter to swell, once again, until it had reached rather sizable proportions, because now "disbelief" was no longer part of the humorous equation.

Eventually, however, even hearty laughter begins to subside in life, and it did in this instance, too, until everything and everyone was nearly silent, once again, which allowed me to quickly add, "but this is probably the first time that he ever objected to that kind of a situation." Now laughter, which had quickly regained its footing, following that indelicate conclusion, began to approach hysterical proportions.

Then, in the midst of indelicacy and laughter and disbelief, all in the confines of an unpredictable late-night bathroom melodrama, a hint of a tear began to form in the eyes of one of those present, which, of course, was at that very moment and on that indescribable night. A night that had followed so many indescribable moments, in nearly a year of those kinds of days and nights, in which three unusual people, only two of whom were married, lived together, and in those improbable circumstances. And, quite inexplicably, I began, of all things, to think about clowns!

With that, the improbable three began to walk back down the hallway, in silence, toward their respective bedrooms. Although they did so quite solemnly now, it was not because of the night's melodrama, but because they all knew that the impending move, by the marital two, of course, was going to change everything, and, maybe, not even for the better, not initially, anyway. Indeed, I think, in that respect, that they all realized, as they entered their respective bedrooms, turned out the lights and crawled under the bedcovers, probably with a hint of a smile still on their faces, that things were never going to be quite the same, not anymore. And for reasons that seemed to be historical, if not inexplicable, life, as it has invariably proceeded, was about to become far more real. And for some unearthly reason, I fell asleep thinking about clowns, once again.

Well, forgetting about clowns, or maybe not, and returning, once again, to the transitional life of our marital couple, things did, in fact, take on a more serious turn, and some of those things did, on occasion, quite a few occasions, seem to become uncomfortably real. Even the move, which did not involve a lot of things, because they did not have a lot of things, proved to be really difficult, because, as hereinbefore noted, they did not have a car. So on each occasion, in which they decided to move some of their things, they had to walk or, alternatively, take a bus, which, incidentally, surprised most of the passengers, because they had never seen anyone move their things, from one location to another, on a bus. Even with those logistical difficulties, however, it actually took our relocating couple no more than three or four days to move into that inelegant, one-room efficiency, but of even greater consequence, it took them no more than three months to move out!

In between was probably the most miserable ninety days of my overachieving life, at least up to that point, which, under the circumstances, seems to be rather ironic, because I don't ever remember being that miserable while growing up in my hometown. And as you may recall, because of a certain amount of repetition, I never particularly liked it there, which is the reason . . . absent a certain amount of others, which have already been set forth in the preceding pages . . . why I ultimately ended up, after a lot of academic and social machinations, over a period of eleven years, in that disgusting place, meaning, of course, that one-room efficiency!

If that had not been ironic, it certainly would have been tragic, and, maybe, that is really the larger story here. Maybe there is something tragic about someone who happened to be so dissatisfied with his life growing up, and with those around him, while doing so, that he took great measures to change everything, in almost every way, and he became even more dissatisfied for having done so.

Well, looking on the brighter side, which always seems to be an historically important thing to do, that miserable situation or that residence, whichever way that you want to look at it, turned out to be only temporary. What's more, with another nod to historical importance, it is obvious or, maybe, not so obvious, that making those kinds of changes, which some may call "life-changing" in nature, often involve a certain amount of risk. And where there is risk, great or not, there is, inherent therein, the possibility of failure, even though that possibility may be only temporary. And it is not too difficult to understand that failure of any kind, even of a temporary nature, can often be quite miserable, sometimes tragically so, no matter how much one may conceivably grow from having overcome it.

Nevertheless, I have always believed that the greatest tragedy in life was the failure to try, especially if it was over a significant period of time, or, even worse, over a lifetime, even though "trying" may well result in a certain amount of misery, on occasion, because of the possibility of failure. In this instance, it is certainly true that my continuing effort to change my circumstances, growing up in the repressive culture of a rural "backwater," by going to college over a prolonged period of time, elsewhere, may well have resulted in the eventual rental of a one-room efficiency that I could arguably afford, but that I certainly could not stand! The alternative, of course, would have been to stay home for the rest of my repressive life, in that stultifying rural culture, which would have been, in my humble opinion, giving up the promise or, at least, the possibility of becoming something more, somewhere else.

That effort, that continuing effort, in and of itself, seemed to have distinguished me at the time from much of my hometown and many of those who inhabited it, and, in my not so humble opinion, continue to inhabit it. And that fact, that distinguishing fact, made all the difference in the world, my world, at least. It was, if you do not mind a bit of repetition, the reason why I left home to go to college, miles away, in the first place. By doing that, I left behind what I found to be a suffocating existence and a resignation that defined many of those who still lived there.

CHAPTER XXXV

AMERICAN UNIVERSITY LAW SCHOOL, THIRD YEAR: LIS HAS "MORNING SICKNESS" ON A BUS, SLEEPING PROBLEMS IN THE LATTER STAGES OF HER PREGNANCY AND TOO FEW MATERNITY CLOTHES

RESIGNATION, OF course, was never part of the life of a young lady, who was capable of walking away from everything that she had once known, after just six weeks, in order to invest in the life of a "budding" young lawyer from another country, by marriage, among a number of other unpredictable things. And that defining characteristic of risk did not change over the course of a complicated first year of marriage, or even of an unplanned pregnancy thereafter. Indeed, at no point during that challenging period of time did the young lady find anything about her marital or motherly situation to be at all uncomfortable, but it is certainly true, in a more limited manner of speaking, that she did experience a certain amount of discomfort in the latter stages of her pregnancy. And sleeping every night on a narrow, foldout cot, with a plywood board underneath, substituting for an inadequate mattress, didn't help very much, either. It was difficult to find a comfortable way to sleep on a board!

The lack of sleep also made it difficult for Lis to continue working, but she continued, even in those challenging circumstances, to make contact lenses, right up to, and until, the last several days of her pregnancy. Getting to work, however, did pose a continuing problem, because she usually felt sort of queasy in her stomach, while riding on the bus to work, often without air conditioning and in the early morning summer heat. It also didn't help that she had to run, nearly every morning, to catch the damned thing.

Invariably, she would have to ask the driver to pull over to the curb, shortly after the bus began moving, having now become rather nauseated, as a result of the run, the heat, the rocky motion and the gas fumes, so that she could quickly get out and "throw-up," normally in the gutter, right beside the curb. Because she usually took the same bus, at about the same time in the morning, nearly every morning, with the same bus driver, not to mention the same passengers, he would ordinarily try to save a seat for her, up front, right behind him. That way, she could easily let him know when it was necessary to stop the bus, so that she could get out and throw up, in order to avoid doing so in the bus. Not surprisingly, when she came home from work on those challenging days, the young "mother-to-be," ordinarily the very definition of stoic, often said that the whole regurgitating scenario, off of the bus, early in the morning, day-after-day, was "humiliating," especially because of the presence of the other regular passengers.

Putting aside, for the moment, buses and heat and queasy stomaches, not to mention overly concerned bus drivers and disbelieving morning passengers, I often wondered at the time if wearing the same four dresses to work, on an ad seriatim basis, week after week, was also humiliating, but Lis never complained about that at all. She was just grateful to have that many summer maternity dresses, which, by the way, had been made by her mother, months ago, in anticipation of the remainder of her daughter's pregnancy.

Actually, notwithstanding her lack of wearing apparel, Lis never complained about much of anything that summer, even in relation to her pregnancy, except, possibly, the summer heat, especially on those days in which the temperature became unbearable in the metropolitan area, which, of course, was compounded by our lack of air-conditioning. But if you knew Lis at all, a subject that I have never mastered, over a lifetime, too, that stoic way of being was not at all surprising. Lis has rarely ever complained about anything, at any time, in almost any situation, a circumstance that, I may add, has never changed over the course of our lives together, now numbering over sixty years. She was, and continues to be, a consummate realist, who deals well with any kind of a situation, no matter how challenging it may be, or, eventually, become, which is certainly an indicium of a lot of character. And that uncomfortable situation, in that horrendous one-room efficiency, while she was hugely pregnant, amidst the heat and humidity of a classic summertime in the Nation's Capitol, without air conditioning, required a lot of character, and, trust me, the girl had, and continues to have, a lot of character, real character!

In that respect, I have often said, privately as well as publicly, that I married "beauty," not to mention more college education than my own, a lifetime ago, and, along with it, I also got "character," a lot of it over a lot years, and I was never sure, over those years, that I wanted that much character! None of our three children, however, were ever as ambivalent about the presence of that defining characteristic in their mother. In fact, because of that characteristic, if not a consequent resilience, my older son, Court, observed, when he was no more than ten years of age, that his "mother was the hub of our family." Sagacious words from a ten-year-old, and he was not even there, not in most respects, anyway, to witness his mother's stoic resilience, during that trying period of her pregnancy, which was spent, as I have now repeatedly pointed out, in that miserable one-room-efficiency, trying to survive in the heat and humidity of a classic summer, without air-conditioning, in the metropolitan area.

CHAPTER XXXVI

AMERICAN UNIVERSITY LAW SCHOOL, THIRD YEAR: THE ASSISTANT DEAN'S ANNOUNCEMENT, IN CLASS, THAT I WAS ABOUT TO BECOME A FATHER; THE AGONIZING TRIP TO THE HOSPITAL; THE DELIVERY ROOM SAGA; THE CORPORATIONS EXAMINATION THAT FOLLOWED, AND THE BIRTH OF MY OLDER SON, COURT EDWARD GOLUMBIC

THANKFULLY, ALL pregnancies seem to come to an end, including that one, and with that, Court Edward Golumbic, my older son, was born on October 1, 1964. That auspicious occasion occurred approximately nine months after my wife's primary care physician implicitly announced, at an examination in his office, that I would be approaching poverty by the end of something called a gestation period. Moreover, he also implicitly announced that my situation at that time would become no different from that of my parents, and, in addition, that my life, because of another life, which would become part of my life, would never be quite the same!

Because of those announcements, implicit as they may have been, and the impending economic doom predicted thereby, which would invariably result from the birth of something that had decided to torture me over a nine-month period, I was not particularly excited about what was going to inevitably happen, at the end of that gestation period, which, of course, would occur on October 1, 1964.

Well, excited or not, the inevitable did happen, as it usually does, and it . . . a baby boy . . . decided to pick that date to get itself born. A photograph of Court, after his appearance had improved, years later, has been included as Exhibit 107 in the Appendix.

Actually, the birth of my older son had its inauspicious beginning, for me, at least, in a class on corporations on that very day. Midway through the class, in which the professor was discussing what, in all likelihood, would be on the five-hour final examination, scheduled to be given on the following day, the assistant dean of the law school opened the door and, as the class fell silent, looked directly at me and said, with a wry smile on his face, "Golumbic, you're wanted at home; your wife is going to have a baby; and she wants you to go home and drive her to the hospital!"

As soon as he was finished with that announcement, the whole class erupted in laughter, and almost immediately thereafter, they began clapping, in a rather animated fashion, I should add. It was then, in the midst of that spontaneous outburst, over my impending economic doom . . . referred to by me, in brighter moments, as the birth of my older son . . . that I formed a life-long opinion of the rest of the legal profession: namely, that you can't trust the "bastards," because they may, in fact, laugh and applaud on occasion over your impending misfortune!

In any event, once I reached home in our little, dark green, Volkswagen "beetle," circa 1963, which was our only car at the time, but certainly not our only debt, Lis . . . the prospective mother of my impending misfortune . . . met me outside of our garden-style apartment at 8668 Piney Branch Road, in Silver Spring, Maryland. The two of us had moved into that apartment, approximately three weeks prior thereto, because it offered a second bedroom for our impending disaster; I mean, our impending family addition.

At the time, she was carrying a small bag, which had been packed several months ago, and which contained about everything that an expectant mother would likely need to give birth to an impending economic catastrophe, and to engage in some kind of a labor to destroy my happiness, or what remained of it, anyway.

Once we were comfortably seated in our little car, or, more likely, uncomfortably seated, for distinctly different reasons, by the way, we began that last fateful trip, or should I more appropriately say fatal trip, historically suffered by countless victims of the French revolution, as they proceeded, step-by-step, toward that inevitable fate, which eventually awaits all of mankind. Unlike those unfortunate Frenchmen, however, who were also on their way to a mortally fateful encounter, I, at least, was not proceeding alone; I was traveling with a very pregnant Dane, who was about to introduce another Dane into this world, except this one would not be entitled to receive a Danish passport, if, and when, it decided to accompany its mother to Denmark, years later.

Meanwhile, its mother wasn't traveling anywhere, right now, except to the hospital, in order to deliver a baby and expand our family by one, in America, which, in her mind at the time, was a far more formidable enterprise! Because it was and because she had never engaged in such an enterprise before, the Danish "about-to-be-a-mother" was slightly anxious and, as we approached the hospital, she became even more so! That was quite apparent from a quick look at her hands, as I was driving, which had, somewhere along the way, become transformed into tight little balls of clenched fists, resulting from hyperventilation, according to a subsequent examination by an emergency room physician.

Interestingly, the hyperventilation came, according to the same physician, from panic. I saw some irony in that fact . . . being panicked about expanding our family . . . because if anyone should have been panicked about that expansion, it clearly should have been me! I was the one who had to shoulder all of that debt; I was the one who had to work several jobs, day and night, while I was still in law school, because of that debt. And because even debtors, like me, have to live in something that virtually screams out, every day, "your rent is due at the end of the month," I was the one who was rapidly sinking into a deeper hole, from which there did not appear to be any ready means of recovery, and, even worse, if that were at all possible, which had formerly been occupied by my parents!

What's more, at least it seemed so at the time, I had a five-hour examination on corporations the very next day, upon which my whole grade for the course would be based, and I was not even finished with my preparation. Forgetting about everything else, which, quite obviously, I could not, that was reason enough to panic! How in God's name could you expect someone to study, while his wife was continually interfering with that effort, while in labor, by constantly worrying, out loud, too, whether everything was all right with a baby that was quite obviously trying to get itself born, and that probably never even heard of corporations, and that, in all likelihood, didn't really give a damn whether you did all right, or not, on an examination on the subject!

Actually, it seemed, as I sat there in the labor room, beside my worried wife, trying to prepare for my corporations examination, that there was a vast conspiracy between my wife, who was inconsiderate enough to get herself pregnant during law school; a baby who was selfish enough to try to get itself born on the day before my examination on corporations; an obstetrician, who was insensitive enough to expect a fee for delivering a baby that I could not afford; and, finally, my corporations professor, who was thoughtless enough to schedule a final examination on the day after this whole depressing episode!

Well, in fact, it all began . . . my eventual undoing, that is . . . when the Danish "mother-to-be" thoughtlessly asked the obstetrician if I could be with her, in the labor room, so that I could keep her company, even though she knew that I had a final examination on corporations on the very next day, and that I needed that time and, probably, even more, to prepare for it. Unfortunately, the obstetrician was equally thoughtless, because, notwithstanding my strenuous objection, outside of my wife's presence, of course, he granted the request. Now I had to try to study in an overly large room, full of inconsiderate "mothers-to-be," located behind a number of curtains, who had no understanding of corporations, or examinations thereon, or the amount of silence necessary to study therefor, and who insisted upon continually announcing that they were about to give birth, or having some trouble in doing so, seemingly every few minutes.

In the case of the Danish "mother-to-be," however, the arrival of an expected miniature being, commonly referred to in more genteel circles as "a baby," was not to occur for several hours, all of which time I had to remain with her, and several other expectant mothers, in cubicles nearby, who were not fortunate enough to be joined by a husband that was about to fail a corporations examination on the following day. Realizing that fact . . . that I may fail that examination and that I may do so imminently . . . I somehow found a way to ignore what was so vociferously going on around me, and to concentrate on corporate principles, instead of maternal principles, at least until the obstetrician announced, following another one of those disturbances, which he liked to describe as examinations, that it was time for the delivery!

With that announcement, panic on the face of motherhood, or, at least, the laboring effort to become, changed into absolute terror! And with that, the circumstances in which I was trying to master the principles of corporations also changed, and rather drastically, too. That was because the maternal principal was being moved, while protesting, quite loudly, that she wanted me to accompany her, into the delivery room, which, upon our arrival, had the steely, sterile appearance of something out of an afternoon horror show, or an evening television drama, starring Count Dracula!

The real drama occurred, however, when the hospital, thankfully, refused "the mother-to-be's" request to have me accompany her into the delivery room. Now, terror, once on the face of motherhood, rapidly changed into rage, which, as the Western world could readily attest, especially in the tenth century, was not a particularly delightful response, not by a Viking, not of the Danish variety, which, by the way, had not changed much, not even in the twentieth century! Now mindful of the terrible cost to their tenth-century forebears, resulting from an enraged Viking, especially the Danish kind, the hospital officials quickly developed a more accommodating response, after consulting with their attorneys, of course, who obviously did not consult with me. Because if they had, they would have left me out of the whole production, somewhere back there in the labor room, with my corporations case book, my corporations notes, my sanity, and what little chance remained of salvaging some part of the rest of my life, or, at least, that part of my life that was about to take an examination on corporations the very next day!

Unfortunately, however, the hospital officials did not consult with me; instead, they relied upon the advice of their forebears, at least those who had survived the wrath of the Dane, and who, by doing so, had decided to choose the medieval equivalent of accommodation, which, given its nature at the time, probably explains why so many people in the English Isles now have red or blonde hair, steely blue eyes, a Scandinavian surname and a rather strong-minded disposition!

Well, because of that accommodating disposition, historically explained, the hospital, with the advice of their attorneys, moved motherhood, still in a rage, me, still objecting, and the rest of the production, including the medical component thereof, into a delivery room. The irony, in this surreal scenario, was the insistence by the hospital officials, not to mention their legal counsel, that I sign a release. Evidently, they were concerned that I may hold the hospital liable for causing me to fail my corporations examination, on the very next day, and, likely, fail out of law school, as a result!

In any event, fearing both kinds of failures, I still tried to study, even in that sterile chamber of horrors, which they called a delivery room, and even though motherhood had a disquieting propensity to continually describe, in minute detail, just how unenjoyable this whole process was . . . in Danish, may I add! By now, however, having become quite aware of my continuing efforts in that regard, even though their professional concerns were more appropriately directed to other, more maternal-like, efforts in the room, the obstetrician commented to the medical resident, who was assisting him at that point, that, in all of his years of an obstetrical practice, he had never seen anything quite like it . . . referring, of course, to my continuing efforts to study in the delivery room, even in those inhospitable circumstances. Then, in words that I have not forgotten, even now, nearly sixty years later, he added, and I quote, that I "must have ice water in [my] veins."

Obviously, the obstetrician, not to mention his medical assistant, was not facing a five-hour examination on corporations the very next day. Moreover, you would think that, at the very least, a medical practitioner could find a more suitable means to describe the husband, in these maternal circumstances, who was currently in law school and whose academic endeavors, related thereto, were now, unfortunately, taking place in such horrendous circumstances. Because of that kind of insensitivity, which has a certain amount of historical precedence in the practice of medicine, I am constrained to point out that an enormous amount of acrimony has grown up between the medical and legal professions over the years.

Nevertheless, I am more than prepared to acknowledge that the medical profession can be quite indispensable, at certain times and on certain occasions, even to an overly critical law student and his "about-to-give-birth" Danish wife. And an obstetrical member of that profession was certainly indispensable on this occasion and, especially, at that moment, because the little creature, who was trying very hard to get itself born, was confronted with a very real impediment, in the form of an umbilical cord that was tightly wrapped around its unborn neck . . . twice! Actually, that medical fact was apparently more than an impediment; it was, according to two quickly reacting members of the medical profession, "a life-threatening situation," for something that, admittedly, may not yet have been technically alive; or to put the matter in other, more recognizable, terms, that strangling circumstance threatened to prevent breathing when, in a very short order, breathing would become an imperative!

Fortunately, however, for everyone involved in this production, insensitive and sensitive, alike, and, maybe, even more importantly, at least in this instance, breathing and non-breathing, alike, the obstetrician called out, urgently, that, "the umbilical cord" was "wrapped around" the non-breathing participant's "neck, twice." Whereupon, the resident immediately cut the cord, with surgical precision, before, I should mention, its owner had entered the world and tried to take a breath. At that point, the obstetrician abruptly removed the poor little creature, with an ugly pair of forceps, from the only security that it had ever known, and if I may become somewhat philosophical about the matter, at least at this point, it would probably ever know, given that it had now joined the rest of us in an existential struggle, as Albert Camus has formerly pointed out, to exist in an "alien universe," whether the little fellow may have liked it or not! See the entirety of "The Myth of Sisyphus" by Albert Camus.

In all likelihood, the little fellow, upon being introduced into a world, described as such, took a quick look around and, very quickly, decided that he did not like it very much . . . the "alien universe," I mean . . . because he immediately began to express his displeasure, by screaming his head off, upon the realization that he had, in fact, been born and, therefore, had become a baby boy, with the name of Court Edward Golumbic, a name subsequently chosen by an exhausted, but relieved, Danish mother.

Well, the Danish mother may have been relieved, as she began to prepare for a departure from those inhospitable surroundings, normally called a delivery room, but the Danish arrival was anything but relieved, and he made that fact known, by continuing to scream. Since he had not yet had an opportunity to master either the English or Danish language, not by that point, anyway, we were left to wonder why the little fellow was that upset, aside from, possibly, some very real existential issues, enunciated in "Being And Time," by Martin Heidegger, involving man's untenable situation on this earth, which, unfortunately, the little fellow probably did not have an opportunity to read at that point.

Actually, his existential anguish, or his insistence upon continuing to scream, whichever you may prefer to call it at that point, could have been for a number of other reasons. Being a Dane, or, at least, a half-Dane, he may not have liked the spelling of his first name, "Court," even though it was a Danish name, but it had been misspelled, in order to capture the Danish pronunciation of "Kurt"; even more likely, he may have actually been ill-disposed toward the Danes, like the whole western world before him, especially in the ninth, tenth and eleventh centuries, because of their brutality, depicted in the "Icelandic Fables," over a period known as the "Dark Ages in European History; or he may not have liked the spelling of his surname, "Golumbic," because it was a Jewish surname that had been misspelled, because his paternal great-great grandparents were probably illiterate; or he may have been a "closet," or, rather, an "in-utero," anti-Semite; or, perish the thought, he may have had some objection to his male gender, because the only member of the human family with which he had any real association at that point was his mother, a strident feminist, who had nine months of exclusive association, in which to persuade him of the merits of her gender's cause; or, more likely, he may have been loath to join a family so deeply in debt, with every indication of becoming even more so!

Then, again, there was always the possibility that, as a matter of social conscience, not unlike that of his "do-gooder" mother, he simply may not have wanted to join a world in which injustice and poverty seemed to have reigned nearly everywhere. Indeed, if he had not been uncomfortably aware of those worldly facts beforehand, while securely encased in a uterine environment, I am certain that he became well aware of their possibility when his comparatively secure circumstances were rudely interrupted by a pair of ominous-looking forceps, acting, rather abruptly, as a delivery agent, into a world where forceps would become the least of his problems.

The forceps, by the way, left a very noticeable dent in the little fella's head, which, by the way, appeared to be somewhat misshapen, but which the resident assured us would blossom out, likely with time and one of God's infrequent miracles. Apparently, that reassurance was issued, because of the apprehensive look on the face of both parents, while a nurse was counting the number of fingers on each hand and the number of toes on each foot. At the time, I could not speak for "motherhood," who now looked visibly alarmed in the midst of that count, but I was already wondering what kind of a return policy the hospital had, and if it was defined by hours, weeks or even months. Certainly, there must have been some kind of an implied "warranty-of-fitness," and, frankly, studying the 'little fella,' once again, following his worldly entrance, I thought that we might have some real issues there. I mean, he really looked like a drowned rat, or, at least, what a drowned rat was likely to look like. That appearance made me wonder, for the first time, whether the obstetrician had agreed in his employment contract to deliver something reasonably human, and whether, as a result, I had some kind of an action for "breach-of-contract."

Naturally, I didn't share any of my lawyerly concerns with the mother of this pathetic-looking waif, who was maternally exhausted, likely because of the whole ordeal, but who was now sort of beaming, while recuperating in the recovery room. Looking down at her, lying there, speechless, but smiling, I realized that it was likely the first time, during that whole ordeal, if you want to call it an ordeal, that I thought about anything other than the possibility of failing my corporations examination on the following day. Now, however, while looking down at my Danish wife, who had just turned into a Danish mother, and who projected, as always, that constantly optimistic demeanor, no matter in what kind of a situation, or how dire the circumstances, it struck me, probably for the first time in my conflicted life, that it was possible that I may never fail, no matter in what kind of a situation or how dire the circumstances, because I had been wise enough to hitch my wagon to a radiant star!

I don't remember what I did following my departure from the recovery room. I don't even remember how I did on the corporations examination on the following day, or if I even took it, but I can't imagine that I did not, and I must have done all right, because I am retired now, after having been practicing law for nearly thirty years. I do remember, however, calling my parents, to tell them that they were now grandparents, and that their grandson's name was Court Edward Golumbic, and that we chose Edward, as a middle name, to honor my father. I also told them that Lis had chosen the first name, "Court," because she wanted a Danish name, and because we had met a Danish physician, at a party, several months ago, whose first name was "Kurt," but pronounced, "Court," in Danish, and that we both liked the Danish pronunciation, so she chose it, or, at least, our misspelled version of the Danish name. Unfortunately, I don't remember much about the conversation that followed, other than, like most conversations with my parents, it was not very long, not because of the cost, but because we never really had very much to say to each other, even in circumstances like that.

What I do remember, however, following the conclusion of that conversation, and I remember that quite well: Before leaving the hospital, although somewhat fatigued by the day's events, I, nevertheless, decided to walk around the corner and down the hall to the nursery, which, of course, was located on the same floor, just a short distance away, so that I could look at the little fellow, who had now become our son, no more than a half-an-hour ago. Arriving there, within minutes, I asked the nurse, who was on duty, just inside the glassed-in nursery, to point out which one of the tiny babies, sleeping peacefully there, was Court Edward Golumbic. Without any hesitation, she immediately walked over to a crib, located right in front of me, which allowed me to easily see where she was pointing, and to whom.

There, sleeping quite soundly, after the enormous ordeal of getting himself born, was the little fellow, now quite oblivious to the world around him, including his father, who was now quietly standing there, intently looking down at him. And for the first time, I began to study his features, in much the same manner that I have done so over the rest of our lives together, now numbering over fifty-nine years at this writing.

Initially, they did not seem to be any different from the features on all of the other babies, who were also sleeping rather soundly there, in that nursery. He . . . because, by now, the formerly misshapen little creature had become a "He" . . . had sort of a pinkish complexion, with just a little tuft of blackish hair on the back of his head, and features that seemed to be quite tiny, not unlike that of the other babies sleeping there. Then, something inexplicable happened, almost instantaneously, while I was standing there, which was beyond my understanding, or my ability to explain, even now. The baby, lying there, peacefully in a crib, among all of the other babies sleeping there in a crib, too, became a boy, albeit a baby boy, who was extraordinarily beautiful, more beautiful than any baby that I had ever seen before, including those sleeping comfortably nearby, even though he looked just like them. After all, he had, in that instant, become my son, an inexplicable phenomenon that has not changed over the course of our respective lives together!

I also remember thinking, as I looked down upon that tiny little person, who was sleeping there so soundly, and who was covered almost entirely by a hospital blanket, that my life and, maybe, even the lives of those in my family who have preceded me, in previous generations, or who may follow me, in future generations, known and unknown, are wrapped up in that blanket, too. I'm not sure that I fully understood the consequences of such a conclusion at the time, but I am sure that it was at that time that I began to think about it, even though it would eventually take me a lifetime to fully appreciate most of it. If however, that appreciation had not come to pass, at least at some point in my life, I can certainly tell you that I would not have written the rest of this account!

I can also tell you that, standing there, immediately in front of that nursery, looking down at my present, my future, and my past, all wrapped up together, in one blanket, one baby, and so many lives, including my own, over so many generations, I began to realize that I was not confronting the limitations of my past, in what appeared to be presently wrapped up in that blanket, but the opportunities of my future, largely because of those who were part of my past.

I also began to realize, while standing there, looking down at that tiny person, that someday, probably sooner than later, I would likely take up the limited circumstances of my forebears, which constitute so much of my past, and walk with it and with them, silently by my side, into almost everything that I may do, and become, for the rest of my life, and so, too, would my new-born son, and his son and their sons!

See the photographs of Court, when he was just a young boy, ranging from a few months to nearly two years of age, which are part of Exhibit 118 in the Appendix.

CHAPTER XXXVII

*AMERICAN UNIVERSITY LAW
SCHOOL, THIRD YEAR: GRADUATION;
AUNT NORMA AND UNCLE CALVIN
AND RELIGIOUS DIFFERENCES
WITHIN MY FAMILY*

MY GRADUATION from law school was rather an uneventful occasion, although I do remember being somewhat grateful for the end of a study that I did not particularly enjoy. Naturally, I did not mention that fact to my parents, who had traveled all the way to Washington, D.C., to attend the graduation ceremony of their only son . . . from law school, no less. My Uncle Calvin Golumbic, for whom I was named, and my Aunt Norma, his wife, also attended. They specifically asked if they could, and although I would have preferred that they did not, I did not let them know that fact, so they came. See the photographs of me at my law school graduation in Exhibit 117 in the Appendix.

I cannot give you a reason for wanting to exclude my Aunt and Uncle, or my continuing discomfort in associating with them, other than a religious one, which may or may not have been a justifiable reason, and which likely depends upon your particular perspective. Mine had less to do with religiosity than its institutional manifestations. I find, for example, institutional Judaism, and its orthodox observation, no more comfortable than its Christian counterparts. On the other hand, I find religiosity to be part of the human experience, encountering that which is beyond description, or even comprehension, just awareness, which, in my case, arose, as a young boy with a fly rod in my hands, while fishing in the headwaters of mountain streams . . . for more, sometimes, than just a trout.

The philosophic, if not theological, understanding of what I encountered in those circumstances, if encounter be an appropriate description, is inclusive, available in the human experience, while its institutional counterparts have always seemed to be exclusive. It is probably for that excluding reason that I have always avoided religious institutions, not to mention those who participate in them.

Armed with this reasoning or, possibly, philosophy, if you prefer that word choice, I was initially reluctant, because of their religiosity, institutionally defined, to visit my Uncle Calvin and Aunt Norma in Bethesda, Maryland, even though I was going to law school in nearby Washington D.C., and they invited me, repeatedly, when they discovered that fact. By that time in my life, I had decided, based on my familial experience, that religious differences among family members, institutionally so, should be avoided, if possible, and, if not, those with the differences.

All of that changed, however, following my marriage to the Dane, who liked the concept of family, because of her own family, and who decided, therefore, to like mine, too, all of them, irrespective of religious differences, not excluding their institutional observance. I didn't object to her interest in my immediate family, consisting of my father and mother, even though there were, ostensively, religious differences between them, because those differences, to the extent that they may have existed, had not become institutional and, therefore, problematic for me, philosophically speaking, if nothing else.

My mother was essentially an orphan when she grew up, and, moreover, she was without any brothers or sisters in adulthood. Therefore, there were no religious problems with her extended family, because, essentially, they did not exist. I was always aware, however, that my father's extended family could eventually become a problem, essentially because of religious considerations, philosophically mine and institutionally theirs. And I had spent a conscious part of my life trying to avoid those problems, by trying to avoid those in my father's family who were part of those problems. That became somewhat difficult now, because of my wife's newfound interest in my family, all of my family, including the problematic part, who were religiously different and, in most cases, observantly so.

So after avoiding those members in my extended family who were religiously different, for years, because of a perception that the difference may become a problem, as a result of their institutional limitations, I was now constrained by my wife's innate sense of decency to confront the problem. And, amazingly, after years of avoiding the problem, which, in reality, was the religious difference within my family, if not those in my extended family who were religiously different, I no longer consider that difference to be a problem, but somewhat of a defining characteristic of who I am!

CHAPTER XXXVIII

AMERICAN UNIVERSITY LAW SCHOOL, THIRD YEAR: MY SUCCESSFUL STUDY FOR THE DISTRICT OF COLUMBIA BAR EXAMINATION IN THE LIBRARIES AT MARJORIE WEBSTER JUNIOR COLLEGE AND THE UNIVERSITY OF MARYLAND

I MAY have graduated from law school and appropriately celebrated that fact with my family, and even with my extended family, at a graduation ceremony, whether I liked it or not, but I was still one monumental examination away from becoming a licensed lawyer. So I enrolled in a bar review course, which was taught by an elderly lawyer, known by generations of law school graduates as "Nacrelli," because that was what most law school graduates seemed to be doing, or have done, in order to pass the bar examination given by the District of Columbia. It was generally believed by most of those law school graduates, present and past, that Nacrelli had become virtually omniscient, at least in his ability to predict the subject matter on the bar examination, not to mention the kinds of questions on that subject matter, and, would you believe, even some of the actual questions!

Accordingly, for recent law school graduates, like myself, who were faced with three days of a grueling examination, consisting of essay questions for six hours each day, that ability to predict the subject matter, let alone the nature of the questions related thereto, if not some of the actual questions, themselves, approached the omniscience of a supreme being, and we treated the man accordingly. In short, we paid his exorbitant bar review fees, willingly, even though, in my case, it meant that I could not afford to eat for the six-week duration of the course. But how can you compare the mundane act of eating to a license to practice a Godly pursuit, or the law, if you prefer less divinely inspired metaphors, acquired only after you pass the bar examination in your local jurisdiction? And, for that matter, you are, to your knowledge, the first member of your family, in over two thousand years, to do so. With all of that in my mind, especially the two thousand years, I knew that I owed it to my family, not to mention to our history and, maybe, even to posterity, to starve for six weeks, in order to pass that bar examination!

Apparently, Bud Menaker felt the same way, because he took that bar-review course, too. So we often drove into the District of Columbia together, to attend the lectures, given three days a week, by, you know, the most important prognosticator since the Oracle at Delphi, over twenty-five hundred years ago, in ancient Greece! When the lectures were over, however, Bud and I went our separate ways to prepare, by way of serious study, for the next bar review class. I don't know where Bud did his preparation, but I did mine in the library of the Marjorie Webster Junior College, during the week, where I was still teaching four classes a semester. In between, before and after, those classes, however, I and my bar-review materials retreated to the college library, for some serious study, at least eight hours every day, not to mention every evening.

On the weekends, however, I usually drove our only automobile, a dark green Volkswagen "beetle," as you may recall, to the University of Maryland, which was only a few miles away in Adelphi, Maryland. There, I did my bar-review study in the rare book room on the eighth floor of the University Library, which accommodated at the time a lot of rare books, a lot of silence and, because of the absence of anything else, a lot of me. For the rest of the time, which was when normal people were normally asleep, I lay awake, cursing my fate as the standard-bearer for my challenging family, in what ultimately may prove to be a futile attempt to escape its academically-challenged history, by achieving a license for a little bit of legal posterity, if not skullduggery.

To achieve any form of legal posterity, while forgetting about the accompanying skullduggery, I had to pass that bar examination, and, as it turned out, I had to do it with hardly any sleep the night before the first day, probably because of a reasonable amount of apprehension about whether legal posterity, with or without the skullduggery, may be beyond my reach, even with the assistance of a modern-day Oracle of Delphi. I did sleep on the nights before the second and third days, however, although somewhat fitfully, probably because of the exhaustion resulting from my lack of sleep before the first day, not to mention the stress occurring during the examination days, themselves. Nevertheless, sleep or not, I had to write a lot of essays each day, for six hours each day, for three days during that week, without the assistance of the Oracle, may I add.

After the first day of writing answers, non-stop, to all of those essay questions, many of which did not seem to conform at all to Nacrelli's predictions, I was sure that I had failed, miserably, at the end of the day. I can't remember much about the second day, on the other hand, other than there was nothing particularly memorable about the day and, therefore, worth remembering about it, probably because of its similarity to the first day. By the evening, however, after finishing two grueling days of writing answers to all of those essay questions, I really didn't care how I would do on the third day of that examination. I just wanted the whole thing, the whole damn examination, to be over, and, then, six hours later, on the following day, which, of course, was the last day, it was!

Days later or, maybe, it was really months, I can't really be sure, anymore, I began to think, upon reflection, that there was very little chance that I actually could have passed that examination. Any doubt about that fact, and I really had very little, was subsequently cured by a review of the failure rate on prior examinations, which exceeded, in some years, fifty percent! For that dire reason, predictably personified, I decided to spend the next several months thinking of alternative means of employment, not temporarily, but for the rest of my professional life. And toward that end, I eventually settled on becoming a waiter, probably because I had been a waiter for nearly all of the years in which I had been a college student, nearly twelve of them to be exact. So I knew that I could keep the proverbial, "wolf-from-the-door," so to speak, if I had to; I would simply work, once again, as a waiter. What's more, every premier restaurant in the country would likely be bidding for my services, because none of their other waiters were likely to have nearly as much education. I would likely even become a novelty; people would probably travel for miles around, even from nearby states, just to see the dumb waiter who failed the bar examination!

There was, however, one major problem with that hypothetical solution, and I had married it. The problem was that the Dane did not leave a family in Denmark, whom she loved, to marry a dumb waiter, who had failed the bar examination in America. Because of that fact, it occurred to me that I may not only become a dumb waiter, who failed the bar examination, but a rather lonely one at that, because my wife may well have decided to return to Denmark, in that event, to find one that passed!

My table-waiting rumination was dashed, however, by a telephone call, late one afternoon, several months later. In that call, a friend of mine, who was a law clerk for a federal judge who was also a bar examiner, called to inform me that my name was on a list of those who had passed the bar examination, which had not yet been, but soon would be, released. To say the least, I was really surprised that I had passed, which is one of the greatest understatements that I have ever made over the course of my understated life. I was not surprised by the telephone call, itself, however, because I had known that young lady, quite well, during law school. Still, she was certainly not under any obligation to make that call. Nevertheless, for whatever reason, friendship or something else, she did, and I was grateful for that fact!

Actually, now that I think about it, I'm not sure that the word "grateful" really captures how I felt at the time. Although I was most certainly grateful and, at the same time, relieved, my feelings, generated by that telephone call, were far more complicated, because, prior thereto, I did not believe that I had passed that bar examination. But I did pass and, maybe, by doing so, I had really passed something more than a bar examination. Maybe I had really passed an examination that was all about myself, at least in part, and, at least, up to that point. Maybe I had passed through an undefined, but eminently personal, barrier, which stood between someone, who had now become someone else. And maybe that person, the latter one, I mean, had now become capable of passing that bar examination and, thereby, licensed to practice law!

CHAPTER XXXIX

FIRST JOB: CONGRESSIONAL OFFICE; I BEGAN MY FIRST JOB, AS A LAWYER, AS A LEGISLATIVE AIDE IN A CONGRESSIONAL OFFICE

IN THE end, however, I wasn't quite sure, not about any of those things, which is the reason why I tried so hard to find a job, my very first job as a lawyer, which might go a long way toward dispelling some of that doubt. Oh, sure, I also needed the money, too, because I had now become the sole support of my family, but make no mistake about it, my primary concern was something far more important to me than money. And I did not forget that fact in every job interview that I had, which, of course, was toward that end. Indeed, it was essentially the reason why I accepted an offer by Congressman Herman Schneebeli, the Minority Leader on The Ways and Means Committee, to work as a Legislative Aide in his Office on Capitol Hill.

Applying for the position, which I didn't know was open, was much like taking the bar examination, because I really did not believe that I had much of a chance of being hired, for what seemed like a very prestigious position. But, then, it always seemed that people, like me, who came from where I did, never seemed to have much of a chance for anything . . . worthwhile, that is. And if they wanted to change all of that . . . who they were, where they had come from, and what was possible as a result . . . they had to take chances, and I did, in that instance and in so many others, before and afterward.

That, in my not-so-humble opinion, was a defining characteristic of whom I was: I was someone who had taken chances, all of my life, or, at least, that part of it that I had already lived, anyway.

Well, to my great surprise, Congressman Schneebeli decided to take a chance on me. Oh, it wasn't because of my overwhelming record, or my charismatic personality, or even my stunningly good looks, although none of those factors was probably going to hurt me. But it was apparently for other, more practical, reasons, likely of a more political nature, which was often true in life, especially in the workplace, and especially in the political workplace. As it turned out, the Congressman and I belonged to the same national fraternity, when we were in college, Theta Delta Chi. Of course, he had preceded me in his college days, by about thirty years, and I didn't go to Dartmouth College, either. But I had discovered, some time ago, from my fraternity magazine, which was distributed to nearly every member across the country, twice a year, that one of our more illustrious "brothers," happened to be Congressman Herman Schneebeli. So I wisely noted my membership in that fraternity on my resume, under the heading, "Activities," and, not surprisingly, Congressman Schneebeli noted that "activity," which, of course, was our joint membership in that fraternity, while reviewing my resume during the interview. In fact, he even said, "I see that we are members of the same fraternity."

Moreover, of no less importance, my voting district also happened to be the same as his, when I was growing up in Lock Haven, Pennsylvania. Indeed, my hometown was only about thirty miles away from his larger hometown of Williamsport, Pennsylvania. He didn't say anything about those facts, but he certainly could see them, because I had very clearly noted my hometown address at the top of my resume. Actually, now that I think about it, he did ask me if I was familiar with a number of his friends, who lived at the time in Lock Haven, which, of course, was part of his voting district. It was obviously very important, in my subsequent hire, that I had grown up in, and was familiar with, his district, and that I knew many of the people who still lived there.

Finally, I am sure that the Congressman must have noted, at least by the end of that interview, that I was a lawyer, or, at least, that I had just passed the bar examination. And lawyers, even of a fairly recent vintage, were ordinarily quite useful in a Congressional office, especially where the Congressman was, like Mr. Schneebeli, the Minority Leader on the Ways and Means Committee. For that legitimate reason, I set forth my law school graduation date and my membership in the District of Columbia Bar on the very first page of my resume. And although I can no longer remember doing so, I must have done it in boldface type, with underscoring in red ink, and with, possibly, an exclamation point at the end. So that there still could not be any confusion about those salient facts I probably left the rest of that page blank.

Well, I don't remember Congressman Schneebeli saying anything about the page, or the profession, or about anything else on my resume, other than what I have already pointed out, which, of course, related to our mutual membership in the same fraternity. I also don't remember him saying anything that was unrelated to my resume, which was of any particular significance, in a rather nondescript interview, defined more by its brevity than anything else, other than I could have the job, if I wanted it, which, of course, said a lot, because I did!

CHAPTER XL

FIRST JOB: CONGRESSIONAL OFFICE;
THE DIFFICULT SECRETARIES;
ROBERT BAER COHEN AND HIS
WIFE; PHILADELPHIA POLITICS AND
STUDENT VOLUNTEERS

I REALLY can't say a lot about my job in Congressman Schneebeli's Office, once I began to work there, other than to say that it was generally office work, in which I responded to letters, did some other administrative work and reviewed, on occasion, some tax journals, in order to brief the Congressman on some of the pending tax legislation. Other than reviewing the tax journals, as well as briefing the Congressman, the rest of the work was rather mundane and, generally, quite boring, and the boring part didn't change much, not for months. For those perfunctory reasons, among a number of others, I guess that you could safely say that I had a very prestigious position, as a legislative aide, for a number of months, in a very prestigious office of a very prestigious Congressman, who was the Minority Leader on the prestigious Ways and Means Committee, in which I generally did secretarial work of a very mundane nature.

Moreover, my associates in that office were a group of elderly women, who had made a career out of working on "the Hill," and who would have made a school of piranhas jealous over their ability to devour any poor creature that happened to get in their way. Thinking of piranhas, not to mention their way of being, I made sure to stay out of their way . . . the elderly women, I mean!

Toward that end, I poured over the Congressional Quarterly, which listed job openings in other Congressional offices, and I listened, carefully, to office gossip, especially in those offices, for the same reason. It was by way of the former medium that, to my amazement, I discovered that Robert Baer Cohen, with whom I had grown up in my hometown, was running for Congress on the Republican ticket in the Fourth District of Pennsylvania. So thinking of piranhas, as well as opportunities, elsewhere, I asked the Congressman, if I could temporarily leave his office in order to work in the Cohen campaign, without, I may add, even asking Cohen if he wanted me.

Nevertheless, as soon as I received the Congressman's approval, in no more than a few minutes, I contacted Bob Cohen, by telephone, and asked him if he could use the assistance of Congressman Schneebeli's legislative aide, who was well connected with the Republican National Committee, from whom Bob could possibly receive some additional funding for his campaign. I also reminded him, as though I really needed to, that we had grown up together, with the implication that such childhood friendships ordinarily form the basis of a loyalty that cannot be purchased by a salary.

I am not sure whether it was funding or loyalty or childhoods that carried the day, although I suspect that it was the former, but after some further discussion, about salary, title and division of labor, he agreed to bring me "on board," as one of the managers of his Congressional campaign. He also made it clear that, in such a capacity, it would be my primary responsibility to obtain additional financial support for his campaign, if at all possible, from the Republican National Committee.

As an aside from that Congressional campaign, not to mention my newly found political ambition, I should note, at least at this point, because of its relevance, that Bob Cohen and I had gone to school together for most of our primary and secondary years. In fact, he was just one grade behind me at Roosevelt Elementary School, which was a differential that did not change all the way through junior and senior high schools in Lock Haven, Pennsylvania.

During all of that time or, if you prefer, those years, he was not a close personal friend, but someone that I knew reasonably well, not only because of our association in school, but because he lived in the same apartment house as a good friend and classmate of mine, Jan Bennett. I often thought, when I was going to school in those days, that Jan Bennett must have been the only friend that Bob Cohen had in the whole world, because, outside of Jan, the whole world, or, at least, that part of it that was going to school with us, seemed to viscerally dislike Bob Cohen.

I can't really give you a reason, other than he was Jewish, while almost everyone else in his class was not, and that seemed to be reason enough to dislike someone when we were growing up in our hometown. He was also rather bright, while almost everyone else in his class was not, and he was not terribly discreet about the difference, which probably did not endear him to those who were not, either.

I don't think that I would surprise anybody, not at this juncture, by pointing out that being different, and being disliked, probably did not create a very nice childhood for Bob Cohen. It meant that he had to engage in a fistfight, likely with any number of people, at recess or after school, sometimes, at least during those years in which he was a student in elementary school and, possibly, in some of the years that followed. Admittedly, I don't remember seeing him involved in any altercations during his first two years in high school, which may be explained at that point by a lot more discretion on his part or, possibly, a lot more tolerance on the part of his classmates. Frankly, however, having grown up in our mutual hometown, almost contemporaneously, I find both of those alternatives to be rather difficult to believe . . . even now. In any event, I can't really speak about any combative situations during his senior year in high school, because I was a freshman at the time at Northwestern University.

I can speak about his situation during my sophomore year, however, because he became a freshman that year at Northwestern University. In fact, he spent his freshman year relatively unscathed, with the possible exception of a university parking violation, for which he was suspended from school during the remainder of the spring semester of that year. That suspension, however, was an administrative problem with the University, not a personality or diversity problem with members of the student body. Given that fact, I guess that you could conceivably say that the students at Northwestern University did not seem to have a problem with their Jewish counterparts at the time, at least not enough to engage in a fight with any one of them In addition, everyone at that university was reasonably bright, Jew and Gentile alike, so that did not seem to be a reasonable basis to differentiate, or even dislike, someone, either.

Actually, Bob Cohen seemed to do rather well, academically as well as socially, among other things, at Northwestern University. In fact, I think that it is safe to say that he was rather well-liked. Certainly, he was liked well enough to join a Jewish fraternity, Phi Epsilon Pi, and to date and, subsequently, marry, Marilyn Wender, who was a member of Alpha Epsilon Phi, a Jewish sorority on campus.

Well, leaving childhoods behind . . . his and mine or, maybe, ours . . . during my first trip to Philadelphia, as a member of Bob's Congressional campaign, I discussed the campaign at that point with him, including, among other political things, the possibility of obtaining further financing by the Republican National Committee. To save money, the campaign's and my own, I stayed in a spare bedroom in his home, where he lived at the time with his two young children and "Wendy," which is what he called his wife at Northwestern and, now, in Philadelphia. Because I stayed with them, repeatedly, throughout the rest of the campaign, I became well acquainted with his family and reacquainted with him, too, by, among other things, learning about the things that had transpired in his life, following his graduation from Northwestern University.

Apparently, he had gone on to law school at the University of Pennsylvania and, following graduation, worked as an associate for a number of years in one of the larger law firms in Philadelphia. At roughly the same time, he apparently became involved in Republican politics, which meant that he developed a reasonably good relationship with Billy Meon, the Republican boss in the city. Because of that relationship and because of a certain amount of success in minor appointed positions, Bob was eventually invited by Billy to oppose Josh Eilberg, the Democratic incumbent in the Fourth District of Pennsylvania.

Because the race began to tighten after several months, following my association with the campaign, and because Cohen was becoming a legitimate threat to unseat Josh Eilberg, I was becoming more successful in obtaining funding from the Republican National Committee. And because of my success in that regard, Bob began to use me for a number of other things in the campaign, too. For that reason, I was traveling to Philadelphia, midway through the campaign, almost every week, and, by the end of the campaign, I was staying there all week, every week. And as the election neared, I also began to utilize some of my students at Marjorie Webster Junior College, as volunteers, in various capacities, on the campaign.

I even brought my wife up to Philadelphia, in the last several weeks of the campaign, to stand outside on the street corners, handing out campaign literature, every day, all day. Unfortunately, however, she hated it, everything about it, the campaign, the street corners, the other political operatives and even, problematically, Cohen, himself.

Her dislike of politics, including the political operative in this instance, began to concern me, because the campaign was really beginning to do quite well and, therefore, on a more personal level, so was I. In fact, I was beginning to think that if we really pulled this off, and upset Eilberg, maybe, just maybe, I might be able to have a real career in politics. There was every reason to believe that Cohen might hire me, possibly as an administrative assistant, heading his Washington office, or, at least, as a legislative aide, handling his committee assignments.

All of that changed one evening, however, including my politically personal ambitions, when we happened to be invited to a dinner for the Republican candidates and their wives, as well as their aides and their wives, including myself and my disgruntled wife. The keynote speaker was Governor Bill Scranton, who walked around the room, following dinner, shaking hands and talking briefly to the candidates, their aides and their respective wives. When he reached our table, Bob stood up, shook hands with the Governor, exchanged some pleasantries with him and, then, introduced my wife and myself. As I stood up to shake his hand, the Governor said, at the same time, "Cal, I've heard a lot of good things about you and your work on Bob's campaign." Before I had a chance to bask in that praise and to consider that God's imperfect universe had just politically, if not personally, improved, dramatically, that is, he turned to my wife, who was still seated, and asked, rhetorically, "is this your lovely wife"? Before I could answer, however, he smiled and extended his hand to shake hers, but the politically deaf Dane, still in a snit about her unwanted involvement in something that she detested, simply looked at him, without any expression on her face, and without rising and extending her hand to shake his.

In those awkward moments, or was it minutes, or was it really the rest of my political life, I began to see my opportunities in Republican politics, or in Pennsylvania politics, or even in politics, per se, simply vaporize before my eyes. It is amazing, isn't it, how such little things, sometimes measured in seconds, or even in minutes, take the measure of your life, or, as in this case, my brief, very brief, political life!

CHAPTER XLI

FIRST JOB: CONGRESSIONAL OFFICE; COHEN LOST THE ELECTION AND, YEARS LATER, I WAS INFORMED THAT HE MAY HAVE BEEN CONVICTED OF A FELONY AND, SUBSEQUENTLY, IMPRISONED, AND, EVEN LATER, I WAS INFORMED THAT HIS WIFE HAD DIED

I'M NOT sure that Bob Cohen would have described the loss of that election as a small thing . . . and we did lose it! And it is not by accident that I have used the pronoun, "we," in that regard, because, in many respects, most of which should be clear from what has already been recounted, the loss was mine as well. For that very personal reason, I can certainly say that it was a very disappointing election outcome and, in the end, a somewhat shocking one, too, because our polls showed that we were well ahead of Eilberg, especially near the end of that campaign, with almost every constituency, in almost every part of the district.

Those polls also showed that we had momentum, with every reason to believe that the numbers would increase in our favor, dramatically, as the election drew nearer. That they did not, in the brief time elapsing before the election, is difficult to explain. In fact, the only explanations that seem to be at all plausible, then and now, is that there was some kind of divine intervention in favor of Eilberg, not to mention his campaign, or, more likely, some kind of political chicanery on the part of the Republican Party in Philadelphia, who were apparently capable of controlling the outcome of that election, and in a manner that did not operate in our favor, either.

Well, whatever the reason, the reality was that we lost the election and that the loss certainly had a major impact on both of our lives. So in the end, Cohen and myself were left with the prospect of returning to our former lives, professionally and personally, with, I may add, a more realistic appraisal of a possible life in politics, or, if you will, God's imperfect universe.

Now armed with that political appraisal, if not a divine one, I decided, upon returning to my life in the Washington metropolitan area, that working in a Congressional office was not so bad, after all, not for the time being, anyway. So I resumed my semi-secretarial work in Congressman Schneebeli's office, mindful, of course, of piranhas and elderly "hill-women," and, yes, divine political risks. Because that work took up so much of my time, being a rather slow typist, and because politics in Philadelphia turned out to be such a disappointing, if not mystifying, experience, I did not stay in contact with Bob Cohen, a circumstance that has not changed, not over the course of our respective lives, even though, in fact, we have shared a lot of history together, some of it worth remembering.

I assumed, however, that he must have returned to his old law firm, or a similar firm, and reentered the practice of law, likely with the same enthusiasm that he had displayed in running for a Congressional office, and that, as the years passed, he probably had become a partner in a very large firm in the Philadelphia area. And I had no reason to change that assumption until about ten years later, when, by chance, I was opposing, following my reentry into the practice of law, a company represented by a large Philadelphia law firm. Following the conclusion of one of the depositions in the case, I happened to ask one of the lawyers in that firm, who was an opposing counsel, if he was acquainted with Robert Baer Cohen, who I assumed was still practicing law in that city.

The lawyer, to whom I addressed the question, paused for a few minutes while looking down at the floor, as though he was considering what to say. Just as quickly, however, he looked up, stared straight at me, with a very serious expression on his face, and said, "you know, he was convicted of extortion and sentenced to a number of years in prison."

I don't remember what I said in reply, or if I said anything in reply, because I did not know whether to believe him, or to believe that he was really mistaken, and that he was really speaking about someone else, named "Cohen." I do remember, however, that I became as uncomfortable as he appeared to be, so I changed the subject. But I have never forgotten about the conversation over the years, or about the person with whom I had grown up and with whom I had so briefly worked, as a political operative, after we were grown, in a Congressional election, which everyone believed that we would win, except, possibly, the electorate, or, possibly, some nefarious political operatives.

Years later, one of Bob's old high school classmates, who was home for a high school reunion, while I was living there with my mother and father, told me that Bob's wife, Marilyn Wender Cohen, had died, and that Bob had subsequently remarried, in the intervening years, and that he was currently living somewhere in the Philadelphia area. At the time, I briefly thought about trying to contact him, but after some further thought, I changed my mind, because some things that are part of our past should probably remain there. So after a brief moment, in which some of my more ambivalent history nearly resurrected itself, with a telephone call to Bob Cohen, I left him and the loss of political innocence, in a Congressional campaign, back there in the past, where they probably belonged, as part of my history, and what I was, not to mention what I have done in the interval, which, among other things, have served, in part, as a basis for what I would eventually become, which is, of course, what I am.

CHAPTER XLII

SECOND JOB: DENNING & WOHLSTETTER; AMBIENCE, THE THIRD REICH AND THE FIFTH GRADE

AT ONE point during my resumed Congressional work, I decided to make some significant changes in my life. In the first place, I decided to reinstate an old, but not forgotten, rule, to leave my childhood, and those who inhabited it, behind, and to avoid it, and them, like the plague, or, at least, like unsuccessful elections. In the second place, I decided to find a position in a law firm in the metropolitan area, because that is where I lived, and because you are ordinarily able to understand why you may have lost in that profession, if, indeed, you do so in a court of law. The loss was because the judge, who decided the case against you, interpreted the law, or the facts, or both, differently than you did, in, among other possible things, your memorandum of law or brief.

Finding a job practicing law in the metropolitan area, however, was no easy endeavor. It meant that I had to find something that I liked and that liked me, and, quite frankly, I wasn't sure what I liked or, just as importantly, whether I liked me, and if I was in doubt, how could I expect a law firm to be otherwise. Nevertheless, casting those doubts aside, or nearly, I certainly liked the idea of making some real money, finally, and employment, as an associate, in a law firm seemed to promise the possibility of making some real money, not excluding someone with failed political experience. Moreover, compared to the public sector, it also seemed to promise the most amount of prestige, and I wasn't above being impressed by a little bit of prestige. When you don't think that you have a lot of that quality associated with yourself, there is something to be said about subsequently associating yourself with something that does!

Prestige, of course, is usually associated with certain qualities that give rise to such a description, and those qualities were generally found, as every recent law school graduate knows, in a large, international law firm. All you had to do was interview in a couple of them, like I did, in order to realize that fact. The first thing that you noticed, upon opening the door to the lobby, was the receptionist, who could just as easily have made it "big," as they say, somewhere in Hollywood, if she had not decided upon a more conservative career, wearing more conservative clothes, while residing, so to speak, in a law firm lobby. And if she were not impressive enough, conservatively speaking, you just needed to look around at all of those opulent surroundings, even in the lobby, which was usually paneled in real wood, once having been part of a forest of walnut trees, in a national park, somewhere, which must have required a virtual army to cut down, in order to cover that much space. And let me tell you, the space was so large, just in the lobby, that the only space that I ever saw, which was even comparable in size, was one or two of our national parks, not all of them, just one or two!

Unlike our national parks, however, the space in those lobbies was filled with steers, not bears or other wild animals, just steers. Well, maybe not the whole steer, just the leather covering, which was now used to cover large inanimate objects, such as overstuffed chairs and sofas. Given the number of overstuffed chairs and sofas in those lobbies, the amount of leather necessary to cover them would have once covered a sizable amount of the cattle herds driven north, every year, from Texas to Abilene Kansas, in the late nineteenth century, for eventual sale in the stockyards of Chicago. In fact, those herds were probably relocated to those stockyards, in order to eventually decorate the lobbies in those large, prestigious law firms.

To reach the individual offices of the partners required the stamina of a long-distance runner, because they were ordinarily found down lengthy halls, measured more aptly by miles than feet, and graced on one side by museum-quality paintings, done by recognized medieval artists, and on the other side by portraits of distinguished looking gentlemen, with grey hair and impressive looking pin-stripped suits, which nobody could afford, except, possibly, the partners who worked in those kinds of law firms.

Once you reached the individual offices, assuming, of course, that you were fit enough to do so, you quickly noticed that they were individually decorated, likely by an interior decorator, and, generally, tastefully so, with walnut paneling on some of the walls, which carefully matched the paneling in the lobby, but which was nearly hidden by an endless array of diplomas from every college and law school in existence, and, possibly, by some that were not.

The bookshelves behind the desks contained rare and expensive antiques, which seemed to be unrelated to the practice of law, except that they were interspersed with leather-bound books that had everything to do with the law and leather and mystique. Looking at them . . . the leather-bound books and the rare and expensive antiques . . . you just knew that it was no accident that they stood there, on those shelves, side by side, in sort of a metaphoric manner. The use of the one, in a manner of speaking, clearly paid for the outrageous costs of the other, which meant, of course, that they were really related to one another, and, therefore, that they deserved to be residing beside one another on those bookshelves.

The desks, in front of those bookshelves, often differed, but not in historic value, which, by the way, would have made a curator envious at the Smithsonian Museum. They were often made of Santo Domingo mahogany, an ancient and rare wood, which was nearly rendered extinct, years ago, by over-logging, for those desks, naturally. Moreover, they were not just any kind of Santo Domingo mahogany desks, either, but, rather, Chippendale, eighteenth-century, slant-front desks, with "beaded" and graduated drawers, corner columns, "O G" bracket feet, original brass hardware and "stepped back" interiors, with inlaid, graduated drawers, which, along with their counterparts in other offices within the firm, had survived the ravages of time for nearly three hundred years. By doing so, and occupying a current position of great distinction and importance in the offices of partners, throughout those kind of law firms, they served to remind the occasional visitor, or client, or, likely, both, who may happen upon them, that the firms, like their desks, have origins that, in the former case, precede, in age and distinction, Methuselah, if not the Old Testament, itself.

I certainly could picture myself behind one of those impressive desks, not simply because I liked antiques, but because I was on a mission, a prestigious one, to become employed by one of those prestigious law firms. Choosing the right one, of course, could be a bit tricky. After all, if the gap between myself and the prestige was too large, I might not be able to bridge it, no matter how hard that I may have tried, and, subsequently, be discharged from the firm, likely for just that reason, so I very carefully chose a law firm that really wanted me. That way, I was able to ensure that the gap would not be too great, because any law firm that wanted me couldn't be that prestigious.

The name of the law firm that I chose, because, among other things, they chose me, was Denning and Wohlstetter, which specialized in legal work before the Federal Trade Commission. The name, itself, was certainly impressive; it just reeked of age and history and class and Episcopalian gentry, lending itself to an assumption that both Denning and Wohlstetter must have come over on the Mayflower. Later, however, I would discover that Denning was actually dead, and that Alan Wohlstetter was, in fact, Jewish. I would also discover a lot of other things about the firm, in the months ahead, that began to seem a lot more important to me than prestige, most of which turned out to be things that I really grew to dislike!

To discuss them, I'm not quite sure where to begin, because I grew to dislike so many things about the firm that addressing them all seems to be quite daunting. I suppose, however, that it is reasonably safe to begin with Alan Wohlstetter, because he really controlled the firm, even though there were other partners, and I did not particularly like the way that he controlled it. Oh, he could certainly be charming enough around clients, but not around associates, and, unfortunately, I was one of the latter. Sometimes, he even reminded me of some of my elementary school teachers, who invariably presided over a classroom in such a manner that you could metaphorically cut the atmosphere with a knife. Unlike those teachers, however, he even monitored the use of telephones by associates, and even by partners, if you can believe that, by continually noting who was on the telephone, why, and for how long. That was Alan Wohlstetter's idea of a well-run law office. Actually, with those kinds of administrative talents, he would have done well as a bureaucrat in the Third Reich. My reaction to all of this so-called administration was not good; I did not go to law school so that I could reenter elementary school or become a bureaucrat in the Third Reich!

Some of this intolerable office administration may have been more tolerable, but not much more, if the work had been at all tolerable, but it wasn't; it was mundane, arcane and mindless, and it grew even more so, every day that I had to deal with it. By work, I mean reviewing the codes for distances, rates and carriers, on a chart format, to calculate the cost basis of certain routes for certain commercial common carriers. And I mean doing it month after month, week after week, day after day, and hour after hour, broken up only by a lunch, for no more than half an hour, followed, possibly, by a clandestine telephone conversation with my wife, for no more than five minutes, of course, to assure her that I have overcome my earlier inclination to avoid all of this by jumping off of the Connecticut Avenue bridge.

If you had successfully completed fifth-grade arithmetic, you could have successfully calculated those common carrier costs. If, however, you had not successfully completed fifth-grade arithmetic, you probably still could have calculated those costs, although you may have been required to ask your fifth-grade teacher to answer a few questions, related thereto, sometimes. Well, I successfully completed fifth-grade arithmetic, I am proud to say, but I began to ask myself a lot of questions, anyway, after about four months of this interminable monotony, and they were not arithmetic in nature, either. I began to ask myself, every day, why I continued to do work that should more appropriately be done by a fifth grader. And by the sixth month of this interminable monotony, in which I had spent nearly every waking hour and nearly all of the other kind, too, trying to find a reason for staying there, I decided that there really wasn't any, unless, of course, you had failed the fifth-grade, which I had not, and, therefore, I needed to find another job, unrelated to the fifth-grade and the Third Reich, which I subsequently did.

So I gave notice, after six months of fifth-grade arithmetic, interminable boredom and a working situation that approached the life of a bureaucrat in the Third Reich, and one month later, I left! To say that Alan Wohlstetter was not pleased with my impending departure is an understatement. Apparently, I had been doing such a good job . . . as a fifth grader . . . that he had ordered a brass plaque, with my name inscribed on it, to be put on the front door, with the other names in the fifth grade, or, should I more appropriately say in that law firm. Since I was now leaving, there was no reason to put it up there, so he gave it to me, with a few disgusting comments and an inappropriate suggestion about what I may wish to do with it. Apparently, there was no historical precedent for leaving the bureaucracy in the Third Reich . . . not sanely, anyway!

By the way, I still have that brass plaque in my possession; it currently resides in the top drawer of the Hepplewhite, curly maple, slant front, eighteenth-century desk, in an upstairs bedroom. On the few occasions in which I inadvertently come across it, still in that drawer, I would always think back to those miserable days at that law firm, and how irate that man became, when I informed him that I was leaving the Third Reich. And I would typically think at the time that there was no reason for him to become that upset, notwithstanding my premature departure, because he could easily find someone to replace me. All he had to do was recruit some fifth grader at one of the numerous elementary schools in the area.

In the six months that I worked, if you want to call it that, at the law firm of Denning and Wohlstetter, I learned a lot, none of which related to the practice of law, and all of which related to the wrong way to do so. And I learned, among other things, never again to choose form over substance; nor would I ever do that again, not in any one of the remaining thirty years in which I practiced law. That lesson, alone, was sufficient to allow me to say, in retrospect, that my six-month interval spent at One Farragut Square South, which was the prestigious address of the Third Reich, was not totally wasted, because I would never again waste my time in a professional situation that was defined by anything other than the actual practice of law, and at the very highest levels. Sadly, I had to discover that such opportunities do not necessarily come in the most opulent surroundings and with the highest-paying positions!

Oh, to be sure, I would come back to Farragut Square, or, at least, the neighborhood, by the end of my career practicing law, but I would do so in quite a different manner, and in quite a different situation. Although that situation was with another law firm, even larger and, maybe, even more prestigious than the firm of Denning

& Wohlstetter, I would ensure, in that instance, that my situation was far more favorable. And by doing that, I would be able to engage in the practice of law at the very highest levels of the legal profession, even though some, but certainly not all, of the remaining practice at that firm was not always consistent with that standard . . . especially in written form.

CHAPTER XLIII

THIRD JOB: NEIGHBORHOOD LEGAL SERVICES PROGRAM; A PRACTICE IN FEDERAL COURTS AND ADMINISTRATIVE AGENCIES OF EVERY KIND, WITH DIVERSE CASES, INVOLVING POOR CLIENTS

PRIOR TO my departure from Denning & Wohlstetter, I began to engage in interviews with a number of legal organizations, private as well as public, all of whom offered me an opportunity to obtain real litigation experience, which was very important to me now. None of them, however, offered a very good salary or a very commodious office accommodation, but that was not very important to me anymore. Now I wanted to learn how to practice law in a courtroom; I wanted to learn how to be a litigator. And I had discovered that the very best way to do that was as a criminal defense lawyer or as a federal prosecutor. So I interviewed for a position with the Public Defenders Office and the United States Attorney's Office.

I also interviewed for a position with the Neighborhood Legal Services Program, which offered me litigation experience, but in a civil and administrative capacity. Nevertheless, that position also included the representation of juveniles, who were prosecuted for misdemeanors and felonies, which were really quasi-criminal proceedings in nature, although they were technically considered to be civil proceedings, because they involved juveniles under a "parens patriae" concept.

After some thought, in which I carefully weighed all of my opportunities, I really became intrigued with the idea of working for the Neighborhood Legal Services Program. The position offered me an opportunity to do work in both civil and administrative cases, as well as in quasi-criminal proceedings, in every kind of forum, including federal district and appellate courts, and even in the Supreme Court of the United States. So after considering some of the other offers to do solely prosecutorial or defense work in criminal cases, I decided to accept an offer to practice law with the Neighborhood Legal Services Program, even though I may be underpaid, and even though I may be working in a neighborhood office, located somewhere in the inner-city of the Nation's Capitol, which I learned, soon enough, would not be too far from the truth.

Actually, apart from that kind of litigation experience, there was probably another reason why I accepted that offer, which was far less apparent to me and far more uncomfortable to think about at the time. I, too, had grown up in a marginal circumstance, and in an impoverished rural area in the mountains of central Pennsylvania. Oh, it certainly was not in abject poverty, although Clinton County, where I had grown up, was, and still is, one of the poorest counties in the State of Pennsylvania. But there was always something about the culture there, if not the economic conditions, that was readily identifiable with the working poor and, for that reason, it was commonly referred to, by most sociologists, as part of "Appalachia." And my family in many ways, if not in most, was certainly part of the working poor in Clinton County, at least it certainly seemed that way, while I was growing up. And if I ever had any doubt about that fact, it certainly was eliminated, quite dramatically, once I became an impoverished, self-supporting undergraduate student at Northwestern University.

Of course, my family was not black, and, therefore, it may not have been subject to the same sociological difficulties as those generally found in some of the blighted neighborhoods in the inner city of the District of Columbia. And, of course, I would be representing those kinds of families, if not the individual members thereof, in the Neighborhood Legal Services Program. Nevertheless, for a displaced son of Appalachia, there was, ironically enough, something very identifiable, in economic and cultural terms, about those that I would be representing in the Program. The irony, of course, was that those individuals, although African Americans, living in the inner city, were not, in many respects, so different from those that I had worked so diligently to leave behind in the mountains of rural central Pennsylvania!

Amazing, isn't it! I was intrigued with the possibility of doing legal work in a program for the culturally and economically disadvantaged, at least in part, because of where I had come from and those with whom I had grown up there, even though I had just spent a significant part of my educational life trying to escape from there and them. Yet, here I was, returning home, metaphorically speaking, although, admittedly, to legally make a difference in the lives of people who were not, in many respects, so different from those with whom I had grown up, and I suppose that made all the difference to me at the time. In fact, I suppose, in some respects, that it still does.

CHAPTER XLIV

THIRD JOB: THE NEIGHBORHOOD LEGAL SERVICES PROGRAM; ITS NATURE, DIRECTOR AND DEPUTY DIRECTOR, MANAGING AND STAFF ATTORNEYS, OFFICE NUMBER EIGHT, DeCOSTA V. MASON, RHODA LACKRITZ AND MY FIRST CASE

THE NEIGHBORHOOD Legal Services Program was largely a black organization that came into being as part of the "War-On-Poverty," and that, consistent therewith, provided free legal services to poor black people, who lived in the inner-city of Washington, D.C. At least, that is what most people believed, probably because that is what they read in the newspapers, but, in fact, the organization was far more complex, organizationally, and racially.

It is certainly true that the two directors were black, or, at least, that they claimed to be. And the managers of all eight of the offices, located in the inner-city, were generally black, too, although they did not have to be. On the other hand, the staff attorneys in each one of those inner-city offices were generally white, with some exceptions, who, in the great majority of cases, graduated at the very top of their class at some of the best law schools in the country.

Instead of following some of their peers into large, prestigious law firms, throughout the country, at exorbitant salaries, they chose an opportunity to legally challenge the status quo, by, among other things, instituting constitutional and statutory litigation on behalf of those whose opportunities in life bordered on an ignoble fiction. Not only was this a noble choice, although an economically unsound one, it also provided the kind of litigation experience, selfishly speaking, that rarely occurs, even after a number of years, in a large, prestigious law firm.

So those of us who chose this "noble" path, also gained invaluable experience, while litigating major constitutional and statutory issues, often of first impression, in the United States District Court for the District of Columbia, the District of Columbia Circuit Court of Appeals, and even, on occasion, the Supreme Court of the United States. The experience, in those kind of courts, although arguably quite noble, because of the nature of the clients for whom the cases were undertaken, also became quite measurable in professional terms, if not in monetary ones, in subsequent years with subsequent employers, who were looking for that kind of experience, and that fact was not lost on any one of us.

On the other hand, the situation involving the directors and the managing attorneys was generally quite different. In most instances, they graduated from lesser law schools, such as Howard University, and as a result, large law firms were generally not interested in them at the time, notwithstanding their experience. So those positions, as directors and managing attorneys, were, practically speaking, the best jobs that they were able to secure over a lifetime, and, therefore, they treated that unfortunate fact accordingly, by, among other things, never leaving.

I really did not think very much about that unfortunate fact at the time. There were far too many other problems associated with that work, which affected me professionally, if not personally, and, therefore, occupied far more of my attention. It is different now, however, because, given my lofty position, in retirement, I think about many of those individuals, every day, who were nominally black, and who were actually my supervisors, with an enormous amount of qualifying experience. They taught me how to practice law in so many ways, and in so many forums and in so many different kinds of circumstances, as well as how to do it competently, even though, in doing so, they enabled me to obtain a future in the legal profession, which was generally unattainable for most of them at the time. And looking back now, I realize that the inherent differences in our respective professional opportunities, which were not based on legitimate criteria, were really quite distinct and quite unfair. Many of them, if not most, were excellent lawyers and very fine people, who deserved to participate, fully, in the great American dream, or should I more appropriately say, legal dream of joining a large, prestigious law firm, with larger compensation and unimpeded expectations.

A glaring example was the managing attorney at office number eight, where I began working, who, incidentally, engaged in oral arguments with a Caribbean accent, probably because he grew up on the island of Barbados. He also had a name, DeCosta V. Mason, that belonged there, too, and a sense of professional pride and responsibility that belonged anywhere, especially in the practice of law. He was, essentially, my very first real supervising attorney, who assisted me in my work in that office, which, incidentally, involved the real practice of law, especially in litigation, as opposed to fifth-grade arithmetic.

Noting, as a reminder, my six-month stint in engaging in arithmetic computations, at a fifth-grade level, for the Third Reich at One Farragut Square South, I probably don't have to remind you that I never really practiced law in any one of my two previous positions, following my graduation from law school, even though one of them was ostensibly with a law firm. So working for DeCosta Mason, at office number eight, was a real educational experience, and most of that education was provided by DeCosta, himself, who had practiced law for nearly a lifetime, before my appearance in his office, that is, which, in years, probably approximated over forty. Over that time, he had become an accomplished litigator, who, fortunately, was not bashful about sharing his knowledge, especially during trial, and we tried a number of cases together, in the juvenile court system, during my tenure in that office.

Interestingly, my very first appearance in a court of law was in the Juvenile Court for the District of Columbia, which occurred on the very first day in which I began working at office number eight. The other staff attorney in the office, Rhoda Lackritz, a Jewish attorney, who had graduated from Yale Law School, was leaving, later that day, to fly home and get married, and, by doing so, become a Burkewitz, somewhere in Connecticut. Because of that matrimonial fact, she asked me if I would attend a status conference on her behalf, in one of her cases pending in the Juvenile Court, scheduled for later that afternoon, even though I had never appeared in that Court, or, for that matter, any other court, with respect to any matter, before that time. I agreed, but with a tremendous amount of unexpressed trepidation, because I was sure, notwithstanding her assurances to the contrary, that something would go wrong at the status conference, and that I would not know enough about the case to be able to handle the problem. As it turned out, however, everything went all right, because nothing more was required of me than the presentation of a simple statement about the status of the case, which Rhoda had provided me well ahead of that time.

That appearance, in that juvenile court, on that day, my first real working day as a litigating lawyer, was likely followed by thousands of others, in a myriad of other courts, over the next thirty years, in which I practiced law in every kind of administrative agency and in every kind of federal court, trial and appellate, including, on occasion, the Supreme Court of the United States. Having now successfully reached the austere age of eighty-seven years, including some additional months and days, it is sometimes hard to believe, in retrospect, that a litigation practice that had reached those dimensions, in numbers and, more importantly, complexity, over the remaining thirty years of my practice of law, actually began with an appearance at a simple status conference in a juvenile court . . . at which I was absolutely terrified! Obviously, in the years that have followed, I gained a lot more confidence, as the result of a lot more experience, in cases of far more consequence and in forums of far greater significance!

CHAPTER XLV

THIRD JOB: NEIGHBORHOOD LEGAL SERVICES PROGRAM; PRACTICING LAW IN OFFICE NUMBER EIGHT WITH LARGE CASELOADS, THE NATURE OF MOST OF THOSE CASES, AS WELL AS FOOD STAMPS AND A CREDIT UNION ROBBERY

OFFICE NUMBER eight was located on the corner of Grant Street and Division Avenue, a poor black neighborhood located in the far northeast of Washington, D.C. The building was once part of the old Strand Theater, which had given way, long before I had arrived, to poverty and, subsequently, a legal services program to combat it. Around the corner, on Division Avenue, was some kind of a restaurant, or, at least, the people in the neighborhood called it that, which, quite frankly, served some things that I had never even seen before, and that I would never have considered eating, let alone doing so. Nevertheless, many in the neighborhood did, on one occasion or another, and paid for the privilege with food stamps, which nearly everyone in that neighborhood received, nearly every month, and which they subsequently turned into some form of currency, legally or otherwise, at that restaurant, or at a number of other commercial establishments in the surrounding area.

Indeed, the back door of our office was also the back door of a consumer credit union, which, obviously, was located in the same building, and which served as a virtual bank for anyone in the neighborhood, who was fortunate enough to be working and to be making enough money, while working, to be able to deposit some of it in a credit union. Most of the people in the neighborhood, however, were far more interested in borrowing money, because they were ordinarily not working, and due to that unfortunate fact, the credit union usually refused to loan them any money.

Some of the less fortunate, however, decided, on one eventful day, while I was busily engaged in the practice of law in my office . . . which, as you may recall, was on the other side of a common back door to the credit union . . . to take matters into their own hands, so to speak, and to rob the place! I don't believe, in retrospect, that their endeavor would have resulted in much success, economically speaking, because more people were withdrawing, or trying to do so, than depositing, in that credit union. For those sociological and economic reasons, there wasn't a whole lot of money available to steal, so even the bank robbers were generally destitute in the far northeast of Washington D.C. You just couldn't make or steal a dime, so to speak, in that neighborhood!

I will say, however, that those who, nevertheless, tried, by stealing, were often rather courteous in their wasted efforts. Indeed, in the case of a credit union heist, they made their "get-a-away," so to speak, by walking straight through the common back door into our office, down the length of our hallway and out of the front door, with guns drawn, no less, while apologizing, profusely, the whole time, for having done so!

There was also a fairly large grocery store, with an accompanying parking lot, directly across the street from our office, where I usually parked my Volkswagen, which was my car of choice at that challenging time. The grocery store was the only one for miles around, and, consequently, it was frequented by nearly everyone in the neighborhood. Since most of them were not working, or obtaining a sufficient amount of money by robbing the credit union, the grocery store accepted food stamps, too. Consequently, it did not take me long to realize, while practicing law in that neighborhood, that food stamps were an acceptable alternative to cash, or any other form of legal tender, for that matter, especially if you wanted to engage in any kind of commercial activity in that area, legally or otherwise. Since our legal services were offered without fees, I never had to confront that fact, or that problem, whichever alternative may seem more appropriate to you in this context.

My confrontations, however, were generally of a different kind, and they ran the legal spectrum, including, but not limited to, such matters as domestic relations, landlord-tenant problems, housing foreclosures, automobile repossessions, welfare fraud, bankruptcies, and Social Security claims. Actually, it was difficult to imagine any kind of a legal matter, involving civil or administrative litigation, on behalf of individuals in that neighborhood, which I did not handle as an attorney in that office. And there was always the ubiquitous defense of a juvenile in an unauthorized use of an automobile, among other more serious crimes.

In that respect, no one in the neighborhood, or very few, could afford to buy an automobile, let alone buy one for their teenage sons. And as you may know, or likely should know, all teenage boys, including those eligible to drive, want to drive, in their words, "a hot automobile." Since they did not own one, and their parents could not afford to buy them one, they usually stole one, or, in the language of more genteel legal circles, "used one in an unauthorized manner," which, if you want to be realistic about the matter, usually resulted in a lot of trial experience on my part and the beginning of a lot of criminal experience on theirs.

Because of that experience, the quasi-criminal kind, I mean, our office was ordinarily flooded with those kinds of cases, as well their civil and administrative counterparts, all day, every day. And, as a result, our caseloads were enormous and increasing enormously, every day. For that reason, among others, it was often difficult to spend the amount of time required to do anything other than resolve litigation by a successful defense on the facts. Sometimes, however, a case may present an issue, in which a collateral attack may, arguably, be made upon an underlying statute, as being, among other things, misconstrued, or even unconstitutional, instead of simply prevailing on a factual defense under the questionable statute. Because of my caseload, however, constitutional and statutory issues were not often raised, in the early years of my practice in office number eight, unless clearly required as part of a reasonable representation.

After several years of litigation, however, including jury trials nearly every other month, I began to realize that I was gaining a lot of experience at a trial level on issues of fact, but very little experience on issues of law, which were ordinarily resolved by cross-motions for summary judgment and memoranda in support thereof, at the trial level, and, more importantly, by briefs on appeal. And given my caseload in office number eight, that was not about to change, because the caseload was not about to change, other than by growing even larger, so I transferred to office number nine, where there was a much smaller caseload and, therefore, a much greater opportunity to raise issues of law, by, among other things, affirmatively challenging the constitutionality or misconstruction of underlying statutes and/or regulations.

CHAPTER XLVI

THIRD JOB: NEIGHBORHOOD LEGAL SERVICES PROGRAM; TRANSFER TO OFFICE NUMBER NINE AND THE ELIMINATION OF THE BACKLOG THERE BY USING VOLUNTEER ATTORNEYS; THE TRANSFER OF EDWARD SCHWAB AND THE ENGAGEMENT IN A NUMBER OF AFFIRMATIVE ACTIONS ON ISSUES OF LAW, WHICH, EVENTUALLY, RESULTED IN A SUPREME COURT CASE

I BECAME the managing attorney in office number nine, which, thankfully, allowed me to carry a much smaller caseload. Nevertheless, I still had to devote a significant amount of time to managerial responsibilities, which, initially, became rather time-consuming, because my predecessor allowed a more than tolerable daily legal practice to turn into an intolerable office backlog. Because of that fact, I immediately devised a means of reducing it, by utilizing a number of volunteer government attorneys, who were more than interested in representing poor people, after their working hours for their respective agencies. And I assigned cases to them, which did not involve the federal government, or otherwise pose a conflict of interests, and which they could handle with some limited supervision. By utilizing enough of those volunteer attorneys and assigning enough of our cases to them, I quickly managed to reduce the backlog in the office to a manageable level, and I eliminated it altogether within a year.

Naturally, utilizing volunteer government attorneys, who had little or no experience doing this kind of legal work, meant that I had to supervise them, sometimes rather closely, which, initially, required a lot of time on my part. In order to reduce the amount of that time, I convinced Ed Schwab, who had previously worked with me in office number eight, to transfer to office number nine, so that, at a minimum, he could assist me in that supervision.

Once the amount of time required for that supervision began to diminish, with a proportional increase in experience by the volunteer attorneys, Ed joined me, as co-counsel, in the defense of major litigation, involving statutory and constitutional issues of first impression, at trial, in the United States District Court, and, on appeal, in the United States Court of Appeals for the District of Columbia Circuit. It all began, rather innocuously, while I was representing a young man, who was charged with a traffic violation, before Judge Tim Murphy, in the old Court of General Sessions in the District of Columbia. The charge was based on a regulation that was less than clear, but it was certainly clear that the regulation did not support the charge and, moreover, I couldn't find a regulation that did, so I prepared a lengthy and well-researched memorandum in support of a motion to dismiss the complaint, because it was not based on any regulation or statute of the District of Columbia.

After reviewing the memorandum and commenting on its scholarship, in open court, no less, Judge Murphy dismissed the complaint and, in a subsequent written opinion, held that the charge was not supported by any regulation or statute of the District of Columbia, including the one relied upon in the complaint. It was not, he opined, "that the allegations in the complaint were unsupported by the facts; rather, the facts, if proven, did not constitute a violation of law under any regulation or statute of the District of Columbia."

Apparently, the Corporation Counsels Office, which was representing the District of Columbia, as the prosecutor in the case, did not disagree, on a subsequent and closer examination of the regulation upon which they had based their complaint, because they never appealed. Moreover, subsequent thereto, they have never, to my knowledge, charged anyone else in a similar complaint, based on that regulation, in the District of Columbia. Clearly, that charge, in that complaint, based upon that regulation, found itself, following that decision, discarded in the dustbin of judicial history in the District of Columbia.

With my recent success in gaining the dismissal of a traffic violation, based on the production of a lengthy and well-researched memorandum, Ed and I began to turn our attention toward similar efforts, by raising issues of first impression, resolved, as a matter of law, by cross-motions for summary judgment, in far more significant cases, many of which were constitutional or statutory in nature. In some of those cases, we were joined by Pat Wald, who would subsequently become, years later, a Judge in the United States Court of Appeals for the District of Columbia Circuit and, eventually, the Chief Judge in that Circuit.

Some of those cases involved juvenile proceedings, in which we asserted, for the first time at trial, and, subsequently, on appeal, that the right to be free from an unreasonable search and seizure under the Fourth Amendment, and the right to be free from self-incrimination under the Fifth Amendment, which were constitutionally applicable to criminal proceedings, were equally applicable to juvenile proceedings of a quasi-criminal nature under the Due Process Clause of the Fifth Amendment to the United States Constitution.

Based on our brief, as well as our oral argument, in one of those appeals, which I presented before the United States Court of Appeals for the District of Columbia Circuit, the Court ruled, in a case involving a tainted confession, that the right to be free from self-incrimination under the Fifth Amendment, applicable to criminal proceedings, was equally applicable to juvenile proceedings, because of its quasi-criminal nature, under the Due Process Clause of the Fifth Amendment to the United States Constitution.

Thereafter, the Corporation Counsels Office, which ordinarily initiated juvenile court proceedings in the District of Columbia, acknowledged that, with respect to those kind of proceedings, which were quasi-criminal nature, they were under the same kind of judicial restraint as their counterparts in criminal cases involving the Self-Incrimination Clause in the Fifth Amendment and the Search and Seizure Clause in the Fourth Amendment to the United States Constitution.

To say the least, this was a major change in juvenile court law in this country, and, significantly, that change was subsequently incorporated into every constitutional law textbook used by law schools throughout the country. And if you will excuse an inexcusable amount of pride, that fact was not lost on all three of us at the time, including Pat Wald, who, if you do not mind a bit off repetition, was subsequently elevated to the United States Court of Appeals for the District of Columbia Circuit, shortly thereafter, where she, eventually, became the Chief Judge in that Circuit!

By careful research, the preparation of an excellent brief and the presentation of a prevailing oral argument, we had done something, as very young lawyers, that few in our profession would accomplish over a lifetime. And as a matter of fact, we, now without Pat Wald, who had subsequently moved on to the appellate bench, were just getting started. In subsequently defending our clients, we raised and prevailed on issues that were never addressed in the curricula of most law schools. Although nearly all law schools included in their curricula at the time a course entitled, "creditors rights," we changed the nature of that course to "debtors rights," because, in case after case and appeal after appeal, the debtors, who were our clients, prevailed on novel constitutional and statutory arguments that resulted in law, for the first time, that favored the debtor!

We moved on to other areas of the law, too, on behalf of those individuals who, at that point, had no judicial voice on matters that affected their ability to live, let alone to live reasonably well. And, in fact, we often prevailed in those instances, too, especially where there were opportunities at trial and, subsequently, on appeal, to make law, or to change existing law, on behalf of those similarly situated. Indeed, in many of those cases, we tilted the scales of justice back to an upright, neutral position, on behalf of the nation's poor, and, by doing so, we left our mark on constitutional law for years to come.

In the end, we turned our interest away from defending the poor on a statutory or constitutional basis, as the years progressed, and, instead, we decided to affirmatively challenge a number of federal statutes and/or regulations under the civil rights statutes in 42 United States Code, Sections 1981 & 1983. Pursuant thereto, we alleged, in a number of those kinds of actions, on behalf of our clients, as well as a class of individuals similarly situated, that the government was denying their rights under the Due Process Clause in the Fifth Amendment to the United States Constitution.

I can think of no better example of our success in that kind of a case than our affirmative action on behalf of a class of Social Security Disability recipients, who had their disability benefits terminated by the Social Security Administration, without notice and a prior fair hearing, because the Administration had determined that they were no longer disabled. Without contesting whether any member of the class was, in fact, disabled, we challenged their termination, because they were not given notice and a prior fair hearing as required by the Due Process Clause of the Fifth Amendment to the United States Constitution.

In that regard, we asserted that Due Process under the Fifth

Amendment guaranteed the right to life, according to well-regarded case law, and that a disability recipient cannot live without receiving Social Security Disability benefits. Moreover, we asserted that well-established case law makes it abundantly clear that any government action that interferes with the right to life, let alone jeopardizes it, by terminating, in this instance, Social Security Disability benefits, requires notice to the disabled individuals, and their right to contest the government's prospective termination, in a prior fair hearing under the Due Process Clause of the Fifth Amendment to the United States Constitution.

The District Court had little interest in what it deemed to be a novel, if not a frivolous, argument and, not surprisingly, it denied our constitutional claim on the merits. In an appeal to the United States Court of Appeals for the District of Columbia Circuit, in which most organizations joined the nation's law schools on the sidelines, as disinterested bystanders, the Circuit Court also rejected our constitutional argument, without a dissent, may I add, and with Judge Wald, ironically, writing the opinion, which, thereby, affirmed the District Court's decision to deny our constitutional claim.

To everyone's subsequent surprise, however, except ours, the Supreme Court granted certiorari and, following a full briefing and an oral argument on the merits, the Court decided, by a 9 to 0 vote, that the denial of notice and a prior fair hearing to disabled individuals, who were threatened with the termination of their Social Security Disability benefits, constitutes a violation of the right to life under the Due Process Clause of the Fifth Amendment to the United States Constitution.

Ed Schwab and I briefed that case in every court in which it appeared, including the Supreme Court of the United States. I presented oral arguments in both the United States District Court and the United States Court of Appeals for the District of Columbia Circuit. Because of the significance of the case, however, and because our claim was against the Secretary of Health Education and Welfare, who was represented by the Solicitor General of the United States, who appeared regularly in major cases before the Supreme Court, we asked Bob Saylor, an experienced litigator in that Court, and a senior partner in the law firm of Covington & Burling, to argue the case, which he did . . . well enough to win!

Still, I must acknowledge that, selfishly speaking, it was enormously difficult to give up the argument in the Supreme Court, after we had done all of the work to get the case there. Nevertheless, oral argument aside, not to mention professional hubris, we prevailed in the end! So, too, did millions of Social Security Disability recipients, a number that must have increased, exponentially, in the more than fifty years that have passed!

Shortly thereafter, I left the Neighborhood Legal Services Program, after having gained an invaluable amount of litigation experience, in the five years in which I had been an attorney with the Program. By that time, I had engaged in almost every form of litigation, in almost every forum, and done so, I might add, quite successfully. Moreover, I had learned how to litigate extremely complex cases, many of which involved statutory and/or constitutional issues, often of first impression, including, in a number of instances, class actions at trial and on appeal. I also learned how to manage a law office, reasonably well, along the way. I had, in short, come along way, professionally as well as personally, in five complex and demanding years.

I left Ed Schwab behind when I left the Program. Well, at least, we no longer worked together after that, although some years later, interestingly enough, we would oppose each other in a number of appeals. And if I ever had any doubt about Ed's competence as a litigator, which I did not, it certainly went away during those cases. He was a formidable foe!

He had also become a very good friend, and remained so, even when we subsequently became adversaries, and long after that, too, when the paths that we had subsequently chosen to follow did not professionally cross anymore. Notwithstanding that dissociating fact, I never forgot about him, professionally or personally. Such individuals are rare, indeed, and when they enter your life, almost by accident, sometimes, they often have a major impact, almost beyond understanding and certainly beyond explanation, which is never limited by time.

Indeed, several years ago and, at least, fifty years after we had practiced law together, while litigating issues of first impression on behalf of the nation's poor, or a class associated therewith, I was invited to a retirement party for Ed Schwab, who was retiring as the Head of the Appellate Division for the Attorney General's Office for the District of Columbia. There must have been close to five hundred people in attendance, most of whom, I presumed at the time, were lawyers. Some were even members of the judiciary in the District of Columbia Court of Appeals and in the United States Court of Appeals for the District of Columbia Circuit, several of whom gave laudatory speeches about Ed's practice before their Courts. Others, of possibly less renown, also gave speeches about their work with Ed, over the years, and what he had meant to that work and to them.

When those speeches had ended, several hours later, I arose, nearly at the end of the evening, to speak about the beginning of his practice, which, in reality, was the beginning of our practice, together, when we were both shortly out of law school. And I reminded him, in that regard, that during those halcyon days, when we were literally rewriting the law together, affecting the economically dispossessed, by major appellate decisions, we also, at the very same time, prevailed in a landmark decision against the Social Security Administration in the Supreme Court of the United States, in an action against the Administration, on behalf of a class of Disability recipients, who failed to receive notice and a prior fair hearing before their Social Security Disability payments were terminated, in violation of the right to life under the Due Process Clause of the Fifth Amendment to the United States Constitution.

Still seated, following my concluding words, my old friend and former colleague hesitated for a moment, amidst the silence that now pervaded in that overly filled room, aside, possibly, from the noise of my chair, as I resumed my seat. Then, with the rest of the room now somewhat in anticipation, because an old trial lawyer had now slowly begun to rise to his feet, just as he had done so many times, in so many courtrooms, far too numerous to recall. This time, however, it was in a far more tentative fashion and with the use of an ever-present wooden cane.

Now standing, momentarily, without saying a word and leaning, somewhat precariously, on that old cane, he finally looked up, at all of those people, anxiously seated there and awaiting for some evening-ending words. Realizing that at last, he turned, ever so slightly, looked over toward me, now seated in my chair, and said, softly, "I nearly forgot!"

At that point, he nonchalantly sat back down, carefully placing his walking stick back down onto the floor, right beside his chair, as he had done on so many occasions, and in so many courts, over virtually a lifetime of practicing law. This time, however, that well-worn courtroom custom was accompanied by a rousing ovation, by a room full of now-standing individuals, for him and, possibly, for another, who, together, had once been young lawyers, that had litigated landmark appeals, even, on occasion, in the Supreme Court of the United States, many of which had almost been forgotten, even by most of those who were, even now, still on their feet, applauding!

CHAPTER XLVII

STONEGATE: LARS IS BORN AND COURT'S REACTION; SATURDAY MORNING TELEVISION CARTOONS AND A RECKLESS DEPARTURE FROM A CRIB

MY YOUNGER son, Lars Calvin Golumbic, was born in 1967; actually, now that I think about it, he barely made it into that year. The actual date was December 27, 1967, just a couple of days before the year came to an end. It was sort of a portent of things to come, because Lars did everything in his life, especially while growing up, somewhat slowly, or methodically, if you prefer to look at it that way; no dramatics, just nice and slowly, or methodically, if you still prefer to look at it that way. See the photographs of Lars, seated beside his brother, when he was two, three and four years of age, which are in Exhibit 119 in the Appendix.

Actually, that's how I remember the way that Lars came into this world, nice and slowly, or, if you will, without any dramatics. The only dramatics that occurred on that day, which, of course, subsequently became Lars' birthday, resulted from the performance of an endless amount of errands by Lis, on behalf of my uncle and aunt, who lived in the area, but who were somewhere else at the time, and who, therefore, were unable to perform those errands themselves. So, somewhat thoughtlessly, they asked a nine-month pregnant Lis, who was "about-to-give-birth," to do those errands for them, even though she had to postpone her trip to the hospital, for several hours, because of that fact.

I guess that you could say, with some accuracy and some inaccuracy, that Lars, or at least his entrance into this world, was unfortunately connected to my problematic family, which now included, much to my dismay, those members living in the metropolitan area, too. Outside of those problems, which, more accurately, should probably be described as errands, at least in this instance, I can't remember anything more about that day that one could possibly describe as unusual, other than the birth of my younger son, Lars Calvin Golumbic!

Oh, yes, there was one other thing, and I almost forgot about that. Lars was born with hair, or, at least, some of it, and it was not the usual kind, most commonly described as brown, black or blonde, but a multicolored variety. That's right, in one small area of his head, which was noticeably in the back, he had sort of an "off-white" tuft, which looked somewhat like a cottontail on a rabbit, and which, naturally, appeared to be rather unusual. Otherwise, like a rabbit, or, at least, the kind that I once hunted in the mountains of Clinton County, the rest of his hair was sort of brownish, which was not so unusual in Clinton County or, for that matter, the rest of God's imperfect universe.

Court's reaction to the presence of another member of our family, who, in this case, was much closer to his age, although a bit younger, was somewhat enigmatic. He simply ignored his younger brother's presence! I guess, with the same logic that he would later employ in the practice of law, if not elsewhere in his life, he simply decided that if you refused to accept that it was there, it might not be; or, at least, if it was there, maybe it would eventually go away. I guess . . . because raising children is a lot of guesswork . . . that Court rightly assumed, with the same kind of historic logic, that the presence of another member of his family, in the form of a newborn baby, was probably going to have some impact on his life, and that it may not be all that good.

Nevertheless, it did not take Court very long to realize, however, utilizing the same unfailing logic, that whatever it was that his parents were calling, "Lars," which was in the form of a newly born baby, was probably not going to go away. Since it was not, which could possibly become a problem, Court apparently concluded, within a short amount of time, that it would probably be better to embrace the problem, before it actually became a more serious problem, utilizing, of course, the same three-year-old logic that had made him a success story, much later in life. And within a short amount of time, likely within the year, that is exactly what he did, metaphorically speaking, that is.

Well, forgetting about metaphors and adopting a little hyperbole, Court became a great big brother, and with that, Lars became a little brother who really grew to like his big brother, because he was such a great big brother. To be more specific, Court included his little brother in whatever it was possible for him to do at that age, and, I hasten to add, in a number of things that were not. One of the latter was watching cartoons on the television set, early on a Saturday morning, before their parents were even awake, or, at least, up and dressed, and ready to confront the family problems of the day.

Court, at four years of age, was more than capable, even at that age, to climb out of his bed, before the cartoon programs had even begun, and to turn on the television set in the living room, to the right channel, no less, and to pull up his little chair, in order to watch the cartoons, which typically filled the "airways" on a Saturday morning. Lars, who was three years younger at that point, was quite another story, because, among other problematic things, he was unable to even climb out of his crib by himself, since the side rails were almost taller than he was. That, however, did not prove to be an insurmountable problem for his innovative big brother, who simply dragged his little chair into Lars' bedroom, climbed up on it, reached over the crib rails and, with his hands underneath his little brother's outstretched arms, literally pulled his younger brother, who had been standing, up and over the rails and, finally, "out," or, should I more accurately say, "down," onto the hardwood floor.

Yes, unfortunately, the "out" part of the operation should more accurately be described as, given the laws of gravity, "down," onto the hardwood floor, sometimes, if not most times, head first! The fall onto his head, fortunately or unfortunately . . . and the jury is still out on the question, even now, over fifty-five years later . . . made it possible for Lars to join his older brother in front of the television set and to watch the cartoons with him, without a chair, of course, because Lars was far too young at the time to sit up in a chair, other than a highchair, unless his older brother would hold him, while doing so, which he ordinarily did on those auspicious occasions.

All of this would normally take place, of course, after Lars ostensibly recovered from the unfortunate fall, which, as you may recall, was sometimes on his head. Years later, given some of his aberrational conduct during his teenage years, especially at boarding school, which shall remain unexplained at this point, because of a lingering familial discomfort, we, as a family, were not so sure about the extent of that "recovery," or, for that matter, anything that could conceivably be construed to be "fortunate" about those falls!

See the photograph of Court and Lars, together, a little more than a year after Lars' birth, likely taken some time in the latter part of 1969 or the earlier part of 1970, and the photographs of Lars, when he was just three and four years of age, likely taken, sometime, in 1972 and 1973, all of which have been included in Exhibit 131 in the Appendix.

CHAPTER XLVIII

STONEGATE: WHILE LIVING IN A GARDEN STYLE APARTMENT AT 1835 PINEY BRANCH ROAD IN SILVER SPRING, MD., WE BEGAN TO LOOK FOR A HOUSE TO BUY AT "SIGNAL HILL" AND, SUBSEQUENTLY, AT "STONEGATE," IN MONTGOMERY COUNTY, MARYLAND

ENCUMBERED NOW with two children, one with ordinary hair and one not, our life began to take on dimensions that seemed extraordinary to my Danish wife. I say, "extraordinary," because she believed that the four of us could not ordinarily live within the dimensions of a two-bedroom apartment, not anymore, because the bedroom where the boys slept resembled a small closet, and the actual closet in that bedroom contained an air-conditioning unit, which sounded, when it actually worked, like the Normandy invasion, on a good day, and the entire World War II, on the others. Because my older son, Court, could not sleep through the invasion, at five years of age, let alone the war, his mother, who had to get up in the middle of the night to calm him down, because of the invasive noise, believed that we needed to leave the war zone behind us, and to find a more peaceful place for Court to sleep, not to mention her younger son, Lars, too, and with distinctly larger dimensions.

Of course, "peace," if not the dimensions thereof, ordinarily comes at a price, and, therefore, I began to worry about the peace process, or, if you prefer, the process of now finding another place to live . . .

with distinctly larger and, therefore, more costly "dimensions." Of even greater concern . . . to me, of course . . . everyone, including my parents, was, unfortunately, now becoming involved in the process, too. And, unfortunately, everyone, including my parents, now believed that a family of my expanding "dimensions," now including a second child, should live in a house of similarly expanding dimensions. That was obviously because everyone, not excluding my parents, did not have to pay for the house, not to mention the expanding "dimensions." The only one who was going to have to do that, in this catastrophic situation, was someone who was financially unable to do so! For that reason, if not for others related thereto, I was rapidly losing my mind, which was the same mind that was spending all night, every night, weighing financial alternatives, which were reasonable and unreasonable, too.

No matter how you looked at the financial basis for my insomnia, as reasonable or unreasonable, the difficulty, for me, at least, was simply that my family had increased by twenty-five percent, causing a family demand for a corresponding increase in the size of our residence, while my income from the practice of law had barely increased at all. That tragic disparity was actually not so surprising when you think about it. Anyone . . . well almost anyone . . . can engage in the process of increasing the numerical size of a family . . . with some reasonable success, I might add. The process of learning how to practice law, however, was far more complicated, if not far more demanding, and far more slowly accomplished, with a correspondingly minimal economic consequence. So in mathematical terms, an increase in the former, family membership, did not necessarily ensure a proportional increase in the latter, which, of course, was a family income, earned, in this instance, in the practice of law. Rather, an increase in the latter, unlike the former, depends solely upon non-conjugal considerations, related solely to the mastery of a more challenging practice, generally known as the practice of law.

Nevertheless, although I was in my foundational years of the practice of law, being more marginal in experience at that point, I was still quite familiar with the general principles of bankruptcy. And the very first bankruptcy principle . . . the golden rule, if you will . . . was to avoid it at all costs! Embracing that principle like a lifeline, and, may I add, like a good lawyer, I refused, or, at least, I tried to refuse, to purchase a home, at all costs, to avoid bankruptcy!

Eventually, however, I had to re-examine my opposition, based on bankruptcy principles, because my principled opposition was becoming too costly. It . . . my principled opposition . . . was not principally viewed by the rest of my interested family as principled at all. It was viewed as myopic, at best, and selfish, at worst. Since I was not interested in appearing to be either one, I spent my evenings thinking about bankruptcy, instead of sleeping. And when one has to choose between sleep and bankruptcy, after three weeks of little sleep, trust me, one chooses sleep, even though the choice may be unprincipled.

I did not principally choose, however, to have my parents involved in the house search. Until that search commenced, I had, essentially, left them back there where they belonged, in the mountains of central Pennsylvania. Oh, I still visited them on occasion, usually when the leaves "turned color," as we are prone to say in those mountains, which, of course, was in mid-October, and, maybe, again, for Thanksgiving and/or Christmas, holidays, with my enlarged family now in tow. But I had worked quite hard, following my graduation from high school, at redefining myself as something other than my hometown in central Pennsylvania, not to mention my parents, who lived there, and I really didn't need to have them bring central Pennsylvania down to where I was living.

Now, unfortunately, I had them visiting me, virtually every weekend, from early October until shortly before Christmas, in order to help us . . . an excited wife and an unexcited husband . . . to search for a house in which to live. Having them visit us, virtually every weekend, for that period of time, was, on top of everything else, distinctly unsettling. There was something unsettling about seeing your face on individuals whose customs and culture were part of your discomforting childhood, in an earlier time, somewhere else, and you wanted to leave all of that back there with them . . . the customs and the culture and the faces, I mean!

Well, whether I liked it or not, the customs and the culture and the faces brought themselves down to my doorstep, or, at least, the one on the house that everyone, except me, was avidly searching for, anyway. I guess that life was like that, full of ironies, I mean, because it was ironic that I had desperately wanted to marry my wife, who, following our marriage, desperately wanted to become involved with my family, which I desperately wanted to avoid, and who, nevertheless, desperately wanted to join in a search for a house with us, because of a request by my newly inclusive wife to do so. Now, however, with houses and searches and parents invading my life, nearly every weekend, it was too late for desperation; now it was time for stoicism, which was the only way that I could ever imagine being able to live in a house that I could not afford, and that was chosen, at least in part, by the customs and the culture and the faces that I had tried, valiantly, to leave behind in the mountains of central Pennsylvania.

Eventually, however, the customs and the culture and the faces found a house that they really liked, and that they thought that we . . . my newly excited wife and her now terrified husband . . . would also like and could possibly afford. For all of those reasons, they wanted us . . . the excited and terrified marital couple . . . to look at it, too, which we subsequently did, and which caused me to add depression, as a daily complement, to my nightly insomnia. The depression was caused by a strange looking structure of very small dimensions, bordering on being uninhabitable, which I preferred to call a "chicken coop," but which the building contractor, and his nefarious real estate agent, preferred to call a house. For some inexplicable reason, the rest of my family preferred the name utilized by the building contractor and his nefarious real estate agent.

Actually, the structure was so small that a midget would suffer from claustrophobia, within hours, if he or she tried to live in it. The only nice thing about that conglomeration of microscopic boards and miniature bricks was the name of the development, "Signal Hill," which must have represented an image in the building contractor's mind, rather than in the actual surroundings, because there was nothing hilly, at all, about those surroundings; the house was only surrounded by flat land, everywhere, which was obviously why the county decided to build a four-lane highway in front of it; and, frankly, the only "signal" that I could find, at least nearby, was the traffic signal out there on that four-lane highway.

Ignoring the highway and the traffic signal and the misnomer, the customs and the culture and the faces of central Pennsylvania raved about the interior of that microscopic structure, especially the kitchen, which, in fact, the four of us . . . consisting of my wife, myself and both parents . . . could not enter at the same time. Actually, the kitchen was only large enough for one member of a family to cook and one-and-one-half of them to eat. Moreover, none of them could get into either one of the two bathrooms. The one downstairs was obviously just for guests, if the guests were very small and very thin dwarfs, and the one upstairs was obviously just for decoration. Otherwise, you would have to take a bath standing up, or, at least, partially so, and you would have to remain standing in the bathtub, in order to wash your hands and face in the sink. Although those features may have been an efficient use of space, in the words of the unscrupulous building contractor and his sycophantic real estate agent, they were a ridiculous use of architectural planning, in the words of a disgusted non-prospective buyer!

Apparently, efficiency was also the goal in the architectural design of an entrance, because there was only one, which was located, not surprisingly, in front of the house. Can you believe that, aside from that one, there was no other entrance to the whole microscopic place, which, again, could, admittedly, be called an efficient use of entrance space. Frankly, however, I would prefer to call it a terrifying fact and, by the way, a firefighter's nightmare!

It is certainly true, of course, that if a fire started anywhere around the front of that house, where the only entrance was efficiently located, you wouldn't have to worry about making the next mortgage payment, which, of course, could be a plus, because the bank that held the mortgage probably would have no way of serving the foreclosure papers on you, somewhere in heaven. It should be evident, in that regard, to anyone at all familiar with banking practices, that a bank has no way of ever reaching any kind of a heavenly location, not even to serve foreclosure papers. There was, of course, the possibility that you may not be a candidate for heavenly rewards, which, of course, would mean, still in reference to their professional practices, that the bank would have a far easier road.

It is also possible that a fire truck may have arrived soon enough to save the structure, with the two-and-a-half-people in the kitchen and a dwarf still in the downstairs bathroom. In that case, you would, in all likelihood, still be obligated to make mortgage payments, but on a structure that would have already been rejected by everyone else, no matter in what time period, including a caveman, if he had lived long enough to see how ridiculous the living accommodations had become in the twentieth century!

Nevertheless, ignoring the opinion of cavemen, not to mention any other reasonable assessment by anyone else, in the intervening period of time, my oblivious wife wanted to buy that stupid structure, which she still insisted upon calling a house, in order to make it a home, for all of us, including, unfortunately, me. Because I still loved my wife, which, at that point, was beginning to become a household tragedy, I stupidly did not object, and we subsequently bought the damned thing, even though the only proportions that were at all sizable, associated with that microscopic structure, were the costs!

Less stupidly, however, I inserted a provision in the sales agreement, which stipulated that if the interest rates, utilized by the mortgage company, exceeded six and one-half percent at any time before closure, I could terminate the contract, without any penalty for having done so, and receive back my full down payment. And, may I add, I would, thereafter, be able to walk away from the whole transaction, with my sanity and my bank account intact, not to mention my back, from not having to bend over, repeatedly, inside that microscopic situation, disgustingly called a house, by the fraudulent building contractor and his sycophantic real estate agent.

Since interest rates had been continually rising over the previous year, and they were actually at six-and-one-half percent at the time that I signed that sales agreement, I had every reason to believe that the rates would actually exceed six-and-one-half percent by the time of closing, approximately three months later, and that I could, literally and metaphorically, get myself out of that microscopic house and its macroscopic mortgage.

Still, interest rates, and their progression and/or regression, were historically fickle, so I really did not know whether I would be able to, eventually, "get myself out of that house," not to mention an associated egregious mortgage. So every morning, before work, I would drive out to that stupid development of undersized and uninspiring dwellings, to water the grass, by turning on a set of sprinklers, which I had set up in the front and back yards, and which I would leave on all day. I did that every day, seven days a week, so that I would, at least, have grass outside of a house that I did not want, because, among other things, it was too small to live in and too expensive to even try. Nevertheless, rainbows can occur, I am told, in the midst of a storm, and if one did occur in this stormy situation, it took place on the ground, not in the sky, and it was all green, or, at least, it was turning green by the end of the second watering week.

When the storm clouds actually lifted, however, three weeks later, interest rates, as I had suspected, now exceeded six-and-one-half percent. So in a morning full of sunshine, I sent a letter to the disgusting building contractor, in which I proposed to terminate the sales agreement and to receive, in return, my down payment in full. I know that the morning was full of sunshine on that day, because I was about to get out from underneath a sales agreement to purchase a house for two-and-one-half people, not to mention one very thin dwarf, which I really could not afford and which was, nevertheless, found to be quite acceptable by, inter alia, the customs and the culture and the faces of central Pennsylvania!

Even better, and, frankly, almost anything would have been better, I had found a house, in the meantime, in a development called Stonegate, which was bigger, nearly all brick, with really nice interior appointments, and which was situated on nearly one-half of an acre of land, no less. Well, for all those geographic and structural reasons, I wanted that house, and after she saw it, following the dissolution of our previous mortgage agreement, for a house fit for dwarfs, so did the Dane, especially because of the brick walls on the outside of the house and on the fireplace in the family room. In fact, she would often stand in front of the house, looking up at those brick walls and, thinking of houses in Denmark, which were always constructed of brick, say, "they" . . . referring now to the brick walls in America . . . "look marvelous!"

Purchasing the house, however, required us to move on from marvelous to miraculous, because I simply could not afford to buy it on the income from any one of my two jobs, and I could barely afford it with the income from both of them. So I knew that I really needed to keep both of my jobs, at least for the foreseeable future, practicing law on behalf of the under privileged, during the day, at the Neighborhood Legal Services Program, and teaching philosophy and political science, during the evening, to the over privileged girls at the Marjorie Webster Junior College. Nevertheless, it seemed to me that it was really worth working two jobs, even though one was during the day and other one was at night, in order to live in a house that I really liked!

Looking back now, I realize that something actually happened during those house-hunting days, something that was probably educational, if nothing else. I believe that I learned that I could not afford to purchase what I could afford, if you can understand what I mean, not if I wanted to enjoy living in it, anyway. Even more, but not at all inconsistent therewith, I believe that I learned, if I had not already been aware, that life is more than simply living in it. Life, if it is to be worthwhile, is doing so much more, and the "so much more" requires a decision to take a risk, quite often, which, of course, has consequences. And one of those consequences is the possibility that you may fail, which, indeed, sometimes happens. Without risk, however, nothing happens; life simply goes on without really living in it; or, to put the matter in other terms, without risk, life becomes a process of dying one whole life long.

With that philosophic observation in mind, I set out, with my family now in tow, to buy a house at 14804 Flintstone Lane, in a development called, "Stonegate," which was in Silver Spring, Maryland, and which, if you can understand me, really "housed" so much more! See photographs of the house during various periods in which we lived in it, which have been included as Exhibit 12 in the Appendix.

CHAPTER XLIX

STONEGATE: WE MOVED INTO THE SPLIT-LEVEL HOUSE IN STONEGATE WITH, INTER ALIA, A MAPLE BED THAT WAS USED NEARLY EVERY EVENING BY TWO OF MY CHILDREN, SUCCESSIVELY, TO SAIL OFF WITH OLD "BLACKBEARD," THE PIRATE, TO PLACES UNIMAGINABLE FOR MOST DISBELIEVING ADULTS

I WOULD be remiss, if I did not point out, at least at this point, that we liked that house at 14804 Flintstone Lane in Silver Spring, Maryland, so much that we lived in it for over forty-seven years, a period of time that did not end until our children had grown up and we had grown old. In fact, it was not until sometime in July 2014, following our retirement, that we finally sold it and moved, over a period of several months, to our newly purchased home at 4 Maass Lane in Rehoboth Beach, Delaware, which was subsequently illustrated in a Christmas card that has been reproduced on the next page.

Prior thereto, however, we accumulated the experiences that, in part, have made up the lives of those of us who have lived, or who have once lived, within the four walls of that brick and block, split-level, family home at 14804 Flintstone Lane in Silver Spring, Maryland. Without any attempt at this point to chronicle or enumerate those myriad experiences, which, in reality, is an effort that consumes a good part of the remaining chapters of this book, it is sufficient at this point to say, however, that they began on a cold, wintry day in January of 1968, when we moved into the house, with the able assistance of my parents, who had departed from their home, early in the morning on that day, in order to transport a number of furnishings to our new home in Silver Spring, Maryland.

The trip was not an easy one for my parents, who had reached an age, certainly by that time, that was long past retirement. Nevertheless, because of the significance of that day, at least to the younger members of their family, children and grandchildren alike, they awoke early in the morning and, working together, loaded a number of furnishings into a small rental van in freezing temperatures. Following that, which was a weighty effort, even by younger hands, they drove the van through snowy mountains, southward, for hundreds of miles, toward our new home in Silver Spring, Maryland, reaching that destination around noontime.

Among those transported furnishings were a number of things that we, as a family, still own and still use, such as my parents' tiger maple twin beds, with two matching chests and two matching mirrors, one of which, because of some condition issues, was consigned to the basement and, eventually, donated, after some years of disuse, to a deserving family. The twin beds and the matching chests, with one matching mirror, however, were, upon arrival at our new home, placed in our master bedroom, where they remained for years. Shortly after the removal to our new home in Rehoboth Beach, Delaware, however, the tiger maple beds and accompanying chests, with the one matching mirror, were given to my younger son, Lars, as a house warming gift, to brighten one of the bedrooms in a new house, which had just been constructed, at a location known as "Terrapin Neck," just outside the town of Shepherdstown, West Virginia.

Considering that they . . . the tiger maple twin beds, chests, and mirror . . . were once residing in his parents' bedroom, for a little over forty years, and in his grandparents' bedroom, for even longer, I can safely say that the "tiger," in those maple furnishings, has some real family history, which is now three generations long. That family history began, as my mother informed me, with a purchase, by her, shortly after she had graduated from college and had begun teaching in a one-room schoolhouse, in the nineteen twenties, in the tiny farming village of Lemont, Pennsylvania.

Unfortunately, the "tiger" does not look quite the same in those maple furnishings now, because, at one point in the nineteen eighties, we had him, or them, if you prefer to think of it that way, refinished with a walnut stain. Personally, I think that "he," or "they," if you still prefer to think of it that way, looked far better before the walnut change nearly eliminated his or their stripes.

My parents also brought along two very tall table lamps, as well as two end tables, upon which the lamps once stood. Upon reaching our home at 14804 Flintstone Lane, in Silver Spring, Maryland, the table lamps were placed, once again, on the end tables, which, in turn, were placed in our family room, where they remained in use for nearly forty-seven years. Following the sale of our home in Silver Spring, Maryland, however, we donated the end tables to a nearby charitable organization, but we included the table lamps in the move to our newly purchased home at 4 Maass Lane in Rehoboth Beach, Delaware. Situated now on a chest of drawers in our master bedroom, on the first floor of our new home, we still use those lamps, following some electrical restoration, that is, even though they must now be more than eighty-five years old. With that accumulated age, those old table lamps fit quite nicely with a number of other age-related objects in that bedroom, at least in the opinion of an avid antique collector, who also happens to be the author of this family "fable."

My parents also brought along a maple single bed, which served me well during the nightly hours of my childhood, while living with them at 269 Susquehanna Avenue in Lock Haven, Pennsylvania. The bed was not accompanied by a "tiger" or, consequently, graced with its "tell-tale" stripes, however, like the twin beds now in my younger son's possession, in his newly built home, outside of the small town of Shepherdstown, West Virginia. But I ask you, why would you want a "tiger" in a bed that subsequently became outfitted, during your childhood, as a magical maple ship, upon which you sailed out, nearly every evening, with old "Blackbeard," the pirate, into an imaginary world, unknown and unreachable by mere adults?!

In those nightly voyages, no one cared whether you could spell, or multiply or, even, divide, or do any of the other things that seemed so important to the teachers in the Roosevelt Elementary School. According to old "Blackbeard," such ridiculous things had become irrelevant, long ago, in the lives of ruthless pirates, and their young crew, who "shipped-out," nightly, in magical maple ships that sailed "the seven seas."

In the intervening years, I had long since grown too old to join old "Blackbeard," on those nightly journeys in a magical, maple, pirate ship, so it remained unmanned and moored in my old bedroom, following my departure for college, graduate school and, thereafter, law school, and, truth be told, well beyond. So my parents thoughtfully packed that maple bed . . . or that magical, maple, pirate ship, if you are unrealistic enough to believe that . . . into that moving van, too, and brought it down to our new home at 14804 Flintstone Lane in Silver Spring, Maryland.

We placed that old maple bed into my older son's bedroom, enabling him, as a young boy, to take my old, nightly position at the helm of that magical, maple, pirate ship, and to sail out, every evening, with old "Blackbeard," the pirate, into an imaginary world of maritime adventure, where only children were capable of going. And, of course, a time came, over the years, when he, too, had become too old to spend his evenings with old "Blackbeard." So following his graduation from high school, he decided to leave old "Blackbeard" behind, with his magical, maple, pirate ship, and to move up in the nautical world and become a Commodore at Vanderbilt University in Nashville, Tennessee.

You might have assumed at that point that piracy had died in that bedroom, with the departure of my older son to Vanderbilt University, and that the magical, maple, pirate ship had remained moored to its bedposts during the intervening time. But that assumption would be incorrect, because, shortly thereafter, Annie, our youngest child, took over that bedroom, and with it, the helm of that magical, maple, pirate ship, after which she, too, set sail with old "Blackbeard," the pirate, into an imaginary world of maritime wonderment, where adults were ordinarily not permitted to follow.

Some might say, of course, that old "Blackbeard" may well have found it to be somewhat unbecoming, as a marauding and ruthless pirate, to set sail with a young girl, among his nightly crew. But those idiotic "landlubbers" must still be living in the nineteenth century, before girls could become anything that they wanted, including ruthless pirates, who sail out, nightly, in a magical, maple, pirate ship to a watery world beyond the reaches and limitations of mere adults, especially those without any imagination.

Now, sadly, all of the pirates, who have sailed, nightly, in that magical, maple, pirate ship, have grown up, and, with that, grown too old to "ship-out" anymore, with old "Blackbeard." Now they are busily fighting other battles, ordinarily taking place in a court of law, which seem far more appropriate for professionally working adults, which is what they have become, so old "Blackbeard," who is far more interested in seafaring conquests, really can't "ship-out" with them anymore. Instead, he remains a strictly nighttime associate, who appears only in the lives of those who are young enough to be willing to pull the covers over their daytime reality, and to set sail, once again, in a magical, maple, pirate ship, to worlds uninhabited by disbelieving adults.

Consequently, that maple bed, which has been utilized by three children over two generations of my family, as a magical, maple, pirate ship, on nightly excursions with old "Blackbeard," the pirate, has been presently consigned to an inauspicious dry dock, in the oversized basement of our house at 4 Maass Lane in Rehoboth Beach, Delaware. There, it silently awaits for another generation of children in our family, to unmoor it from its present dock in that basement, and to set sail, once again, for magical places, known only to seafaring children, who are willing to cast their fortunes, once again, with old "Blackbeard," the pirate, on nightly voyages on a magical, maple, pirate ship to places unreachable by disbelieving adults.

CHAPTER L

AMERICAN UNIVERSITY LAW SCHOOL, THIRD YEAR: I USED THE MONEY THAT WE HAD SAVED FOR MY LAW SCHOOL TUITION TO PURCHASE AN EIGHTEENTH CENTURY, CHERRY, CHIPPENDALE, "SLANT-FRONT" DESK, WHICH RESULTED IN MY WIFE UNFAIRLY TAKING OVER OUR FAMILY FINANCES

MY FRUGAL wife was one of those disbelieving adults . . . with respect to another matter, that is . . . which occurred when I told her, shortly after we had been married, that I had used the money that we had been saving for my law school tuition, the following semester, to buy a Chippendale, cherry, eighteenth-century, "slant-front" desk. Unfortunately, the desk was far from perfect, because it had a brass gallery screwed on to the top, which did not belong there, the feet had been partially cut off, years ago, probably when it had been refinished, and the refinishing job, itself, to the extent that it had been refinished, was poorly done, too. Still, it was a Chippendale, eighteenth-century, cherry, "slant-front" desk, made and signed by the cabinet maker in Erie County, Pennsylvania, and I wanted it! I also wanted to subsequently have the gallery removed, the feet restored and the desk refinished, correctly, this time, all of which was, in fact, done, about ten years later.

I have always loved antiques, probably because my mother did, too, and, therefore, I grew up with a number of them all over our house. Most of them had descended from our Pennsylvania German ancestors, in one way or another, which, of course, made them especially attractive to this historically minded author. I was also interested, however, in acquiring some of them on my own, as I grew older, especially "primitives," such as "red ware" and "stoneware," as well as furniture, painted or otherwise, in the early and middle part of the nineteenth-century, a disease that has lasted over a lifetime. The Chippendale, eighteenth-century, cherry, "slant-front," desk, however, was far beyond anything that I had ever acquired, at least up to that point, especially in terms of cost and rarity. So greatly enamored with the desk, because of the latter and ignoring the former, I impetuously decided to buy it from an antique dealer, located near my hometown, following my marriage.

It cost me five hundred dollars, which, fortunately, had been previously deposited into our checking account by my wife, in order to pay for my tuition, the following semester, in law school. Thereafter, I moved it, with my father's help, from the antique shop to my parents' home at 42 Sylvan Drive in Lock Haven, Pennsylvania. As you will subsequently discover, however, that was the beginning of a family saga, involving an antique desk, a law school tuition payment, a depleted bank account, and an enraged Dane!

Well, there it remained, in my old bedroom, at 42 Sylvan Drive in Lock Haven, Pennsylvania, during the early years of our marriage, which was when we . . . a Dane and a non-Dane and, subsequently, two little half-Danes . . . lived in a series of indistinctive apartments in the Washington metropolitan area. Now that we had acquired a house, however, with more living space, my parents decided to load it, too, into the moving van and bring it along, with the other things, to our new home at 14804 Flintstone Lane in Silver Spring, Maryland.

Having arrived with the other contents in that rental van on that blustery day in January, the desk has remained part of our home, and our lives, over the intervening period of time. Initially, it was placed in the living room, because of its importance, which was a prominent place in our new home. Years later, however, it was unceremoniously moved upstairs into Lars' old bedroom, where it remained, nearly unnoticed, for the remainder of our years in that house. Following our removal to Rehoboth Beach, however, the desk accompanied that move, as you are aware by now, and, eventually, it found an inconspicuous location, once again, in one of the smaller bedrooms, upstairs, in that house. There it has remained for some time, largely unused and unnoticed, but proud and dignified, an artifact crowned by age and history, if not rarity. And no matter in which house, Silver Spring, Maryland or Rehoboth Beach, Delaware, the desk has remained a depository for a number of our valuable papers and a significant amount of other memorable things, too, acquired in various ways and in various places throughout our lives.

Possibly, the most memorable thing about the desk is the secret compartment, not easily found in the interior, but still there. I'm not sure what secrets have been historically associated with that compartment, over the course of our lives, or remain there today, but whatever they are, or may have been, they cannot be as important as its simple existence. In fact, because of its unusual nature, I could not help sharing its location and operation with every one of our friends, through the years, not to mention a few others, too. So suffice it to say, I suspect that the secret compartment has, as a result, lost much of its secrecy, if not its significance, a long time ago.

Nevertheless, the desk, itself, has not lost its significance to our family and, especially, to this generation of our family, which, at this point, is the older living generation. That significance, by the way, does not come from its market value, which, by this time, has become considerable, or its age, which, by this time, has also become considerable, or its attractiveness, which has always been considerable, at least following its refinishing and restoration, or even its longevity with our family, which, by now, has spanned part of two generations, having been transferred fairly recently, as a Christmas gift, to Lars' home, on Terrapin Neck, outside of Shepherdstown, West Virginia.

Rather, its real significance, over that period of time, comes from its controversial origins in our family, which has become, unfortunately, legendary, or, if you recall, a saga, which has never been forgotten by anyone in our family, especially of Danish origins. That is because, as has already been said, I bought the desk with the money that we had been saving to pay for my law school tuition for the following semester. Consequently, we did not have enough money to make that payment, when it became due, several months later. Therefore, we had to nearly eliminate such frivolities as food, clothing, and mortgage payments from our budget, over the next several months, in order to make up the difference, so that I could continue to attend law school that semester.

If that were the end of the saga, which, admittedly, does not reflect well on the storyteller, not at this point, anyway, I would, nevertheless, be quite fortunate, but, unfortunately, the saga does not end there. In fact, the acquisition of that desk, especially in those discomforting circumstances, also resulted in some very significant consequences that were applicable to me, as head-of-the-household, and that are ongoing, even to this day. Among other things, my intemperate Danish wife, in order to avoid a tuition problem in the future, "took over the family finances," in her words, including the payment of all outstanding bills and any other financial obligations, for that matter. Actually, the use of the term, "took over," may be an understatement, if not an actual misstatement; possibly, it may be more accurate to say that there was a bloodless coup, in which I was abruptly relieved of my position as "head of the household," to whatever extent that it may have existed, and, more specifically, any further control over the family finances.

Consequently, for not an insignificant period of time, over the remaining sixty years of our marriage, I was given twenty-five cents in the morning of every working day, so that I could purchase a carton of milk to drink with my lunch, which continued to be prepared by the new "head of the household," and which normally consisted of a ham or turkey sandwich, a small container of yogurt and a banana or pear, depending upon the day and what remained in the fruit tray in the refrigerator. Those consistent gastronomical items, together with the subsequently purchased container of milk, were typically carried by me to work in a paper bag or, subsequently, a children's insulated lunch box, often decorated with such things as cats and dogs or, more rarely, pigs and elephants.

This practice, of course, came to an end, years later, when I became a partner in my law firm, and I had to take clients or, rather, prospective clients, to lunch, nearly every day. But do not be mistaken, it came to an end, not because of the professional necessity of taking those clients, or prospective clients, to lunch, but because, and only because, my firm paid for those lunches . . . in the unlikely event that you may have forgotten about the situation involving the desk, or, if you will, the beginning of this unfortunate saga, years earlier.

Having now reminded you, in the unlikely event that you needed me to do so, you won't be surprised to learn that my unforgiving Danish wife, who now doubles as the family auditor, never told me, for years, where we banked, and when I inadvertently discovered where, some years ago, she immediately moved our accounts to another bank. Consequently, I had little association, bordering on none, with our banking officials over the course of our marriage, at least in the early years thereof. That circumstance resulted in a rather awkward situation, when the Dane decided to take the boys home with her on a summer vacation to Denmark, when they were quite small, leaving me with the responsibility of discharging our family obligations, including the financial part of those obligations, until her return. In that connection, I was given instructions, before her departure, on what bills would become due, how to pay them and where. She also wrote out a check for the amount due, so that I only had to put the signed check in the envelope, which had already been addressed, seal and send it.

In case you may be wondering, which is not at all surprising, not by this point, anyway, I accomplished all of this without much difficulty, by simply following her directions, and, therefore, discharging all of our financial obligations, without incident, may I add, during their absence. Unfortunately, however, I still had to eat something, at least for breakfast and dinner, every day, while she was gone, which required more than the amount of money that she had left behind for me to purchase milk to drink with my lunches every day. So I went to our bank, which I had recently discovered, to cash a check, in order to buy some groceries. Unfortunately, however, I was informed by the teller that our checking account was in her name, only, so he would not agree to cash my check. When I informed the bank manager, to whom I was subsequently referred, that I was her husband, and, as such, her authorized agent, he replied . . . with some derision in his voice, I might add . . . that he was surprised that a lawyer, even one as young and as obviously inexperienced as myself, would even consider that a bank would ever allow a withdrawal from an account by someone other than the named "account holder," who did not, at least, possess a durable power of attorney.

Because the bank manager began to sound a lot like my law professor in agency, a course and a professor that I never did particularly like, I slinked away to a nearby public telephone, in order to call my father and ask him if he would loan me some money, notably to live on, until my wife returned from Denmark. As a result of all this . . . referring, of course, to my futile effort to obtain money from an unrelenting bank manager, requiring a much-needed loan from my father . . . I guess that my father and the bank manager, along with my children, too, not to mention the rest of the uninterested universe, have realized that I was no longer in control of the family finances and, possibly, the family, itself. What's more, I doubted at the time, if not now, that it would ever be in my interest to try to explain to any one of them, or even to all of them, including that insufferable bank manager, that it . . . meaning my economic predicament, if not my family demotion . . . was because of an unfortunate misunderstanding, in the early days of my marriage, that was brought on by a precipitous purchase of a Chippendale, cherry, eighteenth-century, slant-front desk!

CHAPTER LI

FOURTH JOB: AMERICAN UNIVERSITY LAW SCHOOL; LAWCOR AND PROFESSOR NICHOLAS KITTRIE

A HOUSE changes your life . . . trust me; a mortgage changes it even more . . . trust me even more . . . and now I had both! So out of necessity, if not terror, I decided to make some changes, not to the house or to the mortgage, they were part of my life now, and, probably, forever, but to the means by which I could afford to live in the former and pay for the latter.

I needed, in short, to find one job, in which I could make, at least, the same amount of money that I was now making by working two of them. And I also decided that I would like to combine my two areas of professional interest, reflected now in my two current jobs, practicing law in the daytime and teaching constitutional law in the evening, into one job, involving both of those interests and both of those incomes. Such a job, it struck me, would be a teaching position in a law school, somewhere in the metropolitan area, so I began to apply for a position, as an instructor, in the law school in a Washington metropolitan area.

Within weeks, I received a rather encouraging response from the American University Law School. Actually, to be more specific, the response came from Professor Nicholas Kittrie, a criminal law professor, who was a prodigious author with whom I had some acquaintance. Because of that acquaintance, although somewhat distant and removed, Professor Kittrie knew of my extensive litigation experience, and I knew of his extensive publication experience, especially in the criminal law area, which, I may add, impressed us both.

I was impressed, because only faculty members, who were in good standing, authored that amount of articles and books. Professor Kittrie was impressed, because, as a result of his extensive authorship, he was clearly such a faculty member. Apparently, the Department of Justice was also impressed, probably for the same scholarly reasons, because Professor Kittrie had recently received a federal grant to fund, among a number of other things, a demonstration project, in which law students would provide civil litigation support to prison inmates and their families. And he needed someone, with extensive litigation experience, to supervise his law students doing that kind of work. Well, after an extensive interview, in which we were both impressed, he was smart enough to make me an offer, and I was dumb enough to accept it. To be more specific, he was smart enough to realize that I wanted to be a member of the law school faculty, and thought that I would, by accepting his offer, even though I would not, and I was dumb enough to believe that I would.

It was really not so surprising that I believed that I would, by accepting Professor Kittrie's offer, become a member of the faculty of the American University Law School. At the time, law schools across the country were adopting clinical legal practice programs, not unlike this one, as part of their curricula, and they were hiring former litigators, as faculty members, to direct those programs. And this was clearly a clinical practice program, in which the law students, who were participating in the program, would enroll as a three-credit course, which was part of the curricula of the law school. And quite naturally, or, at least, it seemed so at the time, I assumed, as the director of that program, that I would automatically become, or, eventually, become, a member of the law school faculty.

Well, the program that I directed was called, "LAWCOR," by

Professor Kittrie, and it was not only an educational experience for the participating law students, but for me, too, for no more than six months. By that time, I had learned that, when you get yourself into a dumb situation, it takes you about four months to realize that fact and about two months to get out of it.

In the meantime, I must acknowledge that I enjoyed the opportunity of working with the law students, even though the cases in which they were involved did not require much litigation experience, let alone much legal ability. After appearing in the Supreme Court of the United States and, repeatedly, arguing cases in the United States Court of Appeals for the District of Columbia Circuit, in my previous professional life, supervising law students in simple uncontested divorce actions, which made up most of the litigation cases in the program, became rather routine and rather boring, rather quickly. And that kind of work, if you really want to call it that, became even more boring as each successive month passed.

Moreover, it had become clear, without anyone ever pronouncing the fact, that I was not, nor would I ever become, as a so-called "clinician," a member of the faculty of that law school. In fact, as a "clinician," I believe that the janitor actually held a more professionally prestigious position in that law school at the time. Not surprisingly, given my expectation and that janitorial perception, I found this to be rather annoying. I also found it to be somewhat annoying, although not without expectation, that the outcome of each boring case, which I had supervised, would become a statistic upon which Professor Kittrie would base his next book . . . without any co-authorship on my part!

In the end, it appeared that I was doing very little of educational value, because the cases were so simple and so repetitive. Instead, I was just doing research work for a professor that I was beginning to dislike, probably because we had very little in common. Among other things, I liked to work and he did not. He liked academic life, probably because he did not have to work, and I had discovered, as somewhat of an academician, that I did not like that kind of a life, probably for the very same non-working reason. To avoid work, he spent an inordinate amount of time in meetings, and engaged in them, repeatedly, for every imaginable reason. I, on the other hand, deplored meetings, and couldn't imagine any reason for ever meeting with anyone, unless, of course, you were dating them, and I had given up that idea, some time ago, when my wife agreed to marry me .

Moreover, his most distinguished accomplishment in the practice of law, outside of writing some books about it, was his ability to speak Arabic, and he did that at every inappropriate opportunity. Whereas, I could not imagine how addressing the Supreme Court, or any of the Circuit Courts, in Arabic, was going to help me prevail in an oral argument before that Court or those Courts. For all of those reasons, I concluded, near the end of my tenure there, that he was probably well placed as a professor in an academic setting, where inefficiency, if not proficiency in the Arabic language, was normally rewarded with tenure.

I also found it to be somewhat frustrating to work with some of the individuals that Professor Kittrie hired to administer some of his related programs, which, apparently, had also been funded by that federal grant. Those programs really had little to do with LAWCOR, other than they were directed, using that word somewhat loosely, by Professor Kittrie, and they were financially administered by the same obsequious idiot, when in the presence of Professor Kittrie, who financially administered LAWCOR.

The obsequious idiot had managed to graduate from the American University Law School, and, at the same time, befriend Professor Kittrie, while attending law school there. With those two undistinguished credentials in hand, he assisted Professor Kittrie in obtaining government grants, for useless purposes, immediately following his graduation from law school, and he apparently managed to do little else, thereafter, at least up to that point in time. He was a perfect example of how being obsequious can overcome an obvious and distinct lack of ability and ambition.

Then, of course, there was an individual who was in charge of "policy," in Professor Kittrie's currently associated book endeavor. What that policy happened to be was something that I never fully understood, although it must have been related to prison reform. Nevertheless, I don't think that Professor Kittrie, or the individual in charge of policy, ever decided what that policy on prison reform should be, just that everything, related to the subject, should be reformed. I often wondered if that included the institutional breakfast menus, too.

To be quite honest about the matter, I don't think that the individual in charge of policy really had much of an interest in prison reform, including their breakfast menus, and he certainly did not appear to have done much, following his graduation from law school, which would seem to have qualified him as an expert on prison reform. The only achievements that I could observe, following that graduation, were a mustache and a divorce, and the only interests that I could observe related more to coeds than to prisoners, which, probably, explained the mustache and the divorce, if not his employment at that university.

Well, within months, I decided to leave the mustache, the sycophant, and the Arabic language behind, and, in turn, return to the practice of law, which now seemed far more inviting, maybe for all three of those reasons, if for no others. My continuing interest in students, and in instructing them in an academic environment, which, in spite of everything, remained, would have to wait for another day, in a more propitious setting, and, in that respect, another chapter to follow in this tall tale.

CHAPTER LII

STONEGATE: MY YARD WORK, REPLICATING FORESTS FOUND IN CENTRAL PENNSYLVANIA WAS NOT UNLIKE THE YARD WORK DONE BY MY PARENTS, WHO WERE PROBABLY ENGAGED IN THAT KIND OF A PURSUIT, BECAUSE THEY WERE, GENERALLY, WITHOUT FRIENDS

I REALLY did not know what transpired at home, during the day, among the other three members of my family, who remained there, because I was usually away at work at the time. I did know that the two younger members were somewhat disruptive early in the morning, while I was trying to eat my breakfast, and that their mother usually had to restore some semblance of household order, following my plaintiff pleas to that effect.

I suppose that it was quite natural that two preschool children would become that active in the morning. After all, they had just concluded ten or more hours of non-activity during a typical night, which is normally called, for want of a better word, sleep. So in the morning, after returning once again to an upright position, they were simply trying to make up for lost time. And my wife, who, fortunately, was still their mother, during those challenging times, was always trying to instill some sense of civilization, Danish style, in both of them. Now that I think about it, because I never really thought much about it before now, all of that activity, by her two preschool children, which we had unfortunately conceived at an earlier time, was probably why my wife decided to forego teaching, for nearly ten years, and to stay at home with her two little pre-school children. That way, she could ensure that her two little urchins did not grow up to become like their father.

Fortunately, for everyone concerned, according to my now fully grown children, I managed to avoid most of the child-rearing responsibilities, by going to work on most days, nearly all day, whether I needed to or not. And by doing that, according to both of them, I apparently assumed the pathetic proportions, in our family at least, of a drone bee in a well-organized hive. In their uncharitable opinion, after fertilizing the queen and, thereby, ensuring that the consequent progeny would result in a continuation of the hive, or the family, if you prefer to think of it in more human terms, I was ordinarily shunted aside by the hive, or the family, if you still prefer to think of it in that way, as a semi-meaningless fixture, who leaves the hive, or the family, even if you no longer think of it in that way, and goes to work every morning.

Nevertheless, with elements of charity reappearing on the part of my critical children, with age, if not experience, I was, at least, given credit, in retrospect, for reappearing, unlike my drone-like counterparts, on the weekends, at least some of them, depending upon the amount of pending work, still remaining on my desk in the office. I was still, however, no more than someone, in their critical opinion, whose value was found in a former sperm, an income from endless legal work and, time permitting, yard work . . . on the weekends, of course.

I am sure that most people, even in these more progressive times, realize that fathers, especially those born in the earlier part of the twentieth century, were not always held in the highest regard, not by the rest of their family, especially their unappreciative and grown children, which certainly explains the lack of charity in this instance. If, however, I am called upon to address that lack of charity, not to mention those uncharitable remarks, I will readily acknowledge that I was our family's lowly yard man, but that was solely because we could not afford to pay anyone else to do that kind of menial work, when the boys were growing up. And with our house located on nearly half-an-acre of land at the time, with less than half of that amount occupied by a dwelling, something had to be done about the rest of the area. So the "drone" found a niche, which was landscaping the area, or menial yard work, according to the rest of the family, on the weekends, of course, at least those in which he did not have pending work remaining on his desk in the office.

Actually, the niche seemed to work out quite well for everyone in the family. It kept me outside, where I, undoubtedly, could not interfere with what was required in the raising of children. It also involved working with dirt, not high on my wife's value system, which seemed to begin with children, both of them, at least at that point, and which seemed to end long before any form of dirty yard work. And, moreover, given her motherly commitments, which seemed to be extensive, she did not have much time to do yard work, even if she wanted to, and she made it abundantly clear, on more occasions than I might like, that she really did not want to. And while our two children were growing up, especially during their elementary school days, they were far too young, according to their overly-protective mother, to shovel dirt into a large wheelbarrow and to push it around to a number of destinations in our yard. So quite naturally or unnaturally, if you prefer to look at it that way, the yard work fell to the "drone," on the weekends, at least some of them, because there really wasn't anyone else in the family who was willing to do that kind of work, or, at least, interested in doing it, and we couldn't afford to pay someone else at the time to do it.

Actually, it was always rather disappointing when I couldn't do that kind of work on some of the weekends, because I rather enjoyed doing it, even though I am not completely sure why, even to this day.

In fact, it would seem to be rather anomalous that anyone would like to do yard work within the parameters of the metropolitan area, which, of course, was where we lived at the time. It was, after all, carried out, in large part, during the summer months, when the thermometer normally ranges between hot, very hot, unbearably hot, and hell! And, naturally, it is a very dirty business, at any time of the year, which, when you think about it, involves, among a number of other mundane things, moving a wheelbarrow full of dirt throughout the yard, normally requiring more brawn than brains. That, of course, may actually explain my aptitude for the whole dirty business, according to the uncharitable remarks of both of my now-grown sons.

Actually, when you think about it, as I do quite often now, my aptitude, to whatever extent that it may have existed, reflected a certain geographic, if not parochial, perspective in horticulture. Maybe that perspective did not come during the early years of my gardening ventures, in and around our home, but it did come, especially as I grew older. By that time, I had evolved into a gardener, who enjoyed creating landscapes that were reminiscent of my childhood in the mountain ranges of central Pennsylvania. Indeed, with that intention in mind, I tried to plant bushes and trees that normally grew in forests, acid-loving forests, that generally occurred throughout those mountain ranges.

There was something about those forests, if not the surrounding mountain ranges, that aesthetically, or philosophically, or, even, theologically, had a claim on what I was and, maybe, what I am now. The historical, if not geographical, explanation for that claim, or those claims, whatever they may have been, probably lies in the fact that my growing-up years were spent at 269 Susquehanna Avenue, which was at the very foot of the Allegheny mountains. That's right, "Penn's Woods" were literally bordering and towering over my backyard, as part of a major mountain range, the Appalachian

Mountain Range. A photograph of my family house, located at 269 Susquehanna Ave in Lock Haven, Pennsylvania, has been included, as Exhibit 108, in the Appendix.

Because of their proximity, I grew up wondering throughout those mountains or, if you prefer, the forests that had grown throughout them, usually with my dog as company. As I grew older and, therefore, eligible for a license, I began to hunt and fish in them, too, still accompanied my Kerry Blue Terrier. And although I arguably left those mountain ranges behind, following my graduation from high school and entry into an academic life in a metropolitan area, I never really forgot about them, not during all of the educational years that followed, nor, for that matter, the professional years of practicing law that described my life thereafter.

Now, fully in the winter of my years, I realize, more than ever, that those mountains and everything about them, if not within them, including the forests and the streams, were part of what I was and, notwithstanding the passage of an extensive amount of time, not to mention an extensive amount of experience, what I still am, in so many ways, even today. I guess that is why I have been continually trying, over the course of a lifetime, to replicate aspects of them, or, if you will, their meaning to me, in the landscapes that have enveloped my home, no matter where I happened to be living, even in retirement at 4 Maass Lane in Rehoboth Beach, Delaware.

Nevertheless, I must admit that there was always something rather uncomfortable about my continual efforts to replicate part of the forestry of my childhood, probably because, for much of my adult life, I wanted to leave my childhood behind. And although it still makes me somewhat uncomfortable to think about it, even now, that included my parents, too. And I certainly could not escape my parents, not to mention their way of being, by continually working in the yard, replicating plant life, frequently found in those mountain ranges, because they liked to do the same thing, which they traditionally called, "gardening." Not just any kind of gardening, either, but a form that fit nicely within the mountainous terrain partially surrounding their home at 269 Susquehanna Avenue. The fit was so well done that you could not easily tell where their land came to an end and the mountainous region, partially surrounding it, began. That was no less true at their subsequent home at 42 Sylvan Drive in Sunset Pines, both of which, of course, were in Lock Haven, Pennsylvania.

Yes, wherever they happened to be living in that town, my parents liked working in their yard, and, not surprisingly, much, if not most, of their free time was devoted to doing just that. And I always believed, as I was growing up, that the explanation for their rather exclusive gardening interest was because they did not have any close friends, at least not with whom they socialized, anyway. They certainly were rarely, if ever, invited to anyone's home for dinner; nor did they ever, to my recollection, invite anyone to our home for dinner. The only people in town with whom they seemed to be involved, short of some organizational activities, especially in my mother's case, seemed to be individuals with whom they worked, and that involvement generally seemed to occur in the workplace.

Oh, sure, there were always those occasional pleasantries, exchanged with others, on a shopping trip downtown on a Friday or Saturday evening, or even elsewhere, on other occasions, such as at a restaurant, like the Pine Creek Inn, on a Thursday evening, or even at one of the not infrequent church suppers, such as the one occurring, bi-monthly, at the East Main Street Methodist Church. But those pleasantries, exchanged, occasionally, with others, on those kinds of occasions, or situations, were, quite obviously, even to a young boy, simply pleasantries, exchanged, occasionally, with others, who were townsmen, but not necessarily friends. They certainly were not the interchange of meaningful conversation between close friends, who clearly cared about each other, for no other reason than they were close friends!

Because of their isolation during my childhood, I yearned for friends when I was growing up, not for me, because I had so many, but for my parents, who did not. And even now, when I work in the yard, which is quite often, because I still love mountainous terrains and replicating the forest vegetation that you ordinarily find among them, an uncomfortable feeling may come over me, sometimes, probably because working in the yard is still, by its very nature, a lonely pursuit. And that feeling will not go away until I, quite literally, begin to think about the number of close friends that I have acquired throughout my life, some of whom I still have, even at this stage in my life!

CHAPTER LIII

STONEGATE: WELSH TERRIER; THE JOYS AND SORROWS ASSOCIATED WITH HAVING A WELSH TERRIER IN OUR FAMILY

I ALSO had an uncomfortable feeling when my parents came down to visit us one weekend with a dog in the car, ostensively for the boys. At the time, the boys were about seven and ten years of age, and they had been begging for a dog, for some time, but we, their parents, who saw a canine as an additional responsibility, were not too thrilled about the prospect. So we tried to delay the inevitable, but, in the end, we became resigned to the inevitability. We just never anticipated that the inevitability would come to pass in the form of an "energizer bunny," called a Welsh Terrier, sleeping in a basket, in the back seat of my parents' car.

Living with that dog, which is what we had to learn how to do, required a whole lot of effort, and an equal amount of patience, by everyone in the family. Picking up "poop," for example, was a community standard, an individual effort, and not one of the more attractive aspects of living with that little Welsh Terrier. Moreover, teaching that terrier to "poop" outside, rather than inside, was a time-consuming and all-consuming effort, undertaken by every member of the family, on one occasion or another, for very obviously odious reasons.

The lessons began with geography, slowly moved into sociology, then on to psychology and, finally, ended up in criminology. The crime, of course, was "pooping" in the wrong geographic location, and to encourage the dog to avoid doing so, enormous social pressure was exerted by the whole family, so that the dog was psychologically driven, by guilt, to "poop" outside. The result of all of that education, of course, was neuroses, not just for the dog, but for those of us who walked the dog, and who walked upright, on two legs, while doing so.

To offset the dark days of "poop" control, not to mention neuroses, we decided to find a name for our little terrier that would be more consistent with the anterior part of the pooch, who really did have a very cute face, as opposed to the posterior, which, of course, was responsible for all of our neuroses, two and four-legged alike, not to mention the stains on the carpet. The name was eventually supplied by my mother, who did not have to look at all of those carpet stains, because she lived hundreds of miles away, in a "poop" free zone, and in an unstained carpeted house in Lock Haven, Pennsylvania. Because she did, and because she believed that there was something misty about our little pooch, while ignoring the posterior and focusing on the anterior, she selectively named him, "Misty."

Well, I can assure you that there was nothing "misty" about the carpet stains. Nevertheless, carpet stains aside, our cute little terrier became a "Misty," who, nevertheless, continued to struggle with the social standards of "pooping." Eventually, however, I am happy to report, on behalf of myself and the carpet, not to mention my exasperated Danish counterpart, that, after a prolonged period of time, which seemed to approximate infinity, Misty began to prefer lawn over carpet and outside rather than inside to deposit her well-digested lunch. With that, I, too, began to believe that there was something "misty" about Misty!

Forgetting the name for a moment and focusing more on the reason for the name, I think that we all grew to love that little pooch, notwithstanding an occasional violation of "pooping" standards as the years passed. She became so much more than simply the family pet as she began to grow up She became a part of our family, differently, but still a part, a recognizable part, with traits and characteristics that made her as distinctly lovable as her name.

There was never any doubt about how much both boys loved that dog. Each boy did so in his own way, naturally, but that way was as clear to us as it was to the dog, who loved each one of them in return, differently, of course. Being boys, even very young boys, they never actually said that they loved the dog, naturally, but some things were better said without words, and that was certainly true in this four-legged instance.

It certainly explains why my older son, Court, who was no more than ten years of age at the time, would get up before the rest of us and take Misty out for an early morning walk. Admittedly, Misty was normally sitting at the edge of his bed in the morning, hardly able to wait for him to wake up and join her for an early morning walk, which, eventually, Court would sleepily oblige. At the conclusion of those walks, Court would often say to the rest of us, Danish and non-Danish alike, while typically beginning our morning breakfast, that Misty, "had a proud walk." I think, on reflection, that what Court meant was that he was rather proud to walk with his dog, who was equally proud to walk with him.

Then, again, in wrestling matches between the two boys, usually occurring shortly after school, just before dinnertime, Misty would typically try to help Lars, who was four years younger, twenty pounds lighter and, typically, suffering accordingly. Upon hearing the younger brother's screams, down in the family room, where those melees ordinarily took place, the dog would typically race down the stairs into the family room, in order to join the fracas and assist the younger brother, who was always on the bottom of the pile and screaming for help. Within seconds, the dog would ordinarily grab Court's foot, which was readily available and which was covered with nothing more than a sock, a rather smelly sock, because the boys were not allowed to wear shoes in the house. And the dog, now part of the melee, would typically begin to shake the sock, not to mention the foot within, furiously, in a terrier-like fashion!

At that point, Court's screaming, because his foot was nearly being shaken off, usually superseded that of his brother, who still remained precariously on the bottom, although much relieved, even though his circumstances did not seem to warrant it. And the amount of the noise, which now consisted of screaming by both boys, growling by a furious Welsh Terrier and the hysterical laughter of their father, who, by now, had already joined in the fray, was so great that the only responsible individual in the house, who happened to be Danish, usually intervened!

Often in life, however, nice stories, even those about young boys and their dog, eventually have a certain amount of sadness to them, too, because such scenarios, nice as they are, never take place apart from the real world. And, unfortunately, reality almost always involves a certain amount of sadness, at least at some point, and this story is no exception. That is because the wrestling matches and the walks and the "pooping," from our beloved Welsh Terrier, came to a tragic end one afternoon, when a school bus, bringing the boys back home in the afternoon, errantly ran over her, as she eagerly awaited their return, alongside the road, directly in front of our house.

CHAPTER LIV

*STONEGATE: CAMP DEVITT;
MY MOTHER WAS PLACED IN A
TUBERCULOSIS SANITARIUM
FOR SEVERAL YEARS AND,
WHILE RECUPERATING THERE,
SHE CONTRACTED SERUM
HEPATITIS, FOR WHICH SHE WAS
SUBSEQUENTLY HOSPITALIZED, FOR
AN EXTENDED PERIOD OF TIME*

THE UNFORTUNATE loss of our little Welsh Terrier was not the only tragedy to strike my family during my growing-up years. Among a number of others, not really material at this point, was one of far greater consequence, which occurred when I was a junior in high school. The circumstances surrounding that occurrence is really a story about how my family barely survived in the darkest of hours.

The darkness came in the form of a bacteria, called mycobacterium tuberculosis, which caused my mother to become seriously ill with tuberculosis. The illness became so serious that a medical decision was made, after several weeks, to place her in a tuberculosis sanitarium, called Camp Devitt, near Allenwood, Pennsylvania, about an hour away from our home in Lock Haven, Pennsylvania. Sadly, my mother was institutionalized in that sanitarium for over a year-and-a-half, while trying to recover from an illness for which there was really no effective form of medication at the time, other than bed rest, and that was not a very effective means, either. Actually, recovery, as this story makes abundantly clear, was, generally speaking, a painfully slow process, when it occurred at all!

Indeed, at one point during her institutionalization, it seemed that my mother would never recover at all, or that, if she did, it would require that she become a resident of that tuberculosis sanitarium for years. That, in itself, was worrisome enough, if not outright alarming, especially to a boy who was no more than a junior in high school. But the situation subsequently became even more alarming, because, while institutionalized, my mother developed serum hepatitis, accompanied by a raging fever that reached, at one critical point, one hundred and five degrees. At that point, my desperate father had her transferred, following the recommendation of several physicians, to a nearby hospital, called Devine Providence, in Williamsport, Pennsylvania, where she slowly, and I mean very slowly, began an agonizing process of recovery, over a number of months, from a seriously life-threatening medical situation.

Following her eventual release from the hospital, we were advised that the recovery from serum hepatitis may be lengthy, through bed rest at home, and that it may well be a number of months. And that is not even considering the amount of time that was still required for her eventual recovery from tuberculosis. We were also advised that, notwithstanding all of that bed rest, she may never fully recover from the serum hepatitis, because of the possibility of permanent damage to her liver. Consequently, the unspoken concern for all of us, remaining at home at the time, namely my father and myself, was whether my mother would recover at all.

Not during any of the time that my mother was institutionalized at Camp Devitt and, subsequently, hospitalized at Devine Providence was I permitted to visit her, because, as it was explained to me, tuberculosis and serum hepatitis were highly infectious diseases. Some things, however, do not require an explanation, especially given the circumstances, and I did not need anyone to explain to me why my father was rarely at home during much of this time. I knew that he worked all day, nearly every day, and most evenings, too, in order to pay for all of the catastrophic things that were happening to our family. And when he was not working in the evening, which was rarely, he normally drove down to see my mother at the tuberculosis sanitarium, or, subsequently, at the hospital. All of that meant, of course, that I was the only member of our family who remained at home, who walked on two legs, that is, during any significant part of the day or night. It also meant, initially anyway, that I was generally alone at dinner time and, thereafter, at least until my father came home from work, in the evening, or from visiting my mother, later in the evening. And things did not materially change on the weekends, either, because my father continued to work during the day and visit my mother in the evening, with the exception of Sunday, when he usually just visited her in the afternoon.

To say that life at home, in the evenings and on the weekends, had become rather bleak and lonely is an understatement. To say that I constantly worried about what would become of my mother is also an understatement. To say that I was afraid of what would become of my family, or what was left of it, if my mother did not recover at all, is an uncomfortably accurate statement. And to say that I was afraid, in that event, of what would become of myself, is an embarrassingly true statement.

Because I was afraid of the occurrence of any one of those things, or all three of them, I had great difficulty in concentrating on my schoolwork during the day and on my homework during the evening. I was also afraid that I would never be able to go to college, even though that had always been my plan, because my father could barely afford to pay for my mother's institutionalization and subsequent hospitalization. Futility, not surprisingly, had more meaning at the time than possibility.

Actually, the only possibility that I could imagine at the time was that my mother would die, my father would never be the same, and, therefore, I would, effectively, be left by myself, which, for me at the time, and certainly at that age, defined futility. At some point, however, the fear generated by that possibility became so overwhelming that I literally could not live with it anymore, so I decided to do something about my circumstances, not all-at-once, but little-by-little, over an extended period of time. Among other things, I decided not to stay at home, alone, after school, anymore, doing my homework, among a number of other lonely things, not if I could help it, anyway

So I started to go home with my friend, Steve Romeo, after school, and to do most of my homework with him, at his house. But I made sure to finish at least an hour before my friend, Allen Joslyn, sat down with his family for dinner at their house. That way, I could go over there, which only took a few minutes, and work with Allen on our homework in mathematics. Allen was as good at the subject as I was not, which was a matter of common knowledge within the Joslyn household, so it did not seem so unusual, or even unbecoming, that I would be interested in working with him on our homework in mathematics, every day, even though it happened to be just before dinnertime. And I knew from experience, which had begun as early as our friendship, in the seventh grade, that I would always be invited for dinner by Mrs. Joslyn, at the conclusion of our mathematics homework.

The hours following dinner with the Joslyn family always seemed to move along more slowly, probably because I had to go home to feed the dog, at that time, and to take him out for an evening walk. Thereafter, with little to do except feel sorry for my mother, my father, and myself, in ascending order, of course, I would usually try to entertain myself at home, albeit unsuccessfully, for the rest of the evening, or, at least, until my father came home. Unfortunately, however, he was usually too exhausted and too worried about my mother to talk very much about anything after he arrived. Consequently, those hours at home, in the evening, after dinner, with my dog and my thoughts, were the worst time of all, so, eventually, I resolved to change that situation, too.

I did that by making a new friend in high school, after several months of being home alone, every evening, who had a family that I also liked being around, which was the whole point, and which I joined every evening, after dinner, to play a game of cards. Actually, I had known Jim Reichard for a number of years, prior to that time, because we had been in the same math and science classes, all the way through junior and senior high school. I just never realized that he had such a nice family, who would enjoy my company, nearly every evening, after dinner, while playing a game of cards. I guess, until that point, I just didn't need to know, but now that I did, and because I did, I joined them nearly every evening, in order to play a game of "five-hundred-rummy," which usually involved a lot of talk and a lot of laughter, not unlike my own family, in similar circumstances, prior to my mother's institutionalization.

The weekends, however, presented a lot more problems, probably because, in the absence of school, there were a lot more hours to fill. Because of those unfilled hours, I decided to resurrect my old friendship with Nevin B. Greninger, which had begun, years ago, with our mutual interest in coin and stamp collecting, but which had been replaced, in the meantime, by other interests and other friends, especially as I had grown older. Realizing now, however, after a few months of being home alone on the weekends, how much I really liked Nevin, not to mention our mutual collecting endeavors, which had formally occupied a lot of our time, and on the weekends, too, I decided to rejoin Nevin, so that we could recommence our coin collecting together, and on the weekends, once again. And because we now took our numismatic interests far more seriously, requiring a lot more of our time, I often had to stay for lunch and, sometimes, even for dinner at his house, too.

Looking back now, at that difficult time in my life, I am constrained to acknowledge that I do not know when most people discover what they are suited for in choosing their life's work. My Presbyterian friends say that it occurs when you receive some kind of a "calling," and that the "calling" is unmistakable, especially with respect to the ministry. Well, I am not speaking about the "ministry" here, or about some kind of a theological "calling," but I can certainly say, without any equivocation, that it had become quite clear to me, just what I had to do, in order to survive during that very difficult period in my life, and that I did it, without a moment's hesitation, and without any concern about whether it was the right thing to do, or not, at the time. And as I grew older, having graduated from high school and, then, college and, subsequently, graduate school and, finally, law school, I can most assuredly say that I did it, thereafter, for the rest of my life, as a member of the legal profession!

CHAPTER LV

STONEGATE; KERRY BLUE TERRIER; MY KERRY BLUE TERRIER WAS PUT DOWN BY A VETERINARIAN BECAUSE, IN THE ABSENCE OF MY MOTHER AND FATHER AND, EVENTUALLY, MYSELF, THERE WAS NO ONE AT HOME TO TAKE CARE OF HIM

ONE THING that I did not do very well during that difficult period in my family's life was to take care of my very best friend, who happened to be a Kerry Blue Terrier. That old Kerry Blue had been part of my life, for nearly all of my life, at least up to that point in my life. And we did almost everything together, during most of that time, except, possibly, go to school, and that was only because Kerry Blue Terriers were not allowed in school at that time in Clinton County.

Notwithstanding that discriminating disallowance, Terry, which was his name, would normally walk down the driveway with me, nearly every morning, while I was on my way to school. And after a couple of pats, usually on the head, normally accompanied by a few wags of the tail, he would just stand down there, at the bottom of the driveway, and watch me walk down the sidewalk, until I was well out of sight, on my way down Susquehanna Avenue toward Roosevelt Elementary School, which was a few miles away on West Church Street. And when the time came for me to arrive back home, later in the afternoon, after another educational day away from him, he would normally be sitting back down there, at the bottom of the driveway, waiting for me to reappear, with his tail wagging once again, because I was back home with him again. A series of photographs of that big dog, at various times and locations, have been included as Exhibit 109 in the Appendix.

Following my arrival back home and a quick change of clothes, into a more rugged form of outdoor wear, the two of us would, generally, wonder the mountains together, almost every afternoon, which was not at all difficult, because they were located right behind our house at 269 Susquehanna Avenue in Lock Haven, Pennsylvania. Often, I would have to stop, at the most inconvenient times, while he chased a rabbit or two, at least until they were out of sight, at which point he would normally reappear, through the brush, tail wagging, somewhat apologetically, so that, following that brief interruption, we could be on our way once again.

Years later, when I had become old enough, the two of us would often go hunting together, but more out of being together in the mountains once again, rather than a desire to shoot something that would inadvertently stumble across our path. Nevertheless, I would still walk slightly ahead, shotgun in hand, with eyes fixed, in case something would possibly appear, with my Kerry Blue Terrier, ever alert, walking slightly behind me, at least most of the time.

Just as often, Wally Smith and Charlie Lair, who lived nearby, joined us on some of those hunting trips, and they never seemed to mind the presence of a Kerry Blue Terrier, tagging along, even though he had not been invited. In fact, the very first thing that they would do, before we began our mountainous ascent, was to kneel down and place a few friendly pats on the head of our four-footed hunting companion, which was normally accompanied by some kind of affectionate words. If you had grown up in those mountains, as we had, you would understand that young boys, who lived there, often spoke in such a manner to a dog, especially to a big dog, but not to anyone else, certainly not to each other, and certainly not to their parents, not at any time.

I guess that, with the noted exception of school, there really wasn't much that I would do, not in those days and at that age, that I would not do with that Kerry Blue, even if a lot of other kids were doing it, too. If, for example, we . . . meaning most of the neighborhood kids . . . decided to play football in Price Park, which is now called Hanna Park, and which was just up the street, a short distance away, that Kerry Blue would likely play, too. And, may I add, he made some incredible open-field tackles; the trouble, however, was that he tackled anything that was running, which included, on occasion, those on our team, too. So just as many players on our side complained about their pants being torn by an overzealous, football-playing, Kerry Blue Terrier.

Naturally, we didn't play football in the summer; like most kids, we played that "great American pastime," which, of course, was baseball. And our baseball games took place in Price Park, too, except in a different part of the Park, and, of course, that ever-present Kerry Blue Terrier played right along with us. In fact, he usually liked to play in the outfield, probably because he was able reach the balls that were hit out there, long before his two-legged fielding counterparts. That ordinarily should have been quite helpful to the players in the outfield, because there were no fences out there, and, consequently, the balls could, and often did, roll forever.

The trouble, however, was that, upon reaching the ball, the four-legged outfielder would usually refuse to give it to any one of his two-legged, "out-fielding" counterparts, even though they would normally spend a considerable amount of time imploring him to do so. Eventually, however, that continued refusal would pose a problem for the team in the field, because, by now, the batter, who had originally hit the ball out there, was part of the way around the base path and on his way towards "home."

To be quite fair about the matter, it is also true that the four-legged outfielder would often run, with the ball still in his mouth, back into the infield, which, of course, is what any good outfielder should do . . . get the ball back into the infield . . . although, admittedly, with more of a throwing motion. Even aside from that technical distinction, however, there was still an underlying problem, because once he reached the infield, that "outfielder-now-turned-infielder" would absolutely refuse to give up the ball, especially to any one of the other infielders, most of whom would typically spend a considerable amount of time trying to coax him to do so. Meanwhile, the baserunner, who initiated this baseball drama, by hitting one into the "outfield," some time ago, would likely be continuing his journey around the base path, now in somewhat of a sauntering manner, or even in a jaunty-like fashion, while laughing, hysterically, all the way!

Obviously, a run would have now scored, because of the outlandish baseball behavior of a furry, four-footed, "outfielder-now-turned-infielder." And truth be told, once the laughter died down, by both teams now, everyone, "batters" as well as "fielders," all of whom loved dogs, and this one in particular, would normally agree, with barely any discussion, to simply ignore the run as well as the outlandish behavior of their four-footed colleague, in order to continue the game, and on a more serious note, I should hasten to add.

Nevertheless, in order to do that . . . continue the game, I mean . . . the two-legged players needed the ball, and, unfortunately, it continued to reside, even at that frustrating point, in the mouth of the furry, four-legged player. Even more problematic, if that were at all possible, at least at this stage of the game, any effort to continue with the "great American pastime," by dislodging the ball from the mouth of that "major-league-terrier," was usually met with a rather menacing growl!

At that juncture, I am constrained to point out that the baseball game either came to a premature end, or the furry four-legged player got tired of holding the ball in his mouth and simply dropped it at the foot of one of his, now, disgusted, two-legged playing counterparts, whichever alternative came first. And I must conclude my description of this unfortunate and unusual baseball circumstance, at least at this point, by advising any skeptical reader that there really were no other realistic alternatives, not at that point. Based on a certain amount of unfortunate experience, everyone on the field . . . with two legs, that is . . . decided, years ago, when they first began to play baseball with a furry, four-legged, "major-league-terrier," who continually refused to play by the rules, by holding on to the ball far longer than ordinarily permitted, that it was not worth getting bitten, in order to win a game or, for that matter, to simply carry on with it.

I should point out, at this point, anyway, that, notwithstanding his inability to play by the rules, in both sports, by the way, none of the boys, who played baseball and football with us, ever complained about the dog being there, while we played. I guess that was because, being young boys, who were growing up in the neighborhood, they kind of liked that old Kerry Blue, too. After all, he was as much a part of their lives, on a daily basis, as mine, and that statement should not be construed to limit his participation in their lives to just two sports. Everything, literally everything, that boys our age could possibly do, indoors as well as outdoors, we usually did with him, too.

All of that changed, however, after my mother became institutionalized with tuberculosis. I no longer played baseball or football, anymore, not with my friends, not even with my best friend, because I really did not care about doing any of those kind of things, anymore, not even with him. In fact, I really did not do much of anything with him, except feed him in the morning and evening, and walk with him, briefly, thereafter. Even that was sort of perfunctory, because

I just did not care, not even about him, not about anything other than the loss of my family. That was not lost on that Kerry Blue Terrier, because he no longer jumped up on me, excitedly, when I came back home in the evening. He would just greet me, quietly, at the kitchen door, and wait, patiently, for his dinner, and, following that, join me on a nightly walk in the mountains, without much to say, not by either one of us.

In those meaningless walks, we normally followed a mountain trail, beginning right behind the house, which began to rise slowly upwards, in somewhat of a meandering fashion, through a rather dense part of the forest. At the top, however, where everything seemed to open up, we quickened our pace, because we could, even in the darkness, with the dog walking right along with me, sometimes a little ahead and sometimes not, but, generally, right by my side. Now, however, he did not even chase any of the creatures that briefly appeared and just as quickly disappeared, into the darkness, which, of course, was their sanctuary, and, now, maybe even ours, at least over the course of that nightly walk, and certainly at that point in our lives.

I'm sure, now that I think about it, which I do quite often at this point in my aged life, that the feint silhouettes of the towering oak and sugar maple trees, enveloping that mountain trail, at least at the top, which were more than distinctive in the moonlit darkness, must have seemed just as eerie at the time as the two ghostly figures quietly moving among them. And whatever else may possibly be said about their nightly presence, in that haunting scenario, one of them, the taller of the two, must have appeared to be a very lonely figure.

I guess, in looking back, which I do quite often now, the other one, with a smaller silhouette, must have been just as lonely, but, unlike me, he really could not do much about it. At that point, his life consisted of no more than a bowl of dog food in the morning and evening, an empty house in between, and, finally, a brief pat, a couple of strained words and a terribly short walk in the evening shadows of a moonlit mountainside. And it went on that way, nearly every day and every evening, for more months than I would like to say. Then, one evening, when I came home, fully expecting to feed my dog and take him out for an obligatory evening stroll in the mountains, he was gone, literally gone!

My father, who loved that dog almost as much as his son, except, maybe, in his own quiet way, could no longer stand to see him suffer like that. And in a subsequent explanation, to a now tearful and disbelieving son, my father said that he did not believe that either one of us could substantially change the way that we were coping with my mother's absence, and that our dog was suffering, terribly, as a result. So for essentially that reason, he took our Kerry Blue Terrier to the veterinarian, earlier that evening, and had him put down.

I realize now, if I did not at the time, that it must have broken my father's heart to do that; it certainly broke mine. And, maybe, even worse, it made me realize what I had become, in my mother's absence, which was rather disappointing, because, in reality, I had choices, even then, even in that dreadful family situation. And I could have chosen to do more for that Kerry Blue Terrier, than a meal and a short mountainside walk thereafter, even though the absence of the rest of our family, almost on a daily basis, had become intolerable for both of us.

Acknowledging the wisdom that comes from hindsight, especially following a lifetime of experience, some of which may have been rather uncomfortable, I can honestly say, with a discomforting historical perspective, that abandoning those whom you care about, no matter how intolerable your circumstances, may be, in the end, the most intolerable thing of all. That is true, in my retrospective opinion, whether we are speaking about a member of a family, a friend, a professional associate, or even a Kerry Blue Terrier.

I believe that! I believe it even more when I look at a photograph of a Kerry Blue Terrier, sitting obediently by my feet, at an earlier time, shortly before my mother's institutionalization, when we, as a family, were happily seated together in our living room, celebrating the Christmas season. That photograph has been included in Exhibit 14 in the Appendix, although, sometimes, I wish that it had not.

CHAPTER LVI

STONEGATE: LIS; OUR PRESCHOOL CHILDREN'S EATING HABITS DURING LIS' COLLEGE CLASSES; BEING A SUBSTITUTE TEACHER WITH EARLY MORNING TELEPHONE CALLS; THE FIRST DAY AS A PERMANENT TEACHER AND THE RESULTING "KEYS INCIDENT"

AT ONE point during the boy's preschool years, my wife, or, at least, what was once my wife, decided to go back to college, except that, this time, it was, fortunately, in this country. The reason for the academic return was because she was interested in becoming an elementary school teacher in this country, sometime in the near future, but the educational authorities had made it clear that they would not honor her education degree, or even all of her college credits, from the teachers college that she had graduated from in Denmark. They would, however, give her credit for the courses that an education major would be required to take in this country, but that would still leave her about a year and a half short of fulfilling the necessary requirements for an education degree from a college in this country. So one evening, which I would like to forget, she, the woman that I had married and had once loved, at least until that point, informed me that she was going to go back to college . . . at the University of Maryland!

Now that, on its face, may seem to have been a rather innocuous statement to an uninformed reader, or, maybe, even a fairly impressive one to the same kind of reader, but, in reality, the statement was an announcement that life, as I had once known it, and as I had once liked it, was about to come to a tragic end! Now, because we only had one car and could not afford two, I had to come home, immediately after work, once a week, on a Wednesday, in order to enable a former housewife and mother to attend classes, early in the evening, on that fateful day.

I certainly did not have any problem with the classes being in the evening, because I had to go to work during the day, and I needed our only car to drive to work. Nevertheless, there was still a major problem with her academic aspirations, although not necessarily an insurmountable one, because I had to leave work, early enough, to get home, soon enough, to allow her to get to her classes, on time, which was early in the evening. But it occurred to me that I could solve that problem, by getting to work a little bit earlier on that day, and any unfinished business could be completed at home, on the kitchen table, after dinner was over.

Nevertheless, there was still another major problem, and that one was insurmountable, because my wife, or, rather, upon further reflection, my former wife, was going to leave behind two small, preschool-age children that evening, who were one and four years of age, and there would be no one at home to look after them . . . except me! And I could not realistically afford to hire a "nanny" to help me, which meant, in effect, that it would be solely my responsibility, which is why I said, hereinbefore, that the problem was insurmountable!

It was also insurmountable for another, more gastronomically related, reason, because I had always enjoyed coming home at the end of a demanding day, in order to have dinner with my family, in more than a civilized circumstance, insured by my no-nonsense Danish wife. It was a welcome respite from the stress-filled days of practicing law, often in circumstances that were rather unpleasant. It was also a pleasant way to spend time with my whole family, including both children, at the end of a long and tiring day. After all, if one has a family, it is important to spend time with them, and that was a very nice time to do it, at dinnertime, when everyone was happily eating, or, if not, my wife could responsibly intervene. And, finally, I always enjoyed a nice meal at dinnertime, especially when it was well-prepared, and my former wife did everything well, especially in the early years of our marriage, including the preparation of an evening meal.

Unfortunately, however, she would likely be absent during dinnertime, on those occasions in which she attended class, and although she promised to prepare dinner, before departing, that still did not resolve a very serious and potential problem, which, by the way, ultimately became a very disgusting one as well. Yes, it was disgusting to watch my two young children eat their dinner, or, at least, try to do it, and I caution you that I am using the verb, "eat," in the broadest usage possible. For very little food was fortunate enough to reach the mouth of any one of those two little miscreants, and only a fraction of that amount ever traveled its way down to their stomachs. Oh, the food traveled all right, but not in any manner that could conceivably be considered to be part of the digestive process. In fact, even the fraction that did reach their mouths, often decided to change its course, for reasons that were beyond my comprehension, and travel, instead, right back out of their mouths, in a failed process of chewing, which, more accurately, could be described as disgusting!

The only other thing that could possibly be said about the whole misuse of the digestive process, other than disgusting, is that it must have also been tiring, or, maybe, even a little bit boring, too, because it did not seem to last very long. And although that may have actually seemed to be a blessing, initially, anyway, given what has already been described, it actually was not! No, what followed was even more disgusting, because both boys, now tired of the simple act of chewing, and bored with the traditional act of eating, decided, instead, to literally play with their food, by throwing some of it on the floor, and when that did not seem to be exciting enough, on each other. Unfortunately, however, being little children, with under developed throwing abilities, their aim was usually off, way off, which meant that the food, formally on their plates, now decorated much of the rest of the kitchen and, on occasion, each other!

The irony in all of this was that the newly decorated kitchen, compliments of a one and a four-year-old, began to deleteriously affect my marriage. Because my former wife, who, by now, had left the intellectual world of academia, and returned home to the unpredictable world of children, not to mention that unbelievable mess, created by them, did not understand why I had not cleaned it up before she returned home. And, unfortunately, she found my explanation to be wholly unacceptable, if not implausible.

I, on the other hand, found my explanation to be quite acceptable, more than reasonable and, if nothing else, rather imaginative. For one, I said that I thought that it was very important for parents, including mothers, to recognize the creative abilities of their children. And if I had erased their semi-artistic accomplishments in this instance, by cleaning up the mess on the kitchen walls, not to mention the kitchen floor, their mother would never have an opportunity to appreciate what they had accomplished, artistically, I mean, in just one evening, may I add. Moreover, and just as important, at least to my reasonable defense, housework, especially of that nature, was beyond my husbandly job description, and, therefore, if I had, nevertheless, engaged in that kind of work, by cleaning up the mess, it would have constituted a very serious violation under applicable labor law, which, of course, I had fortunately studied, quite recently, in a continuing legal education program, required for all practicing lawyers.

In response, my former wife, who has always been absolutely devoid of any form of humor, and who remains so even to this day, said that it defied explanation why someone, who can manage adults in complex litigation, by day, cannot manage two preschool children, trying to eat their dinner, at night. Faced now with what I considered to be an absolutely illogical response, I countered . . . in rebuttal, I might add . . . that you know that sex is sinful, because it can result in children, implicitly referring, of course, to the two little urchins in question.

Several months later, it occurred to me, in retrospect, that, possibly, I should have waived rebuttal and relied solely on my "case-in-chief," as we say in the law, because my rebuttal seemed to have caused me more harm than good. Indeed, it nearly eliminated "sin" over the last several months!

Fortunately, however, the harm, including the sinful aspect, faded, like most things, into the past, along with my unfortunate rebuttal. Unfortunately, however, the classes and the wifeless dinners on Wednesday evenings, as well as the gastronomical decorations and the unruly children, did not! No, that nightmare, or should I more appropriately say, those nightmares, continued on, for one night a week and one course a semester, ad infinitum, or should I more accurately say, ad nauseam, or, at least, so it seemed!

Actually, upon reflection, they, or, at least, the courses and the "one-night-a-week" nightmare, continued on, until sometime after my older son, Court, began to attend the first grade, approximately two years later. Then, thankfully, the Danish night student, who was formally a wife and a mother, graduated from the University of Maryland with a Bachelor of Science Degree in Education, and, as a result, I had every reason to believe that the nightmares, on Wednesday evenings, would soon be over. Dinner time, all of the time, would regain, I assumed, some sense of propriety, or, at least, some sense of normalization, and I would, therefore, regain some sense of sanity, if not some sense of decorum, on those previously frightful nights, not to mention some of their more sinful aspects. Even more, I could now safely set aside all of my previous thoughts of infanticide, because everything now in my home would, hopefully, return to a "once-upon-a-time" life.

Delusions, however, no matter how happy or hopeful they may seem to make one, have an uncanny way of being interrupted by, or unraveling in the face of, reality. And the reality destroying hopefulness in this instance, not to mention happiness, too, was a broadly stated intention on the part of the newly educated Dane, now in possession of a bachelor's degree in education, to use that degree to teach, as soon as she was able to secure an acceptable teaching position, nearby. That intention, however, was, thankfully, put on hold, at least until our younger son, Lars, began to attend the first grade. Apparently, still possessed of some sense of motherhood, the recent college graduate did not want to work, not outside of the home, until all of her children had, at least, started school. When that did happen, several years later, she began to accept substitute teaching positions, whenever and wherever they became available, while still actively pursuing, at the very same time, a full-time teaching position, as an elementary school teacher, somewhere in the Montgomery County School System in the State of Maryland.

Because it was very difficult at that time to obtain a full-time teaching position anywhere in the Montgomery County School System, given the paucity of new openings, the new graduate continued to work for some time at any elementary school that needed a substitute teacher in the County. That meant, of course, that the telephone would ring, incessantly, not for me, but for the recent college graduate, because a teacher, or a school, or even the school system, itself, needed a substitute for that day or, possibly, the next day, or even one day during the following week. Some of those calls occurred as early as five o'clock in the morning, before a public school was even scheduled to open anywhere in the County, which, believe me, was not a thrilling way to awaken in the morning. The others seemed to occur at dinner time, which meant, of course, that I now had to eat my dinners to the accompaniment of a Montgomery County School System symphonic telephone serenade.

Thankfully, however, the early morning wake-up calls and the dinnertime telephone serenades did, in fact, come to an end. Unfortunately, however, they did, because the object of those calls, who was formerly a wife and a mother, and a rather good one at that, finally obtained a full-time position, as a first-grade teacher, in a public school in Montgomery County. That meant, of course, that I no longer had to worry about dinner-time telephone intrusions, because dinners, at least as I had once known them, no longer existed. They were replaced by a number of inedible, unappetizing apparitions, which masqueraded as grandma's old-fashioned "home cookin'," but, in reality, were nothing more than microwaveable concoctions, in containers, with names that were far more appetizing than their contents.

All of this . . . referring to the unappetizing changes in my dining habits . . . came about because of an administrative "witch," who happened to be a first-generation Scandinavian in the Montgomery County School System, and who, therefore, took an enormous interest in the former Danish household cook. And following several meetings, the Scandinavian School Administrator informed the Dane that she would help her find a full-time position, as an elementary school teacher, in the Montgomery County School System, and, within months, she did . . . at the Wayside Elementary School in Potomac, Maryland.

Well, unfortunately, if not tragically, my former wife and the former mother of my children, began teaching there, at the Wayside Elementary School, several months later, at the beginning of the school year, which, in this instance, was in the fall. What's more, she, the former wife and mother, was incredibly excited on the very first day. In fact, she awoke hours before that elementary school even began, in order to dress, prepare to abandon her family, and drive over to the school, where she was scheduled to begin teaching, for the first time, that day.

I awoke at about the same time, because of all the noise taking place around me, especially that early in the morning. And while making preparations to go to work, myself, in the same manner that I had done for years, I tried not to think about the fact that my former wife and the children's former mother was in the noisy process of abandoning us, for the dubious distinction of becoming a full-time elementary school teacher, somewhere in Montgomery County.

After considering that fact, over the next several hours, while she was continuing, in her words, "to get ready," whatever that may have meant, I began to become even more angry at the unfairness of it all. What we had here, after all, was an unprincipled family abandonment, and I reacted accordingly: I opened our bedroom window and threw her car keys outside in the backyard grass! To say that the "soon-to-be-school teacher" was disturbed by this overly principled action was an understatement; actually, she was furious . . . unjustifiably so, I might add!

Nevertheless, to be quite honest about the situation, which is not easily accomplished at this point in my story, or even at this point in my life, I can't really say, even now, that her reaction was at all unexpected. After all, the reaction to principled actions by principled men and women, throughout history, such as Socrates, Julius Caesar, Joan of Arc, Mahatma Gandhi, Martin Luther King and, of course, Christ, himself, was, similarly, not very good. Those remarkable men and women, as well as their principled actions, were often misunderstood and, as a result, maligned and, on occasion, even hated, with consequences so severe, even mortally so, that I have declined to enumerate them all, in the unlikely event that children may become acquainted with some or even all of this text. And although centuries may have passed in the interval, at least with respect to some of those heroic figures, not to mention their misjudged conduct, you can clearly see, by the reprehensible reaction to the "keys-in-the-grass-situation," occurring on that day, that nothing has historically changed!

I would also like to note, since we are dealing with historical precedents here, that neither Gandhi, King, St. Joan, Socrates, Caesar, nor Christ, himself, had to go outside in the backyard to help find the car keys, in all of that tall grass, too, because of a certain amount of intimate threats, which delicacy does not allow me to presently disclose. And I might add, since we are continuing to deal with historical precedents here, that those historic figures did not have to deal with nosy neighbors, either, asking embarrassing questions about why two adult figures were on their hands and knees, in the backyard, for nearly half-an-hour, looking intently through the grass, rather early in the morning, too, even though it was raining at the time, and they were obviously getting soaking wet.

Well, if you really must know, and I must, in fact, continue to be that truthful, we eventually did find those keys, or, at least, she did, which did not make me terribly happy . . . for obviously abandonment-like reasons! And my wife, or, at least, my former "stay-at-home" wife, subsequently used them to drive across a large part of Montgomery County, in order to teach her very first class at the Wayside Elementary School. And, unfortunately, she continued to do just that, on every other school morning thereafter, for nearly thirty years . . . without having to look for her car keys in the backyard grass, on the first day of class, in each one of those succeeding years, if you really must know.

CHAPTER LVII

STONEGATE: LIS; ELEMENTARY SCHOOL READING GROUPS; FRIDAY NIGHT DINNERS; SATURDAY AFTERNOON MOVIES; SUMMER SWIMMING POOL AFTERNOONS; LUNCH AT DUKE ZIEBERT'S RESTAURANT AND THE BETTY FORD LETTER

AS THE school year progressed and our lives did, too, I often thought, while on my way back home from work, that my wife's elementary school principal must have also wished, during those first few months, that his new first-grade teacher had never found those car keys, too. Because that first-grade teacher made so many changes to the standard first-grade curricula, over those first few months, that the principal must have thought that he, or, at least, his school, was now becoming a protagonist in the book, entitled, *1984*.

Although I'm not sure where to begin to discuss those changes, probably the best place to start is a discussion of the ones that changed my life, too, not to mention the rest of my family. One of them occurred when my wife decided to divide her class into a number of reading groups, by the second month of school, based upon their reading proficiency. That, in itself, was, apparently, not a deviation from a standard first-grade teaching practice, but what followed was!

To encourage those in a lesser reading group to achieve a greater proficiency and, thereby, graduate to a higher reading group, whereby they may become a robin, a cardinal, a bluebird, or, even, an erudite nightingale, there were certain rewards. They included, for the robins, the cardinals and the bluebirds, a trip with the first-grade teacher to see an appropriate movie at a local theatre, located nearby, on a Saturday afternoon. And in the event that a first-grade reader actually became proficient enough to, eventually, move all the way up to the highest reading group and, thereby, alight among the nightingales, he or she was even more fortunate, because they were now entitled to have dinner with the teacher and her family, on a Friday evening, no less.

Well, to be quite blunt about the matter, the only individuals who were really fortunate, in this whole sordid feathery scenario, were the disgusting little robins, the pathetic little cardinals, the nasty little bluebirds and, especially, the miserable little nightingales, who were all able to spread their little reading wings and alight in a higher reading group, and, eventually, at my dinner table . . . every Friday night! That's right, we had some of those little feathery misfits at our dinner table every Friday night . . . every Friday night!

The Saturday afternoons at the movie theater, with the little robins, cardinals, and bluebirds, were, for distinctly different reasons, nearly as disgusting! Until my Saturdays were hijacked by those little popcorn-eating urchins, who, by the way, had to go to the bathroom every ten minutes, I can safely say that a Saturday night movie, somewhere nearby, with my wife, was always a welcome respite from a stress-filled work week practicing law. Now, however, my wife was no longer interested in going to the movies, not on a Saturday night, anyway, because she had already gone to one with those little miscreants of a robin, cardinal, and bluebird variety on a Saturday afternoon.

Even worse, because the little boy robins, cardinals, and bluebirds seemed to go to the bathroom just as often as their female counter-

HULDAH, EDDIE, & ME

parts, my wife decided that she needed an adult male to come along, in order to supervise their continuous challenge in utilizing even the low hanging urinals, which, by the way, were designed, especially, for little feathery creatures like them. Since I was apparently the only adult male available in this whole sordid situation, I had the dubious distinction of supervising a ten-minute routine, whereby a little robin, cardinal or bluebird, who may well have achieved a reading skill level sufficient to reach that group, demonstrated that other, more rudimentary, skills, of a more directional nature, were still sadly lacking, which the walls and the floor of the boys' bathroom were well able to confirm.

Still, if the movie had actually been worth seeing on those Saturday afternoons, that, conceivably, could have offset the cumulative misfires in the boys' bathroom. But I could not, frankly, find anything redeeming about, "Snow White and the Seven Dwarfs," which continually played, for months, as a matinee "feature" for children, at that neighborhood theater, every Saturday afternoon, and which my wife, unfortunately, thought to be more than appropriate for high achieving first-grade readers of the robin, cardinal, and bluebird variety.

Well, to be brutally honest about that "feature," which is a word chosen with some forethought, those dimwitted little dwarfs and their "snowy-white" girlfriend were not an appropriate "feature" for those of us who were fortunate enough to leave the first-grade behind, way behind. And notwithstanding that historic fact, I was, unfortunately, if not depressingly, subjected to a continuously disgusting performance, every Saturday afternoon, by a group of misshapen little creatures, euphemistically called dwarfs, who seemed to have a "thing" for a taller woman, with blonde hair, just because she had a nice smile. By the fourth or fifth time that I had to watch those microscopic creatures, on what otherwise would have been an enjoyable Saturday afternoon, working in the yard, I began to hate them all, except, possibly, "Grumpy," who I found to be somewhat charming, for reasons that I still cannot explain, not even after all of this time.

I also cannot explain why my wife decided to engage in a tutorial program for some of the struggling first graders in her class, for about an hour, every day, after school. Over the course of that hour, she, apparently, helped them with their homework, after the rest of the students had been discharged from the school, following which she drove each one of them to their respective homes, no matter where they happened to be located. I found all of that to be sort of like playing, "Russian Roulette," with all of the chambers fully loaded, except one, and you hope that the unloaded one turns up each time that she drives one of those little miscreants home. With a little luck and an empty chamber, each time, I might not end up on the wrong side of a lawsuit, filed by one of their crazy parents, because their little first-grader happened to become involved in an automobile accident, while being driven home by a misguided teacher, who happened to be my wife.

The situation, if you can believe it, actually went downhill in the summertime, because my "do-gooder" wife decided to tutor some of those little "after school" urchins, in our home, in the mornings, for three days a week, every week, over the entire summer, so that they would be better prepared to successfully make the transition into second grade, in the ensuing fall. With that in mind, she would usually spend about an hour with each one of those little summer miscreants, while the others waited their turn, by playing with my children and their toys. When she finished tutoring all of them, which ordinarily occurred around noontime, she made them lunch and, following that, took them to our community swimming pool, which was private, very private, at least until then!

Since the three or four children being tutored were normally "children of color," so to speak, they did not easily blend into the pale background, normally found in and around that community pool. Consequently, the community, or, at least, the swimming part of it, was no more excited about my wife's summer tutorial program than was I. Moreover, the community, not to mention the "lifesaving" component of it, also found the whole situation to be somewhat unsettling, because most of those little kids, if not all of them, did not know how to swim, not any better than they knew how to do second-grade arithmetic, at least not at the beginning of the summer, anyway. Nevertheless, the little unblended non-swimmers were certainly capable of splashing, which they did on a regular basis, probably as a substitute for their inability to swim, much to the consternation of those in our private, very private, very pale, community swimming pool, who, generally, did not want to get their hair wet!

So if none of those little unblended urchins drowned, or if the middle-aged women of a distinctly paler color did not get their hair wet, or if I was not pronounced, "persona-non-grata," for integrating our private, very private, community swimming pool, I could rejoice, by the end of the summer, over my good fortune, not to mention a renewed belief in God's ability to create a more perfect universe!

Having said that, what was really unsettling, to the point of disbelief, was all of the recognition that my wife received for all of those questionable endeavors. Among other things, when she gave notice at the Wayside Elementary School, several years later, that she intended to transfer to Cloverly Elementary School, because it was closer to home, the parents of all of those insipid little first-grade birds decided to have a lunch in her honor, at Duke Ziebert's restaurant, no less, located in my building, on Connecticut Avenue in Washington, D.C. Can you believe that, at Duke Ziebert's restaurant, no less, one of the classiest restaurants in the city at the time, and in my building, too!

I was invited to attend, but after thinking about it for a while, I politely declined; I didn't think that I could stand watching all of those little first-graders going to the bathroom, every ten minutes, again. I was also concerned that some of those little miscreants might remind their parents of "Mr. Golumbic's" displeasure . . . verbally expressed in a profane manner . . . because of the continual misdirection in the boys' bathroom on one of those Saturday afternoons at the movie theatre. And, finally, I found the prospect of sitting there, with all of those little first-graders, while having lunch in a restaurant full of lawyers and businessmen, some of whom may have been my partners and some of whom may have been my clients, to be somewhat awkward, if not distinctly uncomfortable.

Now that I think about it, however, that, unfortunately, was not my only uncomfortable lunch, involving my wife and her first-grade class, at Duke Ziebert's restaurant. The other one occurred when I naively invited her down to my office for lunch, several months later, during a school holiday. I did that because Randy Ziebert, Duke's son, was ordinarily the host at lunch time, and he knew me quite well, because I took clients, or prospective clients, to lunch there, at least twice a week, even though the restaurant never accepted reservations. Notwithstanding that unreserved fact, Randy would typically single me out, while standing there in the lobby, waiting patiently for a table, among all of the other lawyers and businessmen waiting there, too, and he would typically say, "Cal, we have your table, already set up and waiting for you, over by the window, if you will just step this way and follow me."

That, I was sure, would impress my wife, nearly as much as it impressed me. And given my wife's seeming success, ad nauseam, while teaching little urchins, as reflected by that uncalled-for-lunch on her behalf, a short time ago, at Duke Ziebert's, no less, I thought that such an impression might go a long way in restoring the old boy's status in the family!

Unfortunately, however, things did not go quite as well as I had planned. Oh, don't get me wrong! Randy singled me out, all right, because, if you can believe this, I was standing right beside his "son's favorite first-grade teacher," who, unfortunately, must have made quite a favorable impression on the whole Ziebert family, including their children, three of whom were formerly her first-grade students. Consequently, upon seeing his family's favorite first-grade teacher, just standing there, quietly beside her husband, who is sadly recounting this ironic tale, he immediately exclaimed . . . likely to the whole universe, which, unfortunately, included everyone within hearing range, including some of my partners and some of my clients, who were also planning on having lunch there . . . that "she," referring, now, to the person who had just upstaged me, "was the best teacher in the whole world!"

Then, while I stood there, momentarily speechless . . . to make matters even worse, if that were at all possible . . . Randy proceeded to take "the best teacher in the whole world," by the arm, and walk her over to my table, my table, if you can believe that! And he kept repeating those complimentary words, ad nauseam, as though they had become some kind of a mantra, without even acknowledging my presence, or even saying one word to me, someone who had been kind enough to bring his clients to that restaurant, for lunch, at least twice a week, twice a week, damn it! The whole scenario was absolutely uncalled for, and, certainly, quite embarrassing, if not disgusting! It seemed, at the time, that nothing ever seems to work out for those of us who try to do something nice for someone else.

Oh, yes, I almost forgot, and this one takes the cake, literally and metaphorically speaking! When we finished our lunch, I asked the waiter to bring our check. Instead, Randy reappeared . . . without the check and with a large piece of chocolate cake . . . "for the best teacher" . . . well, you know the rest. And to top it off, he said that the whole lunch was on the Ziebert family. Now that was really going too far!

As it turned out, that lunch was the most miserable lunch that I can ever remember having in that restaurant, and that was not because of the food, either. In fact, the whole miserable meal had such a profound effect on me that I have never eaten another piece of chocolate cake, not over the remainder of my life. And I have developed, in the interim, an obsession for Hershey chocolate bars, the only form of chocolate that my wife will not eat, which, admittedly, seems to have become an inexplicable obsession on my part, short of twenty years of psychotherapy, anyway!

Forgetting about psychotherapy for the moment, if you, unlike me, are able to find something charming and, maybe, even a little bit humorous in my ill-fated luncheon plans on that unnerving day, you might enjoy knowing that you were joined, on the following Sunday, by, none other than, the readers of the Washington Post. Upon being so advised by one of the more sadistic restaurant patrons on that miserable day, who, unfortunately, witnessed the whole sordid scenario, the Sunday Magazine of the "Post" ran a supposedly humorous article, entitled, "Around Town," about my chocolate-flavored humiliation, which, I am constrained to acknowledge, caused quite a lot of laughter in the Washington legal community, not excluding my partnership, for weeks, thereafter. A copy of the article has been included as Exhibit 15 in the Appendix, for your review and, possibly, laughter, too.

Well, laughter or not, as the case may be, I cannot tell you a lot about my wife's teaching performance over the years that have followed, although I don't believe that much has really changed. The little creatures still appeared, from time to time, for tutoring in the summertime as well as for dinner on a Friday evening during the school year, because of a meritorious movement into the highest reading group. And the dumb little dwarfs and their "snowy-white" girlfriend still appear to be a hit with the robins, the cardinals, and the bluebirds at the neighborhood theatre on Saturday afternoons.

Consequently, or should I more appropriately say, incidentally, the walls in the boys' bathroom had to be repainted and the floors had to be resurfaced, several times, in the years that have followed.

Nevertheless, I continued to learn from parents, on my rare appearance at "back to school nights," just how fortunate their children were to be taught by, in their words, the "teacher of the year." And how fortunate they were to have a teacher, who actually takes their children home for dinner on Friday nights and to the movies on Saturday afternoons. Evidently, those parents never talked to the walls or the floor in the boys' bathroom, or, for that matter, to me!

In any event, aside from the walls and the floor in the boys' bathroom of the neighborhood theatre, life seemed to return to normal, for the most part, and to move along rather methodically in the years that followed. And with an abundance of my own work going reasonably well during that time, I became quite successful at ignoring my wife's alarming recognition for her work as a first-grade teacher. Then, one day, which started out like every other day, but, which, unfortunately, became unlike any other day, due to a rather unsettling letter from the White House, where the President of the United States, Gerald R. Ford, lived, at the time, with his overly intrusive wife, Betty!

The letter was addressed to Mrs. Lis J. Golumbic, Teacher, Cloverly Elementary School, and signed, would you believe, by the First Lady of the United States, Betty Ford. In that letter, the First Lady stated, without qualification, that, "Lis Golumbic" was, in her estimation, "one of our nation's greatest teachers." We still have that letter, a copy of which has survived my historical efforts to destroy it, and, consequently, it has been unfortunately included as Exhibit 16 in the Appendix, for your information and review.

I should also note, certainly at this point, while casting wit aside, that I have been dramatically moved by the contents of that letter. Among other things, they have forced me to historically examine the basis for the accolades contained therein. In doing so, it has also caused me to examine the accomplishments, in and out of the classroom, which have given rise to those accolades. Maybe one of the most important is the impact on the children, who were fortunate enough to spend an impressionable year in that first-grade classroom with that teacher. And with that overdue acknowledgment, I must also admit, in print, mind you, that her instructional accomplishments, over a marital lifetime, have certainly not been limited to an early childhood domain . . . just ask Betty Ford!

CHAPTER LVIII

STONEGATE: COURT AND LARS; "LATCHKEY" CHILDREN WHO WERE NEARLY INVOLVED IN A FAMILY BATHROOM TRAGEDY IMMEDIATELY AFTER SCHOOL

UNFORTUNATELY, NOT all of the members of our family were as impressed by my wife's teaching prowess. I'm speaking here of the two, who were still students in elementary school, and who were still interested in coming home to a warm and welcoming household, after school, which likely included an afternoon snack of cookies and milk. Such things were provided, of course, by their mother, who was ordinarily standing in the doorway, waiting to greet her returning children with a welcoming smile on her face. All of that, however, had come to an end, when she, the one who dispensed the milk and cookies, not to mention the welcoming smile, left home for the world of elementary school academics.

Upset by the absence of a welcoming smile, not to mention the milk and cookies, both boys complained for some time about the departure of all three, which, of course, also included the maternal dispenser. When it had become abundantly clear that their complaints had fallen on deaf teaching ears, after a number of months, Lars, our younger son, who was not particularly impressed by those first-grade teaching heroics, or the little feathery creatures that alighted on our dinner table every Friday evening, decided to give his mother a report card, on her performance as a teacher and as a parent, in which she received an "A" for the former and an "F" for the latter.

Unfortunately, the report card has not survived the ages, or a mother's guilt, whichever seems more applicable at this point, and, therefore, it has not been included in the Appendix.

I am sure, however, in looking back now, as former children are inclined to do, that it is not too difficult for them to see that their mother, who once provided milk and cookies, not to mention a welcoming smile, to her young children, arriving home from elementary school, probably served them far better, by leaving home, when and how she did, and by doing really well, if not extraordinarily well, as a first-grade teacher in the academic workplace. Her success in doing so, during the boys' formative years, was likely not lost on any one of them, which probably explains why, as adults, they have clearly emulated their mother's performance in the workplace and, may I add, elsewhere, too. In the end, it would seem that time, and maturity, the colleagues of experience, likely had a way of diminishing in importance the absence of milk and cookies for everyone involved in this workplace saga, although I am not so sure about the welcoming smile.

Still, in the interest of full disclosure, which, of course, is always an overriding interest in any family story, even one involving parents and children, we cannot ignore, certainly not at this point, that both boys had become, in their mother's absence, so-called "latchkey" children, a term that certainly has a rather dubious connotation. Even acknowledging that connotation, however, the "latchkey" situation in this instance and in this family, albeit around the neck of only one of the two children in this family circumstance, has taken on a certain amount of charm, historically speaking, for the members of the family, as a result of a story that I am about to tell.

It is important, in the telling of the story, that you understand, at the outset, that Lars, the younger brother, did not use the bathroom facilities in his elementary school . . . ever! I don't think that he ever gave a reason or really had a reason; he just didn't, which meant that he was desperate to get home, just as quickly as possible, right after his elementary school ended for the day. Home, by the way, was only a few blocks away, but for an overflowing Lars, so to speak, that was a long and agonizing few blocks, even at a dead run, which was ordinarily what happened every day.

Lars, however, did not have a key to the house, but that did not ordinarily present a problem, because his older brother, Court, did. And he kept it on a small chain, hung around his neck, which was long enough to allow him to bend over, without having to remove the chain from around his neck, and to insert the key into the lock on the kitchen door. Whereupon, he would normally turn the key . . . with the chain still attached to it, while continuing to remain around his neck . . . for no longer than ordinarily required to unlock the kitchen door.

What's more, Court ordinarily arrived home shortly before Lars, because his class in the sixth grade was routinely dismissed about fifteen minutes before Lars' class in the third grade of their elementary school. So the kitchen door was ordinarily unlocked, by Court, using the "latchkey," which was hanging from the chain around his neck, at least five minutes before Lars reached home, in an understandable urological panic!

On this questionable day, however, Court spent most of that fifteen minutes standing on the road, just outside of his house, talking with his sixth-grade friend, Dean Bichner, who lived just a few houses down the street, and who almost always walked home from school with Court. Consequently, by the time that Lars reached home, on the brink, once again, of a catastrophically premature overflow, Court, who had just finished talking with his friend, a few minutes prior thereto, was now standing in his younger brother's way, right in front of the kitchen door, leaning over, with the key now fully inserted in the lock, after having just turned it, in order to open the door, while the chain, as usual, remained securely around his neck.

Lars, having now nearly gone beyond the point of desperation, if not urination, without having gone to the bathroom at any point during the school day, as usual, was absolutely oblivious to what was transpiring in front of him, other than his brother was obviously standing in his way, while bent down in front of the kitchen door and taking far too much time in opening it. So, now, focusing solely on the nearest bathroom, and the likelihood that he may not be able to reach it in time, Lars kicked open the door with his right foot, in a urinary panic, while the chain was, unfortunately, still around his brother's neck and the key, to which it was still attached, was, unfortunately, still inserted in the lock in the door. Well, if you can picture that, all of that, and it is important that you do, that kick, not only caused the door to fly open, but the key in the lock, the chain attached to the key and the bent-over older brother, around whose neck the chain was still securely fastened, right along with it!

The door, after swinging open, in somewhat of a jarring-like fashion, eventually came to a rest against one of the kitchen cupboards, after banging against a kitchen chair. Lars, at last, could now see a clear path to a urinary destination, the nature of which you are already well aware. His older brother, however, is a far more interesting subject at this point in this after-school, "latchkey," urinary drama, now being played out in the family kitchen. That is because the chain was still around his neck, and, unfortunately, it was still attached to the key, which, unfortunately, was still inserted into the lock, all of which, unfortunately, had joined the door, in swinging open, far more quickly than the older brother had expected, if, indeed, it could be said that he had ever expected anything like that at all!

The lack of expectation caused the older brother, who, as you may recall, still had the chain remaining around his neck, to swing off of his feet, by the chain and with the door, because of the key still being inserted in the lock, right into the kitchen and onto the kitchen floor, or, rather, should I more accurately say, nearly onto the kitchen floor, in somewhat of a dangling fashion, which can only be described with "gallows humor." Now momentarily dangling there, or hanging there, both of which would appear to be an applicable description at this point, the older brother, understandably, could no longer breathe very well, if at all, because of the chain, which, as you may recall, was still securely around his neck, so he immediately began to struggle to his feet, in order to free himself from that strangling chain or, more generally, from that nonbreathing situation.

At about the same time, his younger brother, who, as you will recall, was desperately seeking some form of urinary relief, quickly stepped over his partially prostate older brother . . . now trying, valiantly, to struggle to his feet, in order to free himself from that strangling situation, or, if you will, the chain around his neck . . . and without a moment's hesitation, he slammed, in sort of a back-handed manner, the door back shut, right behind him, just as abruptly as he had kicked it open. Not surprisingly, at least not at this point in our macabre tale, with the door slamming back shut also went the lock in the door, in which the key was still inserted, as well as the chain that was still attached to the key. And do I really need to remind you that the chain was unfortunately, if not tragically, at least at this point, still around the neck of a somewhat breathless older brother, who, by now, had nearly managed to struggle to his feet and catch his breath, or, at least, a breath, but who was now, by virtue of that door being slammed back shut, hanging once again, by the chain around his neck, in a circumstance that can only be described, once again, by "gallows humor!"

I assume, without going into any uncomfortable details, that, in retrospect, everything, especially of a more fluid nature, turned out all right for the younger brother by the end of this slightly bizarre urinary tale. I also assume, notwithstanding the "gallows humor," that everything also turned out all right for the older brother, too, at the end of this no less bizarre dangling tale. After all, he evidently "survived" that "latchkey" incident, using that term somewhat equivocally, and, quite obviously, has lived well beyond his "latchkey" carrying elementary school days. Indeed, he has lived long enough to confirm this "oft-repeated" childhood story. And aside from some of the less charitable remarks directed toward the younger protagonist in this dramatic bathroom tale, the older brother, on a more or less constructive note, has reached some rather interesting biological and sociological conclusions, growing out of his near-death experience, in this "latchkey" episode.

Among a number of other things, some of which are not repeatable here, the older brother has often said, in the years that have followed, that biologists are wrong in concluding that a human being cannot live, without breathing, for a period extending longer than five minutes. He also says that biologists are wrong in defining human beings as rational animals, and in support of that contention, he suggests that they do not have to look any further than his younger brother. Finally, he says, in looking back upon his childhood, with a certain amount of ambivalence, that his parents have always favored his younger brother, which sociologically explains why he, rather than his younger brother, had to wear that "latchkey" around his neck in the first place. It is not even necessary, in that regard, to point out, according to the older brother, that his younger brother always had a larger bedroom, with heating vents that actually worked, too!

CHAPTER LIX

MUSIC: FAMILY TRADITION; LARS PLAYED THE PIANO AND CLARINET AND COURT PLAYED THE TRUMPET THROUGHOUT MOST OF THEIR RESPECTIVE GROWING UP YEARS

BOTH OF our sons began their musical instruction, as an instrumentalist, in the fourth grade at Stonegate Elementary School. Since our older son, Court, reached the fourth grade three years sooner than his younger brother, Lars, he began his musical instruction three years earlier, too. That instruction consisted of, among other things, Court's participation in the school band as a trumpet player.

Apart from his participation in the school band, Court also began, at about the same time, to take private music lessons, on the trumpet, on a weekly basis. That was largely because his grandmother, who was a musician, wanted him to privately study some form of music, as an instrumentalist, and Court's favorite instrument at the time was the trumpet. And he continued to take private music lessons, on a weekly basis, all the way through elementary, junior, and senior high school. That was, looking back now, a lot of years, a lot of lessons, a lot of practice, and a lot of money. And by the end of his senior year in high school, the years, the lessons and the practice were clearly worth the money, because Court had become, by that time, a rather proficient instrumentalist on the trumpet.

On the other hand, with his grandmother's encouragement, Lars decided that he would like to play an instrument in the fourth grade, too, except that he chose the clarinet, for which he also took private music lessons, once a week, through elementary and junior high school, as well as his sophomore year of high school, too. Once again, that was a lot of years, a lot of lessons, a lot of practice, and a lot of money. Nevertheless, by the end of his sophomore year in high school, the years, the lessons, and the practice were well worth the money, because he, too, had become a rather proficient instrumentalist, except on the clarinet.

Although both boys had become rather proficient on their respective instruments by the time that they had reached high school, Lars seemed to possess something, by that time, that was really quite special, musically, that is, which my mother described as "extraordinary feeling," and which, according to her, "you can't teach; you have it or you don't;" and Lars, apparently, had it!

My mother, who was a vocalist and a pianist, and who taught others to do both, apparently recognized that musical fact, because the two of them would often sit down to play on her grand piano, in the living room, every evening after dinner, when he was visiting her, as a young boy, in her home in Lock Haven, Pennsylvania. Because he seemed to be musically precocious, at such a young age, and, seemingly, interested in the piano, at least in those musical sessions with my mother, she also encouraged Lars to take piano lessons, too, which he did, weekly, until he graduated from high school.

Eventually, it became clear to us, as well as to his piano teacher, that Lars really did have a lot talent as a pianist. Indeed, that fact became quite clear at his first piano recital, if not before, which occurred in his piano teacher's living room, one afternoon, with students of all ages and skills and experience performing in front of their parents. Although Lars was only in the sixth grade at the time, with less than a year of experience on the piano, it became quite clear to all of us, from his performance on that day, that he had a very special gift, at that age, as a pianist. In fact, his piano teacher, who was ordinarily quite reserved, was so effusive about the subject, that we were not sure whether she was simply being overly complimentary. His talent, however, as it blossomed through practice and performance, through the years, proved otherwise. Eventually, it became readily apparent that our younger son seemed to be continuing in a long line of musical tradition, which has existed in our family, or, at least, that part of it that has descended from my mother's side of our family.

Significantly, that musical tradition did not leave his older brother behind. By the time that he had reached his senior year in high school, Court was not only playing first trumpet in his high school band, he had also been selected, year after year, to participate in the "all-state" band, which was a very distinctive honor for student instrumentalists at the time. Even apart from that honor, and that yearly performance, however, Court was also invited to perform at numerous community functions, throughout his junior and senior years in high school, because of his outstanding musical ability on the trumpet. In fact, Court had actually become a recognized instrumentalist, on the trumpet, by the time that he had graduated from high school.

College, however, interrupted the private lessons and community performances, because of academic pursuits in the social sciences and humanities, among other scholastic subjects, in a four-year undergraduate program at Vanderbilt University in Nashville, Tennessee. As it turned out, however, the interruption only lasted for about three years, because Court decided to study the trumpet, in a four-hour elective course, in his senior year at the University. In doing so, he became, as he was so informed, the first non-music major to take, as an elective, a course on the trumpet in the Music Department at Vanderbilt University.

Lars completed his junior and senior years of high school at the Mercersburg Academy, where he continued to study the piano in private lessons there. In fact, Lars was, as we were told, the only student at that school, who took piano, as an elective, or, actually, who took piano at all, and he did so, in both his junior and senior years. Moreover, Lars' accomplishments on the piano became so noteworthy, by the end of his senior year, that he was invited to perform in front of the whole school, by himself, in a piano recital that year. Obviously, Lars bordered, at that point, on becoming, in a comparatively short amount of time, a very fine pianist, at least in ability, if not in interest.

Thereafter, the piano and the clarinet joined the trumpet in retirement, in a manner of speaking, possibly to await the completion of college, graduate school in one case, and law school in both cases. Neither boy, however, has ever decided to play any one of those instruments again, not in any kind of a setting, although, upon graduation from college, Lars bought a tenor saxophone, in order to teach himself how to play the instrument, because, in his words, he would like to play it, someday, in a dance band, likely as a hobby. And Court bought himself an acoustical guitar and taught himself how to play the thing over a number of fairly recent years.

This chapter, however, is more than a chronicle about what those two boys did or did not do, musically, throughout their growing-up years. It is, if you will, part of a story about what they and their family are, and have been, because of a certain amount of things, some of which just happen to be musical. In fact, some of those musical things have defined what we are, as a family, what kind of a family we have come from, and what kind of a family we are likely to become in generations to come.

Although what we will become, as a family, would, initially, appear to be defined by our descendants, those who will follow us in generations to come, I believe that the whole story, generationally speaking, makes it abundantly clear that their story, as descendants, is dependent, in part, on their history. They cannot fully understand what they have become, without understanding what they have come from, by which I mean those who have preceded them in this generation, and even in the generations prior thereto.

Consequently, as I have said before, in commencing this story, it is written about all of us, who are, or were, or will become, part of this family, and, maybe, if interest be there, even the human family, of which we, as a family, are unmistakably a part. But at the expense of repetition, the story, which is this story, is written especially for those who will follow us, and who I may likely never meet, so that, possibly, as a result of this story, they may be better able to understand the whole story, from which they are most definitely a part, or will become a part, if you prefer to look at it that way. And in doing that, understanding the whole story, I mean, they may be better able to understand things about themselves from a different light or, if you prefer, from a different perspective, a historical one. And viewed from that perspective, a historical one, that is, music has always been a significant part of this family, and, frankly, I would be amazed if that does not continue to be so, long after I have any reason to be aware, or even to fully understand.

CHAPTER LX

MUSIC: FAMILY TRADITION; AS IT RELATES TO MYSELF, MY MOTHER AND MY GRANDMOTHER, NOT TO MENTION MY SONS, SPANNING, AT LEAST, FOUR GENERATIONS

I'M NOT sure when I first became aware of a musical tradition in our family. I do remember that I thought a lot about the subject while listening to the boys practice their musical instruments during their formative years. Joining them in their practice sessions, during most of those years, was something that I did, religiously, every weekend, when I wasn't engaged, elsewhere, in the practice of law, because the boys seemed to enjoy having me there, and because I enjoyed doing it. Practice, as I was well aware, from my own experience, can often become tedious and repetitious, and, sometimes, even quite boring, no matter on what form of musical instrument. So having company, even when it is just your father, while doing something that is sort of monotonous, if nothing else, on a musical instrument, can often have a mitigating effect. I think that both boys would likely agree with me, even now, although now, in the late winter of my years and in the early fall of theirs, they rarely seem to agree with me about much of anything.

Often, however, my mind would wonder off, during those practice sessions, to another time, which seemed so long ago, when another individual was practicing the piano, while his mother was seated nearby, intently listening to the music, and how it was being played.

It was a scenario that replayed itself, nearly every day, after dinner during the week and after lunch on the weekends, for years, more years than I would like to remember sometimes.

It began with piano lessons from Alice Christine Siever, when I was no more than five years of age, and which continued until shortly before her death, when I was just a junior in high school. Following her death, I continued to take piano lessons for the remainder of that year, and for the following year, from Mary Mulliner, who lived, several miles away, in the town of Jersey Shore, Pennsylvania. And for most of those instructional years, but certainly not all of them, my mother sat beside me, on the piano bench, while I practiced. And I suppose that it is fair to say that whatever proficiency that I may have gained on the instrument, during those practicing years, was the direct result of my mother's involvement, together with, possibly, a modicum of talent on my part.

Because of that involvement, and a lot of hard work on my part, certainly by way of daily practice, not to mention the ongoing piano lessons, I eventually gained enough proficiency on the instrument to reluctantly play, but only upon request, for various churches and professional organizations, as well as for the local radio station, on a few harrowing occasions, in town. And, then, there were a number of less stressful recitals and graduations, which ranged from a distinct discomfort in the earlier years to an annoyance in the years that followed. I also achieved, notwithstanding a serious case of "nerves," a number of superior ratings, each year, in an annual performance for a statewide musical federation, in which piano and voice students, throughout the state, were uncomfortably evaluated and rated by qualified musical judges.

My mother was present during most of those performances, while I practiced for them and, subsequently, when I received whatever recognition as a result. Notwithstanding that continual presence in my life, at least musically, I am not sure that I knew my mother very well when I was growing up. But there was never a time in which I did not know how much my mother loved music, especially musical performance in voice and piano, and, for that matter, in all other instrumental forms as well, individually and in concert.

Actually, it is not surprising that my mother was so enamored with vocal performance, aside from all of the other musical kinds, because she was, in her own right, a coloratura soprano of remarkable dimensions. Those dimensions became rather clear to me as I observed her, during my growing up years, performing operatic numbers, choral ensembles, classical solos and duets, religious oratorios, and, even, musical comedy, year-after-year, before various audiences and pursuant to various requests, professionally and otherwise. Some of those performances were even recorded and, on other occasions, they were broadcast over our local radio station. Others occurred onstage, with piano or, even, symphonic accompaniment.

Indeed, my mother was chosen, among a number of others who had auditioned, to perform, as a guest soloist, with the Penn State University Symphony Orchestra. A photograph of her holding a bouquet of flowers, to celebrate the successful conclusion of that concert, has been so identified and included as Exhibit 17 in the Appendix. With that photograph in mind, I can't help thinking now about what she might have accomplished, in terms of a professional career in voice, if she had not, thankfully, decided to marry my father and, together, make my life and this story possible.

I guess . . . when you consider the dimensions of my mother's musical performance, even aside from an appearance, as a guest soloist with the Penn State University Symphony . . . it is not too difficult to say that music was a significant part of her life. And given that fact, it is not too difficult to conclude, in light of the previous discussion, concerning myself and my two sons, in this musical chapter, and the one prior thereto, that we are looking at some kind of a musical tradition in this family, with serious historical ramifications. I say that, because the musical tradition did not even begin with my mother; it actually began with my maternal grandmother, Anna Behrer Davis, years before, in the earlier part of the twentieth century.

For years, my maternal grandmother, Anna Behrer Davis, gave piano lessons to the children of Pennsylvania German families, who lived on farms, located up and down the Bald Eagle Valley, in rural Centre County, Pennsylvania. To do that, she hitched up a buggy to a horse, which she kept in my great Aunt Hannah Grove's barn, located in the tiny farming village of Lemont, Pennsylvania. Now seated, somewhat uncomfortably, with the reins in her hands, she traveled a rather wide circuit in that old buggy, teaching piano to farm children for several weeks at a time.

Normally, she would board with some of the families that lived in farmhouses, where there happened to be a piano, and the children in those households received free piano lessons as a result of that boarding privilege. The children who came from farming families without a piano would have to travel, in all likelihood by walking, to the farmhouse where my grandmother was boarding for their piano lessons. Those children, however, were not so fortunate, because they had to pay for their lessons, not to mention engage in that lengthy walk, which, on occasion, could well be miles, according to my mother.

At this point, I should probably point out, if you do not already know, that my maternal grandmother, Anna Behrer Davis, died long before I was born, so I am unable to do any more than repeat some of the stories that my mother has told me about her, and one of those stories was how much she loved to musically perform, not just on the piano, but on the violin as well. That being said, I must confess that I do not know very much about her proficiency on the instrument, because it was not something that my mother talked about, other to say that she often played the instrument at country dances and at church socials. So I am really left with little more than that information about her proficiency, if not her interest, in playing the violin, but I can definitely say, with a great amount of certainty, that whatever that proficiency and that interest happened to be, the latter clearly descended to my mother, along with the instrument, itself, because she subsequently used it to study the violin, following her retirement from teaching school, at approximately sixty-five years of age, in order to gain some proficiency on the instrument.

At that point, my mother began to take private lessons on that "stringed" instrument, once a week, from a violin instructor in the Music Department at Penn State University. And she would practice every morning, all morning, for the rest of the week, a routine that continued for several years, and which only stopped when arthritis, in her fingers, eventually prevented her from being able to continue. Nevertheless, she would get out that old family violin, on those occasions in which I would visit her, in the latter years of her life, and show it to me, with an accompanying request that I study the instrument upon my own retirement.

I never did honor my mother's request, for no apparent reason other than, possibly, lethargy, but I am happy to say, for historical purposes, that I still have that violin. It can be found, in its original case, on an upper shelf of the large closet in the master bedroom on the second floor of our home at 4 Maass Lane in Rehoboth Beach, Delaware. It has been in that closet and, prior thereto, a similar closet in our former home, since my mother died, nearly thirty years ago. I am not inclined to sell it, even though no one in my generation, or the one following mine, seems inclined to play it. But who knows, maybe one of my grandchildren, or even one of my great-grandchildren, will develop an interest in playing that old family heirloom. After all, music and musical performance, even on a violin and, especially, on that violin, have been a significant part of our family, as a family tradition, if not a family heritage. And although I can't be sure, there is no reason to believe that such a time-honored tradition will not continue among my grandchildren, or among my great-grandchildren, or even among a generation of my family that I may never have an opportunity to know.

Actually, I may have misspoken. Even though I may never have an opportunity to meet some members of my family in generations to come, I suspect that I already know something about them. Among other things, I know that they will likely play musical instruments, and I know that their parents will likely sit beside them while they practice on those instruments. And I know that, in doing so, their parents will likely help them grow, musically, to become as accomplished on those instruments as those in the generations of our family that have preceded them.

And if those in our family who follow, in generations to come, wish to know what we were like in this generation, or even in generations that may have preceded us, I would simply say to them, look at your parent, as I have mine, who loved music as much as they have loved you, and who patiently sat beside you, while you practiced your musical instrument. And when you do that, you have seen more than your parent; you have seen generations of parents that have preceded you. Indeed, you have seen part of our history, yours and mine, which, together, have formed part of what we are, and what we have been, as a family, including, among other things, music loved and performed, for generations, by our family.

Oh, yes, lest I forget, whoever in this family decides to take it upon himself to learn how to play my grandmother's violin, in generations that follow mine, and decides to subsequently engage in musical performance on that instrument, will discover, in that instrument and in that performance, a key to unlock a musical history, as well as a musical tradition, that is part of a family that I belong to, and that they do, too!

CHAPTER LXI

FIFTH JOB: CORPORATION COUNSELS OFFICE, APPELLATE DIVISION; APPLICATION AND ACCEPTANCE INTO A WORLD OF LITIGATION ON AN APPELLATE LEVEL

AT ONE point in 1971, Leo Gorman, an attorney in the Appellate Division of the Corporation Counsels Office for the District of Columbia, who had opposed me in a number of appeals involving the District of Columbia, informed me, in a casual conversation at the conclusion of one of those appeals, that there was an opening in the Appellate Division, and that they would be interested in receiving an application from me, because of their familiarity with my work, as an opposing counsel, in a number of those appeals. Because of my disappointment in the nature of the work with Professor Kittrie, and the LAWCOR Program, at the American University Law school, which is an understatement, I decided to apply for the position following my conversation with Leo. I did not need to spend another year around a law school, or one of its more prominent faculty members, to realize that this was an outstanding opportunity to do litigation, especially involving issues of law on an appellate level. So when I received an offer to join the Appellate Division, no more than ten days after submitting my application, I quickly accepted the offer, notwithstanding the absence of even an interview.

Immediately thereafter, I gave Professor Kittrie a thirty-day notice, and, subsequent thereto, departed from the halls of academia, but, as it would subsequently turn out, not forever. No, nearly twenty-five years later, following my retirement from the practice of law, I decided to subscribe to that old and weathered definition of insanity, kindly supplied by none other than Albert Einstein, which is, "doing the same thing, over and over again, but expecting different results," which, in this subsequent instance, was joining the faculty of a university, once again, but "expecting different results."

Unfortunately, or, maybe, fortunately, that story of academic insanity, at least in that subsequent instance, will have to wait for another chapter in my life, not to mention in this story. Now I want to discuss my reengagement in the practice of law, as a litigator, but on an appellate level this time. I realize, of course, that my "re-engagement" may well be characterized, in hindsight, as a different form of insanity, growing out of the continuation of a story about a comparatively underprivileged boy out of the mountains of central Pennsylvania, who was driven to succeed in three different disciplines at three different universities, followed, professionally, by the practice of law, as a litigator, and, now, as an appellate litigator.

I am not quite sure why such a drive may have reached, in a manner of speaking, the proportions of insanity, at least on a metaphoric basis. Possibly, the reasons, although somewhat opaque, may be found in the chapters that have already formed much of this story, or, on the other hand, the reasons may become less opaque in the chapters that form much of the rest of the story. Well, whatever may be the case, the rest of this story certainly involves, in significant part, but certainly not in whole part, and, maybe, not even in the most important part, the practice of law, as a litigator, the manner in which it was accomplished and the individual who accomplished it, who also happens to be your raconteur in this instance. Then, again, maybe the practice of law, as a litigator, and the manner in which it has been accomplished, having already been told, or yet to be told, explain a lot about the practitioner, including, but not limited to, the reasons for the insanity, at least metaphorically speaking.

CHAPTER LXII

FIFTH JOB: CORPORATION COUNSELS OFFICE, APPELLATE DIVISION; FEATURING ECCENTRIC AND HIGHLY COMPETENT LAWYERS IN A DEMANDING APPELLATE PRACTICE

WELL, LEAVING insanity behind in my former ivy-covered employment, literally speaking, my work in the Appellate Division quickly became a major step toward becoming an accomplished litigator, especially on an appellate level. Although most of the work involved briefing appeals, a substantial part of it also involved oral arguments, too. For those two reasons, among a number of others, I began to develop writing and speaking skills that would eventually exceed my expectations and, for that matter, the appellate practice of many of my legal peers. In short, I was beginning to become a highly accomplished appellate lawyer among many who were not.

Admittedly, much of that fact was due to the direction and supervision of the Head of the Appellate Division, Richard W. Barton, a brilliant man and one of the finest lawyers that I have ever known. His judgment exceeded even his writing skills, which, in themselves, were in another world, or should I more appropriately say another legal world. For those accomplished reasons, and so many more, the man was respected and admired both inside and outside of the Corporation Counsels Office. And of even greater consequence, perhaps, he was also admired and respected by members of the federal judiciary, mostly on an appellate level, because of his life-long skills as an appellate lawyer.

With a supervisor who possessed those kinds of skills, not to mention the nature of the legal work, it did not take me long to realize that I had made a very wise decision in joining the Appellate Division. There was no doubt in my mind that I would eventually learn how to become an accomplished appellate advocate. Within months, however, it also became clear that it was not going to be an easy process. During that difficult time, I drafted and redrafted legal briefs so many times that it seemed, on many occasions, that I would never learn how to satisfy the man with my brief writing work. Oh, I learned what was expected, rather quickly, but learning what was expected, and doing it, were two distinctly different concepts, which were often bridged by a seemingly endless process of redrafts. Even though my redrafts reflected, in substantial part, his edits on my prior redrafts, it became apparent that I still had great difficulty in framing my arguments on the following redrafts with enough precision and organization to satisfy the man and avoid more redrafts.

My difficulty, or difficulties, as the case may be, did not ever seem to trouble the man; he simply edited my overstated arguments, with an endless amount of deletions, additions, and other forms of modifications, accompanied, quite often, with comments, which usually ended with a request to redraft the brief, or a part thereof, in light of those edits and comments. In fact, during my first year in the Appellate Division, I sometimes had to redraft a brief four or five times. And, frankly, I can't even remember how many times that I had to redraft my very first brief, but I do remember that only seventeen pages remained of my original thirty-seven-page draft. The rest ended up in my memory and in Dick Barton's waste basket!

I don't believe that the briefs that were written by the other lawyers in the Appellate Division suffered from the same fate as mine. Most of them had preceded me, by a number of years, and, most likely, they had grown quite accustomed, during that intervening time, to Dick Barton's brief writing requirements. Nor did it hurt that they were also rather bright, but, then again, they were also rather eccentric, although, in hindsight, that did not seem to materially affect their brief writing skills.

Maybe writing briefs successfully, for a number of years, which is what most of them had been doing, required a certain amount of eccentricity, along with a significant amount of brilliance. After all, it is a rather solitary existence, and, if I may add, a somewhat unusual way of practicing law, discharged, ordinarily, by research and writing, alone, at one's desk or in a law library.

Oral argument would seem to be an exception to this lonely conclusion, or professional life, but not really, because you are virtually alone, standing up there, too . . . behind the "lectern" and before the "bench" . . . except, admittedly, in a public circumstance. If you doubt that, just spend thirty minutes arguing a case before a three-judge panel, on appeal, in which you are continually interrupted by the three judges, one after another, asking difficult questions, some of which you may not have even considered in your preparation. Standing there, silently, in that challenging situation, even if it is no more than a moment or two, is the loneliest feeling in the world!

Then, again, maybe for all of those reasons, especially the lonely ones, spending years in those professional circumstances, writing briefs in appellate cases and arguing them on appeal, generates a certain amount of eccentricity. And there is no better example of those facts than Leo Gorman.

As you may recall, Leo was the lawyer who encouraged me to join the Appellate Division, and who, likely, encouraged Dick Barton to hire me. So whatever else may be said about the fellow, Leo has always been standing rather high in my esteem, certainly during the years in which I worked with him in the Appellate Division, and, for that matter, even now, nearly fifty years later. But brilliance aside, and Leo was brilliant, make no mistake about it, as much as I may like Leo Gorman, he was and continues to be "one-of-a-kind."

Upon information and belief, Leo was the fortunate son of a well-educated and enormously successful family, for, I believe, a number of generations. In fact, his grandfather, as I recall, established a trust, in which Leo, among others, was a beneficiary, and that trust, alone, may have been sufficient to support Leo Gorman and, subsequently, his wife, and, thereafter, his children, for the rest of his and, possibly, their, natural lives.

Frankly, however, that trust, remarkable as it may have been, was not what made Leo Gorman so unusual. For one, he was incredibly frugal, especially for someone who, seemingly, did not have to be. Leo not only wrote briefs on both sides of the paper on his yellow legal pads, but he also wrote on the cardboard backs, too . . . on both sides! In addition, the ball of string that he accumulated, from the packages that he received, from opposing counsel, or even elsewhere, grew to mythical proportions over the years. With that in mind, it is worth noting that Leo would often say, "waste not—want not," which may well have been a historical quote.

Moreover, frugality aside, at least for the moment, it is possible that Leo did not really have to work, or, at least, work that hard, especially as a trust beneficiary, but he did work and he worked very hard, every day, in which we were working together in the Appellate Division. Still, Leo managed to take all of the paid vacation that he was entitled to receive, which was usually several weeks a year, and, at least, several unpaid vacations, for that amount of time, every year, too. Even then, with that amount of time on vacation, Leo still managed to write more briefs, every year, than everyone else in the Appellate Division. That surprising fact was because Leo was not only a very hard worker, but he was also undeniably efficient in doing his work, which, by the way, was invariably excellent!

Nevertheless, aside from his excellent work, and work ethic, too, Leo was still such an unusual individual, although, admittedly, in a most charming manner, that his way of being often resulted in a situation, not necessarily work-related, that was absolutely hilarious. In one of those situations, which was apart from work, Jim Dulcan, another lawyer in the office, together with his wife, Suzzie, were taking a "scuba diving class" with, among others, Leo and his wife, Nancy Brazelton, in the swimming pool at Marjorie Webster Junior College. At the conclusion of one of those classes, according to Jim, all of the girls, including Nancy, retired to the girl's locker room, in order to change out of their wet bathing suits, shower and dress; likewise, the boys, including Leo and Jim, retired to the boy's locker room in order to do essentially the same.

Unfortunately, however, after finishing his shower, Leo discovered that he had, inadvertently, left his towel with Nancy, who was, at that point, in the girl's locker room, according to Jim, likely in the process of dressing with the rest of the girls. Undaunted by that mistake, or, if you will, the absence of his towel, not to mention its present location, Leo, without saying a word to anybody, calmly walked out of the boy's locker room, down the side of the swimming pool and into the girl's locker room to retrieve his towel, without as much as "a stitch on," according to Jim!

That fact was apparently quite obvious to those who were, at that point, still dressing in the girl's locker room, because some of them became absolutely irate, upon Leo's entrance, which, according to Jim, he could easily hear at the other end of the pool, where the boy's locker room was still located. Finally, Jim said that you had to give old Leo a lot of credit, because, amidst all of those angry outbursts in the girl's locker room, he came nonchalantly strolling back out of there with his towel, just as though nothing had ever happened.

Oh, yes, in case you are still wondering, as I was at the time, Leo was carrying the towel over his shoulder, not wearing it, according to Jim, who was now standing just outside of the entrance to the boy's locker room, so that he could see everything, or nearly everything, that was transpiring down there.

I also remember another situation involving Leo, which, eventually, became rather humorous, in kind of a charming sort of way, at least to me at the time. It occurred during the course of an oral argument in one of Leo's appeals, taking place at the time before a three-judge panel of the District of Columbia Court of Appeals.

As opposing counsel began to deliver his opening argument in that appeal, Leo . . . now seated at one of the two tables, up before the bar, in which both counsel were normally seated . . . began to pour himself a glass of water from a pitcher, typically residing on each one of those two tables, while waiting for opposing counsel to finish the delivery of his opening argument. Actually, to be more accurate, I should probably say that Leo "tried" to pour himself a glass of water, because the water did not seem to want to cooperate, by coming out of the pitcher, not while being held in a normal pouring position, anyway. So Leo, while still remaining seated, became somewhat impatient and, abruptly, turned the pitcher upside down, or, at least, nearly so. As he did, the water changed its mind and decided to come out, except now, it came out, furiously, all over Leo, all over the table, and, after several minutes of significant dripping, all over the courtroom floor, too!

Oh, yes, I nearly forgot, when the top came out of that pitcher, followed immediately by its watery contents, the sound and sight of that whole scenario created a circumstance not unlike that of the Niagara Falls. Apparently, the three judges, who were hearing the opening argument and who were seated at the "bench," almost directly above the "Falls," did not disagree with any of my "Niagara-like" characterization, not at that point, because they immediately turned, almost in unison, to look at the newly created waterfalls in their formerly austere courtroom.

Meanwhile, the Clerk of the Court, who had been busily taping the opening argument, while seated at another table, over by a window, added to the watery drama, by jumping up from his seat, almost instantaneously, and running over to the newly formed lake, now on the courtroom floor, and trying to mop it up, with both of counsels' briefs, if you can believe that, which had been formally resting on his table, awaiting a further review by the judges or, possibly, their law clerks, following the conclusion of the oral argument. As a result of that frenetic situation, involving a lot of dripping, a lot of moping, and a lot of inattention, I don't believe that any one of those three judges ever heard one more word of opposing counsel's opening statement, which, despite the noisy fracas, was still, can you believe this, ongoing!

Despite everything . . . and I really do mean all of those transpiring events . . . opposing counsel, apparently oblivious to the carnival taking place all around him, eventually concluded his opening argument and proceeded to sit down at the table located on his side of the courtroom. At almost the same time, Leo arose from his seat and quickly proceeded over to the lectern, with a few notes in hand, in order to present his opposing argument to the now distracted court. As I watched him, now standing behind the lectern, shuffling through some of his notes, I thought to myself, there, in the form of Leo Gorman, stands a man of, sometimes, comedic proportions, although unintentionally so, who is also an appellate lawyer of gifted dimensions. And if, by chance, that gifted lawyer should lose that appeal, now being addressed by the District of Columbia Court of Appeals, it would not be because of the brilliant oral argument presented by his adversary, because those three judges likely never heard most of it, or even because his adversary wrote a prevailing brief, because that brief was a soaking wet, unreadable mess, by the end of that courtroom circus. It would probably be because those three judges were unable to overlook a little eccentricity, unfortunately, displayed in a liquidly drama, which inadvertently took place in their courtroom, involving a cantankerous water pitcher, the watery contents therein, and a gifted appellate lawyer, who unintentionally precipitated the whole mess.

Well, apart from the eccentricity, charmingly so, Leo Gorman was an extraordinary lawyer in an office full of extraordinary lawyers, all of whom engaged in an extensive appellate practice before the federal judiciary. Nearly all of them were accomplished litigators at the trial level, and nearly all of them were accomplished litigators at the appellate level, if not even more so, which made them formidable adversaries in any judicial forum, especially on an appellate level. Moreover, notwithstanding the above, or, possibly, because of the above, nearly all of them demonstrated qualities, within and without their practice, that were unusual enough to be considered eccentric, certainly by most reasonable individuals, not excluding this storyteller. Nevertheless, eccentric or not, bright or not, they became my associates in the practice of law, for over five years, in a professional circumstance that I will never forget!

In that regard, I can honestly say . . . because of the nature of the work and the nature of my associates doing the work, not to mention the supervisory skills of Dick Barton with respect to the work . . . that my five years in that office had more of an impact on my subsequent performance as a litigator, than anything else that I have ever done in the practice of law, before and after that time. Quite simply, what I learned during that appellate practice would serve me well in everything that I would do thereafter, as a litigating lawyer. Indeed, the fact that I was able to do the things that I have done, as a litigator, in the years that have followed, and do them that well, was because of what I did there, and with them, during that halcyon time!

CHAPTER LXIII

FIFTH JOB: CORPORATION COUNSELS OFFICE, APPELLATE DIVISION; NATURE OF THE WORK, INCLUDING WRITING BRIEFS, DOING LEGAL RESEARCH, REVIEWING THE RECORD AND PRESENTING ORAL ARGUMENTS

I WROTE briefs, among other things, every day, all day, during the five years in which I was in the Appellate Division of the Corporation Counsels Office. It would usually take me part of a week to research and write a brief, more or less, depending upon the nature of the case, and I would have to work diligently in order to finish it by that time. Nevertheless, it was important to finish a brief as quickly as possible, because there were always several more pending appeals sitting on my desk, waiting for me to brief them as soon as possible. And, of course, there would also be several other briefs, which had already been drafted, sitting on Dick Barton's desk, waiting for him to review and return them to me. Upon their return, it may mean a redraft, or, maybe, even two, before approval, as a prevailing brief, acceptable for filing.

Naturally, briefing a case involved more than a simple drafting exercise. Among other things, it depended upon the legal research of an issue, or issues, which, depending upon their complexity, could be quite time-consuming, especially if any one of them presented an issue of first impression. And it goes without saying, that an understanding of the record below, including, and especially, the trial transcript, was also necessary in framing an argument or arguments, based thereon, in a brief. Sometimes those trial transcripts could exceed a thousand pages, or ten thousand pages, or even more, especially if there was a complex factual dispute below, and reviewing and recalling the information contained therein was always a condition precedent to drafting a prevailing argument based thereon. Finally, drafting a prevailing brief often required the kind of organization, if not creativity, that allowed the drafter to present a prevailing argument, notwithstanding a certain amount of case law that may appear to be to the contrary.

In any event, in between the drafting and the redrafting of briefs, or parts thereof, some of which were currently pending on Dick Barton's desk, or on mine, there were oral arguments that had been, or would become, scheduled on those briefs, or on those that had preceded them, which usually occurred, in their presentation, at least every other week. In preparing for those oral arguments, I would ordinarily write an outline, which normally took part of a day. Then I would commit the outline to memory, which usually took the rest of the day, and even part of the evening, too, usually at home. And I would usually present the argument, as I had committed it to memory, before an interested audience, on the following day, in the office, and, subsequent thereto, to the disinterested walls of the courthouse library, just prior to the argument, itself, scheduled shortly thereafter, in the court of appeals. Naturally, I would never be able to deliver the argument in the form in which it had been committed to memory, because of the constant interruptions by the court. But upon completion of my responses to the concerns, expressed in those interruptive enquires, I would normally be able to comfortably recommence my argument, where necessary, because, in most of those instances, it was a matter of simple recollection.

Sometimes, however, those judicial enquires or interruptions may indicate some concern about aspects of your case that did not necessarily follow your outline, which would mean, of course, that you may have to discard the outline, at least in part, if not in whole, and proceed to direct your attention, immediately, to the matter now concerning the court, which, in my extensive experience, was a fairly rare circumstance. Even worse, some of those enquires or interruptions may indicate that the case may possibly turn on a matter that you have never even briefed or, subsequently, addressed by way of oral argument. Although I have often heard about such a dramatic situation, occurring at an oral argument, I am happy to report that it has never occurred in any one of the hundreds of instances in which I have presented an oral argument before an appellate court.

Of course, there were also the endless letters and motions that had to be drafted and redrafted in connection with each case that was pending on appeal. And I am not even going to discuss the interruptive telephone calls that disturbed much of my working day. Actually, because of those interruptions, I did much of my work in the law library of the Corporation Counsel's Office and, following lunch, in the District of Columbia Bar Library, which was located on the third floor of the United States District Court House. I also went to the Bar Library, early in the morning, before each oral argument . . . which had been scheduled, almost immediately thereafter, in the District of Columbia Court of Appeals or in the United States Court of Appeals for the District of Columbia Circuit . . . in order to go over my argument, one more time, before delivering it, about thirty minutes later, at ten o'clock in the morning on that day, before one of those two Courts.

Because of the amount of those oral arguments, scheduled in every appellate court in the District of Columbia, I became, after five years of doing them, a very capable public speaker, especially during oral arguments. Oh, sure, I initially memorized them, but I was never able to deliver them in the same manner in which I had outlined them and, subsequently, committed them to memory, because of the intermittent questions from the three judges, who were sitting on the appeal, by which they continuously interrupted much of my argument, again and again and, frustratingly, again. Those interruptions, as well as their nature and number, caused me to learn how to speak, extemporaneously, in more than a capable manner, apart from my prepared outline, in a rather austere public circumstance. And according to Judge Nebeker, who presided over a panel of three judges in a number of my cases pending before the District of Columbia Court of Appeals, I did just that . . . "speaking extemporaneously in oral argument" . . . better than most advocates who appeared before that Court.

Maybe that was, in part, because I never used notes, or any other means of assistance, in delivering an oral argument. I just arose from my chair at counsel's table and walked quickly over to the lectern, where I waited to commence my argument, which, of course, turned upon receipt of a green light, indicating that I may begin. Until then, I would just stand there, with my hands upon the "lectern," while looking intently at the three judges, who were arrayed before me.

Incidentally, I never addressed an appellate judge in the time-honored manner of most lawyers, who almost always addressed them as, "Your Honor"; I simply addressed them with the prefix, "Judge," followed by their surname, during all of my oral arguments. And with the prefix changed to "Justice, I followed suit in the Supreme Court of the United States. It was important, in my estimation, to have the judges or justices, as the case may be, realize that I had no reason to be deferential, outside of professional courtesy, that is, and that, with respect to the issue before them, I had no peer, including those who were seated before me, during an oral argument on the matter at issue!

CHAPTER LXIV

FIFTH JOB: CORPORATION COUNSELS OFFICE, APPELLATE DIVISION; A COURT-APPOINTED COUNSEL WHO HAD NEVER PRESENTED ARGUMENT IN AN APPELLATE COURT HAD A HEART ATTACK WHILE DOING SO IN ONE OF MY APPEALS

IT IS certainly true that a number of lawyers in large law firms have learned how to write a good brief, if not, on occasion, a great brief. That is because writing briefs and legal memoranda are something that they normally do in their practice, especially if they are litigators at a trial court level. But most of them rarely have reason to appear in a court of appeals, especially in a Circuit Court of Appeals, and in those few instances in which they do, rarely have oral arguments been scheduled, at least not for a full thirty minutes. Unless there were complex issues of first impression, not at all a typical situation, even on appeal, the appeals were ordinarily decided on the merits of the submitted briefs, or following a much smaller time limit allotted for oral argument, normally not exceeding ten or fifteen minutes.

Consequently, oral argument, especially before a three-judge panel on appeal, was, ordinarily, a rather daunting task for most counsel, even from very large law firms, which they assiduously avoided, where possible, or discharged rather clumsily, where impossible. As a result, I have often saved my case, so to speak, by oral argument, especially where I had reason to fear that the result may well have been otherwise, if the case was decided solely on the merits of the submitted briefs. Consequently, I have often refused requests by counsel to have an oral argument waived and to have the case decided on the merits of the submitted briefs, so that I could, if necessary, try to prevail in oral argument.

There were always exceptions, of course, and one of them was noteworthy enough to bear retelling here. It was a criminal appeal, and it was assigned to me toward the end of my five-year tenure in the Appellate Division of the Corporation Counsels Office. The opposing counsel was a rather distinguished elderly gentleman, who was a partner in one of the large, transactional law firms in the city, and who was, not surprisingly, a transactional tax lawyer, who rarely, if ever, engaged in litigation, especially on an appellate level. Nevertheless, he was assigned to the case by the trial court, because the appellant, who was indigent, possibly had a meritorious appeal on an issue of, arguably, first impression.

At this point, nothing that I have already said about the appeal and about the opposing counsel, who was assigned to represent the appellant, may seem, on first impression, to be particularly noteworthy. I hasten to point out, however, that it was certainly worth noting at the time, as it is now, that opposing counsel's law firm was largely a transactional business firm, although a noteworthy one, and that his individual practice was solely a transactional tax practice. And, indeed, I did note both facts, early in my work on this appeal, especially because his brief was extraordinarily well written and quite persuasive on a rather complex issue of seemingly first impression. Indeed, even after having researched the issue and written a brief of my own, in response thereto, which I believed was also well-written and equally persuasive, I was still not too sure about the outcome, because the case on the briefs was, in my experienced opinion, far too close to comfortably tell.

Nevertheless, I knew that I may still have a winning card to play, based on my experience as an appellate advocate, which would become my oral argument, scheduled before a three-judge panel, for a full thirty minutes, in the District of Columbia Court of Appeals. I had regularly appeared in that Court, nearly every other week, for years, and I knew that, in all likelihood, he had not, and that he would, in all likelihood, never appear there again . . . not in his lifetime or mine!

Apparently, opposing counsel was not unmindful of his comparative inexperience, in an oral argument forum, because he called me, about one week before the scheduled argument, and asked me to agree to submit the case for a decision on the merits of the submitted briefs . . . without an oral argument. Equally mindful of his comparative inexperience, at least in an oral argument forum, especially at an appellate level, I politely declined his request, almost before he had finished making it, and, to be quite frank about the matter, the expression on my face at the time was somewhere between a smirk and a snarl! It was the sort of expression that you might expect to see on a predator when it realizes that its prey has been cornered and is about to give up, and that it is simply hunkering down to await the inevitable.

Well, the inevitable came to pass, about one week later, on the day of oral argument. Because opposing counsel was pursuing the appeal, as an appellant in the case, he was scheduled to open with his argument, which he did, and which he continued to do, but only for about ten minutes. At about that point, his demeanor seemed to unravel, and, within minutes, he seemed to become unglued, especially when the inevitable questions began to arise. Now visibly shaken, he seemed to have great difficulty, if not an outright inability, in responding to several of them. And with that, I began to think about winning, and about where and with whom I would have lunch to celebrate my success in this appeal, once the whole trying thing was inevitably over.

At about that point, however, my dining plans were interrupted by something that was completely unexpected, at least I didn't expect it, anyway. Opposing counsel, who was, by now, struggling, but, nevertheless, part way through his opening argument, stopped, abruptly, and said, in a voice that was barely audible, "I think I'm having a heart attack." With that announcement, I immediately stopped thinking about lunches and celebrations and victories. Instead, I began thinking about heart attacks and hospitals and emergencies, and, ultimately, about opposing counsel, who was, by now, ashen grey, visibly, and sort of slumped over part of the lectern, from which he was barely able to retreat to his seat at the "counsels table."

My gaze, then, momentarily left opposing counsel, who was, by now, partially slumped over in his chair at the "counsels table," seemingly unable to either sit or stand, and, then, it moved, quickly upward, toward the three judges, who were intently looking down at him and at his predicament, from their seat at the "bench." For a moment, or, maybe, several, no one in the courtroom, neither the three judges, opposing counsel, the clerk of the court, nor myself, said a word. Then, for reasons that I cannot explain, even now, over fifty-five years later, I jumped to my feet and, like an idiot, requested that the case be submitted for a decision on the merits of the briefs . . . without an oral argument! With that, I immediately turned to the clerk of the court, who was still busily transcribing everything, like an even bigger idiot than the one already described, and I asked him to call for an ambulance, which he did, almost immediately.

Following a preliminary examination of the poor fellow, by a pair of paramedics, roughly fifteen minutes later, right there in the courtroom, with the three shaken judges, the idiotic opposing counsel, not to mention the stupid clerk of the court, as onlookers, an ambulance apparently transported the poor fellow to an emergency room at the nearest available hospital.

In the meantime, the three judges, to my knowledge, never ruled from the "bench," on my request, in open court, to submit the case for a decision on the merits of the briefs, without an oral argument. Indeed, I don't recall those three judges ever doing anything, at the time, other than looking down, in obvious disbelief, at a man who may, conceivably, be dying, right before their eyes, in their very own courtroom.

Actually, I am probably being somewhat unfair; how could you possibly expect those judges to decide on a course of action, even in that mortally threatening situation, when the issue, involving what to do, in the face of a probable heart attack, in their courtroom, no less, had never been briefed, by either party! Maybe, and understandably, especially if you have ever been a litigator, especially on an appellate level, the judges were simply waiting for me to return to my office and to prepare a brief on the relative merits of several alternatives, in addressing the situation, before deciding what to do, and how to do it, in an untimely manner.

In any event, I had, quite obviously, already decided, spontaneously, and without the benefit of a briefing, I might add, that one of the things to do, in a situation like that, was, as opposing counsel, to request, in open court, that the case be submitted for a decision on the merits of the briefs, without oral argument. Of course, my decision, in that respect, was not necessarily in the interests of myself, as an attorney litigating an appeal, and it certainly was not in the interests of my client, who wished to prevail on the merits of that appeal.

Nevertheless, my decision, given the circumstances, was probably the only available option for me, at least at the time, and, even more importantly, for opposing counsel, given his mortally threatening circumstance. And in that respect, it could also be said that my decision, at that moment, to avail myself of that option, by requesting that the appeal be submitted, without oral argument, for a decision on the merits of the briefs, was probably a fairly decent one, especially if viewed from the perspective of a forum much higher than simply a legal one, or, maybe, even an earthly one.

Oh, yes, in case you may be wondering, my decision was apparently viewed by opposing counsel as a rather decent one, too, even from an earthly perspective, if not a legal one, and he subsequently informed me so, in a rather thoughtful telephone call, several weeks later, upon his release from the hospital. The conversation ended with his expression of gratitude for my kindness, or my stupidity, depending upon your particular vantage point. Since I can no longer remember the outcome of that appeal, I am not quite sure which vantage point to adopt now.

That I do not remember the outcome in that appeal is really not so surprising; outside of the medical drama at the oral argument, it was really a rather routine case of very little significance. Although there may have been, arguably, an issue of first impression, according to the appellant's novel legal theory, that was not an unusual argument on an appeal, or as a basis therefor. Many cases, if not most, which were on appeal, involved cases that may have arguably involved issues of first impression, as the basis therefore, especially when you consider the cost, among other prohibitive factors, in noting an appeal, let alone in litigating it. Indeed, based on my experience, as an appellate litigator, such appeals, if not the basis therefor, are somewhat commonplace. And, moreover, with respect to this particular instance, I had already handled hundreds of appeals of far greater significance during my five years in the Appellate Division of the Corporation Counsels Office. Most of them were appeals pending before the District of Columbia Court of Appeals and the United States Court of Appeals for the District of Columbia Circuit. Some others were appeals pending before the Fourth Circuit Court of Appeals, and a few were even appeals pending before the United States Supreme Court.

CHAPTER LXV

*FIFTH JOB: CORPORATION
COUNSELS OFFICE, APPELLATE
DIVISION; I HAD TO ABANDON
MY PLANS TO GO ON A VACATION
WITH MY DANISH WIFE AND
MOTHER-IN-LAW BECAUSE OF MY
PROSPECTIVE PARTICIPATION IN AN
EN BANC APPEAL*

ONE OF the more significant cases during the five years in which I was an appellate lawyer was an administrative appeal before the Superior Court for the District of Columbia, in which the Hotel Association of Washington contested a minimum wage determination made by the District of Columbia Minimum-Wage Board. Following a hearing on the merits of that determination, it was set aside by an order of the Superior Court, which was subsequently affirmed by a decision of a three-judge panel of the District of Columbia Court of Appeals. Thereafter, the Board asked the Appellate Division of the Office of Corporation Counsel to assist it in requesting a reconsideration of that decision by the District of Columbia Court of Appeals, sitting en banc, in which all nine judges in the Court of Appeals would review the decision of the three-judge panel, following a re-briefing and a re-argument.

Shortly after receiving that request, Dick Barton, as Chief of the Appellate Division, assigned the case to me, with an instruction to do whatever was necessary to obtain that kind of relief on behalf of the Board. Toward that end, I subsequently prepared and filed, within a week, a petition for reconsideration by the full court, sitting en banc, as well as a memorandum in support thereof. Following a review of that memorandum as well as the one filed in opposition thereto by opposing counsel, the panel granted my petition and scheduled the case for an oral argument, within thirty days, before the full Court, consisting of all nine judges of the District of Columbia Court of Appeals, sitting en banc.

Shortly thereafter, opposing counsel filed a motion for an expedited briefing schedule, which, if granted, would require my brief, as the petitioner, to be filed within ten days. Over my strenuous objection, supported by a lengthy memorandum, the panel granted his request and issued an order requiring my brief to be filed within ten days. Even apart from the record, which was extensive, numbering well over twenty thousand pages, which I had not yet read, I was not quite sure how I could even write a brief, addressing all ten of the issues, two of which bordered on being issues of first impression, let alone a prevailing brief, within the ten-day period.

Actually, the whole daunting situation, involving an expedited briefing schedule, which, in itself, was unreasonable, given the complexities in the case, and the size of the record, became even more complicated than a simple timing or briefing problem. And, unfortunately, I was married at the time to the complication, which was a Dane with a Danish mother, who was scheduled to arrive within days in the United States. And the three of us, the Danish wife, the Danish mother and the non-Danish husband, now subjected to an expedited briefing schedule, were scheduled to tour the country, for three weeks, with reservations already made in hotels along the way, and with non-refundable airline tickets, already purchased, to fly there!

Well, in case you are already wondering, it took about seven terrifying seconds, after receiving that ten-day scheduling order, to realize that I could not do both the family vacation and the expedited appeal, not at the same time, anyway. In case you are still wondering, it took about five more seconds to realize that I was really in an impossible situation, which most rational individuals, of which I was no longer one, would consider to be quite a quandary. Nevertheless, irrationality aside, but only for the moment, or, maybe, slightly longer, it took me no more than one sleepless night to resolve the quandary, by deciding to do the appeal, instead of going on the family vacation. But it took the whole following day before I could gather up enough courage to inform my Danish wife of that agonizing decision!

Upon being so informed, my Danish wife was, understandably, less than happy, which was probably a gross understatement, and which, along with the expedited briefing schedule, became, quite naturally, a matter of major concern. Until that point, I had always been under the impression, mistakenly or not, that my Danish wife actually liked me, even though she did not particularly like most lawyers, or even the profession, for that matter. And I can certainly assure you, in case you may have some lingering doubts at this point, that her opinion of the profession, as well as its participants, especially one of them, took a serious nosedive, after she realized that I was going to abandon our vacation plans, with her mother, no less, and, instead, write an expedited brief in an en banc appeal.

Following the departure of both Danes, consisting of an excited mother-in-law and her irate daughter, on their holiday trip across the country, I, unfortunately, had to embark on a trip of my own, but it was only to a law library, and for activities that one could hardly describe as a holiday venture. Actually, I had to do whatever was necessary to write an expedited brief, within ten days, on a number of labor subjects, which I, literally, knew very little about. And in doing so, I had to rely on an immense record, consisting of over twenty-thousand pages, which I had never read, not even one page. Because of that fact, among so many other dismal considerations, the prospect of being able to draft an expedited brief, within the prescribed time period, seemed daunting; the prospect of doing a reasonably good job in drafting it seemed improbable.

After another sleepless night, during which I vacillated between guilt, for abandoning my wife and her mother, not to mention their vacation plans, and terror at the prospect of what professionally lay ahead of me, in complying with that expedited briefing schedule, I made a crucial decision, early in the following morning, somewhere between my first and second spoonfuls of shredded wheat: I decided not to try to read that extensive record. Actually, that was not really a difficult decision, because I simply could not have read that extensive record, not even if I stayed up all night, every night, trying to do so, certainly not in a sufficient amount of time to write an extensive brief, in a multi-issued case, like that one, within a ten-day period. So for nearly ten days, which was the time that it took me to draft and file that expedited brief, I figuratively and, sometimes, literally, lived in a law library, along with two labor counsel from the District of Columbia Minimum Wage Board, who, with opposing counsel, created that extensive record in an administrative hearing.

Relying on their extensive knowledge of the record actually worked out reasonably well, because I had become aware of the issues in the case by the time that I had finished preparing my petition for a rehearing en banc. And at the same time, I developed, in conjunction therewith, a rough outline of the legal arguments that I intended to use in a brief on behalf of the Board, in the event that my petition was granted. Finally, I had outlined, at the same time, how I would organizationally present my points in those arguments.

Nevertheless, in order to actually begin writing an expedited brief, I needed to find the facts in the record that would support those points in my legal arguments. Since I could not do that, because I did not know that extensive record, having never had an opportunity to read it, I had the two-labor counsel, who were seated beside me in the law library, every day, and part of every night, find the facts in the record that I needed to support the points in my legal arguments. They also found most of the case law that I relied upon to support those points. As a result, we . . . the two-labor counsel and myself . . . managed to research, draft and file an excellent brief, within the ten-day expedited briefing schedule, partially by an act of God, and partially by the "sweat on the brows" of three overworked lawyers, only one of whom was an appellate lawyer!

The problem, however, was that opposing counsel did, too, and within his prescribed briefing period. Indeed, his brief was so persuasive that I was not sure whether I would prevail on the merits, certainly not on the merits of the briefs. Nevertheless, I still had that extra card to play, which was usually a winning one, because of my extensive experience in doing oral arguments before a three-judge panel in the court of appeals, any court of appeals, federal or otherwise. And this case was scheduled to be heard by the full appellate court of nine judges, sitting en banc, and that was bound to be an unnerving experience for a less experienced lawyer, even one who headed the labor section of his large, international law firm, which, of course, described opposing counsel in this case as well as his law firm.

Well, oral argument before all nine judges of the District of Columbia Court of Appeals, sitting en banc, occurred, as scheduled, within ten days after opposing counsel filed his responsive brief. And it was held in the Ceremonial Courtroom, on the third floor of the United States District Court House in Washington, D.C. Not surprisingly, given the nature of the case, the nature of the appeal, pending before the full court appeals, sitting en banc, and the ceremonial nature of the courtroom, the audience, seated in that rather large and impressive chamber, was extensive. In fact, it is safe to say that it was absolutely packed with people, some of whom were interested individuals, such as relatives of counsel, and some of whom were less interested individuals, such as retirees, who had decided to fill part of their day by watching an oral argument before all nine judges of the District of Columbia Court of Appeals, sitting en banc.

Four members of that audience, however, were of a particular interest to me: They consisted of my parents, who I had invited to attend, several days before, and who had driven to Washington, D. C., to do just that, as well as my two young sons, who had accompanied them. At the time, my sons were about twelve and nine years of age, and although they were rather young to become interested observers, they had never, prior to that time, had an opportunity to see their father present an oral argument in an appellate court, not in any kind of an appellate court. And this, of course, was not an ordinary appeal; it was an extraordinary appeal. And I was not sure whether they would ever have an opportunity to witness that fact again, certainly not in that kind of an appeal. My parents, on the other hand, were quite elderly, and because of geography, among other prohibitive things, they never had an opportunity to see their son argue a case in any legal forum, trial or appellate, let alone in one like this. And given their age and mine, I was not sure whether they would ever have an opportunity to see me do it again, certainly not in a legal forum like this one!

Actually, I don't know whether my parents, or my two sons, really had much of an interest in being there, aside, of course, from our relationship, but I had more than a simple familial interest in having them there, which was equally applicable to both of them, not to mention to their respective generations, even though they were quite disparate in age and time, if not in experience. After all, they were all members of the same family, mine and theirs, and I wanted them to see what their family had done or, in another generation, could become.

When viewed from that perspective, I guess that you could possibly say that I was not just appearing on behalf of the District of

Columbia Minimum Wage Board. I was also appearing, in a far larger, more complicated, sense, on behalf of my family, including those who have preceded me and those who would likely follow me.

For all of those complicated, familial reasons, among others just as noteworthy, including the professional ones, I wanted to win; I wanted to win, badly, and I wanted to win for all of us, referring, of course, not only for myself, but for my family, known and unknown, and for my client, the District of Columbia Minimum Wage Board. But I especially wanted to win for myself. And I did! I knew that I would; I almost always did, if the appeal turned on an oral argument. And I won that appeal in a lengthy one-hundred and forty-three-page decision, issued by the full court, sitting en banc, with a comparable dissent, too, ninety days later.

Funny, though, the decision really didn't change much in my life. My parents, who never commented on their experience that day, went back home to central Pennsylvania, "probably no worse for the wear," as it is often said in the mountains where I had grown up, located, as you are well aware by now, in central Pennsylvania. My two sons, seemingly oblivious to their experience that day, went back to their elementary school, where their friends and the other important aspects of their lives tended to reside. And, of course, I went back to the office to brief another case, and, hopefully, win another oral argument, because . . . oh well, I suppose that you already know by this time!

Considering those predictably pedestrian events occurring subsequently, in all three instances, it might be fair to say that there does not seem to be any significant consequences, following what occurred on that day, to the lives of any one of us. Having said that, I probably should also acknowledge, certainly at this point, my surprise, years later, to learn that both of my sons had decided to go on to law school, which, of course, was at subsequent points in their respective academic lives, one at the University of Virginia and the other at the University of Pennsylvania. Given the enormous demands involved in just becoming a lawyer, let alone in engaging in the practice, which, of course, they certainly witnessed, "firsthand," on that challenging day, if nowhere else, over the course of our respective lives, together, I certainly can't explain their decision!

As a concluding note to this litigating chapter, in an explanatory context, I must now confess, over fifty years later, that I am not sure why I chose to brief that appeal, on an expedited basis, rather than to have it reassigned to another lawyer in the Appellate Division, so that I could join my Danish family on their prearranged vacation. In a sense, however, it may be that I had already made that choice, a long time ago, when I chose to leave my family, remaining at home in central Pennsylvania, in order to go hundreds of miles away to a suburban university in the Chicago area. Maybe, I had already made that choice when I chose to survive in an academic and social environment at that university for which I was initially unprepared. Maybe, I had already made that choice, when I chose to go on to a graduate school, in philosophy, no less, at another university, and to do well enough in that discipline to be awarded a graduate assistantship. Maybe, I had already made that choice when I chose to go on to law school immediately thereafter. Maybe, I had already made that choice, by choosing to work in the legal profession in a manner that provided me with an opportunity to eventually become a partner in one of the largest law firms in the Nation's Capitol. And, maybe, I had already done well enough in all of those choices, at least up to that point, that it was difficult, even in the face of a family dilemma, to choose to do anything else!

CHAPTER LXVI

*STONEGATE: MY TWO YOUNG SONS;
SWIMMING AND BASEBALL LESSONS,
HUMOROUSLY DESCRIBED*

AS SOON as the boys were old enough, I began to teach them how to swim and how to play baseball, both of which I had learned in Price Park, now called Hanna Park, located nearly across the street from my home, as a young boy, growing up at the time at 269 Susquehanna Avenue in Lock Haven, Pennsylvania. I learned how to do those things by doing them every day, nearly all day, every summer, for most of my formative years. Consequently, I did not necessarily do them correctly, or, at least, the way that you were supposed to do them, whatever that may have meant, but I did them in a way that seemed to work, so that was exactly what I taught my two sons to do.

The classroom that we used for swimming lessons happened to be the public pool at Wheaton Regional Park in Montgomery County, Maryland, which was not too far from our home at the time at 14804 Flintstone Lane in Silver Spring, Maryland, and, even more importantly, was virtually free to use by the public, including our family. Because of the size of the pool, which was enormous, and because of the size of the population that used the pool, which was also enormous, learning how to swim often meant learning how to avoid a collision with others, while trying to do so. Nevertheless, with a wary eye on the others, who were also using the pool, the boys became used to the water, above and, eventually, below the surface.

Now reasonably acclimated to the water, above and below the surface, after a period of just a few weeks, both boys began to make some feeble attempts at some kind of a movement, but only above the surface, and only by an indescribable movement of arms and legs. Eventually, however, with a significant amount of repetition, and an excessive amount of encouragement, from both of their parents, who were usually standing right beside them in the water, each boy overcame, by successive stages, a fear of the water, a fear of departing from their stationary parents, who had been holding them up, and a fear that they would never learn how to swim, no matter how hard they tried.

In the end, however, after an endless amount of attempts, countless hours, and an infinite amount of patience, especially on the part of their parents, both boys did, in fact, learn how to swim, or, at least, swim in a manner that approximated the manner in which their parents did it, which may not have been in the same manner that an Olympic swimmer may have done it. Still, they accomplished the art, if we may call it an art, in a manner that was sufficient to discharge whatever concerns their parents may have had about their responsibility to ensure that their progeny would survive . . . at least in the water.

Their father, however, was also aware that survival for young boys, who were interested in reaching their teenage years, without developing some form of a serious neurosis, required that they also learn how to play a competitive sport, or two, reasonably well, also. And responsibility for that achievement, at least in the small community where their father had grown up, usually fell upon the shoulders of a father, who, in this case, learned a thing or two about those kinds of athletic subjects, once again, in Price Park.

To be more specific, since I had grown up when baseball was "king," so to speak, I learned a thing or two about the game, by playing it . . . in Price Park, of course. So I decided to teach the boys a thing or two about hitting and fielding a baseball, Price Park style, by having them do it on the road in front of our house, since we were too far away to practice in Price Park.

That's right, our baseball field was, initially, the road in front of our house, for reasons that I can no longer remember, if, indeed, there were any reasons, other than, possibly, convenience. Actually, looking back now, utilizing the road in front of our house, as a baseball field, really didn't seem to have a good reason, especially when you consider that we actually had a "ball field," down behind the school house, just one block away. Well, whatever the reason, lethargy or otherwise, we used the road in front of our house as a "ball field," which did not make our neighbors, and their front windows, terribly excited.

Nevertheless, the boys avoided the neighbors' windows nearly as well as they did catching the ball. Mindful of the dangers of missing a so-called "fly ball," and the parts of the human anatomy that may be impacted thereby, they spent most of the time trying to avoid those dangers and those balls. Although their efforts, initially, did not seem to be all that unreasonable, when you calculate the probabilities of their actually catching the balls, while trying to avoid being hit by them, it became abundantly clear, after a short period of time, that the whole avoidance process was not reasonably calculated to ever achieve any eventual success in actually catching a "fly ball."

Consequently, after watching this frustrating spectacle, for some time, I eventually announced that they . . . the two boys who, up to this point, gave "avoidance" a new meaning . . . had to get underneath the "fly balls," and stay underneath them, as they came flying down toward them. That way, I announced, "You will either catch the balls, or they will hit you, one way or the other," which was clearly an old baseball maxim that has endured the passage of time . . . even in Price Park.

Having routinely depended upon their parents for safety and

security, not to mention decency, at least up to that point in their young lives, that announcement seemed to both boys to be a radical departure from a previously recognized parental obligation. But I suppose that every parent, who was worth anything as a parent, must have realized that they had an obligation to, metaphorically, "kick their kids out of the nest," at some point in time, if they . . . the disbelieving kids . . . were ever going to amount to anything at all. And, consistent therewith, I suppose that I must have realized, in the face of "catching incompetence," with respect to "fly balls," that such a time had arrived, and that if my two sons were ever going to learn how to catch a baseball, which comes flying down at them, menacingly, they were going to have to learn how to do it the hard way!

The first one to learn how to do it that way, which, of course, was the "hard way," was, unfortunately, my older son, Court, who did not miss the "fly ball," outright; it merely bounded off the side of his glove and onto the side of his nose, which immediately increased the size of his nose, all of his nose, a fact that did not make him terribly happy, or even his mother, for that matter, who still adhered, unfortunately, to the previously announced sociological principle of parental obligation.

Still, when the nose and the mother subsided, a few days later, the boys and their father went back out on to the street in front of the house, once again, for some more baseball lessons, without, hopefully, any more severe consequences for the nose and for the father. And, eventually, the nose, the father, the gloves and the baseballs worked it all out, by coming together, and the boys began to actually accomplish the fine art of catching a "fly ball!"

Catching a "ground ball," however, posed a far more serious problem, which, to the boys, reached the proportions of becoming life-threatening in nature. That was because a "ground ball," unlike its flying counterpart, did not travel in a predictably reliable trajectory.

Instead, the ball did crazy things, because of the crazy topography upon which it traveled, on the way to committing mayhem on the poor idiot, who was still crazy enough to assume where the ball might be, by the time that it had reached him. Consequently, catching the damn thing did not seem to be the object at the time, not to both terrified boys; rather, preventing the damn thing from catching them seemed to be a far more reasonable alternative!

Unfortunately, however, mastering the game of baseball, which, of course, was our ultimate objective, puts a premium upon catching the damn thing, even when it decides to travel, unpredictably, on the ground, no matter how risky that may prove to be. So I, eventually, insisted that both boys, "assume the risk," which I realized was a legal term, but which, in the last analysis, did not seem to be inconsistent with one of life's more important lessons, even when trying to catch a so-called "ground ball." But, then, we have been down that educational road before, in a discussion of other life-related subjects, in other chapters, and in the lessons on catching "fly balls," discussed, at length, previously, in this chapter.

Hitting the ball, however, did not seem to be quite so risky, not to either one of the boys, probably because their father began pitching the ball to them in an underhanded manner, so that there really was not much velocity, and the ball appeared to follow a reasonably reliable trajectory. Moreover, it seemed to both boys that, with an oversized bat, which was the only kind that we could salvage from the basement, they could do more damage to the ball than the ball could do to them. So in the end, and even in the beginning, they liked learning how to hit the ball far more than they liked learning how to field it, because the risk in doing the former seemed to be, comparatively speaking, much smaller, at least in the beginning, anyway.

Their father, on the other hand, realized, very quickly, as a semi-reasonable adult, that hitting a baseball, to the extent that either boy could, may pose a very serious risk to the neighborhood, especially to the neighborhood windows. But after a couple of hits, by both boys, which could only be described as fortunate, given the nature of their "swings," as they say in baseball terminology, it became quite clear that the ball, admittedly a rather formidable object, had no interest in the neighborhood windows. Actually, to be quite frank about the matter, the ball really had no interest in going anywhere, and, generally, avoided doing so, which meant that we had a lot of work to do, just to hit the ball, let alone to do it in a manner that would have satisfied, the one and only, "Joltin' Joe DiMaggio" or, maybe, even "the Babe."

The degree of skill in hitting a baseball steadily improved through the years until it reached, in my older son's case, an amount sufficient to play organized baseball and at a very young age, too. And by that time, his "fielding," in baseball terminology, had become nearly flawless, which probably explains why he was placed at "shortstop," recognized as a demanding position, by his manager. Apparently, having a baseball bounce off your nose, once or twice during childhood, improves the skill level of any "infielder," short of a masochistic one. And although his hitting skills may not have reached the proportions of a DiMaggio or a Ruth, they were certainly sufficient to beat out the rest of the kids, who were competing for that position.

CHAPTER LXVII

STONEGATE: MY TWO SONS; TENNIS LESSONS, TENNIS APPAREL AND PLAYING TENNIS, HUMOROUSLY DESCRIBED

THEIR INTEREST in baseball seemed to fade away before each boy reached his "teens," and it was replaced, in each case, by tennis, which had already been part of their lives, probably since they were old enough to hold a racket. When I say hold a racket, I mean barely hold a racket, because we began to practice hitting a tennis ball, just as soon as they were barely able to hold a racket.

Practice, at first, took place on the road in front of our house once again. Unlike its "big league" counterpart, however, that was a really nice place to start, because the tennis balls bounced, quite nicely, on the road surface, and, if I may say so, rather predictably so. It was also a reasonably safe place to learn how to hit a tennis ball, because the road ended in a cul-de-sac, in the very next block, so we really did not have much traffic with which to contend. And the neighborhood windows really did not have too much to fear, from a misguided hit of an out-of-control tennis ball, because a tennis ball was, quite obviously, far less ominous, in that respect, than a baseball.

So I began, as part of my instructional methodology, by standing directly across from one of my two sons, but within a reasonable proximity, and bouncing a tennis ball, on one bounce, to the awaiting boy, who was more concerned about holding the racket, upright, than about hitting the tennis ball, outright, which, by the way, had, by now, just bounced right past him. Nevertheless, as the years progressed, and the boys did, too, their rackets got proportionally lighter and their game got proportionally better. So in light of those proportional facts, we transported their rackets and their balls, not to mention their "game," or whatever you want to call it, to a number of nearby tennis courts, where we changed our methodology, but not much, in an effort to adapt to the fences and the nets and the lines, as well as other interesting and intervening features, normally found on a tennis court.

Now, for example, I stood on one side of the net, but, actually, right at the net, and I hit the ball, on one bounce, to one of the boys, who was standing, somewhat dubiously, on the other side of the net, not too far away, waiting to hit the ball back to me with a "forehand," enough times so that we could, subsequently, change over, and, subsequently, repeat the same methodology, except now with a "backhand." And, eventually, with each boy having gained more confidence, by hitting the ball in the same manner, over a number of weeks, we repeated the same methodology, once again, except, this time, by using both a "forehand" and a "backhand" stroke, in an alternating fashion. I did that with each boy . . . referring to that alternating methodology . . . day after day, and, yes, month after month, until each boy developed a reasonably good "forehand" and "backhand" stroke, in tennis vernacular, and, possibly, a lot more self-confidence, in everyday vernacular, about hitting a tennis ball, equally well, from either side.

Then, standing beside each boy at the service line, one at a time, we worked on a serve, endlessly, until each one had developed a more than serviceable serve. And within a few years, following a lot of practice over that time, both boys developed a very good "American twist," which was a very difficult serve to learn and, even more importantly, an even more difficult serve to "return," in tennis vernacular, once again, by someone in the opposite court.

By the time that both boys had graduated from junior high school, they were playing, competitively, with friends, nearly every evening and on the weekends, too, as soon as the weather would permit. By doing so, they both developed into very good tennis players, especially "at the net," and I don't even remember working very much with them on a so-called "net game." When you consider the absence of my instructional involvement in their mutually strong "net game," I realize that fact does not comment well on my instructional methodology with respect to the rest of their "game."

I do remember that both boys were very careful to avoid playing against each other, even though, notwithstanding an age disparity, they were fairly evenly matched. I guess, now that I think about it, questions that could have proven to be uncomfortable to answer, especially where brothers are concerned, are better left unanswered.

I don't think, however, that there was ever any question about Lars' natural ability in the game. He had an enormous amount of plain raw talent. Some of the two-handed backhand shots that he could make simply defied explanation, in physics or even in metaphysics, for that matter. And he was simply awesome "at the net"; it was as though gravity no longer existed when he was up there. Notwithstanding his obvious talent, however, Lars saw tennis as a game to play, because it was fun to play, not necessarily because it was fun to win, although he certainly had no philosophical objections to winning, but that was not, as some might say, "the-end-all," for Lars, in a tennis game.

Court, who had a lot of talent on his own part, and just as much skill, which was more of a learned phenomenon, was far more competitive. I suppose that was why he was far more interested in entering tennis tournaments, although both boys did that from time to time. And, maybe, that explains why Court went out for his tennis team in high school and Lars did not, although he certainly possessed enough skills in the game to do so. Court, by the way, made the team, and he played each week, in the springtime, against a player from a tennis team in another high school. As a result, Court played quite well, competitively, by the time that he graduated from high school.

Incidentally, what I remember most about those years, in which Court played on his high school tennis team, had less to do with tennis and more to do with Court. That was because some of his more idiosyncratic ways began to appear, more regularly, on and off the tennis court. Many of them were certainly related to the game, but, in reality, they were more related to Court, as an individual, and as a tennis-playing individual, which was not surprising, because, by that time and those years, Court had certainly become an independent young man, when most young men, at that age, had great difficulty in doing anything, individually or otherwise, that was different from their peers.

I remember, for example, that Court had little time for inefficiency in those days, if not now, and he found it to be terribly inefficient to carry around his tennis clothes, in a backpack, during most of the day, so that he could change into them, for practice or a game, after school. So he decided to wear them to class, instead, on the days in which his tennis team practiced or had a game immediately after school, even though no one else on the tennis team did the same. They did not, we subsequently learned, because shorts, which were part of a tennis player's wearing apparel, were not permitted to be worn by female students, not during the school day, under an academic dress code policy.

We . . . referring to both parents . . . discovered that fact, because the principal's office informed us of the policy, in a telephone conversation one day, and, in turn, requested that Court comply with it, by not wearing tennis shorts during class. We were also informed by that office, in response to our question about the scope of the prohibition, that the rule, technically, only prohibited girls from wearing shorts in school because, prior to that time, no boys had ever attempted to do so. And the school justifiably felt that it seemed somewhat inequitable, if not untoward, that he . . . Court . . . could, and they . . . the girls . . . could not, under that policy.

After thinking about the inequity, in the days that followed, we . . . his totally surprised parents . . . finally decided to ask Court not to wear tennis shorts to school on practice or game days anymore. As we subsequently learned, however, from an inadvertent conversation with a school official about another matter, Court continued to wear tennis shorts to school on practice and game days, by changing into them in his jeep, which he drove to school, every day. Because he did . . . continue to wear tennis shorts to school on those days . . . the school officials, we were subsequently informed, eventually decided, in their infinite wisdom, to change their dress-code policy, and to allow everyone, girls as well as boys, to wear shorts in high school.

Shorts, however, were not the kind of wearing apparel, or lack thereof, that caused tennis officials, on occasion, to interrupt Court's tennis matches, by threatening a forfeiture. It was because, as we were informed by a number of his high school friends, he would take off his shirt on extremely hot and humid days, which had been causing him to perspire, profusely, especially during a hotly contested tennis match. Obviously, he was far more interested in being comfortable than in being suitable, especially on those hotly contested occasions. Some tennis officials, however, were far more concerned about suitability, and they found a half-naked tennis player, who may even have been a winning tennis player, at least at that point in the match, to be unsuitable. When they stopped the tennis match to say so, Court, apparently, found the officiating to be unsuitable, and, apparently, he would refuse to reengage with an overly perspired tennis shirt. I never did learn of the outcome in any of those officiating melodramatic controversies.

Nevertheless, because of those officiating controversies, Court's weekly tennis matches, we were subsequently informed, became a spectator favorite, especially among the student body, whether they liked tennis or not. Apparently, no one could wait to see if the blonde-haired kid, with the weightlifter's "build," would keep his shirt on during the match, and, concomitant therewith, if the official in the "Chair," without the same kind of a physique, would do something about it. Several photographs of Court, in mid-match, without the benefit of an appropriate tennis shirt, have been so identified and included as Exhibit 19 in the Appendix. Unfortunately, we do not have a photograph of the irate tennis official, in the "Chair," at that match.

CHAPTER LXVIII

STONEGATE: MY LITTLE LEAGUE REJECTION AND THE SUBSEQUENT DEVELOPMENT OF SELF-RELIANCE, REVISITED

RELIANCE UPON the opinion of others, even if they are friends, or purporting to be, does not ordinarily come easily for me now. The reason is probably because of a mistaken reliance upon the opinion of others before I had grown up. I say, "mistaken," because their opinion did not serve me very well at the time, or, for that matter, at almost any time. Among other deleterious things, those opinions caused me to believe, when I was just eleven years old, growing up in my hometown, that I was not a very good baseball player. Now that, admittedly, in and of itself, does not, in hindsight, seem to be terribly significant. After all, I was only eleven years old, and it only involved the game of baseball.

Self-perception, however, is a very important part of one's life, and it begins long before eleven years of age. And it certainly involves capability, in almost any capacity, especially if you are a young boy, even in such seemingly insignificant arenas as a baseball game. What's more, self-perception, growing out of a baseball game, or, more accurately, the inability to play the game, or, at least, very well, according to the opinion of others, can survive long after eleven years of age and that game.

Nevertheless, there is, admittedly, a tendency to rely upon the opinion of others, especially when you are growing up, and especially relating to competence, even though some of those opinions may not serve you very well. And make no mistake about it, even some of the opinions of your parents may not necessarily serve you very well, not all of the time, anyway, especially when you are growing up. Their opinions may actually reflect a certain amount of inadequacy, on their part, a concept which, I believe, the psychologists refer to, somewhat critically, as "projection." So if they have some degree of difficulty in thinking somewhat highly of themselves, they may have the same degree of difficulty in thinking that way about another person, too, having "projected," as it were, their feelings of inadequacy onto that person, even if that person happens to be their son or daughter.

I don't even have to address the opinion of others, who are not part of your family, and who, therefore, are likely to have far less interest in your well-being. Their opinion, whatever it may be, is likely to be far less reliable for that uncaring reason. Still, such opinions, especially of an educational nature, voiced by an educational professional, such as a teacher, may have some real value in an educational context, ordinarily found in an academic situation, such as a school. Such opinions, voiced in those situations, may be, and often are, somewhat important in the educational development of a growing child.

They were certainly important in my own educational development. Nevertheless, as I grew older, but not that much older, I began to realize that one should never rely, as a matter of principle, upon the opinion of others, even in an educational context, in determining your self-worth, no matter who the others may happen to be, or how qualified they may seem to be, in expressing such an opinion.

That principle, however, is not easily won in the evolutionary process of self-discovery, likely over the better part of a lifetime, but if it is to be won, it must be won through the agonizing process of trial and error, which is to say, personal experience. And experience, gained over that period of time, may well result, if all goes well, in something beyond the accumulation of knowledge. It may eventually result in wisdom, philosophically speaking, which, among other things, is a realization that whatever you are, or whatever value you may have, comes, in part, from whatever value you have placed on your life, or, if you will, whatever you do with your life and how.

In other words, the meaning of your existence depends upon whatever meaning that you have decided to give to it. Your life should not be defined or determined by the pronouncements of others, no matter who or what they may happen to be, or even how qualified they may seem to be in order to render such an opinion. Rather, your life, or its value, if you still prefer to look at it that way, essentially depends upon the meaning that you have given to it, by, among other things, your achievements and your failures, too, over the course of a lifetime effort.

Of course, one does not ordinarily understand such things after being on this earth for no more than eleven years. It is the wisdom that comes, slowly and painfully, through years of relying far too often upon the opinion of others, while growing up, if not growing old, before realizing the extraordinary cost for having done so. The cost, of course, is believing that those opinions have a theological or genealogical basis, or both, and, consequently, relying upon them, instead of superseding, or overcoming, or even disproving them, by will, decision, risk, and success, and, yes, failure, on occasion, too.

Well, I never did overcome, or even disprove, the opinion of those little league baseball officials, who decided that I could not, at eleven years of age, play baseball, at least at a level sufficient to be on one of their baseball teams. Instead, unable to understand why, if, indeed, there was a reason, I decided that they must be right, because, after all, they were adults, who were baseball officials, and who were vested with the authority to make those kinds of a decision, based upon those kinds of an opinion. So armed with that inescapable opinion, as I grew older, I decided not to even try out for a baseball team in high school. What's more, with that seemingly infallible athletic pronouncement, guiding me, I decided not to try out for any other athletic team, either, not at any time during my years in junior and senior high school.

Obviously, the decision on my part to rely on that little league baseball rejection, at eleven years of age, as a valid pronouncement of my athletic inability, did not serve me very well thereafter. Understand me! I am not saying that the rejection did not serve me very well; that is another issue for another day, or should I say another chapter. What I am saying is that my decision to rely upon that rejection did not serve me very well. If, indeed, I had decided to follow a similar path with respect to the rest of my life, especially of an educational and, subsequently, professional nature, there would have been no aberrational departure, following my graduation from high school, for one of the nation's great universities, elsewhere, no graduation therefrom, with distinction, no graduate degree thereafter, in philosophy, no less, and no law school degree following that. And, finally, there would have been no sterling litigation practice thereafter, which culminated in my retirement, as a senior partner, in one of the largest international law firms at the time in the Nation's Capitol, if not in the Nation.

Oh, yes, and this story probably would not have exceeded the forty-five pages necessary to tell hunting and fishing stories, over a lifetime, with my childhood friends in our hometown of Lock Haven, Pennsylvania. And I am not even going to mention the five or six pages that would have been required to tell some highly repetitive stories about joining those friends in a bar room, nearly every evening, drinking draft beer, while "throwing darts," intermittently, before and after retirement.

In case it is not abundantly clear, at least at this point, just how important I believe in non-reliance, as a lifetime principle in most circumstances, let me point out that it was implicit in the childhood instruction of my two sons, whether, for example, they were trying to learn how to hit a baseball or a tennis ball or swim the length of a pool. In that respect, I don't think that there was ever an issue during any one of those instructional sessions, involving any one of those athletic activities, about succeeding or failing; the only issue was whether they would take a risk and decide to try. That, after all, is the real issue in life, and failing to try, because of the risk, or because of the possibility of failure, or, more importantly, because someone else does not believe that you can succeed, means giving up on life and, possibly, dying . . . "one-whole-life-long!"

With that in mind, I'm sure that it will not surprise you when I say that I cannot really tell you whether any of the boys ever succeeded in becoming great swimmers or great baseball players or even great tennis players, although I do remember that they did some of those things rather well throughout their "teenage" years and, in some cases, even beyond. But apart from those athletic accomplishments, or not, I can certainly tell you, as their more than proud father, that they tried to do as well as they possibly could throughout the rest of their lives, which probably explains, in part, their remarkable success, academically and professionally, thereafter. Because of that fact, or, even, those facts, I am fairly comfortable in saying, while looking back on their childhood now, that I must have been a fairly capable swimming, baseball, and tennis coach, among my other instructional activities, in their developing lives.

CHAPTER LXIX

SIXTH JOB: THE PENSION BENEFIT GUARANTY CORPORATION, OFFICE OF THE GENERAL COUNSEL; HENRY ROSE, INSECURITY AND NON-DECISION MAKING

AT THIRTY-NINE years of age, and with some real litigation experience behind me, especially on issues of law at an appellate level, I became an Assistant General Counsel in Charge of Litigation for the Office of General Counsel in the Pension Benefit Guaranty Corporation. By that time, my perspective, upon encountering unfairness, had improved, dramatically, since my traumatic failure, at eleven years of age, to impress the "little league" baseball officials in my hometown. Now I recognized unfairness when I saw it, made an effort to understand the reasons therefore, to the extent that they existed, and always refused to accept the situation, wherever and whenever I encountered it. And I certainly encountered my share, when I entered the complex world of insecure government lawyers, working in the Office of General Counsel for the Pension Benefit Guaranty Corporation.

Possibly, the most insecure lawyer in the Office was the General Counsel, himself, Henry Rose. When you understand something about his childhood, or, at least, my recollection of it, that fact is really not so surprising. Henry was, as I recall, the only son of a first-generation Eastern European Jewish family, which barely "scraped by," as the owners of a dry-cleaning establishment in Buffalo, New York.

Because of that fact, or those facts, or, possibly, other facts, which may be more cultural in nature, Henry undertook the vocational line in high school, instead of an academic one. And, upon graduation, he joined the armed services, instead of proceeding directly on to college, for which, admittedly, his vocational subjects may not have ordinarily prepared him. After completing his military service, Henry applied to a rather undistinguished junior college, somewhere in upstate New York, gained an acceptance, completed two years, and, upon graduation therefrom, successfully transferred to a four-year school, in the same state, with, possibly, little more renown. There, he did reasonably well, or, at least, well enough to gain admission to an equally undistinguished law school, graduated three years later and, thereafter, joined the Department of Labor, where he served as a labor lawyer, for approximately twenty years, doing more than serviceable work, in a legislative capacity, for the Department.

Sometime near the end of that employment, Henry was assigned to do legislative work on a proposed pension bill, to be subsequently submitted, following a number of appropriate hearings, for enactment by both houses of Congress. Among a number of other remarkable things, that bill established a number of legal standards, for the first time, in the nation's nearly nonexistent pension system. Following lengthy deliberations by Committees in both the House and Senate, as well as on the floor of Congress, it eventually was enacted into law as the Employee Retirement Income Security Act of 1974, as subsequently amended. And with its enactment, Henry Rose, as a legislative lawyer in the Department of Labor, primarily responsible for its origination, became the General Counsel of the Pension Benefit Guaranty Corporation, which was established under Title IV of the Act to regulate, in part, single employer pension plans and, among other things, guaranty a substantial part of the "non-forfeitable" vested benefits for participants and beneficiaries in such plans that terminate with insufficient assets to pay those benefits.

As the General Counsel, Henry, who quite obviously achieved that position through a number of fortuitous circumstances, not including his high school vocational program, supervised, quite cautiously, I might add, an office full of insecure, if not marginally competent, lawyers, looking for a lifetime of security in a low-risk government job with benefits. Their insecurity was clearly magnified, if not compounded, by Henry's manner of being, which, too often, resulted in decision-making that would have made the proverbial "slow and lumbering tortoise" look like "the speedy hare."

There was, however, a certain amount of logic in Henry's inability, if not outright refusal, to make decisions, at least within a reasonable period of time, even though the logic could be quite maddening, especially if you were part of the whole indecisive process. In that process, which had, unfortunately, become a de facto office policy, the fact that no decision had yet been made, or had ever been made, could, theoretically, if you were part of the whole maddening process, be justified on the basis that, so far, no wrong decision had been made, or would ever be made. That assumed, of course, if you were still part of the whole maddening process, that failure to decide within a reasonable period of time, or to ever decide, could not, in and of itself, be construed to be a wrong decision.

Nevertheless, Henry had an answer for that problem, too. His indecisions could retroactively be construed to be the right decision, which they often were, once an eternity had passed and the right decision had become obvious to anyone with enough ability to avoid being institutionalized. Moreover, not to leave anything to chance, or the misfortune of a wrong decision, Henry's decisions, when he eventually made them, which were not often, were so amorphous that you were not quite sure what they were. And there was a certain amount of maddening logic in that fact, too. Since you could not really understand what the decisions were, when he infrequently made them, he could easily construe them, retroactively, so that, by that time, usually measured by decades, any rational person, or, at least, one who was able to avoid being institutionalized, would realize that there were no reasonable alternatives.

CHAPTER LXX

SIXTH JOB: PENSION BENEFIT GUARANTY CORPORATION, OFFICE OF THE GENERAL COUNSEL; MY PREDECESSOR WAS APPARENTLY REPLACED AS A LITIGATION HEAD BY HENRY ROSE BECAUSE OF MY WORK ON A SUPREME COURT BRIEF

IN FACT, although it is somewhat embarrassing to acknowledge, especially at this point, I was likely the product of Henry's decision-making process or, more accurately, non-decision-making process. In that respect, I was hired as an Assistant General Counsel in Charge of Litigation in the Office of General Counsel. What I discovered, however, upon commencing my employment, was that there was no litigation section, and that my predecessor, a Stanford Law School graduate, had been hired to create and head one, but had never done so, probably because Henry would not authorize it. Although that initially seemed to be somewhat confusing, because I was subsequently hired for the very same purpose, I learned, very quickly, that the absence of a decision, or, at least, a definitive one, involving my responsibilities, or even that of my predecessor, was simply part of Henry's decision-making process.

To be more specific, at least to the extent that I am capable, given the subject matter, Henry had apparently decided to hire my predecessor from a large international law firm, headquartered in New York, to create and head a litigation section within the Office of General Counsel. But he apparently changed his mind, once he became familiar with his work, not to mention his personality, or, in other words, once he got a good look at him in action. Nevertheless, in classical Henry style, he wasn't really stuck with his initial decision, because it was so amorphous that it really could not, within any bounds of reason, be construed to be a decision at all, or, at least, not an irreversible one, anyway. So in keeping with that well-tested manner of being, or amorphous process, he just retroactively changed it . . . the decision, I mean, if, indeed, it could ever be argued that he had ever made one in the first place . . . by replacing an understandably offended Stanford Law School graduate with an incredulous Cal Golumbic, as a tentative, very tentative, head of a nonexistent litigation section.

Actually, I can't really fault Henry's replacement decision, or indecision, if you prefer to call it that, because the Stanford Law School graduate had some serious personal and professional deficiencies. In that regard, he had the interpersonal skills of an enraged rhinoceros for one. In addition, his litigation skills were about as astute as a rhinoceros's eyesight. On top of that, if you can actually top all of that, his general appearance was not unlike that of a rhinoceros, either, or, at least, it might have terrified one. Then, of course, there was the issue of judgment: if he had any, it was often difficult to tell. That was because, like the rhinoceros, when threatened, which was much of the time, his instinct, like his horned counterpart, was to charge, like, well, you know, an enraged rhinoceros! And none of those rhinoceros-like attributes served him well in the sophisticated, if not subtle, art of litigation in federal courts around the country, trial and appellate, alike, let alone in the less than sophisticated art of survival in the insecure environment, existing at the time, in the Office of General Counsel.

All of this, of course, posed a rather serious problem for Henry Rose, who, not surprisingly, resolved the problem in the same manner that he usually did, by simply doing nothing. Aware of his indecision, concerning "rhinoceros-like-things," within a short period of time, it became abundantly clear to me that if I intended to develop a litigation section, and head it, Henry's unresolved problem, in the form of a now dispossessed "rhinoceros," was, eventually, going to become my problem.

It was a problem, however, that was not, initially, going to my biggest problem. Oh, no, my biggest problem was going to be persuading Henry to allow me to establish a litigation section, which, after all, was the reason why I had, ostensively, been hired, or, at least, seemingly so. Toward that end, and solely with that end in mind, I decided to choose a significant appeal in the Office, which was pending before one of the United States Circuit Courts, around the country, in which I could write, or, if necessary, rewrite a prevailing brief, in order to demonstrate my capabilities as a brief writer, if not as an appellate litigator. Even better, however, I actually discovered that there was an appeal pending before the Supreme Court of the United States, involving an issue of first impression, concerning a statutory construction, affecting the very basis of part of the Act, which the Office had lost below, at both trial and appeal, and which would clearly provide me with an opportunity to demonstrate my brief writing, or, as in this case, my brief rewriting skills . . . in the highest court in the land, no less.

The opportunity was seized, so to speak, by convincing Henry to allow me to review and to revise, where necessary, a brief that had already been drafted by two of his younger attorneys in the Office, who, quite obviously, had never written an appellate brief before, and who had, consequently, made an unbelievable mess out of this one. The unbelievable mess, however, turned out to be an unbelievable opportunity, especially for someone like myself, who had extensive brief-writing experience, if one could assume, of course, that such a thing as an opportunity could, hypothetically, exist in that office.

Naively believing, at least at that point, that it could and, more importantly, that it would . . .become such an opportunity . . . if I just did an excellent job in revising the brief, or rewriting it, as the case may be, I went to work. And after a careful examination of the brief drafted by the two younger lawyers, as a starting point, I quickly realized that the organization was so chaotic and the manner of addressing several of the issues was so obtuse, that the brief required more than a revision. As I had learned in a philosophy class on logic in graduate school, it was impossible to "make something out of nothing," so I rewrote it, entirely. By relying on the research in the original draft, to the extent that it was sufficient, and where it was not, by simply assigning one of the original drafters to respond to my concerns, by further legal research, I wrote an excellent brief that, eventually, became a prevailing brief, not only in the Office, but, subsequently, in the Supreme Court of the United States. Consequently, I became the brilliant drafter of a prevailing Supreme Court brief, and the two original drafters, marginally competent, became the enraged legal researchers for that brief, all in a disbelieving Office.

I am sure that Henry must have become aware of the rage, at least at some point, because the original drafters moved from becoming enraged to becoming vociferously so, long before that brief had been filed. And I suspect that Henry could hear those enraged voices, just as well as the rest of the Office. Not surprisingly, however, he did nothing about it; he simply waited to see how everything would turn out, or, more specifically, how the redrafted brief would turn out, once it appeared on his desk for review and a signature. Realizing, by now, that this was his modus-operandi, I made sure that the brief, which I was now redrafting, would become a prevailing brief in the view of any knowledgeable lawyer, if not a judicial officer.

Of course, that still would not ensure that Henry would like it. After all, Henry, likely, had no more idea of how to write a good brief than the original drafters, or the rest of the Office, for that matter. Consequently, there was some concern on my part that he would not like my redrafted brief, because he did not know what a good brief looked like. But secure in the age-old proposition, known to all good brief-writers, that if your wife was not persuaded by the simple logic of your well-constructed arguments, neither would the court, I hoped that Henry and my wife would, at least, share some intellectual similarity. So mindful of propositions and wives and Henrys, I wrote a brief whose well-constructed arguments had enough simplicity that Henry and, yes, my wife, too, would understand, without, may I add, a lot of difficulty.

Henry did not disappoint me! He easily met "the wife standard," without too much difficulty, I should add, and complimented me on the simplicity of my language and on the organization of my arguments. He was even rather decisive, if not effusive, in doing so, which, frankly, amazed me, because that miraculous turn of events can only be described in theological concepts. Until then, frankly, I did not believe that Henry was ever satisfied with anything that anyone ever did, including, in all probability, himself. That, in itself, may explain why he was such a cautious fellow.

Far too often, however, his indescribable caution interfered with, or, at least, delayed, his decision-making capability, which I learned, after he had reviewed my brief, was really not so bad, when it, indeed, occurred. In fact, by the end of my tenure, as the Assistant General Counsel in Charge of Litigation in the Office of General Counsel, I can safely say that, if you divorced his emotional system from the equation, Henry Rose was a very intelligent individual, who could, on occasion, make very good decisions. It was just difficult to tell, however, unless you were around him for a number of years, because he did not make them that often and not unless he absolutely had to do so.

CHAPTER LXXI

SIXTH JOB: PENSION BENEFIT GUARANTY CORPORATION, OFFICE OF GENERAL COUNSEL; I ORGANIZED A LITIGATION SECTION TO SUCCESSFULLY LITIGATE CASES IN FEDERAL COURTS, TRIAL AND APPELLATE, BY ELIMINATING MEDIOCRITY, DEMOCRACY AND DECENCY

NOTWITHSTANDING MY draft of an excellent brief in the Supreme Court, which subsequently became a prevailing brief in that Court, it did not change the fact that I was still not authorized to organize a litigation section, the reason why I was ostensively hired, without some kind of an approval by Henry Rose. And that approval, or any kind of an approval, for that matter, for anything, let alone one involving litigation, which Henry knew virtually nothing about, and which he, therefore, had an inherent mistrust, required a decision, and decision-making was never Henry's forte, and that was especially true in this situation.

Nevertheless, I needed to establish a litigation section, which required some kind of an organization, a concept that did not exist anywhere else in that office. And that called for some real discretion on my part, because Henry did not particularly like organization. He sort of found it to be undemocratic, because it tended to result in inclusions and exclusions, and Henry loved democracy, almost as much as he loved disorganization. So I had to move cautiously; but I clearly had to move. Otherwise, I had to move out of there, because a failure to set up some means of engaging in a litigation practice, by way of an organization to do so, would mean a failure in my overall job performance, and I was not, and never have been, big on failure!

Success, however, can be extraordinarily difficult on occasion, and this was one of those occasions, because Henry wanted every one of the young lawyers in that office, as a democratic principle, to be able to do anything and everything that any other lawyer could do in that office, and that, my friends, included litigation, whether they knew how to do it or not. That democratic principle was obviously why the Office had never, to my knowledge, won a case in any federal court, trial or appellate, anywhere in the country, not at that point, anyway.

In order to change that litigation history, and my own professional circumstances in that office, which, in my mind, were synonymous, I knew that I had to change that "democratic" litigation practice, which meant, perish the thought, excluding a significant amount of the lawyers in that office from regularly engaging in a litigation practice. Otherwise, I would continue to have a lot of young, mediocre lawyers, who knew relatively little about litigation, continue to demonstrate that fact, by continuing to lose every case that they litigated in every federal court in the country, trial and appellate.

So mindful of mediocrity and democracy, I decided, carefully, of course, to devise a policy, whereby all of the lawyers in the Office could continue to engage in litigation, but, now, only with the assistance and supervision of the lawyers in a litigation section, who happened to know how to litigate and how to do it successfully. To adopt that kind of a policy, I needed to obtain Henry's approval to hire a few experienced litigators and to incorporate them into a litigation section, which would supervise others, outside of that section, who, quite obviously, needed that kind of supervision.

Toward that end, I proposed to hire Jim Dulcan, an excellent appellate lawyer, largely for litigation and brief writing skills. I also proposed to transfer Bill Hanrahan, from within the office, whose writing skills were quite good, whose judgment was even better, and whose litigation skills were remarkable for such a young lawyer, especially in bankruptcy and bankruptcy was a significant part of the litigation practice in that office.

In my mind, the three of us, forming a litigation section, could, essentially, handle the litigation practice in the Office, by supervising those outside of the section, who had little experience in doing litigation in federal courts, but who were still intent on litigating such cases, pursuant to Henry's democratic and disastrously disorganized office policies. Because this change only involved moving one lawyer into a litigation section from within the Office and hiring one for the same purpose from outside the Office, so that the three of us could supervise all of the other inexperienced lawyers, who had been providing comic relief, for several years, in federal courts, trial and appellate, across the nation, I believed that Henry might find the change to be fairly simple, unobtrusive and acceptable, if not reasonably democratic.

Well, he did, eventually, but only after several weeks of discourse and negotiations, and with a constant reassurance, on my part, that nothing else would change, by adopting that organizational policy. In reality, however, I knew that a lot of things would change, by adopting that recommended policy, inside and outside of the Office, and I think that Henry realized that fact, too, right away. Nevertheless, because his limitations were, generally, emotional, not intellectual, I also think that Henry realized, at least in that instance, that the changes might be, god forbid, for the better. And although the creation of a litigation section sounded sort of elitist, and, therefore, somewhat undemocratic, because it would undoubtedly result in the exclusion of some of the lawyers from that section, I assured Henry that it would just ensure that those, seemingly, excluded, because of a lack of experience in doing litigation, would receive assistance in doing so, by those with far more experience in successfully litigating cases in federal trial and appellate courts, who were in that section. Ultimately, that seemed to Henry to be a reasonably decent thing to do.

I, on the other hand, never thought about litigation in terms of decency; I was just interested in the outcome; and I evaluated the outcome by success or failure, not decency. But, hey, I was not about to argue about decency, when it resulted in the establishment of a litigation section, with enough organization to allow those in the section to successfully supervise the conduct of litigation in the Office. Actually, if we want to speak about it in terms of decency, that sounded more than decent to me.

CHAPTER LXXII

SIXTH JOB: PENSION BENEFIT GUARANTY CORPORATION, OFFICE OF GENERAL COUNSEL; AFTER ACHIEVING AN ENORMOUS AMOUNT OF SUCCESS IN PENSION LITIGATION, I DECIDED TO DEPART THE CORPORATION AND JOIN THE UNITED MINE WORKERS OF AMERICA HEALTH AND RETIREMENT FUNDS AS THEIR GENERAL COUNSEL

HAVING ASSEMBLED a staff, I began to methodically organize a litigation section, right down to a complex filing system, so that we could, immediately, change the course of events, and, eventually, the outcome in pension cases being litigated by that Office in federal district and circuit courts around the country. And the changes that occurred in litigation, undertaken by that Office, as a result of the advent of a litigation section, could not have been more dramatic over the next several years. We went from an Office that had not prevailed in litigation, to my knowledge, in any federal court, trial or appellate, to one that lost only one case thereafter, which was in the Third Circuit, during my three-year tenure as head of a litigation section. And many of those cases actually reached the Circuit Court of Appeals, everywhere in the country, and some of them even reached the Supreme Court of the United States.

They were almost all complex cases of first impression with constitutional and/or statutory issues, resolved by cross-motions for summary judgment and supporting memoranda at the trial level or with briefs on appeal. Some of the largest law firms in the country opposed us, because of the nature of the cases and the amount of money involved, and by regularly beating them in federal courts, nationwide, we, as litigants, began to make a name for ourselves, both inside and outside of the Office. The former posed a problem, however, because of the insecurity within the Office, which, of course, was magnified by our success in litigation, nationwide.

Normally, everyone who practiced law within the confines of that office spent at least half of their working time with an eye on Henry. Now, they spent the rest of their time watching those of us in the litigation section, because our success was viewed by most of them with a considerable amount of jealousy, if not outright hostility.

If there had ever been any doubt about that fact, it was resolved when Henry, because of our success in litigation, decided to promote me to a higher salary level, which apparently was opposed by one of his subordinates, who also substituted, quite nicely, in that office as a "toad," albeit an incomprehensible one, but still a "toad." If you will recall, toads are normally quite small, almost innocuously so, in the world of larger creatures and, therefore, they are always in danger of being stepped upon, by anything with any kind of stature. Aware of that fact, they are generally, if not usually, threatened by anything and everything with any kind of stature, and, apparently, I was not an exception.

Torn now by that opposition, between doing nothing or promoting me, which required an actual decision, Henry, not surprisingly, did nothing. Because of that fact, I decided, within weeks, to improve my situation, professionally, by leaving the Office, including the indecision and the insecurity and the mediocrity and the disorganization, not to mention the democracy, for something more, in a better position, elsewhere.

That was not, in retrospect, a difficult decision. Although it was born out of ambition, and colored somewhat by frustration, the decision was not at all an unreasonable one. I had accomplished some rather remarkable things during my tenure, in an office where accomplishment was disdained or, at least, undermined, and I thought that I may be able to translate those accomplishments into a very attractive resume. Even aside from my organizational accomplishments, in setting up a successful litigation program inside that office, my name had become associated, outside of that office, with nearly every major pension case being litigated anywhere, in a federal district or circuit court, in the country. That, alone, gave me every reason to believe that I may be able to secure a good position, elsewhere, in pension litigation.

Apparently, that was not an unreasonable assumption, because, even before I began to conduct my search, I was approached by the Trustees of the United Mine Workers of America Health and Retirement Funds (hereinafter, sometimes, "the Funds") about accepting a position as their General Counsel. The position had been recently vacated by Henry Ruth, who was, formerly, the Independent Counsel in the Watergate Investigation. Upon his departure, the Trustees had apparently received a number of unsolicited recommendations on my behalf, and, after considering a number of other applicants, they decided to ask me if I would be interested in interviewing for the position, which I did, successfully, may I add, and, after receiving an offer shortly thereafter, I subsequently accepted.

CHAPTER LXXIII

SIXTH JOB: PENSION BENEFIT GUARANTY CORPORATION, OFFICE OF GENERAL COUNSEL; DULCAN, FORD, HANRAHAN, AND ROSE REVISITED, YEARS LATER

IT WAS not with a heavy heart that I left the Office of General Counsel for the Pension Benefit Guaranty Corporation. There were too many organizational problems and too many dysfunctional people to ever consider staying there, certainly for the rest of my professional life. Still, to be abundantly fair, I had gained a significant amount of experience, while working there, including the ability to adjust to, if not overcome, disorganization and dysfunction, which would serve me well throughout the rest of my legal career. In addition, I had become an accomplished litigator, especially on an appellate level, in an employee benefits discipline, which was, essentially, in its origins. Indeed, we . . . the discipline and myself . . . had become quite interrelated over that period of time in nearly every federal district and circuit court in the country, and that relationship, if I may be permitted to use that concept, would grow to proportions, in the years ahead, that I could never have imagined, as I left that office.

Notwithstanding that unparalleled employee benefits litigation experience, for which I was enormously grateful, I have never looked back, probably because I did not particularly like what I saw there, with three notable exceptions. One was Jim Dulcan, my former associate in the Appellate Division of the Corporation Counsel's Office, who replaced me, as we had originally intended, as the Assistant

General Counsel in Charge of Litigation. Jim was a good lawyer, far too good to continue in that office. Nevertheless, he did, but not for an extended period of time, because, unfortunately, that period was cut short by stomach cancer, approximately five years later, which, ultimately, resulted in Jim's death, shortly thereafter, and, may I add, the loss of a good friend.

Although my relationship with Jim Dulcan had obviously come to an untimely end, that was not the case with Bill Hanrahan. It would continue on, over the years, in a number of other capacities and in a number of other positions with a number of other firms. Having said that, I can safely say that, without my continuing professional association with Bill Hanrahan, in whatever capacity and circumstance that it may have been over the years, the quality of my work would not have been the same, the recognition for that work would not have been the same, and the professional opportunities growing out of that recognition would not have been the same. In other words, the light cast upon my professional star by Bill Hanrahan's radiating genius made it glow with a brilliance that would have been absent or, at least, diminished, in his absence. No better evidence of that fact exists than the matters set forth in one of the following chapters about, among other things, our professional association in the Office of General Counsel for the United Mine Workers of America Health and Retirement Funds.

Before commencing that story, however, I need to point out that I also left behind Gary Ford in the Office, too, but not very far behind, and not for very long. Interestingly, I hired Gary, as a law school graduate, shortly after my arrival in the Office, following Henry's decision to put me in charge of the "Hiring Committee." And you will not be surprised to know that I became as careful about making hiring decisions, and, especially, that hiring decision, as I was about making most of my decisions in litigation, which is, obviously, why I have liked most of them. And Gary Ford would prove, over the years of our professional association, which became quite diverse, to be no exception, which is a story remaining to be told in chapters that follow.

I suppose that the same sequential thing could be said about my continuing relationship with Henry Rose, except that story is, by its nature, not to mention Henry's, far more complicated. The complication essentially arose because, notwithstanding my ambivalent feelings toward the man, I continued to have a rather significant association with him over the years. That was because he referred two major pension litigation cases to me, when I was subsequently engaged in the private practice of law, as a partner in my law firm, for which I was professionally, not to mention economically, quite grateful. I also had an occasion to subsequently employ him, as an expert witness, in another pension litigation case, following his entry into the private practice of law with a notable law firm in the metropolitan area.

Because of the change in our relationship, in all of those cases, especially in the latter one, I was no longer faced with Henry's debilitating disorganization and his agonizing indecision, although there were, on occasion, a few frustrating moments. Notwithstanding their occurrence, however, it was not difficult to remember that Henry had just referred two monumental litigation cases to me, even though our former working relationship had been more than challenging, probably for both of us. And to be absolutely fair, even in those challenging circumstances, in which I was responsible for turning around his office's poor litigation history, Henry graciously recommended that I receive an award, in the amount of five hundred dollars, for my success in that regard. His recommendation was subsequently granted by the Director, and I received the award shortly before I left the Office. Several photographs of me receiving the award from the Director have been so identified and included as Exhibit 110 in the Appendix.

The money that I received for that award was used by me to purchase an oil painting, shortly thereafter, of a boy and a girl casually strolling in a woodland setting, painted by an Italian artist of some renown, which, at the time, was over the strenuous objection of the family auditor, who also happened to be my wife and who was far more concerned at the time about the cost of educating our two sons. For nearly thirty years, the painting hung on a wall in the living room of our house at 14804 Flintstone Lane in Silver Spring, Maryland. Upon the sale of that house, however, the painting was removed, along with a number of other contents, and transported to our home at 4 Maass Lane in Rehoboth Beach, Delaware, where it now resides on a wall in the master bedroom on the first floor. There it lingers, along with a few memories, which appear, from time to time, as a nightmare of another time, when I was younger and practicing law in a government agency, surrounded by insecurity, indecision, mediocrity, and disorganization, in the name of decency and democracy!

But that nightmare, awful as it may have seemed at times, was not the worst nightmare in my life. The worst nightmare was geographic and historic, if not genealogical and sociological. Its location was somewhere else, when I was someone else, a long time ago, or, at least, it seemed to be, and I seemed to be. And at the time, I was not quite sure how to change it, any of it, my way of being, or my situation, or both. Nevertheless, futile as it may have seemed at the time, I was obsessed with trying, so with little more than a midwestern destination in mind, and a university seemingly named for that destination, and some indefinable desire to become something else, somewhere else, I boarded a bus. And notwithstanding that historic act, and so many others that have followed, academically and professionally, for much of my life, but not for all of my life, that nightmare has never seemed to go away.

www.ingramcontent.com/pod-product-compliance
Lightning Source LLC
Chambersburg PA
CBHW020242010526
44107CB00039B/1469/J